Best Seat in the House

"AFTER WORKING WITH JUSTIN FOR NEARLY A DECADE I CAN TELL YOU HE BROUGHT AS MUCH PASSION INTO THE WWE RING AS THE SUPERSTARS THEMSELVES. A FAN LIVING HIS DREAM."

- TODD GRISHAM, ESPN, UFC

"JUSTIN WAS THE CLEAN-CUT RING ANNOUNCER WHO OPENED TV SHOWS, PPVS AND LIVE EVENTS. BUT TO BACK ALL THAT UP HE WAS A CONSTANT VOICE ON LIVE EVENTS WITH ME BEFORE THE EVENT EVEN STARTED. HE ALWAYS HAD AN INTERESTING PERSPECTIVE ON THE SMALL DETAILS OF ANY SHOW HE WAS ON."

- DAVID "FIT" FINLAY , WWE PRODUCER AND INTERNATIONAL WRESTLING LEGEND

"JUSTIN ROBERTS STOOD OUT AMONG THOSE WHO HAVE STOOD MID-RING AND INTRODUCED SOME OF WWE'S BIGGEST MATCHES ON SOME OF WWE'S MOST HISTORICALLY SIGNIFICANT EVENTS. RATHER THAN JUST PRESENTING THE WRESTLERS WITH A STANDARD GENERIC VOICE, IT WAS CLEAR JUSTIN KNEW THE CONTEXT OF THE MOMENT, PUTTING HIS OWN SIGNATURE INFLECTION ON THE BIG NAMES HE INTRODUCED TIME AFTER TIME. HIS RING INTRODUCTIONS ARE A PERMANENT PART OF MILLIONS OF FANS' FAVORITE WWE MEMORIES AND MARK AN ERA OF BIG-TIME MATCHES AT BIG-TIME EVENTS."

- WADE KELLER, PRO WRESTLING TORCH JOURNALIST

"NOT MANY PEOPLE ARE AS PASSIONATE ABOUT THE PROFESSIONAL WRESTLING BUSINESS AS JUSTIN IS. WE USED TO RIDE FROM SHOW TO SHOW TOGETHER WHILE LISTENING TO CLASSIC WRESTLING ENTRANCE THEMES. WE GOT ALONG SO WELL BECAUSE WE ARE BOTH LIFELONG FANS THAT GOT TO LIVE OUR DREAMS."

- ZACK RYDER, WWE UNITED STATES CHAMPION

"JUSTIN'S JOURNEY IN PRO WRESTLING—ALL THE WAY TO THE MAIN EVENT OF WRESTLEMANIA—IS NOT ONLY A TREMENDOUS WRESTLING STORY, BUT THE PERFECT ROADMAP FOR ANYONE WHO'S WILLING TO WORK THEIR TAIL OFF TO MAKE THEIR DREAMS A REALITY. MORE IMPORTANTLY, HE'S STILL THE SAME GUY I FIRST MET IN OAKLAND AT HIS TRYOUT 15 YEARS AGO—A DECENT, KIND, TALENTED DUDE, A FAN, AND PROOF THAT NICE GUYS CAN FINISH FIRST."

- SETH MATES, FORMER WWE CREATIVE TEAM MEMBER

"IN 16 YEARS, I SAW JUSTIN NOT ONLY CREATE A STORY THAT CAN ONLY BE WRITTEN BY HARD WORK AND DEDICATION, BUT I ALSO WATCHED HIM LIVE A JOURNEY THAT MOST PEOPLE CAN ONLY DREAM OF. IT WAS HIS PURE PASSION FOR WRESTLING THAT SHINED THROUGH, MADE HIS NAME AND ETCHED HIS NAME INTO THE PROFESSIONAL WRESTLING HISTORY BOOKS. TO BE GREAT AT WHAT YOU DO, YOU HAVE TO LOVE WHAT YOU DO, AND THAT IS EXACTLY WHO JUSTIN ROBERTS IS."

- STEVE ISLAS, 2K GAMES/NAVAJO WARRIOR WRESTLER

JUSTIN ROBERTS

BEST SEAT IN THE HOUSE
YOUR BACKSTAGE PASS THROUGH MY WWE JOURNEY

CREDITS

Cover Design:	Dave Bogart, Adam Mock, Andreas Reuel
Photo Pages Design:	Dave Bogart
Cover Photo:	Matt Roberts
Photos:	Justin Roberts, Wrelano@aol.com, Matt Cardona
Typesetting:	Sannah Inderelst
Copyediting:	Liz Evans
Acquisition:	Manuel Morschel

British Library Cataloguing in Publication Data
A catalogue record for this book is available from the British Library
Best Seat in the House
Maidenhead: Meyer & Meyer Sport (UK) Ltd., 2016
ISBN: 978-1-78255-115-7
Aachen, Auckland, Beirut, Cairo, Cape Town, Dubai, Hägendorf, Hong Kong, Indianapolis, Manila, New Delhi, Singapore, Sydney, Tehran, Vienna
Member of the World Sport Publishers' Association (WSPA)
Printed & Binded: Versa Press, East Peoria, USA
E-Mail: info@m-m-sports.com
www.m-m-sports.com

TABLE OF CONTENTS

FOREWORD

I am best known for my passion for professional wrestling and being the heart and soul of ECW. It is ironic that though Justin and I came from different areas of the country, are 10 years apart, and did different things to achieve our life goals (hell, the smartass nerd used to watch me on TV), we are so similar. We both come from a loving home where our parents, who had similar health issues, supported us in achieving our collective goals, and we also both have one sister. At times, we have shared a collective, immature brain, and most important, both of us have an insane love of professional wrestling. If there was ever a heart and soul of announcing, it would be Justin Roberts. He gave everything to his performance when he was out there in front of the crowd. He was on and amped for three-plus hours a night, every night, when he worked for WWE. In a 12-year career with WWE, Justin drove every mile, boarded every early flight, stayed in different hotels every night, worked while sick, and took a lot of crap from some wrestlers. He was in the trenches with the wrestlers. He gave his normal life up and had the greatest time doing it.

Most people would say that a ring announcer job is easy or it's not important. On the contrary, it is the most important job. The announcer is the voice of the show, the grandmaster of ceremony. Without him, some debuting wrestlers would come out to no reactions. If a wrestler sounds important, he is perceived as important. An announcer sets the tone for the evening. In WWE, the performer's job is to put smiles on faces, and the first spark of that smile and anticipation was Justin's, "Good evening, [whatever town we were in]," and his "Your first match…" always got the people on their feet.

When reading this book, don't look at it as another wrestling book; look at as reading a journey of someone who followed their dream, and use it as motivation to follow your own dream. Justin didn't win a contest or get the job because he was doing something else in news media. This is what he wanted to do, and he paid his dues to get there. This book is an honest depiction of someone who had firsthand knowledge of the inner workings of the WWE, including his dealings with some not-so-friendly wrestlers that viewed him as an outsider and efforts to survive the political landscape in WWE. Justin sat in on production meetings before most shows. Several times, he performed at the grandest show of all, *WrestleMania*. There is a WWE Hall of Fame award and a foundation, Connor's Cure, that wouldn't have been happened if it weren't for Justin Roberts.

I find it funny how he has so many pictures and videos of himself as a total geeky fan, trying to be cool hanging with the wrestlers. Well, this book could also be any movie where a geek becomes cool because Justin has caught the interest of many hot women and still lives a bachelor's life (lucky bastard). I joke around with him for having the inability to love because he is a bachelor, but it's his normal because he knows nothing different. That's his dating, his courtship, and there is no normal in wrestling. I joke with him about the inability to love, but in hindsight, he loves his family, will do anything for his friends, and loves wrestling still to this day. (I can't explain his weirdness for the *Golden Girls* or 1980s and 1990s TV sitcoms, but maybe he can in this book.)

I may be biased, but despite whatever was bothering me in WWE, once I went through that curtain and stepped out to perform in front of the WWE audience, I was at my happiest. The first person I saw was Justin, and his smile and general excitement to see me, even though he saw me all day, made me happier.

I hope you enjoy Justin Roberts' journey. I'm happy to have been a part of it. As a wrestling fan who crossed over the guardrails, this should inspire the reader that if Justin can do it, so can you. If you have a dream follow it, and live life to its fullest. Every night, he had the best seat in the house in WWE because, quite simply, he was the best at what he did.

—Tommy Dreamer

Professional Wrestler, 1989 to present

They say there are two sides to every story. Not this one. This is not a creative writing piece. There is no ghostwriter. This is my story, based on the facts, through my well-documented journey. I never sold out arenas. Heck, I never even claimed to sell any tickets. I did, however, take a long ride on a crazy roller coaster known as the business of professional wrestling. This story is not meant to be a tell-all, nor is it meant to target anyone. It's just my brutally honest story, and if it helps to make any positive changes in the world, or if it helps to inspire one of you or teach you something helpful that you may not have known, it will be worth it. I dedicate this book to my family, friends, fans, all my teachers, and everyone else in my path who helped shape me as a person, and to every performer who put their body on the line in the ring so I could have a job, as well as every performer who ever made me a fan. I hope you enjoy.

PART I

DAYDREAMING

...ty, OK   3/20/16 UR Fight – Phoenix, AZ   11/14/15 House of Hardcore 11 – Queens, NY   11/13/1...
...Hardcore 8 – Philadelphia, PA   10/13/14 WWE Monday Night RAW – Atlanta, GA   10/11/14 WW...
...day Night RAW – Brooklyn, NY   10/5/14 WWE LIVE! – Bridgeport, CT   10/4/14 WWE LIVE!...
...L   9/22/14 WWE Monday Night RAW – Memphis, TN   9/21/14 WWE Night of Champions Pa...
...9/15/14 WWE Monday Night RAW – Lafayette, LA   9/14/14 WWE LIVE! – Boston, MA   9/13/1...
...RAW – Baltimore, MD   9/7/14 WWE LIVE! – State College, PA   9/6/14 WWE LIVE! – Dayto...
...WWE Monday Night RAW – Anaheim, CA   8/24/14 WWE LIVE! – Fresno, CA   8/23/14 WW...
...s Vegas, NV   8/17/14 WWE SummerSlam – Los Angeles, CA   8/11/14 WWE Monday Night RA...
...Melbourne, Australia – WWE LIVE! – Melbourne, Australia   8/4/14 WWE Monday Night RAW...
...7/27/14 WWE LIVE! – Dallas, TX   7/26/14 WWE LIVE! – Oklahoma City, OK   7/25/14 WW...
...r-View – Tampa, FL   7/14/14 WWE Monday Night RAW – Richmond, VA   7/12/14 WWE LIVE...
...VE Monday Night RAW – Montreal, Quebec   6/30/14 WWE Monday Night RAW – Hartford, C...
...4 WWE Monday Night RAW – Washington, DC   6/22/14 WWE LIVE! – Philadelphia, PA   6/21/1...
...W – Cleveland, OH   6/15/14 WWE Monday Night RAW – Fort Wayne, IN   6/14/14 WWE LIVE! – Grand Rapid...
...WWE LIVE! – Rochester, MN   6/7/14 WWE LIVE! – Madison, WI   6/6/14 WWE LIVE! – Detro...
...o, IL   5/26/14 WWE Monday Night RAW – Knoxville, TN   5/24/14 WWE LIVE! – Rotterdam...
...WWE LIVE! – Orchies, France   5/20/14 WWE LIVE! – Sheffield, England   5/19/14 WWE Monda...
...m, England   5/16/14 WWE LIVE! – Leeds, England   5/15/14 WWE LIVE! – Newcastle, Englan...
...E Monday Night RAW – Albany, NY   5/4/14 WWE Extreme Rules Pay-Per-View – East Rutherfor...
...WWE LIVE! – Louisville, KY   4/25/14 WWE LIVE! – Toronto, Ontario   4/21/14 WWE Monda...
...day Night RAW – New Orleans, LA   4/6/14 WWE WrestleMania 30 – New Orleans, LA   3/31/1...
...WWE Monday Night RAW – Brooklyn, NY   3/23/14 WWE LIVE! – Trenton, NJ   3/22/14 WW...
...an Antonio, TX   3/16/14 WWE LIVE! – Dallas, TX   3/15/14 WWE LIVE! – Austin, TX   3/14/1...
...nesboro, AR   3/8/14 WWE LIVE! at MSG – New York City, NY   3/7/14 WWE LIVE – Winnipe...
...E LIVE! – Jacksonville, FL   2/28/14 WWE LIVE! – North Charleston, SC   2/24/14 WWE Monda...
...17/14 WWE Monday Night RAW – Denver, CO   2/16/14 WWE LIVE! – Las Vegas, NV   2/15/1...
...2/9/14 WWE LIVE! – Fresno, CA   2/8/14 WWE LIVE! – San Jose, CA   2/7/14 WWE LIVE!...
.../14 WWE LIVE! – Orlando, FL   1/31/14 WWE LIVE! – Miami, FL   1/27/14 WWE Monday Nig...
...4 WWE LIVE! – Reading, PA   1/24/14 WWE LIVE! – State College, PA   1/20/14 WWE Monda...
...bus, OH   1/18/14 WWE LIVE! – Cincinnati, OH   1/17/14 WWE LIVE! – St. Louis, MO   1/6/1...
...AW – Baltimore, MD   1/5/14 WWE LIVE! – Roanoke, VA   12/30/13 WWE LIVE! – Greensboro, N...
...WE! Fayetteville, NC   12/29/13 WWE Monday Night RAW   12/29/13 WWE LIVE! – Hershe...

CHAPTER 1
WHAT WOULD YOU THINK IF I SANG OUT OF TUNE

It was a brisk Chicago morning in the Northwest Suburbs junior high social studies classroom when Mrs. Mitsokopoulos popped in a videotape and sat down at her desk. The volume of the video immediately rose as high as possible, causing Mrs. Mitsokopoulos to rush over to the television and lower the sound back to normal. As she sat back at her desk, the volume lowered all the way down to the very bottom. She walked over to the television and slightly adjusted the volume back up. While returning to her desk, the volume went all the way up once again. Sure enough, as she tried to slightly lower the volume, the level dropped to the very bottom.

After realizing that a movie wasn't going to work on this day, she proclaimed that the students would be presenting their current event articles to the class. A volunteer offered to start and stood sternly in front of his classmates to begin the presentation. Within 10 seconds, the class interrupted the student by standing up. An appalled Mrs. Mitsokopoulos immediately instructed the class to sit back down. As the student continued on to his second note card, the class once again stood in unison and began clapping. A perplexed Mrs. Mitsokopoulos looked around in awe at the unprecedented, possessed-like behavior taking place before her eyes. This classroom, however, was not haunted; it was just my social studies class. I was armed with a universal remote control watch and note cards that also served as cue cards to my classmates, instructing them to rise if they were enjoying the presentation and next to rise and applaud if they would like me to continue.

I always felt the need to entertain my classmates, to cheer people up, or to add some fun to serious and sometimes boring situations. My name is Justin, and on

December 29, 1979, I was born to two extremely loving parents, the best sister a kid could ask for, wonderful grandparents, a great-grandma, aunts, uncles, and cousins.

My dad, a Vietnam Purple Heart recipient, was the third generation of the family scrap metal business. He took his grandfather's company to a whole new level. Being a part of that business had been his dream since childhood, and he loved waking up early in the morning, getting on his truck and hustling. The super early start time would allow my dad to be home for his family in the afternoon and evenings.

My mom, who is a breast cancer survivor, was a former grade school teacher who left teaching to be a full-time mom once my sister and I were born. We were always her priority and could not have felt anymore love from another human being. I can't say she had a nice home-cooked meal ready for my dad when he came home from work, because dad didn't like the smell of cooking in the apartment. Carry-out or dining out usually fixed that, and she made incredible fish sticks, nuggets, macaroni, and cereal for my sister and me.

I enjoyed coming home early from kindergarten and watching *Batman, The Munsters*, and *The Monkees* and eating mom's deep-fried food. She would also spend the summers taking my sister and me to water parks, go-kart tracks, mini-golf courses, and anything else you could think of. As years went on, a great evening was watching *MacGyver, A-Team, The Fall Guy, The Cosby Show, Dynasty, Dallas,* or *Knots Landing* with my family. When I was five, my sister began babysitting for me on *Saturday nights*. Over the years, we teamed up and babysit for various neighbors and discovered quality TV programming like *Sisters, Amen, 227, Golden Girls, American Gladiators, Showtime at the Apollo*, and then *GLOW. Gorgeous Ladies of Wrestling* was unlike anything I had ever seen. Spike and Chainsaw, Mountain Fiji, Matilda the Hun, Hollywood and Vine...these ladies were nuts. Well, the bad guys were. Tina Ferrari, Little Egypt, and the good guys always overcame the evil in front of a small crowd at the Riviera hotel in Las Vegas. Sis and I were hooked on this show, which would lead right into *Saturday Night Live* on *NBC*. There were some weeks when *SNL* would be preempted for a wrestling show called *Saturday Night's Main Event*. This was wrestling, like GLOW, but with guys and a huge audience. I recognized some of these larger-than-life superstars from the wrestling show that I had seen on tv one time at my cousin Gordie's house. I remember seeing *the Genius* and *Mr. Perfect* causing trouble for *Hulk Hogan*. I didn't know who any of these guys were, but they were strong, colorful characters and I wanted to see what would happen next. I just didn't know how. I figured I'd have to wait until the next time *SNL* would be preempted.

I went to my grade school, kindergarten through sixth grade. I dealt with the usual daily shenanigans most kids deal with at some point—bullying, getting teased, you know. I had pretty ugly glasses, a mullet, big lips, and a big nose. I'm also Jewish, and there were only about six Jewish kids in the school, so kids weren't shy about sharing their opinions on us. I didn't have a ton of friends, but after seven years in the same school, I definitely had a handful of buddies and enough acquaintances to get by. Overall, there were a lot of good kids and very patient teachers who put up with a, I'll admit, very annoying student. Luckily, I had my big sister to look out for me and teach me to be a caring, thoughtful person. She was a great role model for me. I had a pretty high voice when I was young, and most people who called our house telephone thought that I was her. I used that to my advantage at times and had full conversations with people as her.

My family, along with a few of our family friends, spent winter break of 1991 at the Grand Milwaukee Hotel in Milwaukee, Wisconsin, on what would become a life-changing trip. The hotel had a New Year's Eve party for the adults, but, even better, a game room and indoor pool for the kids. My sister and our friends, Scott, Paul, Barry, and I were swimming in the pool, having a great time, when their friend Benjamin came running into the pool area. He was out of breath and very excited. "The Ultimate Warrior is here! The Ultimate Warrior is here!" I recognized the name from my casual WWF watching and knew exactly who that was. We jumped out of the pool and, throwing our towels on, ran up the stairs as fast as possible. Benjamin was young and had a hell of an imagination. We were a bit skeptical until there he was, standing right in front of us. A very large man with big, crazy hair and a denim jacket that contained cartoon images of himself, all muscled out. Wow. This was amazing. I had never seen a real-life wrestler before! There were just a few of us; it wasn't like there was a crowded lobby by any means, so we asked him and the large gentleman with him who I assumed was also a wrestler for their autographs. Warrior told us, "After we eat."

The two gentlemen walked into the empty hotel restaurant and ate their meal as we eagerly, yet patiently, waited outside in the lobby. Just a little over an hour later, standing there in our wet swimsuits which were finally starting to dry off, they walked out. Warrior signed one autograph for a kid who had shown up but wasn't with our group and left the hotel. The other man was very nice and signed for all of us. We asked his driver what the signature said, and he informed us that he was "the Texas Tornado" Kerry Von Erich of the legendary Von Erich family. We were happy to have seen both guys in person, but obviously were a bit disappointed in the Warrior for blowing us off.

I couldn't wait to get home and tell the kids at school about meeting these two huge superheroes from TV in person! I found wrestling in the TV guide and tuned into *WWF Superstars of Wrestling* on Saturday morning and *WWF Wrestling Challenge* on Sunday that week. I was hoping to catch the Warrior or Tornado and I was successful. In the meantime, I got HOOKED. The larger-than-life wrestlers, the colorful characters like Paul Bearer and Brother Love, the storylines that tied them all together—these shows were amazing. I immediately began watching religiously. Saturday morning, Sunday morning, and then primetime wrestling on Monday nights. The characters were nothing like I had seen before. This wasn't a movie with a Freddy Krueger-like bad guy. This was a television show with all sorts of characters battling it out. They were cool, fearless, weird, muscular, huge, tiny, magical—everything was covered. Most importantly, after meeting a couple of them, I knew they were real. People would always talk about wrestling as being "fake." I remember watching my first *WrestleMania* when Jake "the Snake" Roberts battled Rick "the Model" Martel in a blindfold match. As Jake was putting on the blindfold, you could see his hand go up the mask and could tell that the blindfold was see-through! I still never questioned how real it was, and, honestly, I never cared. Movies are not real, and I am entertained by movies. I was just as entertained by this, and it became my escape from reality. I lived for watching wrestling from week to week. I got picked on at school, but at the end of the day, all I wanted to do was go home and watch wrestling tapes, read wrestling magazines, play with my wrestling figures, and play wrestling video games. I loved wrestling and couldn't get enough of it.

My friend Adam was a wrestling fan and he had a family friend who was a promoter. I had no idea what a promoter was, but it translated to Adam getting free tickets when WWF came to the Rosemont Horizon in Chicago. They only came maybe twice a year and Adam would always tell me that there was possibly a chance I could go with him and his family. Well, on April 14, 1991, the opportunity arrived and he invited me (or I begged and invited myself) to go with his father and sister to the matches. I remember being in the car and staring at the Rosemont Horizon, sticking my head out the window and yelling back into to the car, "Wow! Hulk Hogan is inside that building!" We picked our tickets up at the box office Will Call window where his promoter friend left them for us and walked in to see Jimmy "Superfly" Snuka battling IRS and then Tugboat against the Warlord. Bret Hart took on the Barbarian, and I really wanted him to hand me his sunglasses, but that was usually for someone in the front row. Ricky Steamboat wrestled Haku; the Mountie wrestled the Big Boss Man; Legion of Doom fought the Nasty Boys; Ted DiBiase took on Virgil; and the main event was Hulk Hogan battling Sgt. Slaughter!

I was on top of the world. I had the time of my life that night and the next day, I decided that I wanted to be a wrestler and began coming up with possible names for myself. Jake, I liked that name. Harris, I liked that as a last name. Jake Harris… Jake "the Rake" Harris…I would carry a rake to the ring! I would spend my time daydreaming about being a wrestler, running down that aisle, slapping high fives, and signing autographs. My school notepads would consist of my autographs and logos for the Texas Tornado, Mr. Perfect, and the Million Dollar Man. All I could ever think about seven days a week, 24 hours a day was wrestling.

My cousin Duke was a Chicago police officer. On his off days he would work security at the Horizon. He always told me that he could get me backstage and that one of these days he would take me. At a family get-together we were talking wrestling. He saw how obsessed I was and said that he would bring me backstage for WWF the next time they were in town. My hopes were way up, and he came through. My dad bought tickets from the ticket broker at three times the price to land fifth-row seats for my mom, sister, and me. My dad had to be up too early for work to come with us. I watched in amazement as the Undertaker and Paul Bearer (walked to the ring by Chicago cops, including Cousin Duke) passed by me as I was right on the aisle. The security guards all lined up and held hands as the Ultimate Warrior ran to the ring. During intermission, Duke brought us behind the curtain. There was "Hacksaw" Jim Duggan and Kerry Von Erich—all the WWF wrestlers who were on the walls of my room just standing around right in front of me. And there was the Ultimate Warrior. I would finally get my autograph from the guy who was instantly one of my favorites due to his total dominance in the ring. Okay, well, I got lots of autographs and pictures, just not from Warrior. He ignored me when I called out his name and walked away. Maybe he didn't hear me. I was still determined to meet him a third time, but this time I wouldn't let him get away! All of those wrestlers on this night were awesome—Big Bossman, Marty Jannetty, "Hacksaw" Jim Duggan, and even the evil manager, Mr. Fuji. I got to meet everyone, and this made me love wrestling even more!

I collected and played with the WWF Hasbro action figures. Anytime I saw new figures in the *WWF* magazine, I would immediately start calling my local toy stores. The pictures came out way before the figures, so I would call daily. Literally. A nice kid named Chris at Toys"R"Us used to keep an eye out for me and let me know when the figures came in, but I had to have every one of them so it was a never-ending task. I would go home and sit on my floor where I had my Hasbro wrestling ring surrounded by my Hot Wheels car collection. The cars served as my audience for the action figures who would go into the ring and wrestle and then come through the curtain (fabric scraps from art class or even my sister's pom-poms) to the backstage area where they would all talk, just like at the Horizon. I played with my wrestling figures from the time I got home from school until it was time to go to sleep. Once in a while, I'd go across the street to my friend Louie's and shoot hoops or play Genesis, but playing with my wrestling figures allowed me to enter a world of my own. Without even knowing it, I was expanding my world of imagination. I was a wrestling promoter booking matches and feuds both in the ring and backstage. I was announcing the matches in my head. I was constantly redesigning the arena which existed in the corner of my bedroom. Whenever I would go downstairs, I would always run out of my room, through the hallway and down the stairs, pretending I was in a wrestling arena and slapping high fives along the wall and down the stairway railing while making my entrance into the ring. Quite the imagination I had, and truly an obsession as well.

While growing up in suburban Chicago, wrestling consumed my interests, but I also loved watching the Bulls games. We had Michael Jordan, Scottie Pippen,

Horace Grant, BJ Armstrong, John Paxson, Bill Cartwright, and Dennis Rodman, to name a few. Watching the incredible battles they had with rivals such as the Pistons, Knicks, and Celtics was amazing. I'll never forget the night I went with my dad to grab dinner at a pizza place I frequented in the Town & Country Mall called Garibaldi's. Mr. Garibaldi, who I had never met before, was actually there that night. After we ordered our food, he approached me and asked if I had finished my homework for the night. I had. He asked if I was a good kid. I thought so. He told us that he had four tickets for that night's Bulls game, and if it was okay with my dad, they would be ours. Despite having to be up early for work, he took me and a couple of neighbors to see the Bulls! I had a blast, and I never forgot what that felt like—having a random stranger do something so kind.

Our neighbors enjoyed the game, and I was glad that they got a treat as well. My neighborhood was really perfect, made up of friendly, genuine, caring people. Unfortunately, I was somewhat of a pain. I was the kid you didn't want living next door. I had a drum set that I played very loudly and not very well. I tried lessons over the years but didn't have the patience to get through playing the bells and working my way up the actual drums. I would take a small but powerful speaker and play music from my stereo out the window (at times telling the neighbors that it wasn't a tape of "Ice Ice Baby" or "Rico Suave," but rather the artists were in my room performing live). I had a strobe light that I'd put in my window, an emergency red police light, and anything else I could think of to "provide entertainment" for my neighbors. I'd spend much of my allowance money or money that I made from shoveling and snow-blowing driveways on microphones, amplifiers, and speakers from Radio Shack. Totally normal, right? I always, even up till now, felt like I was responsible for entertaining people, cheering them up, or helping them feel better. At the time, I meant well, but I was definitely seen as the annoying kid in the neighborhood. I had a lot of creative ideas. Once, I got my sister to chip in with me and throw my parents a huge 14th anniversary surprise party. All their friends, neighbors, and family came together and we all celebrated, not the 10th, 15th, or 20th, but the big 14th.

In my spare time, I would call in to the radio station Hot 102.3. I would make friends with all the DJs, like JoJo Martinez, and constantly win their hot 9-at-9 contest for free Domino's pizzas. I made them crazy, but I got to be on the air! When I wasn't harassing those poor DJs, I was in school, not really playing sports

(I tried football, but I didn't know the difference between offense and defense. I tried basketball and even wrestling, using moves I saw on TV), and going to Hebrew School three days a week. It's not like Spanish class where you learn the language; you just go there and learn how to read Hebrew but not translate or speak the language. You go three days a week for a number of years, and then when you turn 13, you get to read some Hebrew for your friends and family at the Bar Mitzvah—the huge party that signals you're finally a "man"—and make bank in presents. Well, I got kicked out of class on average two times a week. I brought *Playboys* to Hebrew School in second grade. My dad's friend got an accidental double subscription, so he'd given me the doubles. Brandi Brandt from the October 1987 issue is where it all began with "my" subscription. I got in trouble for bringing them to Hebrew School. Adam, who I only knew through Hebrew School, got kicked out for bringing a blowup doll to class dressed in a "sexy senior citizen" shirt, and each week we would get thrown out for talking too much or arguing with the teacher. I'd be impressed if any of those teachers continued teaching after that year with Adam and me. We were bored and made our own fun—it just didn't go over too well with the teachers.

My friend Anna, who I met on the last day of overnight camp one summer, was in a TV show called *The Torkelsons*. I had never known a celebrity before and was always fascinated by entertainment and learning about the real life of actors. The idea of fame seemed amazing—getting recognized, signing autographs. I was so curious to learn about that world. Anna and I would write letters back and forth, and I never missed her show. She played one of the cousins in the *Home Alone* movies and invited me to the *Home Alone 2* world premiere! This was a red carpet event that featured most of the cast, a screening of the movie before it was released, and an after-party. It was at this after-party where I got to play skee ball with Macaulay Culkin, who I liked because I had seen him on TV at *WrestleMania 7*. Knowing he was a wrestling fan, I told him that *Saturday Night's Main Event* was on while we were there, and there was a title change in the British Bulldog vs. Shawn Michaels match. I loved his movies and couldn't believe we were having a casual conversation. I realized right there that talking wrestling was my favorite thing to do, and it could bring people together from different places in life. He is a celebrity, yet I'm talking to him like he's my buddy because we both spoke the language of wrestling. Now everything in my world was slowly starting to revolve around pro wrestling.

When I graduated junior high, my grandma took my cousin Gordie and me on a Disney trip. We would spend half the week at Disney World and theme parks and the other half on the Big Red Boat cruise ship. I couldn't just take a trip and enjoy it, though. I had to figure out what sort of wrestling would be in Florida, and I happened to hit the jackpot. I discovered that Hulk Hogan would be signing his WCW contract at MGM Studios the week that I would be in Florida for the trip. WCW, or World Championship Wrestling was the rival organization to Vince McMahon's World Wrestling Federation. It was owned by Ted Turner and run by Eric Bischoff. When my favorite wrestlers disappeared from WWF with no mention of their departure, it was usually in WCW where they would magically appear once again. I had been watching WCW for a while at this point and with Hulk Hogan coming in, I knew their shows were definitely in for a change. We chose the itinerary that would have us at the parks on the day Hogan would be there, and of course I begged my grandma and cousin to go to MGM Studios on the right day. When we got to the park, not one employee had any idea about where Hulk Hogan was going to be. We spent the day at MGM, and right when I was ready to give up hope, I stumbled upon the area where the Hulkster would parade down to his contract signing. The scene was filled with random onlookers who had no idea how huge this event was. WCW reps were handing out Hogan signs and merchandise, but the actual fan couldn't get anyone's attention. My grandma and cousin patiently waited as I watched the entire parade and ceremony. I noticed Hulk's wife and kids along with legendary announcer "Mean" Gene Okerlund! When it was finished, I waved down a man in a suit and Hulk Hogan tank top. It was Eric Bischoff, the guy running WCW! I'm 14 years old, and of all things to ask, I asked him for a Hulk tank top! He could have easily laughed at me. He could have easily told me no. But he didn't. He told me to hang on. When he came back, his Hulk Hogan tank top was off his back and in his hand to give to me. That was a moment.

When I was 15, I couldn't just watch wrestling, I wanted to be a wrestler. I lived for wrestling; 24/7 that's what was on my mind, and I loved the idea of this world of make-believe. I would go to Blockbuster Video every weekend and rent *Coliseum Home Video* wrestling tapes and even watch the same ones over and over. I was still playing with my wrestling figures. My imagination would run wild, booking storylines and matches. Is it normal for a 15-year-old high school kid to still play with his wrestling figures? Probably not, but until I could play in a real ring, this was my only option. That got me to thinking, how can I pursue this dream? I actually looked in the yellow pages, but the pro-wrestling section wasn't there. Nowadays, you can find anything on the Internet, but in those days, the Internet could only take you so far. Websites were just starting to come out, and you could send emails, but only if you knew the exact address of a recipient.

Since I couldn't let my fingers do the walking, I began going to the hotels near the Rosemont Horizon when WWF would come to town. For years, I'd hang out near the hotel bar and that's where I could get pictures, autographs and even record videos on my video camera. I would have a list of questions that the guys would usually answer for me: "What was the worst injury you ever sustained?" Al Snow answered, "A broken heart." I would ask Savio Vega if he knew where Kwang (Savio was Kwang under a mask) was. I was young and did not have quality, well-thought-out questions. I just needed an excuse to talk to my heroes.

My cousin Duke was no longer working at the matches, so I discovered this as my way to meet everyone. I'd also stand out back of the Horizon and watch everyone pull up to the arena. I loved the adventure, waiting for a Ford Taurus or Lincoln Continental to pull up and running over to see who it was. Those were typically the rental cars that the wrestlers would drive into town. Once I saw a huge guy step out with a satin "Ribera" jacket. I knew it was definitely a wrestler, and I ran over. I loved watching the matches live, but that was never enough. I always wanted to see what I could get away with. Instead of watching the action in the ring, I'd watch the curtain above the main curtain where guys would peek out and watch the show. Who could I talk to? What information could I find out? I was never able to sit back, relax, and enjoy. I was always thinking ahead and trying to figure out how the whole machine operated. I would watch the road agents—the former wrestlers in charge at these shows. One of these agents, Rene Goulet, was once introduced to me by a security guard. He told Rene that I was a very big fan and always came to all the matches. Rene said the next time they came back, he would take me backstage and introduce me to the guys. The next two times WWF was in town, I eagerly looked out for Rene, but he wasn't there. Finally, nearly two years later, Rene was back! Unfortunately, he laughed at me when I told him what he had promised, as if the conversation had never happened.

When I was a freshman in high school, I met Vince McMahon, the man who ran WWF and blew it up to a new level after taking it from his father. The event was captured on *Chicagoland Television News*, and I still have the clip to this day. It was the 1994 *SummerSlam* charity softball game the weekend of WWF's big event at the United Center. The wrestlers played against Chicago media personalities. I stood along the fence and held up my Undertaker shirt for Vince to sign. He came over, and I asked him if Chicago would be getting *Radio WWF*. That was a radio show that could be heard in several markets where they talked about WWF, and, clearly, I needed an additional outlet to TV and *WWF* magazine. He explained that they were working on it, but I had already figured out how to get it on my own. When you called in on the 1-800-number to ask questions or take part in the contests, you were put on hold where you were able to listen to the show. I would call in and sit on hold to listen. They took my call a few times, and I made up questions for the wrestlers on the show. I also played a game of "Out-Think the Fink" where WWF human encyclopedia and ring announcer Howard Finkel would answer questions. I asked him to name the number on the back of Nailz's uniform, and he did not know that it was 902714, so I won a T-shirt…that never came to me. On this day, I met the Fink and told him I did not receive my T-shirt. He took my address, and a week later, I got my green "I out-thinked the Fink" T-shirt! I wonder how many other kids didn't get their prize and found Howard in person to ask for it?

Luckily, Howard came through for me, but I learned about disappointment pretty early on from experiences with the Warrior and Rene Goulet. I figured I would have to find my own way in, and it wasn't going to be easy. I was at the hotel bar one night when both WWF and WCW wrestlers were all staying at the same place. This was amazing. Rival organizations both in the same bar at the same time! Well, it turned out that the guys who had all worked with each other at some point in their careers were all friends and glad to be reunited. With their tour schedules, they never got to see each other, and this was a very rare moment. During my all hotel visits for shows, never were both companies in the same place at the same time. I had a video camera with me and spent nearly an hour talking with "Lord" Steven Regal from WCW. He was really friendly and incredibly patient with me. He knew I was a fan and took the time to answer all of my questions, and I had a lot of them. Not only that, but I went two nights in a row, and he talked to me both nights. There weren't too many wrestlers that I had noticed taking the time to talk with a curious high school kid, especially because this was their time to relax and enjoy some free time on the road.

Because I read everything I could on the subject, I thought I had a pretty good grasp on wrestling. I was on a cruise with my family in the middle of the ocean when I saw a kid who had to be about twelve swimming while wearing a Bret Hart T-shirt. He obviously loved wrestling as well. Just to mess with him, I told him that I was Bret Hart's cousin. He immediately doubted me and asked me some extremely simple Bret Hart trivia: "What's his brother's name?" He was shocked when I told him that Bret had more than the one brother he knew from TV. I had him convinced, although again I don't know why I would even make this up. This wasn't even a funny joke; it was just an outright lie—which was odd for someone who was always honest. Moments later, my parents were talking to his parents. Out of everyone on this boat in the middle of the ocean and anywhere in the world, the kid's father had designed the boxer shorts that we gave out at my Bar Mitzvah, and they were from my town in Illinois. Karma.

My dad—who looked very intimidating to those who didn't know him well—had a great sense of humor. However, just like it was uncharacteristic for me to tell this kid Craig that I was Bret's cousin, after telling my dad the story about Bret, my dad added to the situation by telling Craig that Bret would be coming on the cruise ship that night. Craig was ecstatic! My dad told him that he would be on the boat at midnight in the theater. So, at midnight, in the theater…Craig stood there wearing his still-wet Bret Hart shirt, hat, and sunglasses along with his video camera in hand.

I walked in laughing hysterically and told him that Bret wouldn't actually be able to make it, which he took okay. We ended up talking wrestling for the rest of the cruise and for the unforeseen future. Craig and I would talk wrestling daily and go to various shows and wrestler appearances together. He became like a little cousin to me.

On one of our adventures, I met Aldo Montoya, who was previously been known as PJ Walker and later on would become Justin Credible. He was 19 when he started and had finally caught his break after being used as enhancement talent for a while. *Enhancement talent* is a term that describes the guys who were put in a match solely to make the wrestling star look good. I figured he was a guy who could relate to me being young but serious about becoming a wrestler. He told me to call his friend Tony. He wrote his name, Tony's name, and Tony's number on a notecard. That Monday, I went to a payphone at my high school with a pocket full of quarters and called Tony in New York. He didn't answer, so I left a message on his answering machine. He didn't call back, so a few days later, with a pocket full of quarters, I went to the payphone and called him again. No answer, no call back. I continued to call every week until I finally caught him. I think it's safe to say that this is where I began to learn that persistence pays off.

"Hi, Tony. My name is Justin. I got your number from Aldo Montoya/PJ Walker, and I want to be a wrestler. I don't want to be one of those guys that loses every week, but I want to be a superstar like Bret Hart." Well, Tony explained how wrestling works as far as needing training. I was in high school in Chicago; he was in New York. We talked a few times, and I realized training with him in New York wasn't going to be practical. I couldn't drop out of school and move out there. Most important, I could look in the mirror and know that I did not look like a wrestler, so I had to start thinking realistically. I had also learned from talking to the wrestlers I had met at the hotel that while wrestling wasn't necessarily "real," that did not mean it was fake. The guys were not going out there intending to hurt each other, but it was more physical than people realize. Every time they go in the air, they have to land on wooden boards sittting on steel with little padding. While I loved wrestling, maybe getting in the ring to wrestle wasn't the right fit for me.

I found out shortly after my call with Tony that he was Tony Devito—a wrestler who I had seen on TV for years and, as I put it in our first conversation, "one of those guys that loses every week." Whoops. I felt horrible about that, but I think he understood. I was young and just a big fan, but as much as I knew about wrestling, I was ignorant of the business, or maybe just uneducated. Tony was always patient and very kind to me. He was another victim of my endless questions but always took the time when I called to talk wrestling. I was happy for him when he had a solid run in Extreme Championship Wrestling (ECW) as one half of the popular "Da Baldies" tag-team.

I had a group of wrestling friends who I would watch the monthly pay-per-views with and discuss wrestling on a daily basis. Bryan, Mike, Larry, and Dave were the regulars. Dave Prazak was brought into the group and had legitimate knowledge of the wrestling business. He was like an icon to us because of his experience, and he even knew some wrestlers as he worked with independent wrestling promotions and wrote a wrestling newsletter called, *Outside Interference*. He even had a book of…wrestler's phone numbers! This group of guys brought me to a whole new level as a fan. They helped me learn inside terms and find out what was going to be happening within the business. I also discovered wrestling hotlines and newspaper articles filled with wrestling rumors. Some resources were accurate, some not so much. On top of all of this, Dave also introduced me to independent wrestling-the minor leagues which I knew nothing about. We would take trips to Milwaukee, Wisconsin, for Mid-American Wrestling and even went as far as Detroit, Michigan, for a show called *Motor City Wrestling* that included future stars such as Rhino, Edge, and Christian.

I signed up with a casting company to do "extra" work because I wanted to be in movies. I stood in the background of *Soul Food*, at one point walking near Vivica Fox. I walked across a street in *Only the Lonely*, which allowed me to talk to John Candy, Anthony Quinn, and Maureen O'Hara. I sat in a crowd and watched Shaquille O'Neill play basketball. I walked across a street again in *I Love Trouble* and met Nick Nolte, I walked through an airport in *Sleepless in Seattle*, and I waved to Al Franken as I—you guessed it—walked down the street for a scene in *Stuart Saves His Family*. The best part, though? I was once called to be an extra as a wrestling fan for AWF TV tapings. I got paid to go to a wrestling show. The promotion was syndicated for a short time and featured tons of wrestlers that I had watched in WWF over the years like Hercules, Tito Santana, Greg Valentine, Sgt Slaughter, Koko B Ware, and many more. It was at this show that I met photographer Blackjack Brown who had been around the business for a long time and was actually friends with some of the WWF wrestlers. We wrote letters back and forth, and sometimes he would even send me shots that he took at WWF and WCW shows.

As wrestling began to grow, WWF raised the bar with their Monday night program called *Monday Night RAW*, which took over for *WWF Prime Time Wrestling*. WCW started a Monday night show to compete with them. Shortly after, WCW's Monday night show *Nitro* was in Chicago on October 9, 1995. I worked my way down to the front row, and I got to enjoy the show and even get on camera a couple of times, which was awesome. I was holding a videotape that I made for Marc Mero. Mero was one of the first wrestlers to communicate with fans over the Internet, which was just starting to become popular. We were using an online message board called RSPW which was short for rec.sport.pro-wrestling. Many fans who went on to contribute to the business later took part in RSPW, from writers to managers to wrestlers. Mero, who was known in WCW as Johnny B Badd, would throw a Frisbee out before his matches and shoot a confetti gun. One night on the WCW Saturday Night show, he held up his Frisbee and flipped it over to reveal "RSPW," which was a shout-out to the fans on there. I had gotten his email address from RSPW and emailed him around the same time, and he wrote back! I thought that was kind of him and wanted to give him something but did not know what. So I edited a videotape of his entrances from various pay-per-views set to his entrance music. Cheesy? Yes. But I was 15 and meant well. I held up that tape all night hoping to eventually get it to him, but he was not there that night. I did meet Diamond Dallas Page after the show by the backstage exit, who was kind enough to take the tape and give it to Mero.

On top of reading RSPW for all wrestling news and stories, I was a loyal subscriber to *WWF* magazine. And just like I couldn't strictly watch a live show, I couldn't strictly read the magazine. I was looking at the credits to see what I could figure out. I recognized one name, WWF ring announcer Howard Finkel. Since he was listed in the magazine, I had to assume the printed phone number to the offices was also a number that the man I once "outthinked" could be reached. I went to school with my pocket full of quarters and dialed the Stamford, Connecticut, number. When the receptionist answered, I politely asked for Howard Finkel. There was a pause. A click. A ring. And then there was that distinct voice that I recognized from television. I froze and quickly gathered my thoughts. "Hi, Howard, my name is Justin from Chicago." I would call Howard numerous times throughout the year and ask him about the various rumors I would hear from my friends and these other sources. "Is it true the Bushwhackers are going to WCW?" Howard would always take my call, even knowing that it was "Justin from Chicago" on the phone. In our last conversation at that point in time, Howard said, "Justin, I'm sure our paths will cross again in the future."

I gave Howard a break as I started gaining even more interest in the business side of wrestling. I'd always be a fan, but how could I get in now? I knew I that being an actual wrestler wasn't the route for me. I'd love to become a manager—that's easy, right? Run around the ring and scream at the wrestlers and fans. A ref? Easy way to get in the ring, and anyone could do it, right? Those were two positions that I assumed (and I was way off) were easy. As I would discover, just like becoming a wrestler, you had to train for these positions.

During all of my classes, I would sit and ponder a wrestling journey. I especially did this a lot during Ms. Glass' class. She was awesome, plus we watched a lot of movies—good movies, not the educational ones—mostly John Cusack movies, because he was her favorite. I also knew she was laidback and appreciated my sense of humor. She would have us read stories aloud and would call on various students to read a paragraph. Every time she called on me, I would read a paragraph in a different voice. Mrs. Doubtfire, Latka, *SNL* voices, anything I had in my repertoire. Most voices were inspired by *SNL's* Dana Carvey. I idolized him and his Church Lady character. I spoke like the Church Lady for most of my childhood. My teachers Mrs. Wituckee and Mrs. Malis could vouch for that. I knew every episode of *SNL* from the first to the last act and what songs the musical guest would perform. I also mocked their impersonations while reading aloud in Ms. Glass' class. I guess this is why I would get called on to read every other paragraph. Of course, I never minded it.

I loved to make my class laugh. In each class, I knew exactly how much I could get away with and how far I could push each teacher. I would raise my hand and reference an episode of *Saved by the Bell*. "Excuse me, Mrs. R, I don't think we should have to take this test today." There was this one episode of *Saved by the Bell* where they had a substitute teacher, and the sub had everyone rip up the tests and give him the grade they thought they deserved. "Can we just tell you what grade we think we deserve?"

"It's really nice out. Can we have class outside today?"

"There's a new episode of *Tempest* today. Can we please watch that?" "Did you ever see that episode of *Full House* where…?"

I had the most obscure comments every single time I was called on, and this happened on a daily basis and in every class. Even the sternest teachers would eventually succumb to my antics and get a kick out of my shtick. I would schmooze the hall guards, the lunch ladies, other teachers I didn't know, the principals, and the van patrol ladies. I never looked at anyone as the holder of his or her position or even as any kind of authority. I just looked at everyone for his or her fun side— even those people who weren't supposed to have a fun side. Our parking lot was big, but only seniors and faculty could park in the main lot. Everyone else had to park far away in a mini lot. My friends and I took over a new Dunkin' Donuts that opened across the street from school. Despite not actually working there, we would go in and run the place, put on the headsets, take orders, even make the fancy iced coffees that we didn't know how to make. They would give me bags of coffee when I left. So, I'd pull into school and find the van ladies who would patrol the lot and make sure that only faculty parked in the front spaces. I'd bring them coffee now and then, and they'd pull away whenever I pulled into the lot, opening a faculty spot and turning their backs to my parking there. I'd go with my best friend Ross into the principal's office and talk about craving Good & Plenty but how they're not in the vending machine and suggest they add that. We walked around the school like we owned it, and we were allowed that unofficial permission just by being friendly to everyone. Being friendly opened every door at that school, and that's where I learned that being friendly could open just as many doors in life.

My parents always taught me to treat everybody with respect and as equals. My dad would tell stories about being friends with the janitors in his school; he'd treat the bus boys, servers, and hosts at restaurants the same way that he treated the owners. It rubbed off on me, and it bothers me when people talk down to others they feel are beneath them. There's no such thing, and you're not always going to be on top, especially if that's how you treat people. Plus, it just feels good to be friendly to people.

I had a pager in high school. It was the best thing you could have in a pre-cell phone era. My dad would page me during the school day, and I would go to my various faculty friends at school and get permission to use the school phones to call him back. "What's up, dad? I'm taking a test." "Nothing. I'm at Sam's Club. Want anything?" It was usually something along those lines. He just wanted to say hello in the middle of the school day. He would come home from work and want to talk to his kids, but we were at school. So he'd page me and get that quick conversation in. He would also drive by the school parking lot on days when it snowed to brush the snow off our cars. He loved his kids and always found a way to go above and beyond for us.

I loved my parents as I knew how caring they were—not just to my sister and me, but to everyone. I was grateful for where I grew up. I really loved my high school. It was fun! Just knowing that I was connected, so to speak, and could never get in trouble was a great feeling. I genuinely enjoyed hanging out with the faculty and guards during the day and just talking anything but rules. I feel like high school gave me the confidence and was my launching pad into entertainment. I continued to use my different voices to entertain classmates, broadening my abilities. A common voice I'd turn to was the "announcer" voice. It was the over-the-top, deep-voiced announcer. Pretty basic, but a hit with the class. I was also a voice on a wrestling hotline at this time. Dave Prazak had a hotline with legitimate wrestling "news" from his inside sources. Meanwhile, a kid named Paul at my school started his own. The only problem was that his hotline was all fluff. Poor Paul was a fan but did not have any real insight to the business. Dave, for good reason, wouldn't let me join him (he had no use for me), so I joined Paul. I would use the news that I got from other hotlines, newsletters, newspapers, or even RSPW. The Internet message boards were becoming popular along with the worldwide web at this point. I used the name Enzo Reed after I overheard my sister mention in a car ride that she liked the name Enzo. She also liked the name Reed. I put the two together and became Enzo Reed. My sister influenced all my television habits, so why not let her influence my name as well? My friend Brian joined me on the hotline as "Stone" (he was a "Stone Cold" Steve Austin fan), and we basically took over from there, which Paul liked because we attracted callers. The callers could then leave voice messages with feedback and questions.

My parents were born and raised in Chicago. When my sister went to Arizona for college, they decided to purchase a small home in Scottsdale to escape the cold weather once in a while and visit my sister. I loved going on those trips as Scottsdale was so different from what I was used to. It was somewhat green, filled with palm trees, and almost every day you could gaze into a sunny, clear blue sky which was a much appreciated change of scenery from Chicago. It was paradise for me. Labor Day weekend my parents brought me along on their trip. The timing was almost perfect as the Monday we were leaving, WCW was going to be in Phoenix for *Nitro*. I begged my parents to take an airline bump so we could get paid in travel vouchers to stay an extra day and fly out in the morning. Coincidentally, that would allow me to go see *Nitro*. My dad had work early the next morning, and both my parents were ready to go home. I begged, but they wouldn't budge this time. We boarded the flight, and I knew that I had lost the battle...until the pilot came on with that John Wayne voice, sounding like he was taking a cigarette drag in between sentences and probably squinting his eyes as he informed us that we had an issue with our aircraft. Everybody would need to leave the plane and head back into the airport. Now we had a problem. Well, everyone on the plane had a problem. I had an opportunity.

That Monday night after a holiday weekend, the airport was slammed. We needed a new aircraft and there were none available. We were told that it would be at least six hours before we would hear any news. I asked my parents if I could go to the show, and they knew me well enough that I would find my way there and back and be safe in between. I left the airport, hopped in a cab, and went to the America West Arena. I bought a ticket from a scalper outside and went to my seat, which was in the fifth row across from the entranceway. As always, I couldn't just go and watch a show. I had to see what I could get away with, make a contact, leave my mark, anything but just sit and watch.

Steven Regal was in the ring with Juventud Guerrera, and I noticed that Xpac, or Syxx as he was called in WCW, was heading down the steps in the middle of the crowd across from the television cameras. I found my spot! I bolted up there before everyone else caught on. While he was talking on the mic, or "cutting his promo" as insiders would say, I stood next to him and mouthed the phone number to my Chicago wrestling hotline. Did I really think that people were going to catch that and call? Would they rewind their videotape to catch that number they missed? I'm not sure what was going through my mind, but I had to do something, and that was my angle. I would market my hotline on television by mouthing the phone number. Once that was done, the only plan I could think of was to wave, smile, and jump up and down in front of Syxx. Thinking about that today makes me cringe, but I still smile when I see that television clip.

I returned from Arizona very early on that next Tuesday morning hours before school began. Numerous kids came up and asked if I was on *Nitro* the previous night. While that part was cool, the best part was knowing that so many people at my school were finally watching wrestling…and admitting it!

PART II

8/12 WWE RAW Live – Dublin, Ireland   11/7/12 WWE RAW Live – Belfast, Northern Ireland
4/12 WWE RAW Live – Nottingham, England   11/3/12 WWE RAW Live – Manchester, England
WE RAW Live – Strasbourg, France   10/29/12 WWE Monday Night RAW – Charlotte, NC
herford, NJ   10/21/12 WWE RAW Live – Hartford, CT   10/20/12 WWE RAW Live – Reading, PA
WE Monday Night RAW – Sacramento, CA   10/7/12 WWE RAW Live – Spokane, WA   10/6/12
W – Oklahoma City, OK   9/30/12 WWE RAW Live – Wichita, KS   9/29/12 WWE RAW Live –
Y   9/23/12 WWE RAW Live – Worcester, MA   9/22/12 WWE RAW Live – White Plains, NY   9/
WE Night of Champions Pay-Per-View – Boston, MA   9/10/12 WWE Monday Night RAW – Mo
ustralia   8/31/12 WWE RAW Live – Sydney, Australia   8/30/12 WWE RAW Live – Brisbane, A
25/12 WWE RAW Live – Peoria, IL   8/24/12 WWE RAW Live – Cape Girardeau, MO   8/20/12
3/12 WWE Monday Night RAW – Dallas, TX   8/12/12 WWE RAW Live – Texarkana, AR   8/11
W – San Antonio, TX   8/5/12 WWE RAW Live – Dothan, AL   8/4/12 WWE RAW Live – Alba
9/12 WWE RAW Live – Louisville, KY   7/28/12 WWE RAW Live – Lexington, KY   7/27/12 W
2/12 WWE RAW Live – Springfield, MO   7/21/12 WWE RAW Live – Little Rock, AR   7/20/1
oney in the Bank Pay-Per-View – Phoenix, AZ   7/14/12 WWE RAW Live – Tucson, AZ   7/13/1
onday Night RAW – Denver, CO   7/7/12 WWE RAW Live – Lubbock, TX   7/6/12 WWE RAW L
Long Island, NY   6/17/12 WWE No Way Out Pay-Per-View – East Rutherford, NJ   6/11/12 WW
ve – Valencia, Spain   6/7/12 WWE RAW Live – Seville, Spain   6/6/12 WWE RAW Live – Mad
6/2/12 WWE RAW Live – Mobile, AL   6/1/12 WWE RAW Live – Alexandria, LA   5/28/12 W
W Live – Guayaquil, Ecuador   5/24/12 WWE RAW Live – Sao Paulo, Brazil   5/21/12 WWE M
WE Monday Night RAW – Pittsburgh, PA   5/13/12 WWE RAW Live – Rochester, NY   5/12/12 W
W – Greensboro, NC   5/6/12 WWE RAW Live – Chattanooga, TN   5/5/12 WWE RAW Live –
H   4/29/12 WWE Extreme Rules Pay-Per-View – Chicago, IL   4/23/12 Monday Night RAW – Detr
WE RAW Live – Toulouse, France   4/18/12 WWE RAW Live – Milan, Italy   4/17/12 WWE RA
Nottingham, England   4/14/12 WWE RAW Live – Berlin, Germany   4/13/12 WWE RAW Live –
ssia   4/9/12 WWE Monday Night RAW – Washington, DC   4/2/12 WWE Monday Night RAW
29/12 WWE AXXESS – Miami, FL   3/26/12 WWE Monday Night RAW – Atlanta, GA   3/25/12
akeland, FL   3/19/12 WWE Monday Night RAW – Philadelphia, PA   3/18/12 WWE Supershov
3/12/12 WWE Monday Night RAW – Cleveland, OH   3/11/1
3/5/12 WWE Monday Night R

RUNNING DOWN A DREAM

WWE RAW Live – Glasgow, Scotland   11/5/12 WWE Monday Night RAW – Birmingham, England
2 WWE RAW Live – Newcastle, England   11/1/12 WWE RAW Live – Nantes, France   10/31/12
WWE Hell in a Cell Pay-Per-View – Atlanta, GA   10/22/12 WWE Monday Night RAW – Eas
12 WWE RAW Live – Trenton, NJ   10/15/12 WWE Monday Night RAW – Nashville, TN   10/8/12
AW Live – Yakima, WA   10/5/12 WWE RAW Live – Everett, WA   10/1/12 WWE Monday Nigh
KS   9/28/12 WWE RAW Live – St. Joseph, MO   9/24/12 WWE Monday Night RAW – Albany
WE RAW Live – State College, PA   9/17/12 WWE Monday Night RAW – Bridgeport, CT   9/16/12
uebec   9/3/12 WWE Monday Night RAW – Chicago, IL   9/1/12 WWE RAW Live – Melbourne
8/27/12 WWE Monday Night RAW – Milwaukee, WI   8/26/12 WWE RAW Live – Rockford, IL
Monday Night RAW – Fresno, CA   8/19/12 WWE SummerSlam Pay-Per-View – Los Angeles, CA
E RAW Live – Biloxi, MS   8/10/12 WWE RAW Live – Tupelo, MS   8/6/12 WWE Monday Nigh
8/3/12 WWE RAW Live – Jacksonville, FL   7/30/12 WWE Monday Night RAW – Cincinnati, OF
AW Live – Charleston, WV   7/23/12 WWE Monday Night RAW 1000th Episode – St. Louis, MC
RAW Live – Jackson, MS   7/16/12 WWE Monday Night RAW – Las Vegas, NV   7/15/12 WWE
Con WWE/Mattel – San Diego, CA   7/12/12 Con WWE/Mattel – San Diego, CA   7/9/12 WWE
arillo, TX   7/2/12 WWE Monday Night RAW – Laredo, TX   6/18/12 WWE Monday Night RAW
y Night RAW – Hartford, CT   6/9/12 WWE RAW Live – Barcelona, Spain   6/8/12 WWE RAW
6/4/12 WWE Monday Night RAW – Greenville, SC   6/3/12 WWE RAW Live – Birmingham
nday Night RAW – New Orleans, LA   5/26/12 WWE Over the Limit Pay-Per-View – Raleigh, NC   5/14/12
ght RAW – Richmond, VA   5/20/12 WWE RAW Live – Glens Falls, NY   5/7/12 WWE Monday Nigh
W Live – Syracuse, NY   5/11/12 WWE RAW Live – Huntsville, AL   4/30/12 WWE Monday Night RAW – Dayton
e, TN   5/4/12 WWE RAW Live – Merksem, Belgium   4/20/12 WWE RAW Live – Paris, France   4/19/12
4/21/12 WWE RAW Live – Rome, Italy   4/16/12 WWE Monday Night RAW – London, England   4/15/12 WWE RAW Live
rt, Germany   4/12/12 WWE RAW Live – Gdansk, Poland   4/11/12 WWE RAW Live – Moscow
i, FL   4/1/12 WWE WrestleMania 28 – Miami, FL   3/31/12 WWE Hall of Fame – Miami, FL
RAW Live – Charlotte, NC   3/24/12 WWE RAW Live – San Juan, PR   3/23/12 WWE RAW Live
New York City, NY   3/17/12 WWE Supershow Live – Providence, RI   3/16/12 WWE Supershow
RAW Live – Buffalo, NY   3/10/12 WWE Supershow Live – London, Ontario   3/9/12 WWE RAW Live
ston, MA   3/4/12 WWE RAW Live – Bangor, ME   3/3/12 WWE RAW Live – Ottawa, Ontario
ight RAW – Portland, OR   2/26/12 WWE RAW Live – Eugene, OR   2/25/12 WWE RAW Live
2/24/12 WWE RAW Live – Los Angeles, CA   2/20/12 WWE
RAW – Minneapolis, MN   2/19/12

CHAPTER 2
PUT YOUR MIND TO IT, GO FOR IT

I was 16 on November 22, 1996, and there was an independent show coming to Waukegan, Illinois, at the Fiesta Palace. The show was run by Sonny Rogers who was a wrestler from the Chicago area who had done lots of enhancement work for WWF over the years. He also ran a training school. A guy named Brian Schenk who I had become friends with from the hotline world knew Sonny. I was somewhat known to a handful of people in the Chicago wrestling scene as Enzo Reed from calling into the hotline. Dave Prazak was going to be the ring announcer on that show. I told Brian I did an announcer voice, and I know it's the one position that doesn't require going to wrestling school. I asked if maybe I could be a ring announcer for one match as Enzo from the hotline. In my head, I thought maybe that would buy me a little credibility, and there'd be a chance one or two fans would recognize the name. Brian talked to Sonny and got it approved. I was going to be stepping into a wrestling ring and announcing on top of that! I was beyond excited.

I wasn't too nervous about being on stage as I was part of a singing and dancing show choir group at my high school. That might not sound cool, but it was a huge part of my high school launching pad, and I thought it was beyond cool. We had a teacher who didn't put up with any nonsense. She took me and many other kids who couldn't sing or dance and made singers and dancers out of us. We competed around the country and actually won. I learned so much about performing and professionalism from being a part of this group. If my nose itched, I would not scratch it. If I had sweat pouring down my face, I would not wipe it. She taught us so many little secrets about what to do and not do while on stage. If you were a strong dancer, you would be in the front row. If it was a good idea to have people blocking your legs, then maybe you danced in the back row. If you were a strong singer, you would be given a solo in a real song. If you sang like me, your solo would be Sebastian's in "Under the Sea" from *The Little Mermaid* or "Day-O" with a gimmicky voice and accent. She knew how to accentuate our strengths and cover our weaknesses. There were 17 guys and 17 girls. We danced in tuxedos and sequin vests. The girls had matching sequin dresses. We even had our own band. The group was a lot of fun, and it was my first experience traveling as a group on something that felt like a tour.

My family always came out to support our shows and enjoyed watching the magic that the teacher had made with us. I had gained a lot of confidence from performing with this group and learned a lot about professionalism that I could use even in the wrestling ring.

I took my show choir experience and arrived that night to the Fiesta Palace in my black suit, black shirt, and white tie. It seemed the perfect attire for Enzo Reed. The venue wasn't the Horizon, or even an arena or theatre. It was a small restaurant/night club. I wasn't sure how Dave would take to me stepping on his toes and announcing a match. This was the same guy who wouldn't let me on his hotline, and I was now interfering in his ring-announcing gig. Luckily, Dave was actually very cool and let me announce both a six-man tag-team match and the battle royal, where a bunch of the wrestlers came to the ring and tried to throw each other over the top rope. I stood in the ring and could not stop thinking about the fact that I was standing in a wrestling ring. It was not WWF or WCW, but it was a real show with a real audience. I was not good. I was actually horrible. I used that deep announcer voice and did what I was supposed to do and said what I planned to say, even though I was unsure of what I was announcing and used incomplete sentences. It was over before I knew it and was only a small taste of wrestling, but I knew that I wanted more!

I introduced myself to Sonny Rogers and stayed on him about future work. He had me come back and work half of his show the next time. Before I knew it, I was the sole ring announcer for his shows during my last two years of high school. I got my feet wet and also got to meet wrestlers I grew up watching—guys like King Kong Bundy who had been to the top, WWF, and even on one of my other favorite shows, *Married With Children*. Again, me being me, I couldn't just work a show with this legend. I had to find an angle to do more. Each classroom at school had a television, and we would broadcast morning announcements on a short, televised news program. This was the perfect gig for me, delivering news off the teleprompter to my high school. I wasn't shy and would usually try to make standard school announcements, entertaining. I asked King Kong Bundy if he wouldn't mind cutting a promo for my school news show. He was happy to help, and we shot a brief clip with him standing next to me, saying our school name, and basically going along with whatever I threw out there. It was a cool moment for me to make this video with a legend who was the main event of *WrestleMania 2* with another WWF legend, Hulk Hogan. *WrestleMania* is the Super Bowl of wrestling and the biggest wrestling event of the year. Hulk Hogan has always been one of the biggest names in the industry, so it was the perfect mix for King Kong Bundy and now for my school! Now that I had this footage I had to think of a way to take it a step further. I loved wrestling; I wanted my school to jump on board and at least tolerate wrestling. Since I was a kid, everyone made fun of me for watching it, but when no one was around, they'd ask me questions. No one my age would admit to watching, as they claimed they "grew out of it." I wanted that to change. So I needed the school to know how cool it was to have Bundy on our morning announcements. I had to grab their attention and then build credibility. How I knew this at 17, I'm not sure, but maybe I was just born to produce wrestling. I used my VCR tape decks at home and created a video of King Kong Bundy vs Hulk Hogan footage, followed by Bundy destroying another wrestler, followed by Bundy's promo about our school. The video was a hit. Kids were coming up to me all day saying how cool that was. I knew that I was on to something and that would not be the end of wrestling on our school morning announcements program.

I always stopped by the school library to talk to the librarians, Mrs. Bass and Mr. G. Mrs. Bass was always very serious, but I knew that in time if I stayed on her with my goofy ways, eventually she would crack, and I could pull out a fun side. In time, I was actually successful. Mr. G was the only male librarian. He was quiet but had a great sense of humor and appreciated the entertainment of my interactions with Mrs. Bass. What he didn't appreciate was students not returning their library books. He enjoyed the videos I made on the morning announcements and asked if I could get the wrestlers to make a video about returning library books. I thought that was really funny, and I knew he was dead serious. So it became a mission that I was determined to complete. Wrestling was starting to get hot. After years of being the number two promotion, WCW was picking up a lot of viewers. The *Monday Night Wars* battle of the two top promotions and their Monday night television programs were on, and my classmates were starting to get back into wrestling—or at least began admitting that they watched. The NWO, Goldberg, "Stone Cold" Steve Austin, and the Rock were not only popular with wrestling fans, but they were also attracting the casual fans and making wrestling cool again for the first time since I was a fan.

I went to a WWF show at the Rosemont Horizon, and it was packed, completely sold out. Every wrestler who came out had a catchphrase, and the people went crazy for every entrance. I went to the hotel they usually stayed at and, of course, brought my video camera. Cactus Jack had just come over to WWF as Mankind and would later become Mick Foley. Mankind, New Age Outlaws, and Ron Simmons all cut promos for my high school about returning library books. So now I was using current footage of these guys who were huge, popular stars in their matches and cutting to them talking about our school and returning library books. I was awesome! The students were enjoying the bonus to our morning announcements, having their favorite WWF stars mentioning our school, and Mr. G was ecstatic to have these stars campaigning for returning library books!

During winter break, my friends and I were going with our parents to check out various nearby colleges. University of Illinois, Indiana, Ohio…I got cold just thinking about those places. That was the problem. The week before our trip, I was on the phone with my sister who was attending school at the University of Arizona in Tucson. It was 8 in the evening, and she was on the balcony where it was 80 degrees. When we hung up, I asked my mom why we should even bother checking out those Midwest schools. I had had enough of the cold that went right through my winter coat and right through me. I wanted to go to college in Arizona. I loved the people and the food at home, but the weather was miserable. That next week, my mom, my friend Scott, and I jumped in the car and drove to Arizona to check out U of A and ASU. It was on this trip that my mind was made up that I would definitely go to college in Arizona for that perfect weather alone.

Back in Chicago, I was continuing to work for PWI, and the sporadic shows were fun. The idea of doing that in the big leagues was not even fathomable. This was a way to live out my dream as a fun hobby. I was now getting paid about $25 to basically watch independent wrestling and, of course, get in the ring and use my announcer voice. Billy Joe Eaton was a wrestler I had seen on WWF TV and worked with at PWI. To me, announcing him was making it. Adam Pearce, Danny Dominion, Ace Steele, Rockin' Randy, Trevor Blanchard, Eric Freedom, Adrian Lynch, Ronnie Vegas, Jinx, Jimmy Blaze, Sonny Rogers, and John Burke were just some of the talent I was able to announce. My friends would always come out to watch. It was a lot of fun! There was a rival organization building up around town. They weren't from a training school, though. They were the LWF, Lunatic Wrestling Federation, and they were self-trained or glorified backyard wrestlers. They may not have taken the suggested channels for training, but they were putting on entertaining shows, and their crowds only grew over time. A few of their wrestlers would typically come to our shows to heckle the talent and amuse themselves. There was a team of CM Venom and CM Punk. At one point during our Crystal Lake show at an indoor volleyball court, the action went out into the crowd, and I was left alone at the plastic ringside patio chairs. CM Punk came over and sat down next to me. He put his arm around me and told me that they were taking over. They didn't actually take any action or do anything wrong, they just made their presence felt in a fun way that amused them and helped add to their buzz.

Over time, Sonny's guys would get tryouts with WWF or be used locally as WWF enhancement talent. The LWF guys had a great run but eventually faded. Punk hooked up with Dominion and Steele who had started their own school and fine-tuned the skills he had learned himself. He worked nonstop with other talent to become one of the best and made everyone he worked with that much better.

Graduating high school was bittersweet. I was comfortable. Really comfortable. I had a great group of friends. As to be expected, we weren't your normal group, either. We weren't going out and doing the usual things in high school. A couple of us had convertibles and would put the tops down in the middle of winter and fly kites out of our cars while driving around the school parking lot. We would take over restaurants that we frequented and play "host" and "server." Ask a girl to one of the school dances? No. Too normal. We would rather drive to a friend's house where everyone would meet before and after the dance and make goofy signs and tie cars together with string. We were not, by any means, the school studs, but we were having fun while not harming anyone else, and that was all that mattered.

My odd qualities had even been noticed by my classmates. When the senior paper came out, I found out that my class voted for me in a few superlative categories. My accolades were 1) best at getting teacher off subject; 2) most likely to win an academy award; and 3) most likely to host a TV show. I was most proud of number 1 as I put a lot of effort into that.

Junior and senior year were really the first point in my life in which I had a group of close friends. I had always been so odd that I only got along well with a friend or two. I was now having fun with good friends in and out of school, and it was great having a friendship with the majority of the school staff on top of it. I was a lifeguard and supervisor at a day-camp pool; I was a server at a neighborhood restaurant; and I even played cards next door at the movie theater in the projector room with the staff. There were many different cliques, but I talked to and liked everyone in and out of school. I thought for an 18-year-old, I also had a lot of connections in Chicago. Mike Lima was a promoter who I had bugged at shows since I was a kid. Later on, he would get me tickets to various shows. I think Mike was my only connection in the wrestling or even entertainment world, but I guess I considered knowing the staff at all of the establishments I frequented a "connection," and it was time to leave that all behind and start fresh at college.

CHAPTER 3
THERE'S A PATH YOU TAKE AND A PATH UNTAKEN

In the fall of 1998, my mom and grandma brought me out to Tucson to begin my education at the University of Arizona. I picked U of A over ASU only because Tucson felt like a college town where everything focused on the university, whereas ASU was in the middle of a major city with lots of things going on. I chose media arts as my major and communications as my minor. I took all the same classes growing up as my sister, so why not follow in her footsteps in college and take the same major as well? I figured I would choose a major that would require me to take classes in which I got to learn about entertainment and how to talk with people. Sounded easy enough! Oh, and I happened to have all her papers and notes as I did in high school...if needed.

Now, I don't condone cheating in school. Maybe I do. Here's the problem: You sit in class every day and learn for hours. You are expected to go home and read or watch something and memorize it for a test, answer some questions, and move on. I don't think you are actually learning or retaining much with that process. I know, personally, I would be too busy stressing over the memorization. My theory was that in life we are allowed to use notes. If that's the case, then we should be able to do the same in school. If there wasn't a way to use notes on a test, the next best thing was using your intelligent classmates. I had a classmate named Justin who, by design, always sat in front of me in sociology. He would leave his question sheet on his lap off to the left and his answer sheet on the desk. For whatever reason, he would visibly circle the answers on the question sheet so I was able to make sure that he knew his material, of course. I would also give him a few dollars as a reward for doing so well. After watching him circle answers and circle the same answers on my answer sheet, I would turn in the test and do very well. Not because I studied, but because Justin studied and I...cheated. At times we would have to write essays as part of an exam. We were told to pull out a blank piece of notebook paper at the start of the test, but why pull out a blank sheet when you can write the essay out at home (we knew the questions before the test) and pull out a sheet containing the essay? While 99% of the class would use the blank sheet, I would think outside the box and use the answered essay sheet. In the end, I got an A. The class got As, Bs, Cs, Ds, and Fs. Even today, none of us remembered the answer to that essay question, so I think I made the right decision.

I wasn't very talented when it came to sports, or anything common, really. I was, however, very resourceful and talented when it came to cheating. My sister always saved her work, and I had a great mind for creative writing which came in handy for essays that I couldn't pre-write as well as presentations. Starting fresh in college, I wasn't sure what I could use from her or how I would be able to beat the system since the rumors state, you can't cheat in college.

I always used wrestling as the topic for my papers and presentations in high school because I knew wrestling and everyone and everything related to the subject. Wrestling was my life, and I was full of wrestling knowledge. I told the right story and just made up the sources. I knew the teachers didn't have a clue, but the stories made sense as they were based on the business, and there was no way the teacher would check these sources. Freshman year in college, I got stuck with the general education courses that no one else wanted and a horrible schedule on top of it. My first major paper for an astronomy class I knew nothing about gave us the option to do a presentation for the lecture hall or write a paper. My friend and I made a movie and did a presentation which had nothing to do with anything from class, just taking the sci-fi road and using examples of things we did in class that we didn't understand and making fun of them in the presentation. At the end, we got a standing ovation from the entire lecture hall. It was straight out of *Bill and Ted's Excellent Adventure:* "San Dimas High School football rules!" As time went on, I discovered that I actually was a good student. I wasn't cheating and was taking the extra steps and extra time to learn the material.

While I am not the frat boy type, I thought joining one might be a good way to make friends. So I joined the biggest party fraternity on campus. It was such a big party frat that they got kicked off campus the year before I joined for lighting the swimming pool on fire. I'm not a big party guy, but for some reason I ended up there. Maybe because the house was an old Howard Johnson hotel and every room had two bedrooms, two bathrooms, a kitchen, a family room, and, of course, that pool. I met a few of the guys through the brother of one of my sister's friends when they had a summer get-together in Chicago. Another kid I grew up with who also caused trouble for teachers we didn't care for was also joining this house. I guess the accommodations, reputation, and few guys I met made me side with them. Pledging was hell for an entire semester. When they found out that I was a wrestling announcer, part of my hazing was to announce things. Every little thing, actually. Certain guys walking through the door, certain guys just standing there, recording voicemail greetings. Haze announcing. We got hazed seven days a week, but also got to enjoy the parties that came with it. In addition to a lot of the Wildcat athletes, Nicole Richie, Kourtney Kardashian, and others frequented our parties and fraternity house, in general.

I was definitely having fun, but I wasn't totally sure how I would ever get wrestling work in Arizona. The one wrestling company that allowed me to announce was in Illinois, and I knew of nothing in Arizona. Before I left for school, I was told that the Honky Tonk Man, a popular WWF superstar from the late 80s, lived in Arizona. One of my wrestling friends got me his number, and I gave him a call. He was very nice and gave me the name of Dale Pierce. I called Dale who had been around the Arizona wrestling scene for a while. He suggested that I call Navajo Kid who also went by the name Navajo Warrior. I called him a few times before I finally caught him. I arrived at the conclusion after calling DeVito and Navajo that wrestlers don't return calls and rarely answer their phones. This was also still the pre-cell phone era. Navajo had been wrestling for a long time all throughout the southwest in the indie circuit as well as working as enhancement talent when WWF came to town. When we did talk, I could tell that he was a very nice and knowledgeable guy as well as very serious and all business. He told me that he would let me know if any shows came up that needed an announcer. That was all I needed to hear to make me optimistic for an announcing future in Arizona.

I was in my dorm room when I read an article on a wrestling website called *Scoops* about the AWA coming back. AWA was an incredible wrestling territory from Minnesota years ago that bred numerous future Hall of Famers and legends. I read the press release and saw the lineup of all of these big names and, most important, this event was to be held in Bullhead City, Arizona. I had no idea where that was, but it was Arizona. I emailed the editor, Al Isaacs, who gave me the promoter's email address. I then sent an email letting the promoter know that I was a wrestling ring announcer and lived in Arizona and that I would love to be a part of the new AWA.

Within days of emailing the AWA, I heard back from a Dale Gagne who introduced himself as a member of the legendary Gagne family. He asked if I could send him footage of my work. So I did. I used clips of my high school morning announcements mixed with various introductions from PWI shows in Chicago. After sending Dale my videotape and résumé, I received an email that he would like to have me as his ring announcer for the show. I was ecstatic! Then I looked up the drive to Bullhead City on mapquest.com since the contract stated that I would be driving. It was nearly a six-hour drive, and I didn't have a car. I let Dale know the problem, and he agreed to fly me out plus pay me $150 and put me up in a hotel. In the indie world, this is unheard of, but this wasn't your average indie show. This was the return of the AWA!

I could not wait to meet and work with the former WWF wrestlers on this show: Val Venis, Jim "the Anvil" Neidhart, Sable, and my old pal, King Kong Bundy. My fraternity brother David drove me to the airport in exchange for a pack of cigarettes. On April 22, 1999, I flew to Las Vegas. At the airport, I met up with "Steve the Ref" and the promoter, Dale Gagne. Dale took us to dinner at the Wolfgang Puck. This was a bit weird for me as I was 19 and had to act mature, but at the same time, I didn't know how to order adult food in restaurants. I had eaten cereal for breakfast, lunch, and dinner for 13 years. I knew simple, common food, not anything on the menu at Wolfgang Puck. I got lucky and recognized a cheese pizza with a bunch of unrecognizable toppings. I had them all removed and enjoyed the dinner with Dale who was full of stories from years of working with the original AWA. Steve was also a wrestling fan, and we picked Dale's brain as he had lots of wrestling stories about wrestlers we grew up watching. Iron Sheik stories came up more than anything that night and on the drive to Bullhead City. Iron Sheik stories are like no other. He was a popular wrestler in the 80s and known for crazy, crazy stories outside of the ring. Both guys were great to talk to and learn from, and that just added to my excitement for this show and also the possibility of being part of a new organization with the potential for many more shows to come.

I went out that night with Steve the Ref to the hotel bar. We had some beers and met some entertaining people. The show was going to be held during bike week for the River Run. We all went to bed late and had to be up early the next morning. I definitely looked like I had been out that night before. I walked out of the hotel and ran into Branscombe Richmond who was an actor on the TV show *Renegade* as well as numerous other shows and movies over the years. I took a quick picture with him and was on my way to meet Jonnie Stewart and head toward the arena.

"The Illustrious" Jonnie Stewart was a wrestler from the original AWA. He was a character in the ring, but out of the ring, he was someone you could only find in a cartoon. I instantly liked him, but the feeling wasn't mutual. I was 19 years old and didn't realize that it was unprofessional to show up to this event in cargo shorts and flip-flops. He also helped Dale run the show and more money spent on a ring announcer meant less money for his pocket. He questioned Dale flying in a ring announcer and paying $150 on top of that, which really is unheard of in the independents. I know that I got very lucky. I got into a promotion that could possibly become a major organization once again. Any company I worked for, I wanted to contribute in every way possible. I was always into theme music, so I volunteered to handle the music on the shows. Part of that was just being a mark for hearing certain music played, so if I took care of the music myself, I knew that the WWF guys would come out to their authentic WWF music.

When we arrived at the venue, I was introduced to the tag-team of Steve and Larry, twin wrestlers from Chicago who wrestled as "Heaven and Hell" and also as the "Twin Turbos." They were super nice guys, and Steve's wife Julie taught me how to use the cuff links on my tux (that I still had from my high school days) as I needed her assistance getting buttoned up. I walked around the venue and noticed a gentleman selling lucha libre Mexican wrestling masks. His airbrushed singlet revealed that he was the Navajo Kid. I introduced myself to him as well as his buddy Lee who worked under a lucha libre wrestling mask. I told Navajo as he went by that I really wanted to start working shows in Arizona and reminded him to please keep me in mind if he ever heard of anything.

We all sat down and signed autographs at a pre-show session. I'm not sure why an unknown ring announcer and even Steve the Ref were a part of this, but I thought it was great! After the session, I met with Dale who went over the card for that afternoon's show. We sat around in this giant outdoor arena surrounded by bike week events. Dale explained how the show would work as well as the order of matches and introductions. The odd thing was that all the names I looked forward to working with weren't mentioned. When I asked Dale about this, he had what sounded like valid excuses for each absence. While the majority of the advertised names weren't going to be there, our show would consist of King Kong Bundy, the Twins, Navajo, Lee, WCW enhancement talent "Playboy" Bobby Starr under a Doink the Clown mask, and the Golden Lion.

I was impressed that this event was going to be huge and would be so without talent that had been television draws, with the exception of Bundy. And then the fans filed in. I was no longer impressed as a very small crowd showed up to this giant arena. Dale was smart; he sold this show to the venue. That meant he got all of his money up front, no matter how well or poorly the event drew. This also meant that we did not have to worry about not getting paid. The advertised talent had not been booked, which included the Nitro Girls who danced each week on *WCW Monday Nitro*. They did, however, find a woman hired off an escort ad in the yellow pages to appear as a Nitro Girl.

Dale and Jonnie were two old-time wrestling business guys, straight out of the carnival. They were smart, and they knew how to work the system. While I was a bit disappointed in not being able to work with the advertised talent and the lack of a crowd, I got some great experience working in a large venue and meeting everyone on that crew. Every one of those guys and girls were extremely nice to a 19-year-old kid who had a handful of Illinois independent shows under his belt.

Dale informed me that he had a bunch of shows throughout the summer, and he would be using me as his announcer. I really enjoyed Dale and Jonnie, as there was no funnier duo, and was stoked to hear that I would be involved in more shows with them. I looked forward to more potentially larger-than-normal independent events.

When I went back to school, I saw a flier for "Fraternity Fight Night." This was an event to be held outside a popular bar area where fraternity members from ASU would take on U of A fraternity guys in amateur boxing matches. I immediately looked up the phone number and contacted the promoter, Scary Larry. I told him

BEST SEAT IN THE HOUSE

I was in a fraternity and a wrestling announcer and would like to announce his event, if he was interested. I told him that I would also help promote the event as well. Any show that I was on, I wanted to do everything I could to make sure the event would do as best as possible. Larry had asked me to help him round up fraternity guys to fight, so I did by visiting various fraternity houses. The event was pretty big on campus, and I got to announce in front of my college mates who probably did not attend wrestling events.

In addition to announcing anything and everything that I could, Navajo—or Nav as I started to call him—actually started getting me booked on local independent shows. Typically a promoter would book a town and a big name or two formerly of WCW or WWF. He would have Nav bring his ring and book the undercard matches as well as the referee and ring announcer. The first show was at Pueblo High School in Tucson where we worked a show in a gymnasium in front of a handful of people. My sister and her friend made up a large percentage of the crowd. It was still a show, and I would take that opportunity, tux up, and run with it. Plus, I got to work with the Honky Tonk Man!

In June of 1999, I found myself a lot more experienced than the previous year of working only for PWI in Chicago. I felt like Dale's show was somewhat of a big deal, and Nav's were a lot more independent guys from the west coast as opposed to Sonny Rogers' student-filled shows. I also had a year of general education classes under my belt at U of A where I learned and retained absolutely nothing in the classroom, but I did learn quite a bit about life. Two of my fraternity brothers had committed suicide six months apart. It was the first time that acquaintances my age had died. I know this might not be the appropriate place bring this up, but I'll take advantage of the opportunity because I went through it with them. If you're reading this and going through a hard time or if things aren't going ideally right now and you feel like you need to escape and you've contemplated suicide, please stop and think about everyone around you and what that would do to them. When you're in that state of mind, you might not realize how much so many people love and care about you, and if you were to do that to yourself, they would be devastated. Just as importantly, you live once, and you have to make the most out of it. You have to do everything possible to make your life as great as can be. There will always be ups and downs. Ride them both out and take everything with a grain of salt. Losing my fraternity brothers was a very depressing experience that I wish had never happened.

I returned home to Chicago that summer and went back to my job as a day-camp lifeguard while taking an English course at a community college to make my Arizona requirement load a little less loaded. Dale gave me some dates for North Dakota, Illinois, Michigan, Indiana, Wisconsin, and Iowa. At one point, I even stopped into the Steel Domain where Ace and Danny were training their students to possibly learn how to take a bump or a fall if ever needed. I saw those two plus Punk and met Colt Cabana, who was training at the time. They were a great group of teachers and students that really worked well together as a team and loved the business. I wasn't so good at taking bumps, but I gave it a shot. The summer shows for Dale were an experience. They were mostly fairs that gave me the opportunity to get better at my craft and also work with many more wrestling stars I had grown up watching: Iron Sheik, Sensational Sherri, Sgt. Slaughter, Nick Bockwinkle, the Bushwhackers, George "the Animal" Steele, and many more. I was learning the business from an insider's perspective and learning how to do my job better. I was also watching the overall production from ringside and figuring out just how everything worked. It was an amazing summer with experiences that I will never forget. I had just taken wrestling 101 on my summer vacation from school.

During my sophomore year back at U of A, I worked a lot of sporadic dates for Dale and even more with Nav and his crew. Nav, Lee, "Outlaw" Mike Knox, and I had the opportunity to set up lots of rings and work many shows. I loved that we never knew which of my childhood heroes were going to pop up at these shows. Most of the Arizona and California events I was working with Nav would feature his guys as the undercard and one to three former WWF or WCW stars. We did a show at a military base in Sierra Vista, Arizona, and Marty Jannetty was booked along with Steven Regal who took the place of Jake "the Snake" Roberts because he had backed out. I never forgot how cool interviewing Regal at a hotel bar was to a 15-year-old kid. I introduced myself to him and thanked him for that opportunity years before. As he did five years earlier, he sat down and talked wrestling with me, which was really cool. I offered to help get him bookings with some of the promoters Nav and I had been working for, but he told me that he had just signed with WWF and that this was his last independent booking, but he gave me his number to stay in touch. I was very happy for him as he was such a unique talent, plus he had the best facial expressions in wrestling—ever. Also, a big time pro-wrestling superstar just gave me his number. I was excited, but playing it cool for sure.

Wrestling even led to an appearance as a guest on the *Jerry Springer* Show. Being from Chicago, *Springer* was a huge deal. During senior year in high school, my friends and I took a trip to the city to see an episode. Now, one of the guys I had met in wrestling, "Big Daddy", suggested that I call the producer he knew from the show. "He would love you. The show has been using a bunch of wrestlers, and you have that young, Backstreet Boys—or whatever it's called—look." I wasn't too serious when I called, but I thought, why not? I talked to a producer and told him to let me know if anything ever came up. Well, that night, something came up. He asked me if I wanted to fly out and be on the show. I asked him to standby. I had a few things I needed to clear up first. I called my parents right away and asked them to put the call on speakerphone. They knew something was up. "Mom, dad, I just got a call about being on *Jerry Springer.* They'll fly me out to Chicago; it's a free trip home…and I get to be on TV!" My mom said she didn't know, but my dad thought that would be funny. So, they were okay with it! Next was a friend that I had asked to a date dash. I called Carrie and explained the situation. I had plans with her first, so I wanted to make sure she was okay with me cancelling before I cancelled. She was. Almost there. The final step was that I had a test scheduled that Monday afternoon when I would be filming, so I needed to talk to the professor of this botany class. General education classes still consumed my sophomore year. "Sir. Something came up, and I need to fly home to Chicago." I looked him straight in the eye with my sad, puppy-dog brown eyes. "I'll show you the plane ticket or whatever you need, but I need to go, and I won't be able to come back until Tuesday morning." He looked me back, straight in the eye, read me, and considered. "Okay. Be in my office at 9 am on Tuesday morning to take the test." High five! I was off to Chicago to be on *Springer*. The trip was fun, and the show was an experience. My "story" was unbelievable: My girlfriend told me she was sleeping with her sister. I told her that was sick and disgusting, and we broke up. Then back on the plane to Tucson. My entire fraternity watched the show the night it aired. Hello, 15 minutes. Anyone I ever knew had ended up seeing that episode as it played numerous times. Word got around, and everyone forgot everything they ever knew about me, and I became the guy that was on Jerry Springer to everyone back home and now at school. It felt cool to be on a show that so many of us had grown up watching, maybe not my proudest moment, but an entertaining experience for sure.

In October 1999, a few of my friends drove with me from Tucson to Phoenix for a *WCW Nitro* taping. They would sit and cheer and boo. I would sit there and drool. All I could think about was what it could be like to announce for WCW. I knew I was small time, but I still had the right to daydream just as I had as a kid about being part of a big show. I decided to take it a little further, though, and feel things out because I couldn't just go watch the show I had to accomplish something, anything. When the show ended, I approached longtime WCW camera man, Jackie Crockett. I asked him how I could become a ring announcer for WCW. He told me the next time I came to a show to bring him my video, and he would see what he could do. I did that for Dale, and it worked out well, so I was determined to do the same and make one for WCW. I knew I could never announce at WWF because the position was never open, and I knew WCW already had their main announcer, and it was the same situation. Plus, I was not at their level. Even though that would have been a dream come true, this was just a hobby, right? It wouldn't stop me from trying.

I enjoyed U of A, but I also liked leaving school on the weekends to do what I loved. Did I learn anything in class? Yeah, I'm sure I retained a few things here and there, but mostly you take general education classes the first two years before really getting into your major. Picking your classes can be rough. Everything sounds intimidating, and if there are one or two interesting classes, chances are you can't get in as a freshman or sophomore. Normally. I found out who my advisor was, and I knew that she had the power to get me into classes I could not get in on my own. I was friendly, I was polite and I genuinely liked her. On top of that, she was a wrestling fan. So I would go in and hang out with Norma in her office, and we would be friends. She would also help me get into all the classes I wanted to take and made sure I had a good schedule. The power of socializing and being friendly. It takes you far, trust me. School became better with the help of Norma, though I still enjoyed the wrestling 101 on the weekends more because that's where I really got the education I was looking for.

I was working a lot and getting most of my announcing on video. Sitting in my room one night at the fraternity, I watched WWF, and I saw Lilian Garcia announcing. I thought to myself, if this was a sign of change being possible at WWF, I had a shot. I always wanted to be there, but I never thought that I was good enough. I just thought I was a kid who would be stuck doing this as a hobby, but that is what I had wanted to do. I wanted to be a WWF ring announcer, and if Lilian—who did not seem like the typical older gentleman ring announcer—could do it, maybe I had a chance as well! I immediately sat down on my floor and hooked up my video camera to the VCR. I began making a demo of my work to send to WWF. I had no idea who to address it to, but just sent it out to the main office and hoped for the best. I would also make a copy of the tape to give to Jackie Crockett later on because while WWF was the place to be, WCW would also be just as great of an opportunity.

In December 1999, I decided to call my old friend Howard Finkel at WWF and tell him that I had sent a video there. I wondered if he had any idea if I was heading down the correct path to become a WWF ring announcer. He told me that he hadn't heard anything about it, and Terry Taylor at talent relations probably got it, but was lost once Taylor returned to WCW. He asked if I would send another, and I said no problem and now felt confident since I had someone to address the package to. It was odd, however, sending it to the person who had the job that I wanted. So while we were on the phone, I inquired about the other announcers. He told me that he, Tony Chimel, and Lilian Garcia were announcing, and they weren't looking, but I still decided to send him the tape hoping it would pay off. And he did request it.

I had no idea if a spot would ever open, but just knowing that someone at either WCW or WWF might watch my tape gave me an ounce of hope. This motivated me even more to keep working shows and to get better and to have more material for future video reels. I remember sitting in health class in high school and staring at a poster on the wall every day. Its message was, "It's better to shoot for the stars and miss than to aim low and hit." I read that poster every single day, and I always kept that in the back of my mind.

I hoped for more work from Dale because his venues and crowd sizes at times were impressive, as were the former WWF names on his show. Dale was a character, and he ran some incredible shows. At times, he was drawing more than WWF and WCW, but usually there was a superstar or even two that would be advertised but not be there. Or maybe it was because an event was called WWF, WCW, and ECW (ECW was Extreme Championship Wrestling, the number three organization that created many stars before they headed to WCW or WWF) present *SummerSlam*, a popular annual WWF event. Either way, his shows were doing well due, in part, to his incredible imagination. Jonnie Stewart even found a "Nitro Girl" for our show by going in to the local Wal-Mart and hiring a random woman to appear. Absolutely amazing. As for Jonnie, well, it wasn't rare for him to appear on the same show as five different personas. That's not an exaggeration. He might come out under a wrestling mask, a women's wig and makeup, another mask, a suit and tie, and his actual wrestling attire all in the same show. It saved the company from having to pay four other people, and it allowed Jonnie to just have fun and be Jonnie. You never knew what he was going to do next, and Chyna (the popular former WWF female wrestler) found out the hard way. She was driving with Jonnie when they "randomly" stopped into a gas station before our show in Gallup, New Mexico. It turned out that, unbeknown to her, when she walked in, she had actually been booked there for an appearance. I'm sure you could imagine the surprise on her face when there just happened to be a crowd of fans cheering for her when she walked in.

CHAPTER 4
PICTURE IT, BROOKLYN 2000

On June 12, 2000, the Twin Turbos and I received an email from Dale with the subject, HUGE OPPORTUNITY: LITTLE MONEY.

Dale told us that he had just signed the agreement for an appearance of a lifetime. He had been negotiating with Bally's Total Fitness on the east coast to provide a mini wrestling production as part of the grand opening celebration of their Brooklyn, New York, club. Bally's goal was to blow the roof off by having none other than The Rock live for an autograph session. The deal was done, and WWF's Rock would be appearing with AWA Superstars of Wrestling.

We were told that we would be sharing the stage and the dressing room with the most recognized performer in this and almost every entertainment industry. We were also told that the Rock would be traveling with agents from the WWF. After the afternoon appearance, Dale planned on attending WWF's Madison Square Garden event.

We were told that the matches would take place inside the club and be broadcasted by video link to a huge outdoor screen. He told us that in order to secure the booking he had to lowball the numbers, which meant that he needed to use local talent unless we wanted the opportunity. He also mentioned that he would be doing a full production for them in Philadelphia September.

If we wanted to be a part of this high-profile event, we would have to take care of all of the travel and lodging expenses. On the flipside, we would be performing in the same show as the Rock. We would also be exposed to their agents and a huge crowd that he anticipated to be over 10,000. He went on to tell us that the clock was ticking, and he was giving each of us this opportunity because he felt that we represented the organization professionally and each of us deserved the opportunity to be noticed.

Wow. I would get to work with the Rock, who is the biggest star in the WWF, if I buy my own plane ticket, car, and hotel. Well, I talked to the twins, and it sounded like a great opportunity, so why not? Being the fan that I was, I flew out to New York City and made my way to Bally's. There were no big screens, no agents, no WWF reps, no WWF tickets, and many fans, but not 10,000. There was also no September event in Philadelphia. We arrived late because we kept getting lost (this was the pre-GPS era). Dale was upset with us (even though he was making money off the event and not having to pay for any of us to be there) and told me that he was going to introduce the Rock. So I stood and watched as Dale welcomed the Rock to the ring and shook his hand and looked over at me to take the picture. The anger and frustration were nothing next to the disappointment that I was feeling as I watched this happen and as I snapped pictures for Dale and the AWA website. This grand opening celebration had matches going on while the Rock sat and signed autographs. Dale had me go over to the table and announce him while he was sitting there. He didn't need an introduction midway through an autograph session, but at least I was able to say that I got to announce the Rock, which ironically would be the highlight of my career at the time. Plus, I reintroduced him later on and made sure to get a photo taken. I had a chance to talk to him in the locker room—well, bathroom—and he was extremely friendly and down to earth. I asked him if he had gotten the eyebrow raise that he did from Dana Carvey's Church Lady, my all-time favorite character. He laughed and made a joke, but I never really got a straight answer. The mystery remains.

While Dale wasn't always totally honest with us, he got us a lot of work, and while it was unfortunate that he would burn these towns that drew huge crowds with advertised talent that was never booked, he still got some suitable names at times to make up for it. This still wasn't fair to the fans, and rather than just taking the pay and the booking and being content, I felt bothered by it. With that said, though, he still took care of the guys, and we always got our pay. There are a lot of promoters who would have taken the money and skipped town without paying the crew. The next week would be another town, another ordeal of missing or unbooked talent, but we all stayed on the team, hoping he would get better since there was so much potential and so many good names out there. He could just advertise actual guys that could and would be booked without disappointing the fans.

While there were indie guys who warned me not to work for Dale because WWF knew about his shows and advertising, I feel that working for Dale was one of the best things to ever happen to me. Yes I once stood in the ring with a lead pipe in my hand when the fans were about to riot after I had announced Mick Foley wouldn't be appearing as he wasn't booked and also was with WWF, but I was working with lots of talent who had been in the major leagues. I learned a lot from them, and I got my name and face out there. Also, most promoters threw someone out there to be a ring announcer, but Dale was flying me in because he liked my work and he liked my connection with the fans. He, too, was a ring announcer and knew the importance of having a solid announcer to run the show. Everything happens for a reason, and running that initial Arizona show put Dale right in the middle of my life's path.

In August 2000, WCW was running a *Thursday Night Thunder* taping in Tucson. When I met WCW cameraman Jackie Crockett the previous year, he said that I should bring him a tape the next time I came out. So on this night, I went to the taping and brought him a tape and résumé. He told me that my timing was perfect because their current ring announcer, David Penzer, had gotten into some kind of (minor) trouble the night before at *Nitro*. He said he would give the tape to Tony Schiavone who was a WCW commentator. I assumed that meant he worked in the office. I was optimistic as I headed back to my fraternity house, which happened to be right down the street from where most of the talent was staying. I walked over to the hotel and let a few of the guys know that we were having a party that night. What did I have to lose, right? Before I knew it, Mike Awesome, Rey Mysterio, even the legendary Arn Anderson had stopped by. Arn was a WCW official, and I told him that I was a ring announcer and had given Crockett my video earlier that night. He told me to send him that video. So I did, at WCW headquarters in Atlanta, Georgia. The only problem was, Arn didn't work at the headquarters.

Junior year kept me in Arizona at a perfect time. This was a pretty significant point in my life. My favorite road trip to this day is one that happened during this time. My fraternity brother told me about a kid that came to the U of A, Danny from California, and he was a huge wrestling fan. Sure enough, we hit it off, and Danny would come with me to most of my shows. If I wasn't traveling with Steve, who lived in Phoenix, Danny was great company on the Tucson-based trips. He would usually help sell merchandise for the guys and record the matches. Eventually, I suggested that we make him a referee so he could be part of the show since he was already at most of them with us. In high school, I thought you had to go to wrestling school to learn how to ref. Now I realized that if you knew the right people, they could make it happen with a foot in the door and just a little basic training.

Danny, a masked wrestler from our crew known as Sin, CC Starr who was a former enhancement talent from years before (and who once lost a match to Brutus Beefcake and got his hair cut), and I all drove in Sin's minivan (yes, the evil masked destroyer known as Sin drove his family's minivan) for 15 hours to Olathe, Colorado. The group of us laughed for 15 hours straight. CC had a really cool mullet until the night before this road trip when he had his head shaved into a skullet (shaved bald with long luscious hair still remaining in the lower back of the head) at a show after losing his match. The hot sun was hitting CC in the freshly shaved bald head, and he was blistering up and oozing, which was disgusting. We stopped at an A&W, and CC ate like a champion, which led to him needing a bathroom along the drive. We were in the middle of nowhere, and there were no bathrooms in sight. He actually needed a toilet, which made the situation worse. After nearly an hour of holding it in, we found a random field that had a port-a-potty. CC was in heaven! We weren't sure what we could do for 5 to 10 minutes while we waited for him, so we decided to amuse ourselves. We pulled the minivan right up to the port-a-potty door and held the horn. After that got old, we pulled the car onto the potty door and began to drive forward a bit, though not enough to actually tip it over because that would be mean. Then we just let the car sit there so the door couldn't open. Poor CC, but he had such a fun sense of humor that he laughed it off with us. We finally ran out of laughs as it had been a long day and were about to fall asleep when Danny hit a skunk out of nowhere and began screaming "Gore! Gore! Gore!" It was such a fun trip that I will never forget with great people that were all just huge wrestling fans, happy to be doing wrestling shows.

In September 2000, Nav was booking a four-night tour for a promoter in Las Vegas, Nevada, and Santa Fe, Gallup, and Albuquerque, New Mexico. The lineup was all former WWF stars that I grew up watching: The Honky Tonk Man, Bushwhackers, Tatanka, Brutus Beefcake, Demolition Ax, Dan Severn, Virgil, Skinner, Public Enemy, Road Warrior Animal, and my all-time favorite, Mr. Perfect. I begged him to get me on the tour, mainly because Mr. Perfect would be there. The promoter had already booked a ring announcer, but Nav said he had personally booked a ref and could unbook him if I wanted to learn. I instantly agreed and went that weekend to Phoenix to jump in the car with him to head out to LA where he was going to be working on a show with riding partner, Lee. They taught me the basics by just getting me in the ring during the show and teaching me as we went. The promoter was Ric Draisin, and he used a lot of Southern California guys. One who really stood out was a guy that I recognized from a wrestling documentary based on a Southern California promotion. His name was "the Prototype" John Cena. He hadn't been at it very long, but looking at him, there was no doubt that he would someday make it to WWF. He was huge, he could speak very, very well, and he was a good-looking guy on top of it. It was cool to meet all the Southern California independent guys that I had been hearing about from magazines and the Internet, but never got to see in person. I refereed the match and got the basics under my belt.

A couple of weeks later, Nav, Lee, Knox, and I jumped in the ring truck with ring in tow and headed to New Mexico. I was in awe backstage. My childhood idols were all sitting around in one room. I had waited hours and hours as a kid to try and catch these guys for a picture or autograph, and now they're just sitting around in a circle. The moment was so exciting, yet intimidating at the same time. I could ring announce no problem, but could I actually ref? It seemed easy, but the more I learned about the role, I found out that wasn't the case. Honky Tonk called me over and asked if I wanted to know the finish, or ending sequence, to his match. Now this was new to me. I never needed to know who was going to win. Sure, it would be cool knowing who was going to win in advance, but as a ring announcer, I had always just announced whatever happened. We never did anything too fancy that I wouldn't be able to figure out. As a referee, I guess the wrestlers would tell me how the match was going to end so I could be prepared for it. So for the first time in my career, not only did I have wrestlers telling me how the match was going to end, but it was these wrestlers I grew up watching.

I never thought the day would come when they would be "spoiling" their own matches for me.

Honky Tonk got the ball rolling on that aspect, and right before I started walking around to each group of veterans discussing their matches, he also told me to take off my jewelry. As a college kid, I had my bracelets, shell necklace, and even an earring. I had never taken that out since I got it. I had asked my parents about getting my ear pierced for years while growing up, and they had always said no. During winter break my freshman year, I came home with a magnetic earring in my left ear. Surprisingly, they didn't think it looked too bad, nor were they angry. I ripped it out and asked if that meant I could get a real one. "So you waited to get our permission?" "Yes! Can I get one?" The next day I accepted their permission despite already being 18 and went to the mall with my friends. Now I would take it out as instructed by the Honky Tonk Man.

The rest of my education came in the ring over the next few nights. The Bushwhackers taught me how to work with a tag-team match and keep guys from coming in the ring illegally. They were a huge help as a tag match has so many things going on at once, and they walked me through every step of the match— knowledge that I will always be grateful for. In the main event, I got to ref Mr. Perfect's, -Curt Hennig, match, which was the reason I had worked that tour. I was always a huge fan of Mr. Perfect's. He was such a great television character and it was very cool when working with him. At one point, he grabbed my scrawny arm, and the next day I had a bruise which I was so proud of that I took pictures of and named it "the perfect bruise."

After the show, Perfect had gotten some beers for the guys, which of course would be the "perfect beer," but by the time I came back, they were all gone, so I never got to drink a perfect beer.

On the final show, Tatanka had rolled up Brutus Beefcake for a pin that wasn't how they had been ending the match, -but I got to three and Brutus never kicked out, so I counted and ended the match. Nav had trained me that no matter what, if that shoulder doesn't come up at three, you count it, and in this case, I did that. Brutus wasn't happy, to say the least, and buried me, by putting me down to the promoter. I had refereed 10 matches each night for four nights straight after only ever refereeing an eight-minute match. I was new, but 41 matches later I had learned a lot. The promoter wasn't thrilled with me, but despite having a great lineup of stars on this tour, he had falsely advertised a bunch of names that wouldn't be there, so he burned most of the towns we ran and didn't pay a bunch of the guys he owed money to, so it wasn't like doing my job correctly was going to cost me any future dates.

Aside from all the independent shows I was working, my junior year in college brought some new opportunities. I wanted to announce everything I could. I asked a classmate of mine about announcing for sports. He suggested that since we had a good women's softball team, it might be helpful to announce for them. That day, I went to the fields and asked around until I found the right person to talk to. I explained that I didn't know too much about sports announcing, but I was a wrestling announcer, and if there was a way to announce the players when they went up to bat, I would be very interested. They already had a full-time announcer, but there were some games that he was willing to let me cover.

He taught me the system, how and when to announce the lineup and keep stats. I grew up watching the Bulls, but aside from that, wrestling was the only sport I really watched. This was all new to me, but I got the hang of it. The team attracted a big following due to some really impressive athletes. Our top player was Jennie Finch who was an incredible player. The only other name that I remember announcing was Leneah Manuma because that was my favorite one to announce and elongate. This wasn't wrestling, but that didn't mean I couldn't pretend it was for practice purposes. During my first game, Finch's Dad walked all the way up to the booth to tell me that the girls had sent him up to tell me they really liked my announcing. I guess they never got wrestling introductions in their past softball games. It was a fun experience, and I enjoyed filling in whenever possible.

I used to watch a show on *FX* called *Toughman*. It was a show in which normal, everyday people who thought they were tough put on headgear and boxing gloves and stepped into the ring with other amateurs who wanted to prove how tough they were. You had police officers, firefighters, grocery store managers, and lawyers, and it was really entertaining. There was a local commercial spot for a Tucson event, and I immediately started trying to figure out how to contact their headquarters. I called the number they gave for people wanting to fight and from there talked to various people until I got an address where I could send my tape. I sent them a demo and résumé and hoped independent wrestling could be used as a stepping stone to get into *Toughman*, and then maybe *Toughman* could help get me into WWF. I called a couple of times after sending out my materials and was told to bring my tux and come by the show that Friday night in Tucson.

On September 15, 2000, I showed up to the Tucson Convention Center in my tux and looked for *Toughman* founder, Art Dore. Art was a tall gentleman with white hair and a distinct deep voice. He was the promoter, ring announcer, and commentator. The show was sponsored by Budweiser, and he would enjoy drinking their product while tearing into the fighters, egging them on during his commentary. He was very accommodating and invited me to sit beside him at the ringside table.

At one point in the middle of the show, he handed me his microphone and said, "Let's see what ya got, kid." I was totally thrown off and not expecting to work during the show. Maybe before, maybe after, but mid show? I took that mic, pretending there was no hesitation, and got in the ring. I worked up the crowd and introduced the fighters. When I sat down to give him the mic for commentary, he told me to keep it. I had never done commentary let alone trash-talk commentary mid fight. In wrestling, my job was to put over the talent, never to talk down to them. Despite my lack of practice, I got through the match and wasn't horrible. Art said we would be in touch.

Lydia and Susan from their Arkansas office had called me about working a couple of weekend slots. They would run one to three cities in a weekend, doing Friday and Saturday tournament-style shows in each town. Art could only be at one place at a time, and they had a couple of other guys who they used, but they had room for me in the rotation if I was interested. I had just turned 21, and I was getting to fly out to Iowa, Arkansas, Texas, Tennessee, and Oklahoma. The shows consisted of my two boss ladies, me, and the local fighters and ring girls. There were no boundaries. It wasn't like wrestling where there are a bunch of stars or future stars, and my job was to enhance introductions. In *Toughman*, you had local guy in yellow vs local guy in black every match. I had to take their stories and put them out there for the arena to get behind. "Joe Smith in the yellow corner and headgear got a $500 jaywalking ticket last week. Bob Smith in the black corner with black headgear happens to be the officer that gave him the ticket. Who do you want to win? Black? Yellow?"

Toughman was so much fun. Between the introductions, which I had down, the trash-talking live commentary brought interest to the matches so they wouldn't get stale. The commentary worked up the crowd, and I even found talent. Yes, we would have shows in which no women signed up, or maybe just one, so I would tell the crowd that if any woman thinks she's tough, she has to step up! Women would come from the crowd, take a pregnancy test, and fight as long as they were cleared by the local athletic commission. I loved the opportunity to do these shows, and I was becoming a better wrestling announcer with all of the experience the events were giving me. Susan and Lydia were always a pleasure to work with. I was a kid and had a lot to learn, but they were good to me. I didn't have a car for these shows, so I would just stay locked up in a hotel room or wander around a nearby mall.

I used *Toughman*, indie wrestling, and even my high school announcements to make yet another new tape and send it out to WWF and WCW. I also found out from asking talent who had worked with WWF that Kevin Kelly was in charge of talent relations. Wrestlers would send him their tapes in order to get booked for tryout matches. I directed my materials to any name that was suggested, and especially to Kelly, although I never knew if he handled the ring announcers. I had sent this most recent tape to Kelly and decided in December of 2000 that I would try giving the office a call and asking for him. As I expected, the call went to voicemail, and I left message. What I did not expect was Kevin calling me back a few hours later. He told me that he liked my tape and sent it to TV production because they hire the announcers. He also said I shouldn't let the guys beat me up so much. (I had gotten beat up in the video to show I was willing and capable, if needed.) He told me that it took two years for WWF to hire him, so I had to just wait now. But I was too hungry to just sit back and wait!

In March 2001, I went to a WWF show in Tucson. I still remember them playing Kid Rock's *Lonely Road of Faith* that night. I watched Tony Chimel ring announce and was so eager to get in the ring and give it a shot myself, but it just seemed so impossible. That ring was so close, yet so far away. I came back to my place that night and told my roommates about the show and how badly I wanted to work for

WWF. It was my passion, and it was my life. It was what I enjoyed watching and thinking about. I worked on the weekends to try to make it happen. I needed to make another tape. I had been working quite a bit with Sgt. Slaughter at Dale's shows. Sarge was a respected wrestler and now a WWF agent as well. I would always ask him for his advice at our shows, and he had offered the opportunity to send him my video reel, so I jumped on that. He said that he liked it and passed it on to Vince McMahon's son, Shane. I don't know what department Shane worked in, but I trusted Sarge and was thankful. I also sent a new tape to Kevin Kelly since it had been a few months. Nav was going to be working a show where he would see Terry Taylor, and I asked him to please give a video to him as well.

In February 2001, I called Terry Taylor to see if he had a chance to watch the video that Nav had given him. I left him a message, and later that evening he called me back. He told me that I was very talented and inquired about where I live to determine if I was still young and living with my parents or out on my own. When I told him that I was in school, he was surprised because he thought I was out of school and looking for a job. He basically said to call him every couple of months to check in, and that he would like to introduce me to Eric Bischoff since I lived in Arizona (Bischoff lived in Phoenix). So I explained that my classes were only on Tuesdays and Thursdays, and I would love a job!

Well, following up with Taylor would be futile because on March 23, 2001, WCW, the number 2 wrestling organization which had become number 1 at one point, was bought out by WWF. I was really hoping that a new WWF show would be produced using the newly acquired WCW talent, so I called Kevin Kelly again. He told me that he had received my latest video as well as a video from WCW's newest ring announcer, Keith Butler. I called Steve Regal to pick his brain, and he thought that things were looking good for me. It seemed like maybe, just maybe, there was hope. Maybe WWF would run a WCW brand and could possibly use me as their ring announcer, if they did not use WCW announcer David Penzer.

Around this time, I saw online that Gary Michael Cappetta was writing a book. Cappetta was the WCW ring announcer for many years. A book written by a ring announcer who once worked for WWWF (WWF before it was WWF) and WCW? I couldn't wait to read that! As always, me being me, I couldn't just read the book, either. I wanted to contact Cappetta and offer to help him out in any way I could. I sent him an email, and he wrote back. We continued to talk, and he told me about a book tour that he would be doing over the summer to promote his book. He asked about having me come on board as a "pitchman" after looking around my website and seeing my some of the content I had posted.

I can tour with someone who has lived my dream, pick his brain, and help him promote his book? Sign me up. I told him about sending tapes to WWF and talking with Kevin Kelly and that I would only back out if I got a call from them, which he understood. My friend Danny and I would read Jim Ross' *Ross Report* column online every week and hope that he said something about me or a ring announcer or a spot.

The rule in wrestling is that you always bring your gear, just in case. I packed my clothes and my tux, and I headed out to New Jersey where I would stay with Gary for two weeks and work the Meadowlands Fair, starting on June 24, 2001. We would arrive early in the morning to get through the gates and set up our area, and then we would stay all night until we were able to tear down and leave. Early the next morning we would be at it again. All day, I would call out to people walking by and try to sell Gary's book for him. He would wander around and make calls and relax. If someone was interested, he would come in for the close. I understood where he was coming from, but talking all day to everyone walking by was pretty grueling. I ended up using a mini disc to record a pitch, and I would play it on repeat. Great success! We had former WWF stars Road Dogg, Sunny, and Jimmy Snuka come to the booth to sign and hopefully bring in more wrestling fans. I always loved Road Dogg's singing, and his version of "With My Baby Tonight." We actually ran through the Meadowlands Fair in an attempt to get people over to the booth. I even started singing his "With My Baby Tonight" song, and he joined in! The Iron Sheik was in town and heard about the appearance, so he booked himself and showed up. A golf cart with Sheik and three security guards pulled up. He got off the cart, sat down at the table, moved everybody's pictures out of the way, and started selling 8x10s and Polaroids. "Okay, come on over. You want a picture of de Iron Sheik bubba? Tell me your name. $25. Too much? Okay $20. Uh, what do you mean too much? Okay, for you, friend of Iron Sheik, $15 bubba." He was amazing. This is the same guy I once went to pick up at Midway Airport in Chicago for a show in Iowa. I couldn't find him anywhere, and I waited and looked around for hours before we finally had to get on the road to make the show.

He ended up recognizing a fan in a wrestling t-shirt at the airport and got him to drive Sheik to Iowa in exchange for getting to be his manager for the match.

After the Meadowlands Fair had ended, we drove in a van to Ohio, Iowa, Michigan, and Indiana. If the drive got long, I might ask Gary to do a WCW introduction for me. He didn't want to, but I definitely requested a Bunkhouse Buck (accompanied by Col Rob Parker) introduction more than a few times before finally doing my own version of it instead. A month into the two-month tour, Gary and I were butting heads. We had a few big arguments over him leaving me at the booth alone all day. I was talking to everyone that came by all day by myself. "Gary, I understand my role here, but I'm doing everything. Can you work with me just a little bit?" "I think the way it is now is perfect, and I'm not going to change anything." I felt stuck. I sat at the booth at the Porter County Fair in Valparaiso, Indiana, and looked up as a man approached, checking out the book. "Gary Cappetta. Is he here?" I looked at his eyes, and I knew those eyes. I had seen them somewhere before. It was WWF's Doink the Clown, WCW's "Big Josh" Matt Bourne. I was pretty excited and thought, wow that's random! Gary came over, and they started talking. Bourne was part of an indie show that would be taking place that day at the fair. I jokingly told him that if they need a ring announcer, I was there! A couple hours later, he took me up on the offer. The promoter, Bobby Fulton, wasn't there to run the show, and they didn't have a ring announcer. I asked Gary if I could announce and then talk about his book and sell them during intermission. It was a wrestling book. His "audience" was at the show, which was perfect. He simply said, no. "But Gary, you will sell more books at a wrestling show than you will just being set up in the middle of the fair. I'll talk about it on the mic and totally push the book!" "You're here with me, not to work their show. You either stay with me, or if you want to work that show, you go work that show and don't come back." Well, it really didn't take much thought.

I grabbed my belongings, thanked him, and went to announce that show. Sure, I brought my tux, but I never packed black socks. So I wrapped my feet with the wrestler's athletic tape. Mia Martinez, who I had met at the Steel Domain, was on the show and offered to give me a ride back to Chicago because that's where my parents still lived. After the show, we drove back, and I surprised my parents at two in the morning, and they were definitely surprised. I spent some time in Chicago and then flew back to Arizona for the rest of the summer and my final year of school. That wasn't the way I planned on leaving the tour, but I think the way it worked out was for the best. One of my favorite parts of that tour was seeing my photographer friend Blackjack Brown when we were in Michigan. I had kept in touch with Blackjack since high school, and he always took the time to talk to me. He told me that I was going to make it. He didn't say that he thought I would, he assured me I would and told me he had never been wrong about anybody else. Those words really motivated me to keep going.

My senior year at U of A was a bit daunting. I really had one semester of classes and then maybe a class or two the second semester before I would be done. I would be in the real world. Graduating college is really scary. Hey, I have this piece of paper. Now I have to choose a career for the rest of my life and do so in the next few months? I had no idea what would happen when I graduated. The only career I wanted to do was become a WWF ring announcer. That was it. I had been sending out videotapes and résumés to WWF every three months since sophomore year to Kevin Kelly and everyone whose name was tossed around by anyone in the industry. I would email and call Kevin Dunn's office at WWF. He was the executive producer, and I wouldn't have known he even existed if it weren't for seeing him on the *Tough Enough* show (WWF's reality show for finding a new superstar). I had never met him, nor did I know if I was sending my work to the right email and mailing addresses. I didn't let that stop me, though.

CHAPTER 5
I RESPECT YOU, BOOKER MAN

I got a call from Steve Turbo who was running a show during my winter break right outside Chicago in Hammond, Indiana. He had booked most of the talent and asked if I could book, or write, the show for him. I had never written a show before, but I knew I could put those puzzle pieces together and figure it out, so I accepted and thanked him for the opportunity. He had wrestling legend Terry Funk booked as well as a lot of local talent. He wanted one more well-known name to advertise but didn't have a big budget. I tend to think outside the box and do things that other shows aren't doing, so my big idea was using one of the *Tough Enough* kids. These kids had been training with WWF and learned how to wrestle for the reality show, which aired on *MTV* so the public—especially wrestling fans—would be familiar with the talent. The show had just ended, so I assumed the guys who didn't win would have to be available and probably interested in working an independent wrestling show. No one had ever used a *Tough Enough* talent on an independent show, so I had to figure out how to track down Josh Mathews, a memorable wrestler from the cast who lived nearby in Indiana. This would be perfect! A guy fresh off WWF/*MTV* television and most likely inexpensive to book and no flights or hotels to pay for. I used the Internet to find him and to track him down in Indiana. I found his mom and left a message with her for Josh to call me back about an upcoming booking. He called me early the next morning and was very excited about the opportunity to work a wrestling show. There was a documentary prior to *Tough Enough* on *MTV* about a guy named Rory Fox who wanted to be a pro wrestler. He wasn't far from Indiana, so Steve booked him as well and I made an "*MTV* match" between the two. The fans who attended were skeptical that Terry Funk would really be on the show because it wasn't common to see him on an indie show in the area. I wrote the show with that in mind.

We began with Big Daddy, the manager that the twins and I had become friends with through the AWA, who had also been responsible for my *Jerry Springer* appearance. I started making an announcement that unfortunately in this business we run into travel issues, and tonight...the crowd immediately started booing. They knew the announcement would be that Terry Funk wasn't going to be there. Big Daddy interrupted and cut a promo, running down Terry Funk—of course he wouldn't be there because he was too old and too scared to take on the client he represented. As he ran down Terry, Funk's music hit, and the place went nuts. It was an entertaining show and a fun learning experience. All of those years of booking shows for my Hasbro wrestling figures, and now I got to do it for real!

I went back to Tucson after my winter break and decided that I really wanted to run my own show. I had enough friends in California and Arizona to make it happen, and I wanted to give it a shot. I went all over looking for venues and finally stumbled upon a roller rink. I asked if they had any down nights where they would like a special event to bring in some extra money. Steve would donate his ring, and all of the men and women he booked came out with no money demands. That really took a lot of the pressure off. I would call my promotion MSPW (Mountain Strength Pro Wrestling). The hotspot bar on Wednesdays for U of A was a place called Bumsteer where they had $0.01 beers. I made that the official after-party place in return for their sponsorship donation. I got a donation from the University of Arizona Hillel, the Jewish organization, as well as Tens—a local strip club. So you can imagine how thanking the list of sponsors sounded that night.

I was an intern at KVOA, which was the *NBC* affiliate in Tucson, and my main responsibility was to scroll the teleprompter for the anchors. When word got around the studio that I was a wrestling announcer, they talked about doing a story on me, and doing it while I was promoting this show was the perfect time. I got some television exposure from KVOA and also made fliers that I personally handed out all over town from the Wal-Mart parking lot to the local schools. The U of A newspaper—a staple around campus—even covered my story in the *Daily Wildcat*. Nav, Lee, Knox, "Hardcore Kid" Aaron Aguilera, Lexie Fyfe, Lawrence Tyler, Gallo, CC, Hawaiian Lion, Hollywood Yates—who would later play Wolf on the new *American Gladiators*—and my favorite tag team, Shane and Shannon, the Ballard Brothers, all came out for the show. We didn't sell the place out or even get close to it, but we had a small, decent crowd. I was proud to have run my own show. It was a big accomplishment. Between the sponsorship and the tickets that we sold, I had enough money to pay everybody a small amount, but most of them wouldn't accept money anyway. I was really fortunate to be able to work so many shows with such a great group of people. Everybody got along well. We all loved the business, and as much fun as we had at the shows, we really enjoyed going to Denny's afterward and laughing. Lots of laughing.

I knew MSPW wouldn't be a career after college, so I called Steven Regal, at this point known as WWF superstar William Regal, to pick his brain. I explained that I had been sending out my videotapes and résumés, but I hadn't heard anything at all back from WWF. He told me that they were looking for writers and asked if that would be a path I might want to take. I said I would do anything to get my foot in the door and immediately began the application process. I needed to write an episode of *Monday Night RAW*. Once I did that, he said he would hand it directly to Vince McMahon's daughter, Stephanie McMahon, who oversaw that department. I had watched every episode of the show since it began in 1993 when I was 13, and by 22, I could incorporate my crazy ideas plus what I learned from running Steve's show and write my own episode. I did so and sent the piece out to Regal.

WWF had a developmental territory in California, and I had tried for a long time to get on their shows, even if I could do one match for them. WWF officials would go there to scout talent. I just wanted to be able to get under that WWF microscope. Unfortunately, they wouldn't budge, and I would have to figure out another plan to get noticed by WWF.

While I waited to hopefully hear back from WWF, I continued to work shows for Dale. One particular show happened to be in northern Arizona. In April 2002, Dale was staying in Phoenix, and Danny and I had also gone down to my parents' house after a show in Prescott. Dale told us that WWF was in town for *RAW* and had gotten tickets from Sgt. Slaughter. The three of us went to *RAW* and sat in the front row, which was really cool. As we all sat and watched, I just stared at that ring and pictured myself standing in the center of it. I just wanted to announce one match so WWF could see what I could do and hire me, or at least tell me they're not interested. I knew what Howard told me about there not being a spot, and I knew what Kevin Kelly told me, but I wouldn't let that stop me from wanting it and going for it.

After the show, we went to the Phoenix Hyatt where Slaughter and the WWF crew were staying. We sat outside and had dinner while we waited for Sarge to get back. I looked across the way at the front doors of the hotel, and I recognized Kevin Dunn from *Tough Enough*. I asked the guys if I should go say something to him. Danny, who I love but always seems to be wrong, said no. Luckily, Dale said I should. Asking their opinion was like my sister asking me when we were kids about which shoes to wear. It didn't matter. She knew what she wanted to do, and I knew what I wanted to do. I ran over to the front entrance of the hotel and caught Kevin.

"Excuse me, are you Kevin Dunn?"

"Yes."

"Hi, my name is Justin Roberts. I am a ring announcer. I have been sending you tapes."

"I know who you are. Maybe one of these days we will get you in the ring and see what you can do"

"Thank you!"

For the first time ever, I thought there was legitimate hope; there could be a chance of an opportunity to show them what I could do!

I was ecstatic. My face was red the rest of the night as we had a couple of beers with Sarge. At one point, Mr. Perfect came into the bar as well and bought a round of beers for all of us. He looked at me and told me I looked like I could be wrestler Tom Zenk's brother. This was probably the third time I had met him and the third time he said the exact same thing, and I loved it. On the same night as my conversation with Kevin Dunn, I finally got to drink the perfect beer with him as he told me Tom Zenk stories!

The next day, I got back to Tucson and saw a missed call on my caller ID from a Stamford, Connecticut, number. To this day, I still have no idea who that was and if it was actually someone from WWF. No follow-up, however, and back then, I didn't have the courage to just call it.

I had a pretty light schedule the second semester of my senior year. I had taken a couple of summer classes in Chicago before and after freshman year, plus a post-year summer semester each May, and I only needed three more credits to graduate. Getting everything done early—a class here and there—certainly helped to make my final semester easier. Those final credits were coming from an internship with Nav and *Toughman*. The "class" was keeping a journal of my internship. The journal along with reports from my bosses would get me my final college credits. So basically I was on campus and living the college life without having to go to class. My journal entries were based on the shows that I did, plus some creative writing, so I had a lot of extra time to have fun in Tucson as well as work a lot of shows.

PART III

LIVIN' THE DREAM

E RAW Live – State College, PA   1/21/11 WWE RAW Live – Trenton, NJ   1/17/11 WWE Monda

e – Beaumont, TX   1/14/11 WWE RAW Live – Chattanooga, TN   1/10/11 WWE Monday Nigh

AL   1/7/11 WWE RAW Live – Augusta, GA   1/3/11 WWE Monday Night RAW – Phoenix, A:

E RAW Live – Wilkes-Barre, PA   12/27/10 WWE Monday Night RAW – Albany, NY   12/26/1

E Tables, Ladders, and Chairs Pay-Per-View – Houston, TX   12/18/10 Tribute to the Troops airs o

2/7/10 WWE SmackDown Taping – Dayton, OH   12/6/10 WWE Monday Night RAW – Louisvill

E Monday Night RAW – Philadelphia, PA   11/28/10 WWE RAW Live – Salisbury, MD   11/22/1

/10 WWE Monday Night RAW – Hershey, PA   11/13/10 WWE RAW Live – Milan, Italy   11/12/1

N Live – Innsbruck, Austria   11/9/10 WWE RAW Live – London, England   11/8/10 WWE RAV

– Birmingham, England   11/5/10 WWE RAW Live – Cardiff, Wales   11/4/10 WWE RAW Live

sland, NY   10/31/10 WWE RAW Live – Montreal, Quebec   10/25/10 WWE Monday Night RAV

– Winnipeg, Manitoba   10/18/10 WWE Monday Night RAW – Calgary, Alberta   10/17/10 WWE

– Spokane, WA   10/11/10 WWE Monday Night RAW – Seattle, WA   10/10/10 WWE RAW Liv

10 WWE Monday Night RAW – Wichita, KS   10/3/10 WWE Hell in a Cell Pay-Per-View – Dalla

W Live – Luxembourg   9/22/10 WWE RAW Live – Saint Etienne, France   9/20/10 WWE Monda

WWE Monday Night RAW – Cincinnati, OH   9/12/10 WWE RAW Live – Peterborough, Ontari

Monday Night RAW – Washington, DC   9/4/10 WWE RAW Live – San Juan, Puerto Rico   9/3/1

w – WWE Monday Night RAW – Boston, MA   8/29/10 WWE RAW Live – Newark, NJ   8/28/1

– Tokyo, Japan   8/20/10 WWE RAW Live – Tokyo, Japan   8/18/10 WWE RAW Live – Honolul

os Angeles, CA   8/9/10 WWE Monday Night RAW – Sacramento, CA   8/8/10 WWE RAW Liv

Antonio, TX   7/25/10 WWE RAW Live – Beaumont, TX   7/24/10 WWE RAW Live – Shrevepor

WE Money in the Bank Pay-Per-View – Kansas City, MO   7/17/10 WWE RAW Live – Omaha, N

) WWE RAW Live – Rockford, IL   7/9/10 WWE RAW Live – Peoria, IL   7/5/10 WWE Monda

Live – Wheeling, WV   6/26/10 WWE RAW Live – Youngstown, OH   6/25/10 WWE RAW Liv

iew – Long Island, New York   6/14/10 WWE Monday Night RAW – Charlotte, NC   6/7/10 WW

nville, SC   6/4/10 WWE RAW Live – Asheville, NC   5/31/10 WWE Monday Night RAW – Austi

RAW Live – New Orleans, LA   5/24/10 WWE Monday Night RAW – Toledo, OH   5/23/10 WW

WWE RAW Live – London, Ontario   5/15/10 WWE RAW Live – Kingston, Ontario   5/14/10 WW

WE RAW Live – Mexico City, Mexico   5/7/10 WWE RAW Live – Puebla, Mexico   5/6/10 WW

Live – Monterrey, Mexico   5/3/10 WWE Monday Night RAW – Jacksonville, FL   5/2/10 WW

5A   5/1/10 WWE RAW Live – Mobile, AL   4/30/10 WWE RAW Live – Huntsville, AL   4/26/1

Richmond, VA   4/25/10 WWE Extreme Rules Pay-Per-View

CHAPTER 6
I WILL NEVER WORK FOR WWF

May 5, 2002, was a big day in the wrestling world and the day when my chance of announcing for WWF had ended. The WWF had lost their initials to the World Wildlife Fund and quietly changed their name to World Wrestling Entertainment. It's all good, though, as I was now determined to work for WWE!

By the time I graduated college, I had that piece of paper my parents wanted me to get and a ton of experience in the field that I wanted to work in. My parents, sister, and grandma came out to Tucson for graduation. My grandma was adorable. In her 70s and 80s she had more energy than I did. She was very sweet and a very proud grandma of her four grandchildren.

After the ceremony, my dad flew back to Chicago. My friend Paul, who was with me for the Warrior encounter, and his brothers lost their father who was one of my dad's best friends. He was one of my favorites, and I was proud of my dad for coming to my graduation and then going back there to be with them during an awful time.

The day after my graduation, I worked an indie show in Tucson and then moved my belongings from the Tucson house that I had been living in for the past two years out to my parents' house in Scottsdale. That night I pulled out my laptop and sent yet another email to this address that may or may not have actually been the correct address for Kevin Dunn. I mentioned that I had just graduated college that week and moved to Scottsdale, Arizona. If there was ever anything I could do for a show in LA, San Diego, Phoenix, or Tucson to please let me know, and I would drive there.

With that sent, I closed my laptop and went to sleep. The next day I drove my mom and grandma to the airport. I got home around 3 pm to a friendly sounding voice on my answering machine.

"Hi Justin, this is Sue calling from Kevin Dunn's office at World Wrestling Entertainment. Please give us a call back when you have a chance. Thanks!"

It was 3 in the afternoon on Friday in Arizona, which meant 6 pm in the east. If I didn't catch Sue, I might have to wait until Monday to find out why she was calling. I picked up my cordless phone and began dialing the number. I fumbled and had to try again. I fumbled again. On the third try, I dialed correctly. I couldn't think straight, and my heart was pounding.

"World Wrestling Entertainment, Kevin Dunn's office, this is Sue."

"Hi, Sue, my name is Justin Roberts. I received a message from you." I felt like there was a lot of stuttering on my end.

"Hi, Justin! Kevin would like to give you a tryout on June 17th in Oakland before *RAW* and in Sacramento on the 18th before *SmackDown!*"

I thanked her. A lot. And probably a little more after that.

I sat there frozen as my eyes slowly filled with tears. All that work, every event I had announced, every tape that I mixed and sent out, everything had paid off. That was my proudest moment, just knowing that I was getting a tryout.

I couldn't wait to call my parents and tell them the news. Once they heard, they were just as happy and proud of me for getting to that point. It wasn't easy, and it was actually very unlikely that it would happen, but I never gave up. They used in-house people, and the position had just never been open for someone to "apply".

That afternoon, I popped in one of my favorite movies which seemed to fit best on this day, *Rudy*—an inspirational story about a kid who wanted nothing more than to play football at Notre Dame. Despite not having a chance due to size, lack of funds, and lack of grades to even get in to Notre Dame, Rudy persevered and accomplished his dream of eventually making it to the team.

While I hadn't gotten signed to a contract, or even stood in a WWE ring, I felt like my dream came true, and this was really happening.

In just a few weeks, I would finally be able to step into the middle of a WWE ring. I started telling everyone back home in Illinois. I reached out to old friends who knew about my desire to get this. I reached out to former teachers. I even called my high school show choir teacher who I felt like I owed a lot to for teaching me so much about performing.

There were so many guys that I had worked with for years in the independents. We would always talk about getting a shot and wondered if it would ever be a possibility. It became a possibility for me, but the support wasn't there like I would have imagined. Out of all those guys I traveled with, I only heard from a few. That was okay, though. I was excited and determined!

While working the independents over the years, I always wondered what that moment would be like if I ever got the opportunity to stand on a WWE entranceway. When I walked down that ramp and into a WWE ring, would I freeze? Would I even be able to speak? Or would I be too nervous? When doing local independent shows in Arizona, Nav, Danny, and I would always eat at a restaurant in Tempe. Along the parking area was a metal cover in the grass that reminded Danny and me of the *RAW* entranceway. We used to stand on top of the metal and pretend we were on the *RAW* ramp.

It was my weekly tradition to go to my friend Jen's house on Mondays to watch *RAW* because it came on earlier with her satellite. Every week, we would hang out and watch *RAW*. I wanted nothing more than to one day announce on that show so she could watch me on TV!

As my tryout got closer, I became increasingly nervous. The Sunday before *RAW*, I messaged various independent friends who had tryouts over the years. I asked Ace Steele for advice, and he told me to make sure to shake everyone's hands and introduce myself to everybody. I also watched *Beyond the Mat*, a documentary that showed very rare behind-the-scenes footage of WWE events. I tried to pick out any information I could and study the scene, so to speak.

I couldn't sleep despite having an early flight to Oakland. Eventually I got a couple of hours and then was on my way. I landed and got into the car WWE had rented for me. As I approached the building, the first person I ran into was D-Lo Brown. I had met D-Lo the previous year through Steve and Larry. He asked what I was doing there and was surprised to hear that I was getting a tryout because I think he saw me as just a big fan. I asked if he had any idea who I was supposed to talk to or where I was supposed to go, so he introduced me to Jason, one of the floor directors who brought me to a room where I could leave my suit and bags. I opened the door and was face to face with WWE chairman, Vince McMahon, wrestling legend Ric Flair, and talent relations head, Jim Ross. If there's any meeting you don't want to interrupt in your first five minutes at WWE, it was that one. I apologized and shut the door as my face turned bright red and my heart raced out of my chest.

Jonathan "Coach" Coachman walked by, and I introduced myself. I mentioned the name of a mutual friend, and he asked me where I was changing. I told him that I was brought to that room, and he told me that was bad information and brought me to the room where he would hang out. Coach took me under his wing and introduced me to everyone that walked by. I was unbelievably nervous and uncomfortable, but having Coach with me helped a lot. Rather than just approach everyone and shake their hands, his introductions made saying hello a lot less awkward.

Eventually I was brought to Lilian, the woman who was ring announcing *RAW* on a weekly basis. Lilian was told that I would be announcing the dark (non-televised) match featuring California's own "Prototype" John Cena against Shelton Benjamin. Cena and Benjamin had been signed to WWE and worked out of the WWE developmental territory OVW (Ohio Valley Wrestling) in Louisville, Kentucky. They would work the weekend WWE live events and then wrestle for the WWE officials in dark matches on TV days. We talked for a bit, and she asked me what the plan was for me going forward. I told her that I had the two tryouts and knew nothing past that. When she mentioned Howard Finkel, I told her the story about how I called him as a kid. She told me that I had to tell Howard the story and brought me over to see him.

When we met, I informed Howard that he predicted our paths would cross again in the future, and here we were. I asked the two announcers if they had any advice for me. They told me which cameras to face, the cues I should speak on, and to not say "his opponent" when introducing the second competitor. They gave me the weights and hometowns for both wrestlers, and then it was time to memorize and get ready for my big match. Ring announcers at WWE don't use notecards, teleprompters, or in-ear IFBs (a small ear piece that many broadcasters wear to receive directions from their producers) to receive direction. They get a bell or a hand cue to speak. Whatever comes out when given the cues is up to the announcer, which was somewhat nerve racking.

I ran into the biggest icon in wrestling, Hulk Hogan, and asked if he had any advice for me. He really didn't have any advice, but the idea that I was talking to the Hulkster was cool enough. He even told me a "Macho Man" Randy Savage story. That may have been better than any advice.

I changed into my dance tuxedo from high school and headed toward the backstage area and ramp entrance. This was it. I went from standing on the metal cover in Tempe to the real deal, and I would find out what happened while I stood on that ramp. The dreams I had about being too nervous to speak or even think would either become a reality or simply a bad dream.

Gorilla position was the area directly behind the entranceway curtain where Vince sat at his monitor and watched the entire show. He could also talk to the commentators, Kevin Dunn, and the referee from there as well. The agents or producers also sat there to give direction as well. Sgt. Slaughter was in one of the seats. He said that they didn't know if there would be time for a dark match, so we waited to walk to the ring. I didn't know that this was a possibility, and now I had one more thing to stress over. Sarge looked over and said, "Justin and Lilian, go." This was it. I walked through that curtain. As a kid, I would run out of my bedroom, into the hallway, down the staircase, and into the kitchen. In my head, however, I was running through a curtain, down the aisle, and into a wrestling ring, slapping hands along the way. On this night, I wasn't running and no one wanted to slap my hand, but I was walking through a real WWE curtain and heading down the very ramp I had dreamed of standing on.

A floor producer named Todd gave me my instructions. This was simple. I had done this a million times at independent shows around the country. I announced full shows. What's one match? The cameras weren't broadcasting to the millions of WWE viewers around the world. This would be easy: Smile. Introduce the wrestlers. Say their weights, hometowns, and names. And don't say "his opponent."

Todd gave me the thumbs-up, and I walked into the middle of the ring in the unlit arena. I stepped through those red ropes that I saw every week on TV. I stood on that clean white canvas in the middle of a WWE ring. I looked out at the largest crowd I had ever stood in front of. To me, this was the greatest moment of my life. To the fans who were shuffling into the arena, it was early and quite a while before *RAW* would go live on TV. They were probably looking at me and wondering who I was. The bright lights came up and the music hit. Once Mark Yeaton, who I had seen on WWE ringing the bell and tossing beers to "Stone Cold" Steve Austin for years, rang the bell, I would start introducing the participants. With the most serious face I had ever made and in a deep voice that wasn't my natural voice, I introduced John Cena as "the Prototype!" The music changed, and I saw his opponent come out from the back, which was my cue to introduce him. "And his opponent, Shelton Benjamin!" His opponent? Well, at least I was facing the cameras.

After the match, I watched *Monday Night RAW* in the room backstage with Coach. The room was called pre-tapes, and various talents came in and out of the room throughout the night to record promos for *RAW*, as well as all of the other WWE programming that needed footage. Coach introduced me to every talent that came through and made that whole aspect just a little less intimidating and overall much easier. I could never thank him enough for that.

I drove away from the building and called my parents to let them know how it went. I was hoping for a better idea about the future after the next night. My throat was feeling a bit rough, which seemed weird. I abused it as a kid doing growly impressions of "Macho Man" Randy Savage and the Bushwhackers. The thing was, I had announced long, full shows and never had an issue. Now, after one match, my throat felt weak. I called my friend who was a singer and took voice lessons. I asked her for advice on what to do and explained that I had another match the next night. She suggested lemon drops and hot tea. So I went out and picked up lemon drops and hot tea. I started wondering what would happen if I got hired and then my throat gave up on me. I hoped it was just nerves as I never had a problem with my throat in the past, especially after announcing one simple match, and proceeded with my drive to Sacramento.

In each TV event city, there's a hotel where most of the crew and some talent stay called the TV hotel. The next morning at the Sacramento TV hotel, I left my room for the elevators. The elevator door opened, and Stephanie McMahon and her husband, Triple H, were in there. As if elevators aren't awkward enough, I was in a closed space with these company executives, Vince McMahon's daughter and son-in-law. I was bright red and only remember saying hi and just anxiously waiting for that ride to end. Ten long minutes, or more realistically, two floors later, we finally arrived to the lobby floor. Paul Heyman, who was part of the writing team at the time, was the last one at the front desk when everyone else cleared out. Paul was the mastermind behind the ECW, which as I mentioned, inspired both WCW and WWE as well as groomed a ton of great talent for both companies. Paul is an absolute wrestling genius, and I was a huge fan of his. I said hello and asked if he had any feedback for me from the previous evening. He said, "It was superb. Word going around was what was Tucson's loss could be our gain, and I am almost positive you will be picked up. If you ever need a reference or recommendation, just let me know." I shook his hand and thanked him as we wished me luck for the second shot that night.

The arena setup was similar in Sacramento as it was in Oakland. While we were at a new arena, all the rooms were made the same with various signs. Male talent, female talent, TV office, TV locker room, Vince's office, catering, etc. Once again, Coach let me hang out with him in the pre-tapes room where the men and women would come in and record various promos for the television shows as well as for home video. Tuesday was a *SmackDown* taping, so the roster was a totally new crew of talent. The Rock would also be coming back on this night for a surprise appearance. I enjoyed meeting everybody, and they were all very welcoming. I could see how the crew and talent all seemed like one big, happy family. I wanted to be part of this family so badly. This was the industry that I loved and wanted to be a part of for so long, and this was the place to be. I loved the idea of having a job where my "work" was to be at wrestling shows.

As I left catering, I got into an elevator at the same time as Shelton, Cena, Rob Conway, and Vince McMahon. One of them thanked Vince for having him, and Vince responded with "Welcome. You guys are the future of this company." I guess Cena really took that to heart! I knew of all his work in California, and that day the Brooklyn Brawler was recording Cena for various promos. I remember how excited he was about this new talent: "He's got the look; he can talk. This guy's got it all!"

My dark match on this night would be John Cena versus Shelton Benjamin once again. In addition to that, I would get to announce Rey Mysterio's very first WWE match against Funaki. I walked down to the ring before the show started, and the same crew was on the floor. Todd, Mark the timekeeper, and Frank Bullock the audio engineer. Mark had been ringing the bell for WWE television as long as I could remember. He got caught in the middle of numerous storylines over the years for being in the right place at the wrong time. And, as I mentioned earlier, he was the guy tossing beers to a thirsty "Stone Cold" Steve Austin each night during the Attitude Era. This guy was "Mr. WWE" to me. I thought sitting with him was one of the highlights of this tryout.

I announced the two matches, and things went exactly as planned. I didn't say anything that I shouldn't say, and I said everything I should have said. As a ring announcer, I know that my job is not to stand out. My job is to give talent a great introduction and enhance their entrance as best as possible. On this night, I was way too scared to do anything fancy, but I still got the job done.

At the end of the night, a producer by the name of Kasama brought me to the production truck where I was able to meet with Kevin Dunn. He said I did a good job and asked if I could do anything besides ring announce. He said they might have me do backstage interviews. In one of those "I'm really nervous, so I'm going to say something stupid" situations, I just said "Sure, I'm multitalented. I can do anything you need." Multitalented…?

I got to walk down that ramp, get in the ring that I saw each week on TV, and ring announce, showing WWE what I could do. That opportunity was all I could ask for, and now the future was in their hands. The dream was achieved, but the journey was just beginning.

CHAPTER 7
I'M GOING TO DISNEYLAND

I jumped in my car and headed to the airport to fly back to Arizona. It almost felt like the entire experience was a dream. I wasn't told that they liked me or disliked me. As far as I knew, I didn't do a good job or a bad job. I flew home, and it was like it never really happened.

I enjoyed living rent free at my parents' vacation house. That living situation definitely helped take some pressure off of me, and it was also just a nice, quiet, older neighborhood. I would sit at the pool and observe. Lois, Fran, Bruce, Bernadette, and Pat were the regulars. I was friendly with all of them. I loved hanging out with this crew of retired folks. Unfortunately for years, all of them had various rivalries that kept them from talking to each other. There was virtually zero interaction between any of them. This one didn't talk to that one. That one didn't like this one. So each day I made it my goal to be friendly and make the pool fun on my end. They would all sit there in silence, and no one would interact with each other—even though we were all there just about every day! Over time, it became a more friendly atmosphere. I would slowly get one of them to engage in conversations with me and someone else. Before I knew it, everyone forgot about their past differences, and we all became friends. I loved that. I loved hanging out with them because they were genuine people who had been around, and I could learn from them.

Solving the social problems at the pool was one thing, but making money was another. Independent and *Toughman* gigs here and there wouldn't be enough. I lived in a new city and didn't really have more than a couple of friends. I decided to get a job waiting tables at California Pizza Kitchen. I had waited tables when I was 15 and loved it. I was actually the takeout guy at the Italian restaurant before moving up to helping the servers with salads, bread, and drinks. I liked helping tables more than dealing with people over the phone because I have always been a people person. Plus, I wasn't good at writing down directions for the drivers, and GPS was unheard of back then. New owners took over and asked me if I would like to do more than run the items out. They thought I would make a great server. I asked if they knew how old I was and their response was, "we don't care." That was the end of that conversation, and I became a server and had a blast. I was so young that I would say things other servers wouldn't say. Instead of learning the 10 different cheesecake flavors, I would just describe them by their color. Awful, but I could get away with these things at 15. I made up magic tricks for my tables and did everything possible to get a good tip so at the end of the shift I could go to the movie theater next door and have money to gamble with on top of the projector room with the theater staff.

I knew that CPK would be different because I was older and in a different city. I hoped to make friends and, of course, make some money while I was attempting to get my feet on the ground in "the real world". That phase where you graduate college and enter the real world is intimidating! You have just finished college, and you have this degree. Now whatever job you choose is your career for life. That's part of the reason I decided to take a serving job instead of a corporate job. The only job I really wanted was to be a WWE ring announcer. I got my tryout which was awesome, but if they didn't like me, I needed to figure out a plan. Or just stall at CPK.

Fortunately, during my training, I got a call from an unavailable number on my phone. That's usually how WWE office numbers came up on caller ID on my cell phone. I bolted to the bathroom to answer. The office was calling to inform me that they would like me to come out to Stamford to try out for a commentary position. I have watched wrestling forever and have always admired the commentators. They have a very, very challenging job. They call the action, help get storylines across to the audience, and constantly talk so there's no awkward silence. There are so many people who have been mastering the art for so long. I felt like this was a wasted opportunity for someone that actually deserved it. I knew that I did not deserve the opportunity and that I would not be good, as this was an art that I never mastered or even once attempted.

Despite this feeling, I still had to take a chance. So on July 15, 2002, I flew out to New Jersey. I took a cab from the airport to the arena in East Rutherford. The plan was to go to *RAW* (because I wanted to get to go to another show, and it was in town that night), meet up with Coach, and head back to Stamford with him. As I pulled up, Coach came outside and met me. The show had already started, and he seemed really excited. "The NWO is done. There is a huge surprise here, a new general manager to run *Monday Night RAW*. No one knows who it is. Big night. Come on in!"

We walked back to the TV locker room—the locker room used for most of the televised locker room scenes. I watched the show from that room and couldn't believe it when Eric Bischoff was revealed as the GM. For years, Eric tried to be the number one wrestling promotion, which was, according to WWE, "trying to put them out of business", until WWE finally won that battle and bought WCW. Now Bischoff is working for Vince McMahon? This was one of the most surreal moments in the business, and I was there for it! After the show, I saw William Regal. He told me that he wanted to introduce me to his friend Chris. We walked over to the monitors and approached Chris Benoit who immediately stood up and shook my hand. Benoit was one of the most intense wrestlers that I had ever seen in the business. He was a wrestling machine and definitely one of the best to ever put on a pair boots. He was extremely kind, soft spoken, polite, and had the biggest forearms I have ever seen. He and Regal were good friends, and I was glad to be able to meet him, especially with an introduction from Regal.

Before long, Coach and I were on our way to Stamford where he would drop me off and then pick me up in the morning, grab some breakfast, and bring me to WWE headquarters. WWE headquarters is the Holy Grail, the Wrestling Kingdom, my Disneyland. I could not wait to get into that building. There was so much history there, and it was filled with my kind of people, wrestling people. I could never relate to anyone anywhere else. I couldn't talk football, baseball, or hockey. I knew obscure wrestling references that no one else got. Inside WWE headquarters, I would be united with people who spoke my language!

Or so I thought. I walked into the building and immediately started pointing out various rooms and decorations. "This is where they filmed *Livewire! Mania! Primetime Wrestling!*" "Those are the letters that used to spell out 'Superstars' in the beginning of each *Saturday Morning Superstars* episode!" Coach looked at me like I was out of my mind. There was an area with a bunch of monitors, and an old match was playing. "Hey, is that Tommy Rich versus..." The guys who were working just looked at me like I was nuts and said they had no idea. Then I met a gentleman named John McColl who has been a cameraman at the WWE studio at headquarters for many, many years. He could tell that I was fascinated by the studio and offered to show me around. He was there when all these shows were taped and gave me the backstories. I was amazed.

Eventually it was time to show off all of those alleged multiple talents that I mentioned to Kevin Dunn. Whoops. Step one was sitting with Coach in front of a producer named Jenn, who worked under Kevin. Jenn played a match, and Coach and I were going to do commentary over it. We would start with Coach doing play-by-play while I would do color. The play-by-play guy calls the action, move for move, while the color guy explains the story surrounding what we are seeing. Well, I was speechless for most of this. I moved my hands, nodded my head, and even moved my eyes a lot, but that doesn't come through on the commentary microphone.

Strike one.

Then we switched roles.

Strike two.

Now I had to prove that I could easily handle a backstage interview. Ask a question and hold the mic, not very difficult. Jenn explained that I was interviewing the Rock (who would be played by Coach). So I turned to Coach and said "Rock..." Coach immediately turned into the Rock. I started laughing. Remember when Jimmy Fallon was on *Saturday Night Live* and would lose it and start laughing in most sketches? That's the same issue that I had. Coach as Rock threw me off, and I instantly earned my third strike. Well, it was fun while it lasted. They must not have liked me as a ring announcer, and now they definitely were not going to like me as a commentator or interviewer.

So it was back to Arizona and back to California Pizza Kitchen. CPK was pretty fun, and I liked my coworkers and general manager. On top of that, my U of A friends and I would go out to the bars near ASU, basically reliving our U of A times at ASU without having to go to class. One night during my shift, I got a call from my friend Josh in Florida. Josh was a family friend who, when I found out he liked wrestling many years before, I drove nuts trying to find out wrestlers' real names and any insider info he had, just like Craig did with me years later. Josh had called to tell me that Lilian was announcing on *RAW*, and a team by the name of 3-Minute Warning had attacked her! He thought maybe this meant there would be an opening for me. My hopes were up, but that night as I watched the tape of *RAW* that I had recorded, I never got a call from WWE that night.

The next afternoon, I was washing my car outside when my phone rang with an unavailable ID. My heart started pounding. "Justin? Hi, this is Sue at WWE. Kevin wanted to know if you could be at *RAW* in Seattle next Monday night. Are you available?" While frozen, I told her, "yes!" She asked if I watched *RAW*, to which I said "yes!" again and asked how Lilian was doing. She told me that Lilian was unlikely to be there Monday to work *RAW*, and I asked if that meant I would be there for that reason, and she said "yes." I was totally psyched! I immediately called my parents and asked them to put the phone on speaker. I told them the news and couldn't believe it. I would be announcing on *Monday Night RAW* in less than a week! A dream come true! I was on top of the world!

Until the next day.

I called all of my good friends and told them the news. Luckily, I had enough battery left in my phone to get the call from Sue the next day when she told me there was a change of plans. She said, for storyline purposes, Howard would be announcing Monday, and they would not need me, but said Kevin assured her that they would contact me within the month. Well, I went from the top of the world to the bottom. The only redeeming point of the call was that Kevin would be calling me sometime within the month. Or so I thought.

On September 5, 2002, the month was up, so I figured that they had forgotten. I emailed Sue when I saw WWE would be in Arizona the next month and mentioned that I'd be willing to help with anything they might need. Usually when I emailed, it would trigger a call. So that next day at 2 pm, the phone rang with unavailable ID, but it wasn't Sue's voice. It was a man's, which threw me off. "Justin, it's Kevin Dunn." I didn't know much about horoscopes, but I happened to read it that day, and it said to accept an incoming call, you never know who it might be. Deep, right? He said he hadn't forgotten about me. He was ready for me last month, but they ran the angle with Lilian and Howard. Now they were ready and would call me on the following Wednesday with some numbers. I wouldn't be full-time, but about 90% four days a week, ring announcing house and TV shows. That was huge! It seemed like I was in. I went out that night, and I'll never forget the confidence I had walking around town, knowing that I was going to be part of World Wrestling Entertainment!

Kevin didn't call that Wednesday or Thursday afternoon, so I called Sue, and she said he would call Thursday evening, but the phone never rang. It did, however, ring the next day at about 2:30 pm. He told me they don't just let anyone into the family, and I could have a three-month exclusive deal getting paid per show. I couldn't be Justin Roberts because of Justin Credible, and I asked about being Jason Roberts since people have mistakenly called me Jason most of my life anyway. He told me that on Sunday I would shadow Howard Finkel in Montana and then shadow Lilian Monday at *RAW* in Denver and announce *Velocity* and *SmackDown* in Colorado Springs Tuesday for Tony Chimel, who would be on vacation.

Sunday in Billings, Montana, was exciting. I was sitting at ringside with Howard Finkel, learning how to do his job from the man himself. On Monday in Denver, I was already nervous, and then Lilian approached me with some notes. She had written out a page-long announcement that was a disclaimer. This announcement needed to be made to the live audience before the show began. The announcement was about photography being ok, laser pens/video recording equipment not ok, don't throw anything at or toward the ringside area, violators will be ejected from the building and are subject to arrest, and so on. Okay, this was long, plus the audience did not know me, so I could totally see the audience booing me as I made this speech right before they got to see the first match.

The next day, I had my disclaimer announcement memorized and used WWE. com to gather everybody's biographical information for their introductions. I got through the show with no mistakes, but, wow, was it nerve-racking. My only cues were from Mark who rang the bell or pointed at me. I was really on my own for what to say when I had the green light. I felt okay about the show, but that next day, my throat was killing me. I couldn't swallow without intense pain, and my glands were swollen. I revisited this fear of finally getting the job of my dreams, but now maybe my throat wouldn't allow it. This was never something I could have ever imagined while daydreaming about freezing on the ramp and all the other possibilities. My logic was, well I did it. I made it to WWE and got to announce. That's what I wanted, and I achieved my dream. If it ends now, that would be disappointing, but the bottom line is that I still got to live out my dream. I also managed to get an 8x10 of Shawn Michaels signed for my U of A advisor Norma, who was a big fan of his and helped me to make my college classes tolerable junior and senior year. Mission accomplished, right?

I rested for two weeks and healed up in time for my next run which was shadowing Tony Chimel in October 2002 in Kansas City, Missouri, followed by San Angelo, Texas, and then Tucson, Arizona. I loved working with Tony because he was willing to give me all the matches to announce. I thought maybe I'd get a match or two, but Chimel was more than happy to let me do everything. I guess the office wasn't happy with that decision, though, and the next show we split the card down the middle.

That night we were in Tucson, so we flew into Phoenix. I grabbed my car, which was already at the airport, and John Cena asked if he could hop in with me. We drove down to my alma mater, and I took him to a couple of my favorite food spots—Los Betos and Beyond Bread. John taught me how he adapted to the locker room and some do's and don'ts. He would always be the first to show up to the building, do what was asked, and stay out of the way. He was very respectful to everyone around him, and when it came time for his match, he would go in there and do what was asked of him. When he was done, he stayed quiet and watched the rest of the show to learn from the other guys. Then he was the last to leave. I appreciated his thorough advice, especially since he was the perfect role model.

That night, Tony and I split the show again. At one point, Crash Holly fell off the ring apron and right onto me. Billy Kidman did the same. I realized that being at ringside wasn't always going to be a safe place, and anything could happen at any time, so I had to be prepared for those kinds of ribs, as well as do my job. At live events, I would announce, ring the bell, and take jackets and accessories to the back at the beginning of the matches. The shows went well, and I was getting the hang of it. That night, I brought Cena out to Maloney's, one of my favorite night spots at U of A. We had a fun night, and he met up with some of his buddies who were in town. He went back to Phoenix with them, and I drove to the *SmackDown* taping the next morning. Tony announced the televised *SmackDown* show, and I announced the pre-show, *Velocity*, which aired on Saturday nights.

After this tour, my throat wasn't beat up as badly as the previous tour, but it was still shot. I had a few days at home to rest and heal and then left for Edmonton, Calgary, London, and Toronto in Canada. I was stoked to be in Canada for the first time, and I rode with Tony and referee Mike Chioda for this loop. People always wondered how we all got from town to town, and, for the most part, the company would fly us into a town, and then you get a rental car for yourself for the tour until you flew home. At times, the towns were booked so far apart that sometimes there would be mid-tour flights and drives. A lot of back and forth, too. It wasn't out of the norm to drive 300 miles between towns A and B and backtrack 200 miles to get to C and then drive back again for down D.

You could also ride with more people to save costs or for the company. Chioda had been in the company for about the same amount of time as Chimel. They used to drive the ring truck from town to town, and then Mark Yeaton got Chioda hired as a referee. He went on to become one of the best. A WWE referee is a very difficult job despite how easy they, especially Chioda, make it look. I sat in the backseat of the car and made wrestling, television, and movie references because that's what I was into. They thought I was nuts. They didn't want to talk wrestling, and they hadn't heard of any TV shows I mentioned and maybe knew of only one or two of the movies. They thought I was crazy, but I thought they were insane. I realized that they live in this bubble where they are constantly on the road, and they don't have a chance to watch much TV or go off to the outside world. This is also a point where they didn't have access to all of that on their computers or phones.

The loop went well, as did the shows, and I enjoyed being on the road. I learned a lot from Mike and Tony. I would always walk in the door at home and felt the same way I did after the tryout—like every WWE tour was a dream that never happened. Once I got home, I was away from that world, and it didn't seem real. I ended up spending the next couple of weeks in bed, nursing another bad sore throat. My glands were swollen, and I couldn't talk or swallow, so I began seeing an ear, nose, and throat doctor.

My short-term contract expired, and I never heard anything from WWE about future dates. It was a really weird feeling to not know whether this would happen or not for me. Was I done? Would they offer a new contract? If they did, could my throat hold up?

I did an independent show on October 30 in Phoenix, and I loved every minute of it. I wanted to get back in a WWE ring, though. I would constantly call Sue. Eventually she told me that she knew Kevin liked me, but he hadn't talked to Steve Taylor, a very good guy who I believe was scheduling announcers for house shows at the time. In March 2003, I got an email from HR regarding the script that I had sent in. I asked Sue how to respond, and she told me the original plan was to use me, but business was bad. They liked me and didn't want to lose me, so they just didn't tell me anything. She had Palma at HR call me, and I was going to meet with Stephanie McMahon, who headed the creative department, about joining the writing team.

I had written numerous independent shows by this point, and my mind revolved around wrestling. Maybe my throat wasn't going to hold up, so this was a sign, another way in to the company. I already got to announce, so why not give this a try?

I was eager to meet with the executives in Stamford, and they flew me out from Arizona. When I landed in New Jersey, WWE sent a car service to take me to Stamford. They put me up at a hotel the night before where I got some good sleep despite being nervous. I was ready and I was hungry for this. Before the interview, I connected with a WWE.com writer I had become friends with named Phil Speer.

Phil knew how big of a fan I was and offered to give me a full tour of WWE Headquarters—the actual building that I hadn't yet seen since I had only been in the studio portion. Once again, I was in awe. I wanted nothing more than to get this job and be a part of WWE. Phil brought me to HR, and I filled out the paperwork. I waited for my interview with Stephanie McMahon. After waiting quite a while, I was informed that Stephanie would not be meeting with me after all because I did not have enough television writing experience. Wait. Did they not realize this before they flew me out? I was in shock.

I shared a taxi back to the hotel with a gentleman who did get the opportunity to interview. He told me he was from LA, so I started naming independent promotions out there, asking if he had worked with them. He hadn't. He wasn't a wrestling writer. He worked with the *Lifetime Network*. I told him I loved the *Golden Girls* and that was the end of the conversation. I got back to my hotel room and stared out the window. It was cold and miserable outside with mist and grey clouds in the air. It was the epitome of a horrible day in every possible way. I wanted to leave the east coast as soon as possible as I really felt like the company that I loved so much had slapped me in the face. Why get flown all the way out there and spend two days there for nothing? I thought about giving up, but that's just not something I do. Unless they told me that there was no chance, I was going to stay on WWE for something. Anything.

Between November and December, I worked at CPK. I would call Sue every week and ask her if there was anything I could do. I hated bothering her, but I was persistent, and I wanted this to happen. Every week she would tell me the same thing, that there was nothing available, and she would let me know if anything came up. I had no announcing dates until December 22 when I was asked to fill in for Tony at TV. I gladly accepted, but still wanted more. I figured it was a good sign that they were using me, but it was so inconsistent. Tony was still announcing all live and televised *SmackDown*'s, while Howard did all live *RAW* events and Lilian did the *RAW* TVs. I realized my only shot was filling in for Tony who liked taking vacations. Howard wasn't interested in those.

I was able to announce a fun *SmackDown* episode due to the tag-team match between the team of Edge and Billy Kidman and Eddie and Chavo Guerrero. Chavo and his Uncle Eddie, who was one of the greatest and most entertaining wrestlers I have ever watched, were trying to get disqualified so they wouldn't lose their titles to Edge and Kidman. Every time they attempted to get disqualified or counted out, the referee had me make an announcement. It was a lot of back and forth between them and the announcements which was something I was never able to do before. The majority of my job was saying, "the following contest is scheduled for one fall," or something to that effect. Doing something outside the box was fun for me. It was also fun announcing names like Guerrero and Mysterio. I would roll my Rs a little...well, a lot. Kevin Dunn despised that, and I was asked to stop shortly after I began.

After this episode of *SmackDown*, another long period went by before I heard anything from the office. I worked some *Toughman* shows in Des Moines, Iowa, and Jackson, Tennessee. Jackson was always a lot of fun. There is a great nightlife there! As a 22-year-old announcer, I appreciated that type of thing.

My throat was still giving me trouble now and then, and I took speech lessons at a Phoenix hospital to try and correct whatever I was doing wrong. No one taught me how to announce; I just did whatever felt right. Maybe I wasn't speaking or breathing correctly I thought, so my doctor and I agreed to try this, which I think it helped buy me some time.

The *SmackDown* loops I was working really took me out of the indie show mentality that I previously had. While working indies, I was basically self-trained on how to do my one job, but no one really ever sat me down and explained that the show was more than anything, about the wrestlers. I was working up the crowd and bantering between matches. These loops allowed me to improve on how I showcased the talent instead: little things like cowering from bad guys. Small details like this helped get the characters over making them even more popular with the fans.

There was one night, though, when I learned my lesson the hard way. We had an afternoon show in Worcester, Massachusetts. You are supposed to stay clear of the Undertaker—the dead man, the phenom—who basically has superpowers in the wrestling world. I didn't know how to adjust from the fan's perspective to now as someone who was part of the magic. He had come outside the ring right by where I was seated to ring the bell. He went to attack his opponent by the steps, and the opponent ran out of the way. He looked right at me, and I looked right back at him as if I would shrug my shoulders and think, well he got away.

He instantly changed his look as if he was going to kill me, and I ran from him for real. When I got to the back, he explained that people sell for that character, meaning that they react how they are supposed to react to whatever he is doing. When the Undertaker was anywhere near you, you did whatever you could to get away from him. From that day on, I would look and really be uncomfortable anytime he was near. I always walked, ran, or looked away from him, depending on the situation. Undertaker has always been very well respected by the fans and his peers for his long run within the company. He would work no matter what, no matter how sick he might be. We were in Texas when he was in a room all day with a bad case of bronchitis. He left to work a match that you would think would be shortened for his health but ended up even going longer than planned. When he came back, he was immediately treated by paramedics. He also had an *Elimination Chamber* match where he was burned by the flames during his entrance and remained locked up in the chamber, burning up! Nothing ever got in the way from Undertaker doing his job.

I would come home from the loops and wait to find out when my next booking would be. The real estate market was booming in Arizona, and like many other people, I decided to go to real estate school and get my license just in case wrestling didn't work out. I took the crash course which was nine jam-packed days so I could finally have a back-up plan. The class was filled with way too much information that I could not retain and just wasn't interested in. I finished the class but never took the test. I guess becoming a realtor wouldn't be plan B, so I really needed to make WWE a full-time job!

On March 11, 2003, I worked a local show with my Phoenix crew. Nav had booked a kid from California to drive in. He was on *MTV's Real World* and training to wrestle, so Nav gave him a shot. I don't mean this the way most people talk about "flipping through the channels," but I was literally flipping through and saw this kid holding up a toy WWF belt and cutting a promo, so I stopped and watched. That was the only minute of the show I had ever seen, but he got me to watch. Mike Mizanin, a long-time wrestling fan, was a very friendly kid with a great attitude who found fame from *MTV* and was now determined to use that to become a wrestler. I watched as the people came up to him after the show and quickly realized just how popular he was from his *MTV* show.

The next night, we ran another Phoenix event, and then I was off for a couple of weeks until a *Toughman* weekend in Cedar Rapids, Iowa. WWE had called to book me for *SmackDown* at the end of April in Nashville, Tennessee, and I asked if I could also work the Chicago show on April 8. As I grew up going to shows in Chicago, I dreamed of announcing at the Rosemont Horizon (now known as Allstate Arena). WWE allowed me to go there and announce on *Velocity*. My family and friends were ringside, and all I could do was look out at the seats I used to sit in as a kid. Now I was in the ring at that arena! It was amazing. On the same day, I got a call from a friend in Tucson. A woman was looking for entertainment at the upcoming Pima County Fair and was looking into the possibility of a wrestling show to open for Blue Oyster Cult. Tucson legend Jim Click's son, Chris, gave her my number, and we discussed what she was looking for. My little book of wrestling phone numbers was all the way back in Scottsdale, so I had to figure something out because I only had three weeks to assemble the entire show. Again, this is a time before everything was available right on your cell phone.

Money for the event was guaranteed, which made this completely different from the last time that I ran a show. The fair would pay me an agreed-upon amount, and then I would use that to cover all the expenses for the show. The fair guarantee was very good, and I, of course, rented the ring from Steve and booked him as well as all the men and women that worked my first show. I told him that there was money in the budget, so I wanted all of them well taken care of this time around.

I wanted to think outside the box to find a draw (someone who is a big enough star to bring people to the show). Who would be a cool name to book that no one else was using on their shows, I wondered. My first thought was Mike Mizanin with his Miz character. He appealed to the *MTV* audience and was trying to get as much wrestling experience as possible. I liked Bull Buchanan a lot when I worked with him at WWE when he teamed with John Cena, and he was now working independently, pretty fresh off TV. He was friends with the Big Boss Man, one of my favorites growing up. I had never seen him on an independent show, so Bull connected me with Big Boss Man, and he was in. I had worked with Greg Valentine and Tito Santana in the AWA and called them as well as I slowly rounded up numbers from friends. If you're even a casual wrestling fan, those are some names you will definitely recognize. I was able to pay everyone what they asked for, plus cover hotels, transportation, rent, and transportation of the ring. The fair was very happy with the attendance and the show. More important to me, everyone in the crew I assembled was very happy with the show and the experience.

I couldn't wait to book that fair again the next year with more notice and access to more wrestlers. Unfortunately, Lana had told me that Valentine had called the next day and offered to book the show next year at a lower cost. Regrettably, the fair committee decided to avoid wrestling all together the next year.

The rest of the spring was pretty slow as far as WWE shows went. I had a couple of shots for Dale's AWA and a decent amount of *Toughman* events. I felt like I was in a weird position because I had no idea what my future was going to be with WWE. Was I done filling in? Would I ever actually be brought on board full-time? Should I find a new career? WWE wouldn't give me a solid answer. They wouldn't tell me one way another. Did they want me to get lost? Did they want to keep working with me? I had no idea. I eventually learned that it is a regular practice for WWE to never definitively say no. They keep hope alive in all aspiring talent because then those people are always available and continually hungry for a job—and at WWE's beck and call all year round. The "carrot" of a prestigious and sought-after job with WWE ensures that hundreds of thousands of wrestlers and other sports entertainment hopefuls around the world happily go along with it and say "thank you".

The end of summer approached, and I found out that the Harlem Globetrotters were based in Phoenix. Wrestling is sports entertainment, a rare genre, and the Globetrotters are somewhat similar. My mom mentioned to me that she knew the daughter of Abe Saperstein, the former owner and coach of the group, so I put together a videotape and résumé package and sent it out. When I followed up with them, they mentioned that they would like to have me in for an interview. I went in and learned how their tours work. The position was part-time, as were their shows, and the pay wasn't going to cut it as a career. I was told "you have to do it for the love of the game." As is often the case in life, however, the "love of the game" wasn't going to pay my bills. Although my bills and rent weren't really a demand at the time, I realized that eventually I had to start earning a living. I passed on the Globetrotters.

I sat next to Tom Ambrose on a plane a while before this. He was one of the executives with the Phoenix Suns, and I had given him my card. I told him that I was a wrestling announcer working part time with WWE, and if they ever needed an announcer or host for any of their charity events to please let me know. Well now I had gotten a call that the Suns were looking for a new announcer. I thought, how great would that be? I could announce a game a half hour away and come home from work without having to fly. That sounded terrific, but again, the pay wasn't enough to live on. Plus, it would interfere with my sporadic WWE work. So I passed on a potentially great opportunity in the hopes that I would acquire something stable with WWE because that was what I truly wanted.

At the time, I was working maybe one week every three months for WWE, with an AWA show sprinkled in here and there and a *Toughman* weekend every once in a while. I wondered if I let WWE know that the Globetrotters were interested in me that would make them hurry up and decide on me one way or another. I decided to find out. I reached out to WWE knowing that a Globetrotters deal was technically still on the table. They suggested I take it since it sounded like a good opportunity, and there wasn't enough work available. Sue had given me the bad news and ended the conversation with, "I'm sorry things didn't work out for you here." I felt utterly disappointed. But what did I expect? I was the one looking for something steady. They were more than okay using me once in a while when there was a need. I had to laugh, because the situation was like my love life, but in reverse. For the first time I was the one who wanted a steady relationship (in this case, a stable contract), while the other party (WWE) was just looking to casually date.

As you might expect, hearing no from WWE definitely didn't motivate me to take that the Globetrotters deal. My heart wasn't in it. I wanted to do something that I would really enjoy. Even though I knew the games would be fun, it just wasn't me. Since I was a kid, I knew I wanted to be on TV. I always liked being on stage. I loved performing. Even before I knew what wrestling was, I wanted to live in LA and be an actor. So, if WWE was plan A, going to Los Angeles and doing absolutely anything at all in entertainment could possibly be plan B.

Lana from the Tucson fair had previously advised me to have business cards made. I finally took her advice and had some printed up with my face on them, as she suggested. I decided that I needed some headshots, too. Being the resourceful guy that I am, I took out a bed sheet, draped it from the ceiling, used a camcorder in black and white and posed. I snapped a shot, plugged my video camera into the computer, and saved a video frame of my face, giving me a "headshot" to get by.

CHAPTER 8
PLAN B, WATCHA GONNA DO?

In October 2003, just before I headed out to LA, my sister got married. Oddly enough, her big day was the happiest day of my life as well. As far as wrestling goes, I had gotten to announce in a WWE ring (and even do it on TV), and I was just about to head out to Hollywood for my next big adventure. I had that in the back of my mind as I mingled with my family and friends. Everybody was there, and everybody was smiling. It was such an incredible day. I gave a speech welcoming my caring and selfless brother-in-law to the family and letting all our relatives and friends know how much my big sister had influenced me over the years. She really did. She influenced the shows that I watched growing up, and I learned so many other traits from her to help me in life as well.

The next morning, I loaded up a U-Haul. Nav was kind enough to come along and help with the move, and we drove to LA. He had always been there for me and was a true friend. He also laughed at all the childish things I would do to him and say or even sing to him, which I appreciated as well. I was glad he came along for the ride and paid him with entertainment for six hours. Whether it was impersonating friends or acting out Avril Lavigne songs, Nav was amused. I had gone out a few weeks prior to find a place to live while helping my buddy Seth move from LA to Rancho Cucamonga. He still had a couple of weeks left on his lease and let me camp out on his floor while I tried to find an apartment.

Nav and I headed to the apartment that I found in a neighborhood in the Valley called Sherman Oaks. It was a nice little one-bedroom apartment that was both affordable and in a decent location. A Costco and Target were nearby, and if for some crazy reason there was anything else I needed, it was all within a 20-minute drive (or two hours, depending on traffic). While I was getting settled in, I received a call from Sue.

"Hi, Justin. Just when we thought we were saying goodbye...We have some shows coming up this month and would like for you to fill in on the *RAW* live events. Are you interested?"

Of course I was interested. *RAW* events? Maybe there was still hope after all! I flew out and worked the loop. The company rented my cars and booked my hotels, so I usually rode by myself. I was friendly with everybody but didn't really have any friends I could travel with. On this loop, I ended up meeting with a wrestler named Stevie Richards. I became a fan of his when he was in ECW. Eventually, he was in both WCW and then WWE. I learned early on that most of the people in this business are very quirky characters, myself included. I think you have to be. Stevie was no exception; he was certainly a character. He was also very technically savvy in and out of the ring, an all-around good guy, and a cardio freak.

I got a call while I was already on the road that I was going to be needed for *RAW* TV on Monday night but was told not to wear a tux anymore. The office said that's Howard's thing and asked me to save the tux for events like *WrestleMania*. Stevie and I went to the mall, and I got a new shirt and tie that I could wear with the tux I had to make it look more like a suit.

Doing *RAW* TV was, of course, a huge deal for me. My parents were never into WWE. They would take me to the matches when I was a kid, but IRS (Irwin R. Schyster) was the only wrestler my dad was into. (I had worked an indie show with him a while back, and he was kind enough to record a promo on my video camera for my dad, and he loved it.) When I announced on *Velocity*, my parents would always watch, and my dad actually started taking a liking to it. Velocity was the late Saturday night show that now WWE filled with mostly talent that wasn't being used on *SmackDown*. This was the show where John Cena really started connecting with fans who watched regularly. (For you ultra-fans out there, *Velocity* was also the home of the epic A-Train and Funaki feud that would take place almost every week as Vince once proclaimed in a production meeting that it would "continue until they got it right.")

When I told my dad that I was going to be on *Monday Night RAW*, he was extremely proud and happy for me. He mentioned that he doesn't usually watch *RAW* but would obviously watch on this night.

Like a child, my 59-year-old dad was hooked. He enjoyed *RAW* and the different array of talent there and added the show to his schedule. He took a liking to Chris Benoit and Batista. As we talked on the phone, I noticed that he sounded like a younger version of myself, discussing all the talent on the different shows as well as what was happening in the storylines. Now that he was genuinely interested, I was looking forward to bringing him back to the next Chicago show.

I mentioned that my dad went to work extremely early in the morning. By doing so, he would be home early to nap, sit outside in the sun, and call my sister and me daily. He didn't need a reason to call and most times didn't have one. He just called to say hi. He liked hearing our voices. Now we could finally talk wrestling together.

When I came back from the last tour, I had to head right out to a *Toughman* weekend in Oklahoma. The *Sunday Night Heat* episode I taped on that loop would be airing the Sunday after the *Toughman* shows. I was excited to be a WWE announcer working on these *Toughman* shows. I had used indie wrestling to get to *Toughman* and *Toughman* to get to WWE. I decided to take a few liberties during *Toughman* shows and boast that I could now be seen on worldwide television. I was most talkative about this during early Saturday shows when I would remind fans that they could go right home and catch me on *Velocity*.

The bosses weren't thrilled with that. I don't blame them. But I was 23 years old, and I wanted, more than anything, to be a WWE announcer. That was the bottom line. I no longer viewed myself as a *Toughman* announcer. I was the WWE announcer who happened to announce *Toughman* shows on the side. Bartlesville, Oklahoma, would be one of my last bookings for the *Toughman* contest. Pumping WWE at their events was clearly not professional, but I blame it on being young and, well, just being honest. I couldn't hide the fact that my passion was strictly WWE. By the time I was in Jackson, Tennessee, shilling my WWE appearances nonstop, the two ladies who had hooked me up with the *Toughman* gigs, Lydia and Susan, were done using me. I can't thank them enough for the opportunities they provided. I learned a ton and had so many great experiences.

CHAPTER 9
WELCOME TO THE JUNGLE

In December, I was asked to work my first WWE (overseas) international tour. I couldn't believe that they asked me to go! South Korea, Singapore, and Australia were the three countries where we would be doing shows. Not only would these be my first international events, but this would be my first time leaving the country to head overseas for a WWE tour, and I was thrilled for the opportunity.

Some of the talents were teasing me about this being my first international tour, making it sound as if I should be scared. Why would I be? What could be so bad? I'd done a bunch of tours, including Canada, and never had an issue. Well, I never imagined the hell that I would be going through when I flew to San Jose, California, for the *SmackDown* taping. I was sick. My throat was really bothering me again. It was a bronchitis-type breakout. I was coughing up a bunch of junk and not feeling well. My voice was barely there, but I squeaked through the show. When the taping ended, we boarded a charter plane for the group. I didn't have very many friends that I felt comfortable with. Okay, that was being generous: I actually did not have a friend on that plane. I had guys that I've worked with over the years, but no one that I felt comfortable with as a friend. I had the feeling that everyone was out to get me, and, as I soon discovered, I couldn't have been more right. I was the new guy. I was a measly ring announcer, and I was with an established family that I simply wasn't a part of yet. In short, I didn't belong, and I could definitely feel it.

This plane was pretty small. It was probably from the 1970s and had two seats, an aisle, and another two seats in each row. They were the big, leather, old-school, first-class seats. I sat next to one of the referees, Nick Patrick. Since it was a small plane, we had to make numerous gas stops. Our first stop was in Alaska. We landed, gassed up, and proceeded to the next stop, which was Russia.

At this point in my life, I had been on a fair number of airplanes. But I never experienced a flight like the one to Russia. The winds were taking our plane on quite a ride. We were trying to land in a blizzard and would fly side to side, make giant drops, and go nose down. I had never been so afraid on a plane. The rest of the guys seemed to feel the same. It was pure silence as we were trying to land again after one failed attempt. Paul Heyman would try to lighten the mood with a joke here and there, but then it would be silent again. We tried to land. We failed again. On the third attempt, the pilots were heard arguing that they couldn't see the runway, but we were out of fuel. Ric Flair was sitting across from me one row ahead, and I just thought to myself, there was no way he was going to be in another plane crash. That didn't really reassure me, though. I was scared out of my mind. On our third attempt, we landed safely and were all relieved. At least we were until we found out that after we quickly fueled up we would be taking off again right away in that weather. Same pilots, same plane, same blizzard.

When we finally got to Seoul and in one piece, we had a few hours to roam around the hotel. There was a mall attached which was cool to explore. Shortly after, it was time to head to the arena. We would travel on two buses. The good guys, or "babyfaces" on one bus, and the bad guys, "heels" on the other. I rode with the good guys. We got to the arena, and I met with Dean Malenko and Sgt. Slaughter, the agents in charge of running the show. Brock Lesnar, A-Train, Chris Benoit, Undertaker, Bradshaw, Bob Holly, John Cena, Big Show, Eddie Guerrero, Rey Mysterio, Nunzio, Scotty Too Hotty, Nathan Jones, Ultimo Dragon, and Tajiri were some of the guys on this tour. Good guys like Brock, Undertaker, Eddie, Jones, Charles Robinson, Scotty, and Tajiri were all business. They were there to do what they were there to do: their jobs. No screwing around. A few others had more on their mind: namely, making my life miserable. Bob Holly didn't like me very much. He modified his ring entrance to include knocking me out of my chair each night. It was only three shows, but they were pretty far apart, and three days felt like three weeks. I was in a whole new world in every respect. The guys would also yell at and degrade me. I was told to introduce them when the music played, but then they wouldn't walk out. So afterward I would get talked to for announcing them when the music played before I saw them. I just wanted to do a good job, but I couldn't as the rules would change. The producer would tell me to do something, and then when the other producer would chew me out for it, the producer who gave me my instructions would stand there and watch.

The last day of the tour was in Australia. It was the native country of Nathan Jones, who was set to be in the main event that night. Before intermission, Derek from the merchandise department came up to me at ringside and told me not to mention anything about Nathan. He left the building. He had enough and walked out before his match. At the time, it was a good thing that I didn't know he was going to be leaving the building and going home, because I probably would have joined him.

By the next day, I wish I had. I was still sick, I was given a hard time by a bunch of the guys, and I just wanted to quit. They had driven me to that point. The guys had transformed from my coworkers to evil monsters. The travel was lousy, being sick was lousy, and being the new guy was—you guessed it—lousy. JBL, or Bradshaw, who has a reputation for being a bully, did a wonderful job of keeping that reputation. He found any excuse possible to get the rest of the locker room to hate me. He would twist everything I did in order to stir the pot and turn people against me. At one point, Paul Heyman stood up for me. No one ever stood up to Bradshaw, so I appreciated Heyman speaking up on my behalf.

JBL was a fixture in the company and future overseas tours, and I couldn't do anything about it. Every tour he was on for the next few years involved him and his bullying. Every day I saw him, he asked me why I was still alive and told me to go kill myself. Sadly, there are some people out there who probably would have been driven to that point had they been faced with his treatment for that long. Maybe he never had friends who actually went through with it and had no problem encouraging others to do it. He would verbally abuse guys, force them to drink, and even force guys like Palmer Canon to quit mid-tour. That's one guy I hope to never see at the company's Be a Star anti-bullying campaign. Ric Flair had privately approached me and tried to explain that it was all ribbing and if I really got bothered to let him know. That was very cool of Ric, but I kept it to myself. I should also mention that I always brought old wrestling DVDs on those tours and on this one I was watching my favorite *Royal Rumble* from 1992. Bobby "The Brain" Heenan made that whole show, endorsing Flair in the Rumble match. While watching this match as I had so many times since 1992, I noticed Ric Flair over my shoulder as I watched it on the plane. Never in my life did I ever expect to watch that WITH Ric Flair. Moments like that were my silver lining.

I always brought old wrestling DVDs on those tours, and on this one, I was watching my favorite *Royal Rumble* from 1992. Bobby "the Brain" Heenan made that whole show, endorsing Flair in the *Rumble* match. While watching this match, I noticed Ric Flair, also watching it over my shoulder. Never in my life did I expect to watch that with Ric Flair. Moments like that were my silver lining.

Finally, the tour was finished, and it was time to head back to the US for TV. We took off from Australia for San Diego. Unfortunately, we landed in a different city in Australia instead. There was a problem with our same plane from the trip over, and we had to get out at this airport. I got off the plane onto the same jet bridge with Jamie Noble and Chris Benoit. They had wrestled down Nunzio. All three were highly skilled grapplers you wouldn't want to pick a fight with. As I walked into the airport, Chris Benoit walked over to me and asked how my tour went. As I started answering, Jamie Noble grabbed my leg and took me down from behind. Noble put me in a massive crossface, and I instantly tapped out, hoping that he would break the hold. Instead, Benoit picked up my leg and twisted my foot, which felt like it cracked. Each hold is a legitimately powerful and painful maneuver, and the combination of the two put on me at once by these athletes...well, words don't really do it justice.

They say you're not supposed to sell a rib. In non-wrestler speak, that means you aren't supposed to let the guys know a prank (a "rib") bothers you ("sell it"). In even simpler terms, the boys were just having some good ol' fun, and I should ignore it. The problem was, my ankle swelled up, and I thought it was broken. I couldn't walk, and it was throbbing with pain. The crossface didn't feel great either. These professional wrestlers laid both moves in very solidly on a defenseless 160-pound guy. I spent the next long flight to our first gas stop in the Marshall Islands in pain, and it got worse as we flew on to San Diego. I was honestly contemplating never coming back again. I had wanted this my entire life, and now because a handful of evil people, I was going to walk away. (Maybe on crutches, but walk away, nonetheless.)

Almost 23 hours after the journey began, we had finally arrived. Benoit approached me when we landed and told me to take his number. He wanted to go to the hospital with me if I needed to go, and he apologized for what happened. He told me that he was drunk and just messing around and that he wouldn't try to hurt me on purpose. He sounded sincere and came off as a totally different person than the guy who took me down. The trainer planned to take me to the hospital for an X-ray, but instead we let it sit until the next day.

The bronchitis or whatever it was had finally cleared up the next day, and my ankle was feeling better once I wrapped it. I arrived at the arena and was called in for a talent relations meeting with John Laurinaitis. Company official Dave Hebner had told me the office heard about what happened, and they were pissed. They received a report about the incident at the airport and wanted to talk about it, but I told John that I didn't know what he was talking about. He read off a report to me that basically nailed most of what happened. I didn't know what to say. I didn't want to rat anybody out, but he already knew all the details and all the names. I simply told him that I didn't know if I wanted to be there anymore. He told me the ribbing was wrong, and it should never have gotten to the point where I lost my passion. We had a good conversation, and I realized that I wasn't ready to leave and definitely wouldn't give up because of a few bullies.

The next show was in Chicago at the Rosemont Horizon which was really cool because it was the first non-televised show that I was doing in my hometown. I met my parents and grandma for Gino's deep-dish pizza beforehand. Chicago has the best food in the world—it's not up for debate. There's Portillo's, deep-dish pizza from Gino's, Edwardo's, Lou Malnati's, Girodano's, thin-crust pizza from Barnaby's, Wapaghetti's, Rosatti's...I can go on and on. It was actually at Gino's where I got a call from Jenn at WWE studios. I had posted what today would be called a blog on my website before the company encouraged social media updates—before "social media" was even a thing. I had talked a little about the tour, not about the bullying, just the scary plane ride. Once the office caught wind, I was immediately told to pull that off my website. I did as they asked to avoid any issues or heat from the company and headed over to the arena.

I introduced the family to my coworkers, who were also my dad's newfound heroes. He took pictures with the Big Show, John Cena, Chris Benoit, Brian Kendrick, Tajiri, Nidia, the Basham Brothers, and Akio & Sakoda. This is the arena where, as a child, I took pictures with my favorite wrestlers in the early 90s, and 12 years later, my dad was doing the same thing. Working this arena with my dad now in my shoes as a fan was a very special moment for us.

Before the show started, I was changing in a room with Paul Heyman. Once he was dressed, he left the room. I decided to do the same since the show was starting in less than 10 minutes. I went up to the big blue door to the hallway and pulled, but nothing happened. I tried again. Nothing. The knob moved, but the door would not open.

In less than 10 minutes, I was going to announce a full live show for the first time ever in the arena where I grew up watching the live WWE and WCW shows as well as concerts like REM and New Kids on the Block, but I was trapped. I started to bang on the door even though it was a thick, heavy one. After a decent amount of pounding, I heard a familiar voice. Our security guard, Jimmy Tillis, was on the other side. "What's going on?" he asked. I told him the door was stuck, and I couldn't get out. The next voice I heard was the Big Show, a 7-foot tall giant. He asked Jimmy what was going on and then told me to step back. With one giant kick, Big Show busted open the door and gave me my opening to run to the ring to start the show. I had a blast announcing with my friends and family in the crowd. The one *Velocity* episode I did was a just couple quick matches which translated to maybe a total of 60 seconds of announcing. This was a nearly three-hour long show! I was honored to host it and to guide this live hometown audience through the journey of a WWE event.

Following my first international tour and first Chicago event, I headed back west. I soon realized that my "LA lifestyle" was going nowhere. The positives were that I met a few people I considered friends, and my good friend Adam from back home was still out there, so socially I was okay. But as far as work goes, I needed an agent to get gigs, and I needed gigs to get an agent. It was a puzzle. I had done a lot of pushing to get into WWE and was exhausted about starting that process all over with acting. I figured if I was able to make my way into working for WWE (where there wasn't even an opening, I might add), then surely I could break into a commercial or a TV show or a movie in an industry where there were literally unlimited spots and unlimited gigs.

CHAPTER 10
FULL TANK OF GAS, HALF A PACK OF CIGARETTES, AND A BUMP IN THE ROAD

I hadn't heard anything from WWE in a while, and they were going to be in Bakersfield and Fresno, so I decided to drive up and see if I could talk to Kevin Dunn in person. As I left my house, I got a call from my dad. He was using the snow blower outside and felt chest pains, so he went to the doctor. He had a heart attack when I was in 5th grade. When that happened, my mom was out of town, so my sister and I were alone with him. He was clearly in a lot of pain, but we had no idea that we were watching our father have a heart attack. Now when he felt the pain, he immediately went to see the doctor. He said "something came up," and the doctor was concerned about a shadow that they found in his chest. I didn't know what to make of that, but I assumed it wasn't good. I began to worry but hoped for the best.

I had a lot of time to process what was going on while I drove to Bakersfield. I tried to think positive. Because I didn't have any other information, I knew there was nothing I could do at this point. I got to the arena and waited around to see Kevin Dunn. I hoped for a solid answer. Did he want to bring me on board, or was this going to remain a fill-in thing here and there? While in catering, I saw both Batista and Benoit. These were two of my dad's favorites, but I was disappointed in Benoit for what took place on the international trips. So I just went up to Batista and told him about my dad and what I had just found out. I asked if he might be able to say hello to him on the phone because maybe that could possibly cheer him up. My dad wasn't the type of guy to ever be nervous, but I heard it in his voice that day. Batista happily obliged. Benoit overheard the conversation and asked if it would be okay for him to give my father a call. I didn't know if Benoit would actually call, but I gave him my dad's number anyway. I was happy to see

Batista and even happier that he spoke to my dad. The call definitely put my dad in better spirits. I wasn't able to talk to Kevin Dunn as every time he walked by he put his phone to his face. I didn't want to interrupt, so I would try again the next day in Fresno at *SmackDown*. I drove off, got a hotel room in Fresno, and thought about the conversation earlier in the day with my dad as I tried to get some sleep.

When I got to the arena the next day, I saw Jim Ross, who was still the head of talent relations while he groomed John Laurinaitis for the spot. JR was very knowledgeable about the business. As the greatest overall announcer to call wrestling matches, he had seen and done it all with incredible runs in both WCW and WWE, making so many moments in wrestling history memorable. Now he was handling WWE's talent, and I wanted to pick his brain and see if he could give me any advice. JR had always been kind enough to respond when I emailed him over the years about trying to make it to WWE, and I appreciated that. He told me that everyone in the company wore multiple "hats," meaning that no one did just one single job so they could be useful to the company in more than one way. He suggested that I ask the office about taking on a different position and additionally announcing when dates were available. That sounded like a great idea. I knew that I would enjoy just about any role I could get working for them. When I finally got a second to talk to Kevin Dunn later in the day, I mentioned this idea. Kevin said there wasn't a permanent ring announcing spot and that I should call human resources and see what options were available. That was all I needed to hear.

Once again, it sounded like there was hope on the job front. Unfortunately, my dad's shadow turned out to be a tumor in his lungs. When it was tested, it came back malignant. My dad had a cancerous tumor. That was a blow. A massive blow. I love my parents more than anyone or anything. They were so great to me for 23 years. This was a horrible nightmare, and I couldn't wake up from it. Surgery was scheduled right away, and I booked a flight home to Chicago.

On March 2, 2004, after trying to find any random job I could do, I landed a spot as a contestant on a TV show called *Street Smarts*. I did my homework and realized that the game wasn't won by using common knowledge, but rather guessing which person on the street would give the correct answer and then choosing someone else. My theory was way off, and I lost. I even wore a dunce cap on the show. As soon as the taping ended, I rushed to the Burbank airport and flew home for my dad's surgery.

I was scared out of my mind. After his heart attack, my dad had quadruple bypass surgery years. Despite the surgery, he had continued to smoke and to eat whatever he wanted. More recently, however, he liked the idea of the WWE Cruiserweight Division, and he got it in his mind that he jokingly wanted to get down to 150 pounds like the cruiserweights! He had been eating healthy and going to the gym when this all happened. Even so, his arteries were once again clogged, which made us even more worried about this procedure. The whole family was there, which helped. But I was petrified for my dad's life as the doctor said it was risky to remove the tumor from his lungs in the condition that his arteries were in.

The hours went by, and finally the doctor came out to tell us that the surgery was a success. They had removed the tumor. It would just be a while before my dad was up and out. He told us that everything was fine, and he did not need any chemotherapy treatment or radiation. That seemed odd to me, but I'm not a doctor.

I spent a little time at home before flying back to LA. Shortly after I arrived, my dad called me.

"Jus!" he exclaimed. "You'll never guess who called me!"

I really had no idea.

"Chris Benoit!"

Chris Benoit had called my dad earlier that morning to see how he was feeling. I wasn't with Chris. He hadn't seen me in a while, but he was thoughtful enough to randomly think of my dad and give him a call. My dad told me that they had a long phone conversation, and I was both proud and appreciative. The same thing happened on the morning of *WrestleMania 20*, the biggest day of the year. On that night, Chris Benoit won the world championship, but that morning—again, with me not even being there—Chris called him to check in and see how he was doing. I will never forget that because I know that call helped my dad with his recovery.

I worked some WWE and *Toughman* shots, but coming back to LA each time was getting old. When I was a kid, I wanted to move to LA and act. I moved out there in October 2003. By May 2004, I was done. After just seven months in LA, I got it out of my system. I was over the name-droppers, the broken promises, and the traffic. I wanted to move back to Scottsdale. Days after I made that decision, I was back in Arizona. On my dad's birthday in May 2004, I packed up a U-Haul and moved back into my parents' house in Scottsdale.

On the drive, I had gotten a call from Nav about starting his local indie organization again. He found a venue and asked if I was interested in coming on board with him. He and I worked really well together. We both shared a love for pro wrestling, and we each had creative, but different, minds. He could come up with an idea, and I could envision it and then add to the concept. I could have an idea, and he would be able to then add to my vision and make it even better. Together, we made a great team. I agreed to help run IZW—Impact Zone Wrestling—with him. We would produce the shows at a bar called The Sets in Tempe, Arizona.

As I was pulling into the neighborhood, I got another call-this time from the birthday boy in Chicago. He sounded great and was recovering well from the surgery. He had an early birthday dinner so he could get home to watch WWE. He was just like me from a decade earlier, and I got a kick out of that. He would tell me what he saw on *RAW* and *SmackDown*. He would tell me all about the guys that he liked: Batista and Benoit. Then he would tell me about Coach and Chris Jericho, how he didn't like them at all. I'd say, "Dad. Coach is awesome. He was so good to me when I first came around and still is. Jericho is a great guy, too. It's just a character that they're playing!" My dad didn't care to hear that. He was sticking to liking the good guys and disliking the bad guys. It just goes to show they were doing a great job.

Coming back to Scottsdale felt like a huge relief. I was really comfortable in that town and was glad to be home in Arizona. Running IZW with Nav also gave me something to do. Sure, going to the ASU campus bars was fun, but I needed to do something productive. WWE work was still sporadic, so I contacted HR about the conversation that I had with Jim Ross and Kevin Dunn, about employees wearing "different hats," in order to see if there were any openings in the company. They got back to me shortly after with the offer of a media librarian position in Stamford. I didn't need to know the Dewey Decimal System, and I would get paid to go through the WWE mega library and notate all of their footage. I thought, "Wow, what a job: I'll get paid to watch old wrestling tapes." Living in Stamford, however, wasn't really something that interested me. I grew up in the cold and really wanted to live somewhere warm. My sister lived in Arizona, and my parents came out to visit just about every month. If I moved to Stamford, I'd be far away from everyone. I politely declined and hoped my decision wouldn't burn a bridge with the company. I picked up a job working the front door at a bar called San Felipe's Cantina where Nav eventually joined me as well. It was good socially and for making some extra money. Plus, we had a fun crew and a great camaraderie.

On May 25 2004, IZW had its debut show at The Sets. Nav had been working with local talent, some of whom he trained at his training school. In addition, he brought in guys from California who loved to wrestle but couldn't get booked as much as they'd like mostly because they were not physically huge. We didn't care how big or small a guy was. We had big guys like Mike Knox, Derek Neikirk, Jack Bull, and Hollywood Yates. But, we also loved having Lil Nate, LT, Gallo, Peter Goodman, Hawaiian Lion, Jack Durango, Mucha Lucha, Showtime, Storm, Amber, Erica D'Erico, and anyone else who had passion for wrestling and just wanted to work.

We had an entertaining assembly of talent and ran really fun shows every other Tuesday, drawing a pretty decent crowd. IZW was starting to catch on, and before long, we had a full house for each show. A-Train, who had wrestled in WWE as Prince Albert (and most recently, Tensai, now NXT head trainer, Matt Bloom), lived in Arizona and wrestled in Japan. When he was in town, he loved working our shows, and he was a great addition to the crew. He was not only a WWE attraction for our fans, but a great coach for the talent. Nick "Eugene" Dinsmore, who now runs a training school in South Dakota, also lived in Arizona around this time and would come around to share his knowledge with the IZW guys while he was on the WWE roster. Everyone loved IZW and wanted to see us succeed.

Nav and I had a blast producing those shows. We met at Venezia's, a local pizza place, and casually caught up, ate pizza, and had some laughs. Once we had our fill of pizza and laughs, we worked together to write our entire show on a little pizza shop napkin. We took into account what special guests we had, the pertinent elements from the previous show, and, of course, where our future storylines were headed. We wrote up the whole card in about 10 or 15 minutes. We had incredible booking chemistry and just clicked when putting the shows together. The frequent shows had an ongoing central storyline, and it was fun to watch the talent, as well as the company itself, evolve.

Looking back, I realized that I was the bad cop to Nav's good cop. Sometimes no matter how hard I tried to be nice, if I said something to someone or gave them any direction, I came off looking like a jerk. In this case, I was working for WWE and had a really good grasp on the business since I was learning from some of the best former and current wrestlers and producers. When I tried to help the guys who did not have that experience, my attempt to help could have been taken as something else. I wish I had been a bit nicer either way, but sometimes passion can take over. I would always act with the big picture for the entire show in mind, whereas some of the talent would only be able to see things from their character's perspective.

On June 22, 2004, I was in Orlando, Florida, for *SmackDown*, talking in the back with Eddie Guerrero. Eddie was always nice to me from day one, which I especially appreciated during the times of a very rough locker room. He introduced me to his wife, Vickie, and his two daughters. I couldn't say enough to them about how great their dad was on top of being the incredible talent that he was, and I truly meant it. While speaking with them, my phone rang, and I walked outside to take the call. It was my dad.

"Whattup?!"

"Not good."

I felt like a bolt of lightning had struck me, and my body prepared for the worst. "What's wrong?"

"I went back for the checkup today, and it spread. My other lung, chest, and ribs," he said.

I didn't know what to say. I don't even know what to say now trying to type this. We always wanted to keep him positive, but I just couldn't think of anything positive to say. My heart was instantly filled with sadness. We talked, and I told him he was going to be okay. He's a champion, and he's overcome all other obstacles. He was going to be fine because he was a tough man.

I got through the show and eventually to the next tour. I asked Jonathan Coachman and Chris Jericho if they would mind getting on the phone with my father to say hello. They all spoke to him, and my dad was on top of the world. He was so excited to tell me that I was right. Those "bad guys" were actually "really nice," as he put it. "See, I told you, dad!" Jericho even signed a T-shirt and gave me some of his Y2J wristbands for my dad. Well, those "bad" guys gained a new fan on that day.

On July 16 and 17, I was very excited to work two WWE shows in Tokyo, Japan. I figured that I was "hazed" plenty on the last international trip, so hopefully I was in the clear on this one. I had very long flights both to and from Japan, which gave me too much time to think about my dad and his condition. I wanted to wake up from this nightmare of my dad being sick, but I couldn't. Unfortunately, many of the same guys who contributed to making my first international trip miserable came back to do the same thing on this one. Bradshaw did a fine job of rallying everybody against me. He found anything about me that he could, even something as innocent as sitting in the wrong seat, and twisted it and used it against me with his army of bullies. If I sat at the front of the bus, I should have sat in the back. If I took a window seat, it should have been an aisle. Every move I made was the wrong move, and there was no way to win.

At one point during a long drive, Bradshaw had both buses pull over. He sent two of his henchmen on to our "babyface" bus to notify me that the "heel" bus wanted me to grab my bags and join them. One of the wrestlers, my buddy Paul London, was sitting near me. He was close to my age, a talented performer, and a really good guy. I'll never forget the fear that was going through me as I grabbed my bag and walked off. I looked over at Paul, and his reaction terrified me. It was as if his expression alone said, "This is not good at all. Good luck." In the middle of nowhere, somewhere in Japan, our two talent buses sat on the side of the road for the only purpose of having me switch buses. On the heel bus, it was everybody versus me. They all took turns yelling at me for whatever excuse they could find. The heels were really heels; even the referee Nick Patrick took advantage of the opportunity to chime in and tell me what a horrible person I was. They asked me if I talk to the dirt sheets, the wrestling newsletters and websites that put out behind-the-scenes information. I would never give anything away from behind the scenes to those sites, but in my days as an indie announcer, I would advertise our dates and news. There's a difference between working with them in the indies and leaking information from WWE. I never did the latter. I was even honest with the bus and admitted that I used the newsletters and websites to help promote our indie shows, but that was it, no contact with them once I was in WWE. They got to the point where they were just making excuses to hate me, as they drank beer after beer.

You never know what someone is going through on a given day. My dad was heavily on my mind, making me scared and depressed for the first time in my life. I had been bullied as a kid, but this was beyond that. This was pure evil, and it was even harder to handle on top of everything else I was dealing with. This was my dream job? At this point, it was more of a disappointment than a dream. I would get heat for anything I did. I got heat from the bosses one night for saying, "On behalf of everyone here at WWE, I want to thank each of you for coming out tonight," in my goodnight/thank-you announcement. Once I reworded to "we want to thank," it was acceptable. There were a lot of good guys in the crew, but the other guys made this a miserable experience. After I was verbally abused and they had their fun, we arrived at the hotel. I thought I was in the clear, but I was wrong. They sent guys to call and even come to my room—all night long. I kept hearing keys in my door—they had gotten keys to my room—but luckily there was another lock in the room that kept the key from working. Mike "Nova" Bucci later said Chris Benoit and JBL were hunting the hotel for me and trying to find my hotel room. He said they did this so violently that he was praying I wouldn't open the door. I remember sitting at my computer, messaging with Colt Cabana, who was probably on the road working indies and wanting to be at WWE. It was hard not to mention to him how awful it really was to work there and tell him that I would never wish working there on anyone.

After three days of hell for these two shows, I had another long journey back to the US. I sat next to Luther Reigns who went by the name Horshu when I worked with him quite a bit in the indies. There are a lot of gimmicks in wrestling, but Shu was a real-life gimmick. He had died and come back to life numerous times. He had a drug addiction at one point that would have killed anyone else, and he had his throat slashed open and survived. He lived in a house on top of a mountain and had a bunch of cars along with a porn star girlfriend. Everything he did was big; he was big, and his heart was and still is big. That was the last trip the company would fly us in business class (which made the long flights somewhat tolerable). Sitting next to a friend in a comfortable seat made the trip home a bit easier, especially knowing I wasn't going to get messed with. I don't think anyone, no matter how tough they thought they were, would mess with Shu. We landed in LA that day, and I immediately called my parents to let them know that I was back in the country. At the time, my phone didn't work outside of the US. My dad told me that he started losing his hair. That hit me hard. My dad had perfect black, wavy hair. I felt horrible because I knew that was rough on him. He told me that he was going to start wearing hats, so I immediately called Sue and asked if there was a WWE hat I could get for him. She responded quickly, and within the same week, thanks to Sue, he was alternating between his new *RAW* and *SmackDown* ball caps.

On August 5, I flew home to spend some time with my dad. My mom was leaving town and asked if I could fly in to accompany him to his chemotherapy appointment. Looking back now, I feel like an ass for not going back earlier. There was no good reason for staying in Arizona; I easily could have spent more time in Chicago because I wasn't working full time. My dad was always there for me. Everything he did was for his family. He got sick and needed me, and I was hanging out in Arizona for no reason. That still really bothers me.

When I walked into the house, I noticed his hair had become thin and grey. I could tell that he was waiting for my reaction to his appearance. It was different from how it used to be, but I downplayed it and just told him he looked great, which he really did. We had a really special week together. I went to work with him for a few of the days. He was a very respected and well-liked man. Going to work with my father was like being out with a king: Everybody loved him, everybody respected him, and everybody was intimidated by him. I think of a line from one of our favorite movies, *A Bronx Tale*, "Is it better to be feared or better to be loved?" My dad was both.

One morning, about 3:30 am, before we went to work, I came downstairs, and he told me that he had just seen a mouse. I had lived in that house for a good 15 years and had never seen a mouse, so that was a very weird thing to hear. But then I saw it! We spent the next 20 minutes chasing this mouse around. It was a very different bonding experience with my dad, mostly because it was so ridiculous. The whole thing was funny: the two of us grown men running all around the house, chasing this tiny little mouse. I threw plastic bowls at the creature at one point. (Because what else are you supposed to do during a mouse attack, right?) We chased the little guy into a closet in the family room and then trapped it in there by placing towels under the closet doors. After work, we stopped at the store and picked up a mousetrap, which we placed in between two of the towels. Sure enough, the mouse came out and ended up in the trap. This was teamwork at its finest with the best tag-team partner a son could ever ask for.

My dad was fighting like a champion, doing everything the doctors wanted him to do and bravely battling all of those chemo sessions. I wanted to keep him entertained and as happy as possible on those horrible treatment days. I brought my computer with various comedy and wrestling videos and even introduced him to *Chapelle's Show*. He got through his chemo session as he had all the others and never complained. He didn't have much of an appetite, but we still went to one of our favorite regular spots for dinner. Part of me wanted to talk about life, and part of me just wanted to be positive and not talk about anything that was going on. I was sad and could only imagine how he felt. I didn't want to make anything worse.

After a short but meaningful trip with my dad, I headed back to Arizona. I spent the next few weeks working IZW, WWE, and even World Extreme Cagefighting in Lemoore, California. My parents came out to Arizona at the end of the month, and we got to spend a lot of time together. A week later, I drove them to the airport. I pulled up to the American Airlines terminal and got out of the car to say goodbye as I had many times in the past when my parents left Arizona to head home to Chicago. This curbside goodbye was a bit different. I hugged my mom and told her I loved her as I did every other time. I did the same for my dad, just like every other time. He hugged me hard and cried. Until now, I can remember only two times I had seen my dad cry. He cried when his mom passed away. I was four years old at the time. He cried when his dad passed away four years later when I was eight.

We all had an idea of what could happen, we just didn't want to believe it. The whole time my dad was sick, we just tried to keep him positive by telling him he was going to beat this and having wrestlers call him to lift his spirits. We didn't want to even think about him losing the battle.

I headed out shortly after for a *RAW* tour through Texas and rode with Mike Chioda and Randy Orton. My dad took a liking to Randy's "Legend Killer" character, so at one point when my dad called during the drive, I gave Randy the phone. My dad was ecstatic. It was that easy to lift his spirits, and I appreciated my superhero coworkers using their superpowers to help my dad.

When I got back to Arizona from that loop, I continued working on a project that I started during the past month. On top of running two monthly shows, IZW also ran a pro-wrestling training school where people with dreams of becoming a wrestler could learn the craft. Wrestling was pretty popular, and I had an idea: We could give away one year of free training at the IZW school. We hoped to get publicity for IZW by having anyone in the state who wanted to become a wrestler send in a videotape of them cutting a promo. The best promo would win free training.

The local *Fox* station bit on my press release and wanted to send a crew to cover our next show. That was perfect because that show was headlined by *MTV*'s Mike "the Miz" Mizanin. In September 2004, Mike came to town from California. We roamed around the ASU campus where everyone recognized him. He helped us promote the event for that night, and we stopped to get some lunch. I was very preoccupied with the show and excited that it was going to get exposure live on *Fox News*.

My phone rang. It was my dad.

"Whatttup?"

"Hey Jus, not feeling too well. I left work early today. I was having trouble breathing, and my friend took me back home. They're going to be putting oxygen on me and around the house."

I told him to take it easy and not push himself.

He asked how I was doing, and I told him how excited I was for that night's show and about all the promotion we had done. He then told me about a newspaper article he had found related to wrestling, and he was definitely short of breath. It seemed like he was struggling just to talk. I again told him to take it easy and just rest. As always, we ended our conversation exchanging I love yous. He didn't sound good at all, and I hoped it was just from a long day at work and that he would be better once he got some of that oxygen. It was hard to picture my dad surrounded by oxygen tanks, as that's something that wouldn't sit well with him. I hoped by the morning he would feel better.

Everything went well that night. We had at capacity crowd, and Miz was very gracious about doing anything and everything to help promote the company. I was interviewed for the broadcast, and Miz handled the rest of the TV time. It was great for us to have him on camera since he was so well known from *MTV*. It was a perfect night for IZW. We went out to eat after the show, and then I returned home. My nightly ritual when going to sleep was to completely shut off my phones and turn on an air purifier, which blocked out all outside noises. There was also a gate that I kept locked, preventing anyone from getting to the doorbell. I didn't like to be woken up and took all the proper measures to prevent it.

The next morning, my do-not-disturb mode and habit of sleeping in proved to be a problem. My brother-in-law had been trying to reach me all morning but, of course, was unable to. I woke up to the sound of him banging on the metal gate. I jumped out of bed and opened the outside gate to let him in. He told me my dad wasn't doing well, and my sister and I should fly to Chicago right away. He booked us both tickets for the next flight out. I didn't know what to do. Subconsciously, the song "Papa Was a Rolling Stone" was playing in my head. More specifically, the line: "The day I'll always remember 'cause that was the day..."

I looked at the empty suitcase and started throwing in clothes for the trip. In my head, I was wondering if I needed to bring a suit. I wanted to ask my brother-in-law, but I couldn't, so I just asked him what I should take. His response was whatever I thought I'd need. I didn't want to think about the fact that I may need a suit. I didn't want to believe it, so... I didn't pack one. I threw a bunch of clothes in a suitcase, got dressed, and went out to the car where my sister was already waiting. We drove to the Phoenix airport and got to our gate. My bag was a bit larger than a typical carry on. The gate agent stopped me and told me that I needed to check the bag. I looked her in the eye and as tears filled mine explained that I didn't have time to wait for a bag in Chicago and needed to get to the hospital where my dad was as soon as I landed. Without any further hesitation, she let me on with my bag. My sister and I sat in middle seats across from each other. The worst thoughts crossed my mind as I sat there for three hours. I lowered my hat in front of my face and escaped into my own world. I still wasn't sure what was going on. Part of me wondered if something happened and my brother-in-law didn't want to tell me, but I also remember him calling after he dropped us off, saying it wasn't good and that this was very serious. Tears rolled down my face thinking about what might very well happen when I get to Chicago. I didn't want to face that. I wanted to get there and cheer my dad up, so that was what I'd do.

Our good friend Niki picked us up from the airport, and we headed straight to the hospital. We took our bags, went to the main desk, and asked for my father's room. He was in intensive care, so we got the room number and headed straight there. I was wheeling my bag down the hallway, watching the numbers get closer and closer. I was eager to see my dad's face light up when he saw us, and I knew he would instantly feel better.

As I approached the room, I saw my aunt in the room and then got closer and saw my mom. And then I saw my dad on his bed. But there were no machines. No tubes. My dad was lying on the bed with his mouth open and his eyes closed. He was gone. My hero, my idol, the best dad any kid could ask for, was gone.

We all hugged each other, and then I hugged him. My sister's wedding was the greatest day of my life. This day was the worst.

My world had just changed forever.

We drove home. Various close friends and family members came over. We discussed funeral plans and let everyone know what happened. A part of me had died when I lost my dad. I wasn't sure I could ever be the same. He lived a very full 60 years, but that wasn't enough. I was lucky to have my dad for 24 years, but that wasn't enough either. We were finally at a stage where we were buddies and more than just father and son. My brother-in-law flew in later that night, and we could all be together at a time when we really needed each other's company more than ever before.

The next day, I went out with my sister and her husband to get our clothes set for the funeral. My phone rang, and it was Sue. Sue is one of the kindest, most thoughtful people I had ever been honored to have as a friend. She had asked how I was doing and told me this probably wasn't the best time, but there had been some talk at the office. They wanted to put me in Howard's spot on the road full time. I was to work *RAW* live events Friday through Sunday, and then announce the *Sunday Night Heat* taping before *RAW* went live on Mondays. She gave me a start date a couple of weeks away, but told me to think about it and if the date was too early to start whenever I was ready.

I hung up the phone, and my eyes filled with tears once again. Anytime I got a call from WWE, I immediately called my parents on speaker to give them the update. That's how it works. Or, that's how it used to work. I realized I couldn't call my dad to tell him the big news. That hit me hard. I told my sister and then called my mom. They were thrilled for me, which I appreciated, but it still felt weird not being able to tell my dad. After these years of wondering about making WWE a real career, and now one day after I lose my Dad, it happens. I thought to myself, "His first day up there, and he's already pulling strings." I smiled, looked up, and said, "Thanks, dad." There were a lot of things going on that week that really made me think he was around and looking out for me. It helped the situation a small bit.

My father owned his business. He was third generation, meaning he inherited it from his father who had inherited it from his father. The business could be mine now. I could take charge and be the fourth generation to keep it going. Or I could accept the new WWE deal, the job I always dreamed of. The family scrap business was a great one, lucrative and secure. My dad had worked hard to make it successful after three generations, but I just knew that it wasn't where my heart was. He had never, ever put any pressure on me to get into his business. He encouraged me to follow my dream, so I had to decide if I should keep his dream, the family business, going or follow mine. Because there was never any pressure from my family either way, the decision was easy to make.

I had a very uncomfortable feeling about the funeral. It was a mix of sadness and disbelief. I remember it very well, but when I play it back in my head, I don't see it clearly like most other memories. There's a hazy filter. When my dad's friends or business associates passed away, he would always send the largest floral arrangement. He would joke that it shows you cared the most. In our case, though, we had asked that instead of flowers our friends donate to the American Lung Cancer Society.

My dad had really taken a liking to WWE and had a collection of memorabilia, some of which I left with him. His favorite song (and personal credo) was Frank Sinatra's "My Way," which we played throughout the pre-service.

A line of people walked up to greet my family. I saw close friends, relatives, neighbors, former neighbors, acquaintances, teachers, local business owners, and other familiar faces from the past 24 years of my life. This was a gathering of everyone that I had ever known who had come to pay their respects to my dad. The line did not stop. The entire room was jam-packed. A second room was opened so that everyone could hear the service over the speaker system. The turnout at my father's funeral was incredible, and he had to be smiling. It was two fully "sold out" rooms, standing room only, and eventually the line had to be stopped.

I wrote a eulogy with my sister. The opening was "When I hear the song 'Cat's in the Cradle,' a song about a father's relationship with his son, it reminds me of how much it…does not remind me of my relationship with my father." My dad always made time for our family. We spoke about how wonderful a dad he was to us, how wonderful of a man he was, and how great of a friend he was.

The procession from the service to the cemetery went on for miles. As a Vietnam veteran, my dad was honored by the military and by the hundreds of people who had shown up to pay their final respects to this incredible man who I was lucky enough to call my dad.

When I headed back to Arizona, I would start a new life. I was now the head of the family, looking out for my mom and sister. Beyond that, I also had a real career now—a full-time job, five days a week, and even a salary. This was it. It was exactly what I wanted. The only thing missing was my dad to call bright and early in the morning when I was heading to the airports and every day in general.

CHAPTER 11
YOU GOT IT, DUDE

I worked an IZW show on October 12, and it wasn't easy. I couldn't stop thinking about my dad all day, every day. On the 21st, I flew to Lemoore, California, for World Extreme Cagefighting. I worked their event and then flew to Green Bay, Wisconsin, for WWE the next day. As I grabbed my rental car, I got a call from Jenn at WWE who was calling to give me the details of the new contract. I was still numb from everything going on and just glad to have a full-time deal. I accepted whatever they offered. I'm pretty sure there was room for negotiations, but what did I know and what did I care? I just wanted the job. I think they even bumped it up $5,000 on their own.

Walking into the arena for the first time as the full-time *RAW* live events announcer was surreal. I had worked a lot on *SmackDown* as a sub, but I had only worked with the separate *RAW* crew a handful of times. I felt a lot more comfortable with *RAW*. On *SmackDown*, it felt like everyone was out to get me. *RAW* was a lot more relaxed and filled with guys who weren't interested in bullying. I stepped into the production office and checked in with the bosses for the evening. Orton approached me and expressed his condolences. I thanked him as my eyes watered up. The subject wasn't something I could talk about. I continued down the hallway where I ran into Jericho. He said hello and asked how my dad was doing right away. I had to get my response out without breaking down. The show wasn't easy. The weekend wasn't easy. The next week wasn't easy. The next month wasn't easy. All I could think about was my dad. I drove the loops by myself and spaced out on the open highways. Lots of thoughts, lots of memories, and lots of tears.

As time went on, things became a bit easier. Time was really the only thing that could help, and it did. That first year was the worst. I still think about my dad every day, but time made things a bit easier. I still feel like he is always with me, and that also helps. I also wish that I could pick up the phone and call him or see him, but since I can't, knowing he is with me helps. I noticed as time went on that so many things I do now I never would have done in the past. Little things like the way I carry myself are more like him as are my mannerisms, sense of humor, and personality. In a way, I've unknowingly become a lot like my dad.

I wondered how I was going to hold up working full time, knowing that my throat was breaking down a lot. It would become sore very often. Talking, swallowing, announcing—everything hurt. Once it cleared up, it would instantly break down again. When that happened, I got sick. Whether it was a cold or anything else, it would turn into bronchitis and immediately clog up my throat, making it sore, and I would be out of commission for weeks. Something wasn't right, and I needed to find out what was going on before it kept me from living my dream now that the opportunity was here. I went back to the ear, nose, and throat doctor in town, who suggested a tonsillectomy. If you get your tonsils out as a kid, it's an easy procedure. If you wait until you're an adult...not so much. The doctor assumed that the recurring sore throat and all the associated problems might go away if I got rid of my tonsils, so I moved forward with the procedure.

Luckily, my mom stayed with me because that recovery wasn't fun. It felt like I was going to choke on my own uvula, which was swollen and touching the back of my tongue. I could even feel it touching my tongue at times. I couldn't talk for two weeks. I lived solely on slushies and ice cream. I was worried I might never talk again as that surgery put me in pretty bad shape. Maybe I could just act out the introductions if that happened.

The good part was quality bonding time with my mom. I've always been my mom's baby, and I always will be. I'm sure she would rather spend time together under better conditions, but I know she enjoyed these days together as much as I did. We played a lot of cards in that time and got to hang out, which we hadn't been able to do in a while. The loss of my dad was hard on all of us and having each other's company helped. My mom is very sweet and caring, and I am lucky to be her son.

Eventually I started feeling a bit better and got back on my feet. I also went out for my first dinner and was so excited to eat real food. I was disappointed when I finally got that food, and it was bland. How do you mess up pasta?! My next meal was bland, too. I was a bit suspicious. I called the doctor, and he informed me that one of the side effects of the tonsillectomy is losing your sense of taste. This was really, really strange, and I just hoped it would come back soon. Some foods still had taste, but most were bland. Within a month, however, my sense of taste was back to normal. Lilian, who was still just announcing on Monday nights, needed time off, and I had to come back sooner than expected which scared the hell out of me. I hadn't talked for about two weeks and now had to go from barely talking at all to announcing full shows. There was no easing into it. I dove in headfirst. Luckily, in the long run, I feel that the surgery definitely helped me. I stopped getting sick, and I stopped getting sore throats.

So it was back to the ring and back to belting out announcements over blaring music, which seemed to go ok. I mentioned that I was always a fan of wrestling theme music. I knew after half a second when music hit exactly who would be coming out. I could name every entrance song in WCW and WWE history. When I went to shows at the Horizon, the WWF production crew had a briefcase of cassette tapes that had everybody's music on it. That inspired me to do the same. I taped the music from video games and from TV. I bought national anthem CDs... anything I could do to get wrestler's theme music. I played the theme music when I played with my wrestling figures as they walked to the ring. As I grew older and the Internet made obtaining cleaner versions of songs easier, I was able to procure better versions of all those wrestling themes. I distinctly remember typing in the keyword "WWF" in America Online and finding downloadable songs right there.

Eventually my entire theme collection made its way to my computer where I was able to safely keep and manage my music. I was at a *RAW* live event the same time Stephanie McMahon was there to observe. As the show began, the 360 Player, the name of the fancy music machine they used instead of cassette players, broke down during one of the entrances. Theme music really sets a tone for each aspect of a live wrestling show, and with the 360 going down, I worried about the quality of the show. Obviously, the matches would still be great, but the atmosphere created by the music is so important to the fans' experience.

Derek from merchandise happened to come to the ring, and I told him that I had my laptop with me, and it had most of the songs on it. He ran back and asked

This is the kid that my neighbors were stuck with.

My dad was a very special man, who made me a very lucky son.

My family

My sister and me, standing backstage at the Rosemont Horizon with the Big Boss Man.

The Big Boss Man, making his way to the ring along with his security, my cousin Duke

Standing at MGM Studios in 1994 and watching Hulk Hogan sign his WCW contract and talk to "Mean" Gene Okerlund as WCW President Eric Bischoff watches on.

With Shawn Michaels in 1992. In 12 years, I would get to stand in the ring and announce him.

"Hacksaw" Jim Duggan said, "Thumbs up, Buddy," and that's what I did, having no idea we would become real buddies and work together numerous times down the road.

In 1994, standing with "Mean" Gene Okerlund at MGM Studios while we waited for the arrival of Hulk Hogan.

Sitting with Adam next to Chicago TV personality Rich Koz at one of my first WWF shows. Plus, my Hulk Hogan camera allowed the Hulkster to appear in every shot it took!

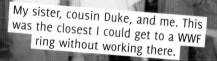

My sister, cousin Duke, and me. This was the closest I could get to a WWF ring without working there.

Craig and I meet Razor Ramon.

Standing in my Ultimate Warrior jacket, handing Virgil a $ necklace to go with his newly won Million Dollar Championship.

My bedroom arena, where I spent most of my time playing with WWF Hasbro action figures.

My briefcase of pro-wrestling theme music cassette tapes.

Mr. Perfect

JAKE The Snake Roberts

MACHO

After he was nice to my sister and me at the Grand Milwaukee, we became big fans of the "Texas Tornado" Kerry Von Erich as we met again backstage at a WWF show! I had my camera this time to get a picture.

Craig, his brother Marc, and his idol, Bret "Hitman" Hart in Dayton, OH, after Hart returned to WWE.

Because he was proud to swim in this T-shirt, Craig would one day meet his idol.

Ross and I made friends wherever we went, especially after taking over Dunkin' Donuts.

By the back exit of the Rosemont Horizon with Bret "Hitman" Hart in 1992.

Excused from my high school senior year lock-in, I drove to Peoria, IL, to see a WCW Thunder taping, met Bill Goldberg, and got back to Chicago and the lock-in event.

Before I could stand on the real WWE entrance ramp, I would stand here with Danny and pretend that I was doing exactly that.

King Kong Bundy cutting a promo for my high school morning announcements.

The Ultimate Warrior racing past me as he to the ring to face Undertaker at my se live WWF show.

Wearing my giant Undertaker T-shirt by the back exit of the Rosemont Horizon and getting a picture taken with his manager, Paul Bearer.

Ring Announcing Toughman was different from wrestling, but it gave me experience that I needed to grow in wrestling.

Enzo Reed, ring announcer for Pro Wrestling International.

At age 20 and in New York City with Larry and Steve, the Twin Turbos, who were always looking out for me on the road.

Working for Dale Gagne gave me lots of unique experiences and made for some unpredictable and unforgettable moments.

While Dale's promises didn't always come through, he delivered on the biggest wrestling star showing up to our event at Bally's in Brooklyn. My first time standing in the ring with the Rock in 2000.

At the AWA autograph table with Jonnie Stewart, Larry Turbo, Steve the Ref, and Lee.

After our AWA show in Fargo, ND. It was the first time I would dine with the wrestlers I grew up watching: Sensational Sherri, Lee, Julie, Steve Turbo, Steve the Ref, Bushwhackers Luke and Butch, George "the Animal" Steele, Dale Gagne, and Jimmy Van.

After Mr. Perfect grabbed my arm during his match, I had the perfect bruise!

FOX News came out to The Sets in Tempe, AZ, to cover IZW.

I learned to referee just so I could stand in the ring with one of my all-time favorites, "Mr. Perfect" Curt Hennig, as he teamed with Road Warrior Animal against Public Enemy, Rocco Rock, and Johnny Grunge.

On the book tour with Gary Cappetta and guest, "Road Dogg" Jesse James.

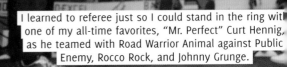

The old crew: Mike Knox, Nav, and Lee.

Watching in amazement as the Iron Sheik showed up, not booked, and took over the Gary Cappetta book tour!

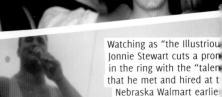

Watching as "the Illustrious" Jonnie Stewart cuts a promo in the ring with the "talent" that he met and hired at the Nebraska Walmart earlier in the day.

I idolized Dana Carvey on SNL and tried to be the Church Lady, but there was only one!

Betty White and I in LA, wearing our matching T-shirts.

Pee-Wee Herman, holding the Polaroid of me at 10, wearing my Pee-Wee Herman footie pajamas.

Reunited with Jerry Springer as he came to WWE to host RAW.

Right before introducing the band Tool—Adam Jones, Justin Chancellor, and Danny Carey— before their soldout concert.

In Chicago with Bea Arthur!

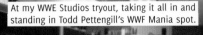
At my WWE Studios tryout, taking it all in and standing in Todd Pettengill's WWF Mania spot.

I was lucky to have my grandma come to all of my performances, including WWE.

Standing in a WWE ring for the first time and introducing John Cena at my WWE RAW tryout.
(Photo Credit: Wrelano@aol.com)

Word Life with John Cena in our early WWE days

Jonathan Coachman earned his nickname. The Coach really helped me out when I came into WWE.

Getting direction at my WWE RAW tryout, before I stepped into the WWE ring for the first time.
(Photo Credit: Wrelano@aol.com)

Real World/Road Rules star Mike Mizanin wanted to be a wrestler, so he came back to hone his craft at IZW in September 200.

My mom recorded every show I announced on TV and came to the live shows whenever we were in the area.

In Tucson, AZ, with fellow ring announcer, Tony Chimel.

about using it, which the production guys were okay with. During the match, I ran backstage to get my computer. I turned it on and headed to the production table. Triple H asked what I was doing. He asked if I had his, and I said, yes, every version. "Good, that's all that matters," he joked. I ran it out to the table, and just as I did, the 360 Player began working again. The production crew thought it was great that I had the music on my computer as a backup, however. That night they asked their one-man music department, composer Jim Johnston, to email me the few songs that I was missing. He even sent me the authentic versions of some of the others I had. Jim Johnston was my WWF theme idol, and he and I were corresponding! It was a proud night for me.

At age 24, I was on the road full time as the ring announcer for *WWE RAW* live events and *Sunday Night Heat*. I also filled in on *RAW* TV and *SmackDown* TV whenever those announcers needed time off. The *RAW* crew was, for the most part, established talent: well-respected veterans like Kane, Goldust, and many others who showed up, did their job well, and moved on to the next town. The *SmackDown* roster was a mix of established talent and newer guys, which meant that there was a lot more self-policing and unneeded dictatorships among the guys. Established guys abused their positions to bully respect out of the new guys and used fear to have full support from everyone on the tour. I was very comfortable working the *RAW* tours. I was scared for my life to work *SmackDown* tours, however, because the nature of that particular locker room was brutal on new guys, especially a puny ring announcer who didn't have many allies.

I was asked to cover an upcoming *SmackDown* overseas tour for Tony Chimel. For the first time ever, I declined. The office was well aware of what happened previously, but they insisted that I went, so I had no choice. The domestic dates on the tour were fine. Fast forward to the overseas portion of the tour. It was like a zombie movie in which people instantly changed. This particular tour, the "Summer Bash" as it was billed, was a nightmare for me. On top of it, this was my first Father's Day not having my father. That made it harder to keep my mind off the hazing. At one point on Father's Day, legendary wrestler Ricky Steamboat, a producer who meant well, offered to let me use his phone to call my father. I politely declined. I appreciated the thought, and I privately wished that the call would have been a possibility. After dates in Glasgow and Aberdeen, Scotland, Dublin, Ireland, and Manchester, England, I was ready to get back to the United

States and to the *RAW* crew where I wasn't picked on. The tour was miserable, and I was miserable. The only highlight of this trip was having "Stone Cold" Steve Austin with us. He had always been cool to me from when I was a fan, and he still was, even though it seemed like everybody else still hated me, and if they didn't, they still had to distance themselves from me so the others wouldn't give them a hard time as well.

I started out the tour by sitting on the front of the bus. That turned into JBL telling everybody loudly and publicly that I have no respect and made the guys who had been there for a long time, the veterans, have to walk all the way to the back to find a seat because I sat in the front. Then I moved to the back, and again I was taking up a seat in the back of the bus when other guys had to sit two to a row. At each hotel on the tour we would have to load our bags on and off the bus, and JBL would throw my bags down the street. Whatever I did was declared wrong. When I was sick, I got on the bus and went all the way to the back to be out of the way and slept from the hotel to the airport. It was early in the morning. When I arrived at the airport, everything was fine. We checked in for our commercial flight, and I sat away from everyone and kept my mouth shut. JBL was walking around to everyone and eventually grabbed Benoit, and, drunk and angry, they approached me. He told me because I was sleeping, I took up a seat on the bus, and Benoit didn't have a seat. They were pissed and screamed at me in the middle of the airport. JBL would twist anything I said, and the majority of the other guys would stir the pot. There were a handful of the good guys who didn't take part, but they couldn't try to stop it either. Fit Finlay was the other agent on the tour and would privately tell me not to give up. Nova, who also got bullied, later said that everything started on day 1 when they told me I would be throwing T-shirts in the crowd from the ring, and I joked that I never learned to throw as a kid, so I probably wouldn't be any good. I never refused to do it. I just made fun of myself for not being good. JBL ran with that story to the roster and made it seem that I didn't want to throw T-shirts because I didn't know how to throw. Everything I said would be taken, twisted, and used against me.

The tour was finally over. We were scheduled to fly from Manchester back to the US where I would announce *RAW* in Phoenix for Lilian and then *SmackDown* in Tucson. I got to the airport and looked for my passport in the bag pocket where I always kept it. It was gone. My stomach dropped. While the rest of the group flew to Phoenix, I was stuck in Manchester, England, with no passport. I found out later that this was a rib. Stealing a passport out of someone's bag is a pretty evil rib, and not giving it back means it's no longer a rib.

I was trained to never miss a show. I had to find a way to get to *RAW* at all costs. I flew with one of our production girls, Hannah, on a domestic flight to London and took a cab to the US Embassy. I waited there until I was approved for a new passport. Then I took a train by myself to Heathrow airport. I don't even know the train systems in the US! From there, I got on a flight to Boston, stayed overnight, and booked a flight from Boston to Phoenix the next morning. I didn't make it in time for *RAW* and headed straight to Tucson for *SmackDown* when I landed. That was an awful experience, all because one of the guys who just didn't like me thought it would be funny to steal my passport. After the production meeting that morning, Vince McMahon walked past me, stopped, and whispered, "Don't forget your passport," as he walked away with a giant grin on his face.

In any other company, the company officials would be upset over what happened and find a way to fix it, discipline the guilty parties, or at the very least, investigate. In WWE, however, the powers that be love that stuff. The people in power seemed to have no sympathy and to even enjoy seeing people in bad or embarrassing situations. For example, if someone was ever unlucky enough to be part of an embarrassing photo or video, it would eventually get into the wrong hands and air during rehearsals on the large screen in the arena for everyone in the crew to see. That business card Lana suggested with my face on it? That was up there for JBL's amusement. Everybody looked up and laughed at the screen as Vince joined in.

One Monday afternoon, Vince called for a mandatory meeting for everyone involved with WWE. Wrestlers, producers, cameramen, seamstresses, caterers— everyone. We assumed he was pissed, and we were all in trouble. Nope. Someone had made an entrance video on YouTube from the WWE video game with Kane and Undertaker to *Nitro* and Melina's entrance. Vince got a kick out of that and played it for everyone who was part of the show to see. Kane and Taker included. I realized then Vince loves a good rib and loves to embarrass people or make them feel uncomfortable in any way possible. So many of the characters you thought were awful were simply there to entertain the chairman.

BEST SEAT IN THE HOUSE

In late March 2005, I received a phone call. It was Sue.

"How would you like to announce *WrestleMania*?"

My jaw dropped. Sue told me they wanted me to announce the show. *WrestleMania* is the absolute biggest show in the entire industry. It was in Los Angeles that year and only weeks away. I could not believe it, and I was on top of the world once again! I didn't want to jinx anything, so I called my Mom on speaker and only told her and my sister. By the Friday before the show, after the office had closed in Connecticut, I figured it was a sure thing. After all, if the plan had changed, I definitely would know by now. I began to tell all of my close friends. I went out and bought a new tuxedo, shirt, and tie. It was expensive, but Horshu had told me that back then the *WrestleMania* paychecks were really big. I assumed I would get paid well for working the show, so it would work out in the end. I went to a popular Scottsdale bar called Barcelona where I was friends with a lot of the staff. I was so proud to tell my friend who worked there, Loy, that I was officially the ring announcer for *WrestleMania*. I really felt like I had made it. I would be part of history, another huge career highlight.

Until the morning of *WrestleMania 21* came.

They flew me out to LA, put me up in a hotel, and told me when to arrive that next morning. I was in the room where a pre-show meeting was to take place. I looked everywhere, but I didn't see my name next to any of the matches. Kevin Dunn came into the room and called me outside. "There was a change of plans. Howard is going to do the show. You'll announce next year."

I walked out of the room heartbroken. I repacked my brand-new tuxedo into my suitcase. As I said before, higher-ups in the company seemed to enjoy making people miserable purely for the sake of doing so. At times, it even seemed that amusing themselves was more important than doing what was best for business and making money. Was this one of those times? Was this a rib? I couldn't help but wonder. I honestly don't know if the decision to go with Howard was simply to toy with me, or if they legitimately changed their minds at the last minute. Maybe the decision was made days before that, but lack of communication in the company, which was common, kept anyone from telling me until that morning.

Howard Finkel did announce the show, just as he had for years and years before. I always loved hearing him. He had a very distinct way of dramatizing the wrestlers' names. (In years to come, when I made big introductions, my immediate superiors would mockingly refer to me as "Howard," meaning my intro was too long, too big, or both.) Even though I loved Howard's work, the point still stood: I was not announcing *WrestleMania* after I had been offered the opportunity. The only silver lining was that next year, *Mania* was in Chicago, and Kevin promised me I would be booked. That could be amazing.

By March 2006 I hadn't heard anything about Chicago. I was on the road every weekend for every single TV and live event, covering mine as well as Tony's and Lilian's when needed. I never missed a show. That year, I was in Japan for a *SmackDown* tour, anxiously waiting for an upcoming break in the schedule. My mom had planned to come out as I was going to have a few days off, but then I got an email that Lilian wasn't able to cover the Manilla tour during that period, so I would be going rather than getting the break. I accepted and said thank you. At some point leading up to Mania, I discovered that all talent was booked to be in Chicago except for me. I asked Sue what was going on, and she told me they didn't have anything for me to do there. I told her what Kevin had said the previous year, but she just said there was nothing for me, and that it wasn't in the budget.

It happened again. I worked hard every day, every week, and this was how I was repaid. Not only was I not working the biggest show of the year (after I was promised I had the spot), but I also wasn't even going to be there. Oh well, at least I had a weekend off!

I thought, well, if money really was part of the issue as Sue had claimed, then I had a solution. At the time, WWE booked all my hotels. A lot of the time, the rooms were pretty expensive. So I started negotiating and saving them money left and right. I would keep an ongoing list of how much they had reserved something for and the price they ended up paying once my negotiating skills came into play. I would send Sue updates not to be a jerk, but to say hey, I'm saving the company this much money, hopefully that will allow for me to be at *WrestleMania* next year. After a few months, I was asked to stop, and I did.

I may not have been able to go to *WrestleMania*, but around the same time, I was able to take the coolest field trip of my life. WWE Films released a movie called *See No Evil*, starring WWE superstar Kane. On May 8, we were all in Anaheim, California, for *RAW* and bused to a movie theater for the premiere. I never imagined sitting in a movie theater filled with WWE wrestlers, let alone vendors walking around with full-sized movie candy, popcorn, and drinks. We were spread out over multiple screens, and even some fans were able to join. I'll never forget the entire theater cheering for the bad guy, Kane, to chokeslam the poor babyfaces at the end of the movie. The overall experience was one that could never be repeated.

On June 5, 2006, I announced my matches for *Sunday Night Heat* in Pittsburgh, Pennsylvania, at the Mellon Arena. I went backstage and changed out of my suit so I could sit in the arena by the TV camera section and watch *RAW*. No one really knew who I was, so it was easy to sit out there and watch the show. I looked up from my phone just in time to see Charlie Haas enter the ring. Just like every other night, he got in the ring, ran the ropes...uh oh. What happened next wasn't just like every other night. Lilian had finished her intros and was standing on the canvas just outside of the ropes. Charlie didn't see her as he was bouncing off the ropes, which was part of his routine, and he ran right into her at full speed. She fell off the side of the ring and folded like an accordion.

I saw her go down from where I was sitting, but I didn't see her get back up. Hoping she was okay, I quickly walked backstage and made myself available in the event anyone was looking for me. Sure enough, agent Pat Patterson said I was needed in Gorilla (position). Pat has one of the most brilliant minds in wrestling. He and Vince used to book the shows that had captured my interest as a kid.

When I got there, I saw Gerry Brisco sitting in his seat where he would time out each segment. Gerry was always good to me and gave me great advice. I had instantly taken a liking to him and had a lot of respect for him. He told me that I had three minutes of a commercial break left to get into my suit and into the ring.

I ran backstage where Vince McMahon's son, Shane, was filming a pre-tape segment in the locker room. Oh no. Vince's son is filming in there, and I need to get in there and get my suit! I didn't want to interrupt, but I had less than three minutes. In that company, many of my coworkers and I always worried about "heat." It was easy to upset any one of the many officials by doing anything that could be perceived as wrong. In this case, it would be wrong to interrupt, despite interrupting for the right reasons, so you would fear getting "heat" from doing something that you had no choice. I apologized, ran in, threw my suit on, and ran back to the ring. As I fixed my tie near the ring, a couple Pittsburgh Steelers players who were seated in the front row were nice enough to help me fix my tie and collar. I jumped in the ring just as we came back from commercial, announced the next match for the women's championship without a hitch, and successfully got through the rest of the show on the fly. I knew and now the company knew that I was dependable and would be ready to jump into any spot at any time. Getting into the groove really helped with my confidence. I was slowly learning how to master the art of ring announcing.

My mom had grown up with a well-known director from Chicago named Andrew Davis who directed *The Fugitive, Above the Law, Code of Silence, The Package,* among others. We become close with his family over the years and often got together with them in Chicago. He called me and asked about reading for a part in his upcoming film, *The Guardian.* The role was for a drill sergeant character. I didn't think I looked like a drill sergeant, but if he saw me as one, I could make it happen. If I was getting the ring announcing role down, acting in a film could even help me to grow.

I was an independent contractor for WWE, the same classification as all the wrestlers, but I still had to run anything like this by the company, which seemed weird, because I was an independent contractor. Anyway, I got the company's permission and put together a videotape with my camcorder. In the tape, I tried to show the type of drill sergeant I could be: I was angry, yelling, and basically transforming into my WWE and *GI Joe* hero, Sgt. Slaughter. If you saw the movie, you know that's definitely not the kind of character they were looking for. Andy flew me out to California where I did a swim test to audition for a role in Ashton Kutcher's group. I used to be a lifeguard, so I thought this would be easy. But I was swimming alongside actors that were expert surfers and swimmers. I had nothing and was totally out of shape. I'll blame my asthma. At one point while swimming laps, I jumped out of the pool and ran to the other side. I looked at the studio executives, channeled my inner Eddie Guerrero, and said, "If you're not cheating, you're not trying. Cheat to win!" It didn't work though. They did give me a part as Kevin Costner's assistant in the film. I was only on set for one day, so I wouldn't miss any WWE events. On that day, we shot a scene where Kevin Costner walked into a lecture hall where Kutcher, the class, the sergeant, and *Home Alone* dad John Heard were waiting for him. I walked alongside Costner, carrying his bag and watching him as he talked with Heard.

Everybody on the set was really friendly. I spent most of the day standing with Costner in the back of the room. Andy came over and introduced us, which was very kind of him (as was finding a spot for me in the film). He told Costner what I did and that sparked a conversation about wrestling. He told me that he hadn't seen much wrestling, but that he liked "Macho Man" Randy Savage and the Undertaker. He had good taste! When we eventually shot the scene, I positioned behind Costner so I would be out of the shot. I was very programmed to get out of the shots by Kevin and Vince in order to "be small" and highlight the featured talent, the wrestlers. I'd stand in the center of the ring as the first entrant came out and hide in the corner while we waited for the opponent so I wouldn't get in the camera shot with them. As is often the case, aspects of wrestling do not translate well to other facets of show business: Andy cut the action and told me to move over so I could be in the frame of the camera. It's a very, very small part, but I still get tweets to this day asking if I was in *The Guardian*. The answer is yes, and what a cool experience.

CHAPTER 12
E-C-DUB, E-C-DUB

Originally, my goal was to one day become the permanent ring announcer of either *RAW* or *SmackDown*. That is, until June 2006. WWE had bought the rights to ECW in 2003. In 2005, they revived the innovative, entertaining, rebellious, game-changing brand with a cult following for one night only, a pay-per-view event called *One Night Stand*. In 2006, the company decided to bring the show back permanently, and a new ECW went back on the air. ECW would have its own run of weekend live events as well as a one-hour live show on TV. I remember watching the second *One Night Stand* from home and noticing the classic ECW ring announcer, Steven DeAngelis. I was a fan of his style, but after working for the company and having an idea of what they looked for, I wondered if he would make it working under Vince and Kevin. The next afternoon Sue called me and asked if I could be at TV the next day in Trenton, New Jersey. She didn't give me any details whatsoever, just my travel itinerary. I flew out Tuesday morning and arrived at the building. As I walked toward the ring, Steven was being escorted out. I had an idea of what was happening, and even though it was good for me, I felt bad for him.

I was told that Kevin Dunn wanted to speak with me, so I walked into his production truck. Kevin stood up and asked, "Where have you been? Let's go for a walk." We stepped outside, and he told me that he wanted me to be the face of ECW, the ECW ring announcer. I was stoked! I loved ECW, and to be on one of the live shows permanently would be amazing. I'd get to work with all of the ECW guys that I used to watch! Part of me worried about going in reverse, though. I endured all the *SmackDown* nonsense and had been accepted by the *RAW* crew. Because the ECW tour was made up of mostly just the old ECW crew, would they put me through hell as well because they didn't know me? I was concerned, but at the same time, I was excited. I just wished I had more allies there. Either way, it was time to start over again. From the indies to *SmackDown*, I started over going from *SmackDown* to *RAW*, and now I'd be a rookie once again in ECW.

On June 18, 2006, I worked my last *RAW* show in Syracuse, New York. The main event involved Triple H and Shawn Michaels who revived Degeneration X (the fun, rule-breaking, anti-authority faction). After their match, Triple H called me into the ring. He announced to the arena that I was leaving *RAW* to go to ECW, which of course would get the crowd to boo me. Shawn hugged me goodbye, and before I knew it, Triple H came up from behind and pulled my pants down. I was in my boxers, which Triple H was also trying to pull off until I could finally run out of the ring and to the back.

He loved humiliating people in the ring, on the mic, backstage, anywhere he had an opportunity. You can see this when you watch WWE. He will always make a snide remark because that's his character, but it's typically about him looking stronger than anyone else on the show. He has made the Great Khali sing happy birthday on the microphone because Khali had a very heavy accent that he liked to make fun. He did so when mocking Jinder Mahal's Indian background during a non-televised DX Segment in Cleveland, Ohio, along with a Slurpee reference. There's a long list, a very long list. He typically referred to me as dipshit and numbnuts despite my always trying to do a great job and make his ideas that weren't totally thought out get executed properly. He would make fun of anyone he could. Big Show once sat on a folding chair backstage in Iowa, and it broke. Hunter had me take the chair back to Show and ask him to sign it for the company to auction off on the website. Big Show was embarrassed about the situation and was going to kill me until he saw Hunter there laughing at him. He also came over to me and Fit Finlay during one of John Cena's first house show matches on the *RAW* brand in New Jersey. Cena had the old, spinning WWE championship belt, and Hunter got out of the ring and spun the belt like a record and told Fit, "This guy's sucks" as he made a record scratching noise while spinning, "Get Me Outta Here." He just always had to knock everyone and get everyone to laugh at others, and everyone always laughed no matter how dumb his jokes were because he was the boss' son-in-law; he was the game.

One night in Wheeling, West Virginia, word got out that it was my birthday.

Triple H hog-tied me after his match and rolled me into the ring where I was hit in the face with a giant cake. Then to finish off the rib, he had been backstage watching me hop to the back when the show ended. He ran out and again pulled my pants down while I was still tied up. The next night in Erie, Pennsylvania, someone found my old résumé on my website and noticed that on it I claimed I could do impersonations, including Triple H. My old résumé listed anything I could think of, and impressions were one of my miscellaneous skills. It had been a long time since I had worked on this particular skill, however. Triple H made his entrance first that night for his match against Ric Flair. He grabbed the mic for an unplanned promo. He told the crowd that he heard I did impersonations. He said he read it on "some gay website" that my face was on. He was always big on "gay" jokes and references. As always, he was leading the crowd to boo me, but I still have a video from this night, and it's clear they were actually cheering and giving me a chance. He would name a character, and I would have to do the impersonation. The final one was him, and he said it better be good. I did it, and it was pretty good. The crowd agreed. He did not. Of course not. I was being set up to fail. I knew that. He reached into my suit, grabbed my boxers, pulled them over my head, and Flair came out to interrupt and get the match started. He could do that sort of thing because he could say it's a show and it's his character. In reality, it's just how he is. He constantly needs to be reassured that he's the best. As part of the ECW crew, I wasn't going to miss any of that.

That night in Erie wasn't the only memorable one. A while back, we had flown in from another town on a Sunday afternoon for a show. I drove with security pal Jimmy Noonan who you might know as Galikanokus from *Super Troopers*. We jumped into the Toyota Camry from the rental facility as the snow started to come down and picked up some Subway before heading to the building. As soon as the show ended, we were off to Penn State for the following night's *Monday Night RAW*. Unfortunately, we walked outside to see that the snow was now a blizzard. We jumped in the car and slowly made our way to State College. The roads were really bad, and we were sliding everywhere even while driving slowly. At one point, I completely lost control, and the car spun out and ended up facing the opposite direction and on top of the metal barrier that keeps cars from falling off the cliff. I tried to drive, but the gas pedal didn't get us anywhere, which is when we stepped out of the car and noticed why. Fortunately, no cars spun out into us while we were stuck. Finally, a car slowly drove by, and I happened to lock eyes with the driver. It was Nova. In his car were fellow wrestlers Gene Snitsky and Chris Masters, two of the bigger guys in the company. For the record, it wasn't Snitsky's fault. They pulled over and joined Jimmy in lifting the car up and over the rail to set me back on the road, where I drove forward and turned the car back to the right direction. I let Jimmy drive the rest of the way as I had enough for the night. Not too long after, he wiped out into a snow bank. By the time we got to State College, that car didn't look too good, but we got there in one piece, even if the car was in a few.

Anyway, it was now time to start my new adventure. That following Tuesday, we had TV (how we referred to television days) in Albany, New York. I was still learning about the roster as well as the format of our show. The camera positioning, entranceway, and everything else was different from the standard TV setup. I even tried to change my style up to make it a more "extreme." I would hold names longer and growl my Rs because that felt…a little more extreme. That Saturday, we would be running our first ECW live event at the infamous ECW arena in Philadelphia. The ECW arena was known for its hardcore, outspoken, passionate fans. They defined extreme and played a huge part in the ECW shows as well as in the success of ECW. In a way, ECW was a big family that included the wrestlers and the loyal fans. This place, the original ECW arena, was intimidating. I was one of a few people there who was not an ECW "original," and I suspected that the fans weren't going to accept me as their announcer, but I had no idea just how bad they'd let me know it. I remember doing an interview before I went out there, saying how excited I was, which I most definitely was, but also knowing that this would be the most challenging crowd I would ever work in front of. I asked Paul Heyman, the genius behind the original ECW's success, what I should do. I asked if I should give it right back to them. His advice was that I got to where I was because I was a professional. Tonight, I needed to be professional. He said that whatever those fans throw at me, I should simply take it and be professional. As much as I wanted to give it right back, I knew that his advice was golden and that he was usually right. Paul had approached me at one point when I was sitting around the arena on a TV day and playing on my phone. He asked if I knew everything there was to know about the business. I did not. He asked why I wasn't standing around the ring learning. From that day on, I would stand by the ring throughout the day and listen to Vince McMahon and the producers teach talent and soak up all the knowledge that I could.

With Paul's advice in mind, that night I walked out through the tight entranceway filled with fans to a chorus of boos. The entire building was booing me. I never had that experience as an announcer. I was a "bad guy" authority figure at one point in IZW, but in WWE and everywhere else, I was the host, a friendly advocate and guide on their journey through a live wrestling show. The ECW faithful booed me to the ring, and they booed me as I welcomed them to the show. They wanted their ECW ring announcer, and I did not blame them one bit. If I were them, I would want the ECW announcer, too. Instead, they got me. I was proud to be there and happy to be there despite the reaction. Between every match as I stood in the ring, they would chant "You suck dick!" It was nonstop. "Welcome to ECW, Justin," I thought to myself. I could only hope that eventually I would earn their respect and that they would accept me.

I wasn't the only one welcomed to ECW with derogatory chants. The fans also gave a hard time to ECW and WWE newcomer Kelly Kelly. ECW newbie CM Punk, on the other hand, was welcomed with open arms as he made his WWE, ECW debut that night. I was very happy that my old friend and I were starting on this journey together. I knew big things would come from his love and drive for the business. Just about everybody else on the show was an ECW alumni, and the crowd was happy to have all of their favorites back home. After the show, ECW icon Sandman shook my hand and told me I earned his respect that night. He was impressed that I never let the crowd get to me and that I did my job like a professional. Thank you, Paul.

The next week, we started our full ECW run at an ice rink in Belle Vernon, Pennsylvania. It was my first time meeting ECW security agent Big Todd. Big Todd, as you would probably guess, was a big guy who became my very good friend on the ECW run and beyond. Aside from always looking out for all of us, he was always a smiling, joking, and caring friend. Wrestler Tommy Dreamer, who had been working in WWE talent relations, was considered the heart and soul of ECW. I would also consider him the heart and soul of the locker room. Tommy made everything fun. I could write an entire book just based on Tommy stories. He had the greatest sense of humor, got along with everyone, and was respected by all. Deep down, he is a 10-year-old goofball posing as a responsible adult. Tommy's moniker is the "Innovator of Violence." He's also the innovator of "Tommy Ball," and I will get to that.

I fondly recall the entire ECW crew as super nice guys and girls. They were over-the-top characters both in and out of the ring. Each one had a unique personality and made going to work a lot of fun and always interesting. A lot of times I would get a call from one of them on the first day of each loop asking about riding together. Some didn't have a driver's license or credit card, which made it difficult to rent cars. Sometimes it worked out, and I got to spend a full weekend with an ECW original, which was beyond entertaining, to say the least. Everyone got along very well, and we had nothing but fun at these shows. For the most part they were at smaller venues with smaller crowds. WWE put their focus on *RAW* and *SmackDown* and sort of let ECW just happen. From the indoor sports facility in Schenectady, New York, to the small room in Racine, Wisconsin, to the major arena in Glens Falls, New York, it almost felt like I was back in the indies but getting a WWE paycheck. No drama. No bullies. I loved every minute of it! It's safe to say that the "Summer of ECW" was my favorite time in WWE. I could no longer be at IZW on a regular basis and eventually had to stop writing the shows as well because I wasn't there to gauge the audience's reactions. I really enjoyed IZW but having a great experience with ECW was well worth it. Unfortunately, as the weeks went on, it became clear that the ECW originals were on their way out the door and that the WWE guys were coming in to replace them. Test, Kurt Angle, Hardcore Holly, and Big Show came on board. The company was starting to get away from retro ECW brand and moving toward a newer, more "WWE" version of the company. Vince isn't big on helping a business that he did not create to thrive. He is more likely to squash it as he squashed the WCW name shortly after he bought the rights to it.

It was always believed among some of my coworkers and me that Vince hated the ECW chants "E-C-Dub, E-C-Dub" that would still take place and by calling this new ECW, ECW, fans would be less likely to chant those letters.

The large pay-per-view events would typically feature half *SmackDown* matches, half *RAW* matches, and one ECW match. *WrestleMania 23* was approaching, and I had been announcing the one ECW match on the pay-per-views, so I could only hope that I would announce the ECW match at *WrestleMania*. If any year could have been the year, this was it! There was an eight-man tag-team match booked as the ECW match on the *WrestleMania* card. It featured a team of the ECW originals—Tommy Dreamer, Sandman, Sabu, and Rob Van Dam—going head to head with the "New Breed" which consisted of Matt Striker, Marcus Cor Von, Kevin Thorn, and Elijah Burke.

As far as I knew, I would announce this match. I tried not to get my hopes up too high, though, because I knew what happened in Los Angeles and Chicago and even that previous November when I was flown into Philadelphia for the ECW match and they ended up not using the ECW announcers for the *Survivor Series* pay-per-view. Each brand had a match or multiple matches on the show, and each brand had their official commentators, ring announcer, and referees. The company brought Taz, Joey Styles, and me out to Philadelphia but decided not to use us on that event, and the same thing could happen at *WrestleMania*.

I walked around the massive stadium that day in Detroit, checking it all out and imagining what it would look like full of 80,000 people. I was so close to getting to be a part of it, and I wanted to get excited, but I had to keep fighting it. I felt like Rudy from the movie *Rudy* once again when it came to announcing Mania. Just like he would check the roster for his name before every game, I was doing the same for every Mania. There was no one at the events that would approach you and tell you what you were doing on a given night. You were there but pretty much had to figure out where you were supposed to be. I could only assume that I would be announcing that match. As the show got closer, I got more and more pumped up, and it looked like I would be working since no one told me otherwise. So I headed toward the ring. I was ringside in my tux for the whole show, and it seemed as if I would actually be able to announce a match at *WrestleMania*, the biggest night of the industry put on by the biggest company in the industry.

The match before ECW was Undertaker versus Batista. They came near the announce tables, and I ended up getting knocked down to the floor. Jim Ross had a thermos of tea that had been knocked over, and sure enough, I landed right in his tea puddle. My pants were drenched in tea. Good thing it was black so no one else would notice, but I definitely felt it. As the Undertaker/Batista match continued, I wondered if the ECW match would actually take place, or if it would be cut due to time constraints. Could I finally get into a ring at *WrestleMania*?

The match ended, and as far as I knew, we were next. No one holds your hand and walks you through a show. The lack of communication would keep all of us at ringside, wondering. I stepped in the middle of the ring, and it was a good thing I had already wet my pants because it kept me from doing it on my own. I stared out into the sea of 80,000 fans surrounding the ring. There's something soothing about looking out at a crowd so big. It's almost as if they're not real people; it's just a mirage. People ask me all the time if I get nervous being in front of a crowd that big. On that night, I have to be honest: Yes, I was. It was *WrestleMania*, and it was the largest live crowd I had ever announced in front of. Now, however, many years later, I can say that speaking in front of 80,000 is easier than 20,000 or 5,000 and without a doubt, much, much easier than speaking in front of 15 people. Because it is so mind blowing, so surreal, even an almost quiet-like feel, it's easier. It happened. I was able to announce the match after all. I announced at *WrestleMania*, and that was an unbelievably proud moment! With all the wrestlers in that one match, I had the opportunity to announce quite a lot of names.

As we approached January 2007, the ECW live events weren't drawing a lot of fans. The new plan was to combine ECW and *SmackDown* live events and still shoot ECW TV with *SmackDown* on Tuesdays. That meant Tony Chimel would announce both *SmackDown* and ECW live events, and I would move back to the *RAW* live events. My schedule was *RAW* live events Friday through Sunday, travel on Monday, and ECW TV on Tuesday. Wednesday was a travel day, and I had Thursday at home. I enjoyed being with the *RAW* crew for part of the week, and the *SmackDown* days were much better now that guys like Dreamer were around. The crews were much more positive than in previous years, so I had the best of both worlds.

On February 19, 2007, I was at the gym in Scottsdale. I had a late afternoon flight to San Diego for an ECW taping the next night. I had been talking to a girl named Crystal who I had met on MySpace. Yes, MySpace. Not having a lot of time to go out and have a social life left very few options for meeting a girl. We had been very casually talking for a while, but with my crazy schedule, I was never able to get to San Diego. This was my chance to finally get there early and have time to go out for dinner. Having a social life outside wrestling was a challenge, so I looked forward to finally meeting a girl with potential that night. I would finish at the gym and fly out late that afternoon where I would have that extra evening before the San Diego show.

I got a call at about noon, mid-workout. It was Sue. She told me that Lilian had walked into a pole the night before and that she was unable to announce *RAW* that night. The show was in Bakersfield, California, and she asked if I could make it to Bakersfield by show time. I looked at my watch and told her if it's possible, I will be there.

I bolted home and threw a together a suitcase. I put my suit and tie on because I knew timing was going to be tight. There were no flights available from Phoenix to Bakersfield or anything easy like that. The closest I could get was San Luis Obispo, California. I took it. To save time with a rental car, I called the rental company ahead and gave them all my information over the phone. That way, when I landed, I could simply flash my license and jump in a car. We were delayed taking off due to rain, and I landed a little later than expected. My stress level was through the roof of the plane. The longer we sat after landing, the more anxious I became. Finally, I got off the plane, and sprinted to the rental facility. I flashed my license and grabbed the keys. I was on my way to *RAW*!

I didn't know this ahead of time, but it was mostly a one-lane route 142 miles to Bakersfield, and I was approaching rush hour. I swerved in and out of oncoming traffic to pass up the slow cars. I called Sue and told her that I was on my way. I asked what plan B was, as traffic was picking up, and my time was starting to run out. She told me that Kevin liked plan A (i.e., me getting there on time), and he was going to stick with that one. I knew there wasn't room to fail, so I drove that much faster, without breaking too many laws. I'm usually an eight-over kind of guy. I didn't have time to get pulled over for a speeding ticket. I asked what the first segment of *RAW* was, and I found out that it was a Vince McMahon promo. That was great. I knew that would buy me a few minutes, if I needed it. At 5:30, matches would be taped for *Sunday Night Heat*, but I needed to be there at 6:00 to go live for *RAW*. I factored in the Vince promo, which gave me until maybe 6:08.

At 5:48, I called my friend Todd who was working security that night. I had never been to that arena at the time and wanted him to give me a feel for the place. I didn't have time to search for the back entrance. Some arenas, like the Horizon, had an easy back entrance to find, and others like LA, Houston, and Cleveland, were somewhat hidden. He gave me a tip to find the back entrance easily and told me that he would be outside waiting. He was a true friend, and I appreciated everything he did for all of us. At exactly 6:00 pm I pulled up to the building and saw Todd's smiling face. I tossed him the keys like they do in the movies and ran straight from the back entrance right into the arena and up to the Gorilla position. They notified Kevin in the production truck that I was there. Vince was in the ring. Talented and entertaining broadcaster Todd Grisham, who would later go on to join Coach at *ESPN*, covered the pre-show matches and introduced Vince to start off the show.

Immediately after Vince's promo, I walked to the ring. We passed each other on the way, so he knew that I had made it. The next segment was an intercontinental championship match. The participants were already out there, and I announced the winner as well as the rest of the live *RAW* television show for two hours, all on the fly with zero preparation. My adrenaline was flowing, and after the show ended, I was beat. Mark Yeaton took his headsets off, dried the sweat on his pants, and handed them over. I was being paged. Kevin Dunn was on the other end. He asked me if I traveled in my suit. I said yes and explained why. He thanked me, and then Vince's voice came through in the other ear and said, "Good job." I hadn't been around that long, but I knew compliments weren't commonplace. People usually only heard things if something was wrong. Frank, who heard the exchange, looked at me with a big smile on his face. He told everyone that I got the ol' 'atta boy from Vince and Kevin. He loved to give me a hard time, but he was happy for my rare moment in the sun. When Vince and Kevin talked on headset, lots of production folks could hear whatever they said. If you got a compliment, a large audience hears it. If they yell at you, everyone gets to hear that as well.

At the end of the long day and night, Big Todd joined me in the car for a long drive to San Diego. I had to cancel on Crystal for earlier in the evening and then again after the show since it was a 230-mile drive, and I wouldn't arrive until late. Crystal ended up marrying Hugh Heffner, so it probably wasn't going to work out anyway.

On March 18, 2007, I had just flown into Chicago and driven to Valparaiso, Indiana, for a *RAW* live event. I had watched *E!* one day and caught a show about a kid who hosted a talk show in his parents' basement in Valparaiso, Indiana. His name was Michael Essany. I loved the concept of the show, and every character in it. It was so real and so genuine. I was determined to meet him. I do that a lot.

If there's someone who I think is cool, I'll immediately start figuring out how I can get in touch with them. In this case, I researched Michael and his sidekick Mike and asked if they were wrestling fans. They were! So while doing the show in Valparaiso, we met for lunch at Chili's. I really respected the fact that Michael had always wanted to be a talk show host; he legitimately wanted to be the next Jay Leno and was following his dream by hosting a local show in his hometown. *E!* thought it was cool, too, and gave him a national show. I like go-getters. I find them to be very admirable. Even my old buddy Colt Cabana was a huge fan of Essany's and joined us as we met again at Chili's after the show.

In addition to being go-getters and dream-chasers, I had something else in common with Michael that blew my mind. He, too, was bullied by JBL and didn't even work for WWE! Michael interviewed JBL when he was in high school. His mom was there, and Michael was eagerly standing with his mom, waiting to interview JBL when he nervously dropped the blue index cards with his questions on them. JBL then asked his mom if she had any children who weren't mentally disabled. Unreal. We talked about better wrestling memories and eventually called it a night.

Following that, I drove back to Chicago to catch a flight the next morning. As I pulled into the hotel, I received a voicemail from Kevin Dunn. Kevin didn't usually call me, so I assumed it was important. He told me to get back to him as soon as possible and as late as needed. I immediately called to find out that Lilian injured herself while skiing. He asked if I could be at *RAW* the next day in Indianapolis. Of course I could be. So the next day I drove back to Indiana and headed to Indianapolis to cover *Monday Night RAW*. Over the next three months while Lilian was injured, I would cover *Monday Night RAW* TV, *RAW* live events, ECW TV, *SmackDown*/ECW Europe tour, pay-per-views, and even various *SmackDown* TV episodes that Tony would take off. I loved every minute of it. Announcing *Monday Night RAW*, ECW TV on Tuesday, and *SmackDown* on Friday all in the same week made me feel like I was finally in the groove. Kevin Dunn had told me I was becoming a staple around there, and that wasn't easy to do. Another 'atta boy!

In June 2007, I left home for the *Extreme Rules* pay-per-view, TV, and an international tour that followed right after. My sister had been pregnant, and I was very anxious to have my first-ever baby relative. I got the call as I landed in the first town of the tour, Jacksonville, Florida. My sister had gone into labor, and by the time I got to the building, I received pictures of my niece. It was an unforgettable moment realizing that I was an uncle. Unfortunately, I had to wait 10 days to meet her. I was beaming, and the first person I ran up to at ringside when I got the news was Chris Benoit. He had been asking about my sister and how she was doing throughout her entire pregnancy. I proudly showed him the pictures of my new niece. "Isn't life amazing? Aren't babies a miracle?" he asked as he smiled and congratulated me.

It took a lot to get through that tour as the technology wasn't then what it is now, meaning I couldn't get fast, immediate updates from my sister. I finally got home and went straight to meet my niece for the first time. I'll never forget holding her little head in the palm of my hand and looking at her big blue eyes. It was a very special moment. I had only lost family members over the years. This was my first time gaining one.

At the end of that month, on June 26, I was in Houston, Texas, for the *WWE Vengeance: Night of Champions* pay-per-view. I was scheduled to announce the ECW title match between Chris Benoit and CM Punk. Throughout the day, no one had seen Benoit. I ran into Dean Malenko, a WWE producer and close friend of his. He mentioned that Chris had said something on the phone about his son being sick. That was the last anyone had heard from him. It wasn't like him at all to be late, let alone miss a show. I was told that the match was plan A, and if for whatever reason Benoit didn't show up, John Morrison was to take his place. As we got closer to show time, we went ahead with plan B, knowing that if Benoit came in time, he would obviously be back in the match. Benoit never showed up. That night I drove alone (as I usually did) to Corpus Christi. I had a horrible feeling in my stomach, and I didn't know why. Maybe I was worried about Benoit or maybe it was something else, I didn't know what the cause was. I drove to Corpus and tried to keep my mind busy.

This episode of *RAW* was a combined show and was to be the night that Lilian returned from her injury and resumed announcing *RAW*. She was adamant about having me announce the pre-show matches because she felt her big return should be made on *RAW*. She always tried to avoid doing anything before the main show.

I didn't mind it. I liked announcing whatever I could and agreed to do the openers. The theme of *RAW* this week was interesting: It was Mr. McMahon's funeral. The previous week, Vince's character exploded in a limo, and we, the audience, assumed the character had "died." This three-hour special show featured talent from *RAW*, *SmackDown*, and ECW, as well as many stars from the past. It was a very unique script, featuring not only the entire roster, but also names from the past.

As we got closer to going live, we were asked to assemble into the arena. All the talent sat around the ring, and we waited to find out what was going on. I knew that we weren't getting good news. The few people I saw whispering to each other were tearing up and covering their faces. Within a few minutes, Vince walked into the arena and took a microphone into the ring. He told us that they had sent the police over to check on Benoit when he suspiciously didn't appear at the show. The news they got was that Chris, his wife, and son were all found dead, which made it sound like all three had been murdered. We were shocked and sad. Vince told us that *RAW* was cancelled, and we could all leave as that night's show would be a three-hour tribute to Chris Benoit.

As I walked around the arena, I saw the casket, the hearse, the black wreaths, and all the other props planned for the televised Vince McMahon funeral. Seeing these somber props didn't make getting this news any easier. I called my mom to let her know. Chris had been very good to my family, and I didn't know what to say or do. I didn't know how to feel. He had his moments when he was my friend, but I do recall being terrorized by him on those tours early in my career. All in all, however, he was very kind to my family, especially my dad.

We all found out the next day that Chris wasn't a victim, but that he had killed his wife and son and then taken his own life. The atmosphere in San Antonio for the *SmackDown* taping was really uncomfortable. We were all affected by what had taken place and were trying to come to terms with the details. I had a rare run in with Kevin Dunn as I was putting on my tie in the dressing room. I asked him if I should start the show how I normally would, or if I should use the appropriate tone. I got my answer: normal. It was rough on all of us, but we got through it.

The following week, my grandma, who had been visiting Arizona, ended up in the hospital. She was 83 and typically had more energy than anyone in my family. She was very social, too. If I called her at midnight she would put me on hold because she was already on the line with someone else. She was one of my strongest supporters ever since I was a kid and was always entertained by my performances—school plays, impersonations, and now wrestling. She went from being in great spirits and the picture of health straight to the hospital and on a breathing machine. I visited her late at night as much as I could. Sadly, the nurses assured me that she would never recover. It hurt me each time I had to leave her side to fly out for work because I didn't know how much time she had. Over the next few weeks, she didn't make any progress. Our family decided to keep her in the hospital and on the breathing machine anyway because we knew she was a fighter and wouldn't give up.

On July 23, 2007, I finished an early west coast pay-per-view event, *The Great American Bash*, and left the San Jose arena. I returned the many missed calls from family and discovered that my grandma had a "rally". She was out of her coma and talking to my family. My eyes teared up as I drove down the highway, knowing that I would be able to speak with my grandma again. Up until that point, I didn't think that would ever be a possibility, and I felt very lucky for the opportunity. As soon as I flew back to Arizona, I went straight to the hospice that she had been moved to. She wasn't her normal self and often gazed off into the distance while I spoke to her, but she was able to hold conversations. I called a few of her friends back in Chicago so she could say hello. The conversations were short, but at least they were able to talk.

Later that week, my mom and I stopped in to see my grandma before we drove to Las Vegas together. I had a show there that night, and it was great to share a road experience with my mother. We watched movies and caught up. She was able to see what life was really like on the road and how I was spending all of my weeks. Unfortunately, she also got to see how things go on the road after a long day when you check into your hotel and have a long walk to your room (especially a Las Vegas casino hotel) and then get there to find someone else was already in that room. Surprisingly, that happened a lot with our late hotel check-ins. The day after the show, we drove to Prescott Valley for another one and then made our way back home. That week, the ECW taping would take place in Phoenix, which was perfect. I loved riding that loop of shows with my mom. She is the sweetest, most caring, thoughtful, and positive person I have ever known and is always in a good, upbeat mood. My mom is so kind to everyone, not just family. She once came to one of my shows and took a little boy who was there (with his grandfather who was working security) to the concession stand to get him food since he was sitting alone. She is an overall friendly, loving person who taught me that we are all here for just a short visit and to do whatever makes you happy as long as you don't hurt anyone else. And she is so right.

The next weekend, I worked my loop and came home. I woke up to a voicemail from a woman in a friendly tone informing me that my grandma had passed. That was not the ideal way to hear the news. The reality didn't hit me as I lay there in bed. My spunky, energetic, funny, always positive, sweet, and caring grandmother, my last remaining grandparent, was gone. She had flown to Arizona to meet my niece and caught a virus on the plane ride out.

It was a horrible situation and very unfortunate to lose such a wonderful person. I never called in sick for work, or for vacation, or any other reason. Many of us feared that asking for time off could result in losing our jobs. The company frowned upon talent even asking for time off, so it was assumed that if we did, we could easily be replaced. Therefore, I was anxious about having to ask for time off, but I needed to be with my family in Chicago for the funeral. I never took time off and was never offered time off, and I didn't want to upset the company, but I needed to make this funeral. Lilian couldn't cover for me, and Tony had his own family issue that week, but luckily, they made it work. *SmackDown* general manager, Teddy Long, covered one tour, and Extreme Expose (a three-diva dance group from ECW) covered the other tour.

The time with my family helped. I returned to work the following week in New York City for a *Saturday Night's Main Event* taping at Madison Square Garden. I worked MSG, the world's most famous arena, for a second time. Unreal! From there I continued on to the *RAW* tour and worked the ECW television show. ECW was going well. I developed my own style and started receiving feedback from fans on social media who were picking up on the little subtleties in my announcing that made me and the introductions different from other announcers. The growling, the energy, making the bad guys sound like bad guys, the good guys sound like good guys—everything was done for a reason, and the fans seemed to like it. Vince, however, was not a fan of me doing any big introductions. He told me to tone it down, and I began delivering plain introductions hoping he would tell me to bring it up a bit. Unfortunately, he was happy with plain. It was pretty weird growing up enjoying his over-the-top commentary and then working for him and doing that in my own waywith him not liking it at all.

CHAPTER 13
RUTHLESS AGGRESSION

On September 18, 2007, I returned from a tour in South Africa, where we had shows in Cape Town, Durban, and Johannesburg. Hiking with Dr. Rios, Santino Marella, Paul London, Randy Orton, and Dave Taylor was an incredible way to see a city versus going to a local gym, which I had started doing on the tours. Our last night in Johannesburg, we were advised to stay at the hotel due to safety concerns. I felt like they just preferred that we didn't get out and into trouble, so staying in for "safety concerns" was a logical suggestion. A large group of us sat on the patio of the Hilton, and two guys came out and said they recognized John Cena. They told us that they were the 70s music group Air Supply and asked if they could join us. Why not? So Air Supply and the *RAW* roster hung out on the patio, talking and listening to music, which was the perfect way to end a perfect tour.

When I arrived at TV in Atlanta, Georgia, I was informed that from then on I was the new official ring announcer for *SmackDown*. I would announce the *SmackDown* portion of the TV taping and also handle the *SmackDown* live events. It seemed like just when I became comfortable on any tour, I was moved. I was very excited about this promotion and new opportunity; I just had to hope for the best with going back to the *SmackDown* locker room. That night, Tony Chimel announced the ECW matches as the first part of the show, and I came out for the beginning of *SmackDown*, which kicked off with a wedding for Teddy Long.

I was definitely glad to be on the full *SmackDown* schedule. Now I wouldn't have a down day like I did being out Friday through Sunday with Monday off, but on the road for Tuesday's show, and I would be out four-and-a-half days each week, rather than my current five-and-a-half. That one extra day made a huge difference. I actually spent most of my two-and-a-half down days running errands to prepare for the next tour. One of those errands was my weekly haircut. Yes, it grew back that quickly! I had been going to a girl named Stacie for many years, and every week she was amazed at how quickly my hair grew. She knew how tight my schedule was and always managed to squeeze me in, which I appreciated!

In addition to announcing on the live events, television shows, and pay-per-view events, I had also begun announcing on the WWE video games. Each year, THQ, and later on 2K, would make a WWE video game, featuring the majority of the roster. When I was announcing for ECW, they brought me in, and each year after that, I was doing more and more voiceovers for the game. A THQ employee named David was producing me, and since I did not have much spare time and David lived in Arizona, I would typically fly in from a tour and head straight to the recording studio. It was fun at first, but after belting out each line as a major announcement 700 to 1,000 times, it became tedious. I would announce, "Here are your winners and NEW WWE tag-team champions…Name! and Name!" Then I would do it again and switch out one of the names, and go through it over and over, inserting new names each time. We made it fun, though, and got through it year after year, game after game.

In 2008, David let me know that he was going to be leaving the company. He had worked with Nav in "mo cap," who knew all the wrestlers in the area and coordinated with them and THQ to come in and do motion capture for the video games. David thought Nav would be perfect to take his place in the company and asked what I thought. I agreed and told him there would be no better person for the job after him than Nav. I let David know that if I could be of any help to please use me as a reference. It wasn't because Nav was my friend; it was because I knew that was his calling.

Sure enough, I received a call from Mike at WWE offices asking about him. He was very hesitant, simply because he was viewed as an independent wrestler. They didn't want someone coming in to that spot and using it to get a spot as a wrestler. I explained that wouldn't be an issue for him, and he was the absolute best person for the job. He was responsible, and he knew how to deal with all talent from booking talent on shows over the years. He even had experience with many of the guys on the WWE roster from his independent days, and he was well respected. I guaranteed that he was truly a great guy and would be efficient in this role. The office doubted me despite the high praise, but still gave him a shot. He had worked many enhancement matches over the years for WWE, and I was lucky enough to be able to introduce a couple of them, but I knew that wasn't something he needed to do anymore and could focus solely on this new position. Within three months, I received a call back from Mike, who was one of the passionate guys that really cared about his job and the company, which is why he put so much thought into Steve taking that position. He was a great asset to them over the years and wanted to keep up his good reputation, and I didn't blame him. He apologized for doubting me and told me how happy they were with Nav. He was basically the liaison between the company and the video game and would handle getting the guys photographed and recorded. This also meant that we got to work together again in WWE because he was producing my VO sessions. I was thrilled for him to have this job and loved the long VO sessions because he was there.

It was also actually fun being back on the *SmackDown* live events combined with ECW. Some of the ECW guys were still around, but it was predominantly WWE guys. Dreamer was still there, so it meant that the locker room, which was once the toughest and hardest in the world, one in which you could get in trouble for pretty much breathing the wrong way, was now the most fun and easy going atmosphere in the company. Like Nav, Tommy was also well liked and respected by everyone—office and talent. His sense of humor was on a totally different level. I also believe a big part of the overall change was due in part to what I mentioned earlier: Tommy Ball.

What's Tommy Ball? Let me explain. Tommy, Edge, Hornswoggle, Kane, Chavo Guerrero, Matt Striker, and I were once in a locker room in Charleston, West Virginia. Tommy was getting undressed near Kane and just being goofy as usual. In response to Tommy's behavior, Kane, "the big red monster" reached into his bag, retrieved a tennis ball that he carried with him, and fired the ball at Tommy's...how can I put this delicately...balls. In that weekend, this turned into a locker room past time: Tommy Ball. The male wrestlers, both good and bad guys, refs, and I lined up in a locker room while Dreamer let his testicles hang out of his pants, and we all took a turn tossing the tennis ball and trying to hit the target. A light, underhand toss or a light overhand toss with a bounce were okay.

If you broke the rules, you were banned. Who would allow an entire wrestling roster to do this? Who could make something this crazy into a game? Ladies and gentlemen, the innovator of Violence and Tommy Ball, Tommy Dreamer.

Dreamer was also the innovator of the Mr. Fuji Game. Mr. Fuji, for those who don't know, was a wrestling manager famous for throwing salt into his opponents' eyes so that his team would take advantage and get the win. We were on an overseas trip and stopped at a buffet to eat. While we were eating, Dreamer asked Hornswoggle a question that garnered a "who?" response. Dreamer responded with, "Mr. Fuji" as he threw a handful of salt into Swoggle's face. That became known as the Mr. Fuji Game. No one was safe; at any point, anyone anywhere could get Mr. Fuji'd. If someone asked you a question, and you answered with, "Who?", you were immediately vulnerable to attack. Edge came to the ring on that tour in front of thousands of fans doing his normal entrance. Posing on the ropes, but also walking up to me and asking if I knew who was coming to the show tonight. I quickly responded with yes, and he growled and threw a handful of salt on the mat outside the ring. In catering later that night, Dreamer Mr. Fuji'd a couple people with ceremonial rice (well, white rice from catering). Unfortunately, this game that could have been as popular as Monopoly over time ended as fast as it began. The last person to get Mr. Fuji'd with rice was the Big Show. Dreamer noticed an unsuspecting, sweaty Big Show in catering. No one thought he would do it, so when it happened, the room got awkwardly quiet. Big Show did not get Dreamer to say, "who," yet Mr. Fuji'd Dreamer with a fire extinguisher...while still in catering. The room once again filled with awkward silence, just like a classroom of children when one of the kids takes things too far, Mr. Fuji had gotten to this point and the teacher, or, in this case, the Undertaker, stepped in and had both kids—er, superstars—clean up their mess.

We once had a meeting before an ECW show. The meeting involved the late legend, Dusty Rhodes, and all the ECW talent. Everyone was talking before the meeting, and out of nowhere, Tommy Dreamer casually announced in his monotone speaking voice, "By the way, today is Daylight Savings, so make sure you set your watches back an hour." This created lots of commotion as everyone was discussing how this would affect their night. I turned to Tommy and said, "It's summer. Daylight Savings isn't 'til November." He turned to the room and said, "Oh, never mind. It's not." So now whenever Dreamer tells me anything that's questionable, I respond with, "Daylight Savings?" Sometimes it's factual, sometimes it's out of nowhere with no validity. I'll never forget our drive through New Mexico where he was happy to see the sun. He stripped down to his underwear, opened the sunroof, and reclined his seat all the way to tan. Everything he did and everything he said made me laugh.

Unfortunately, laughing was a problem when working with him. Sometimes at the live events, we would have a little fun, because back then it was allowed. If we had fun, the fans had fun. We would do things each night to entertain each other and, in the process, entertain the fans. When the TV cameras and the politics that came with them weren't at shows, we would do little things. One of which was altering Dreamer's intro. I would slip in little things during his introductions that the fans wouldn't catch, altering his weight or his hometown and so on, but he would, and they would make him laugh. Unfortunately, I would make myself laugh in the process, and I wasn't able to introduce his name without laughing. So I would start saying his introduction and then have to stop and try to contain myself and then start again and usually end up laughing in the mic. At times, I would switch the mic off mid introduction and pretend it wasn't working because I knew I couldn't get the rest of the announcement out without laughing into it. Every time, he would get to the ring with a huge grin and tell me that I robbed him of an entrance again! I couldn't help it.

I was in a good groove with a good group and having fun. My throat was holding up with the exception of a South Carolina tour in December 2008 when laryngitis got the best of me. Aside from the recovery, the tonsillectomy was exactly what I needed. I felt fine, but did this show without a voice, because if the wrestlers could wrestle hurt, I could announce "hurt." Fit Finlay was the agent that loop and asked if I was sure I wanted to work, and I was. The next night, he didn't give me an option and told me that *SmackDown* general manager Teddy Long would be announcing. I sat backstage trying any remedy I could find. As I sat there, Triple H received a message from Vince about an overseas flight he had just been on where apparently JBL was egging on former announcer Joey Styles. He got away with that from me, but this time, I was glad to hear that a smaller announcer stood up to him as we were told Joey had punched JBL. It was weird because shortly after that, JBL had disappeared from the company. I've always hated bullies and was glad karma, or Joey Styles, had finally come back to stand up for himself.

CHAPTER 14
I LOVE IT WHEN A PLAN COMES TOGETHER

In late May 2009, I caught wind that Lilian was leaving to focus on her music career and to start a family. I wondered if I would be chosen to announce *Monday Night RAW*. As the days went on, I saw news on the Internet that **"WWE is looking for a young, attractive female to sing the national anthem and be our regular ring announcer every week, for one of our most popular TV shows."** WWE was searching for an attractive female who could sing and announce. Casting agencies everywhere were notified. I assumed with all the talent applying, a new girl who knew how to sing and announce would get the spot. I had been with the company for about seven years at this point, five years full time. I had worked my way up the ladder and truly, truly hoped I would be able to be the permanent *RAW* ring announcer since that was the main show.

I never had a buddy-buddy relationship with Kevin Dunn as I did with most others in the entire company, both at the office and on the road. He knew that I did my job and rarely bothered him. He would usually go out drinking in the hotel bars after the shows and associated with the group of guys that joined him. I never got into that and usually stayed away from the company hotel just to avoid getting sucked into anything like that. Work was work. So without the relationship, it was a little harder to talk. If I had to go in the truck to ask him a question, he would typically humiliate me by announcing loudly, "Everybody stop what you're doing. Justin has a question." So I didn't make a habit out of that. This question was important and worth the embarrassment it might cause. On June 23, 2009, I announced a *SmackDown* taping in Milwaukee, Wisconsin. After the show, I built up the courage to walk into Kevin's production truck. I told him that I wasn't an attractive female, I couldn't sing, but I could definitely announce and that I would like to throw my name into the hat to be considered for the *RAW* ring announcer. He said, "Vince and I already discussed it. You're the new ring announcer for *Monday Night RAW*. Congratulations, and don't tell anyone."

Well. That was awesome. I did it! I got into the company when a spot didn't even exist. I worked hard nonstop, and now I would be announcing the flagship show. I just couldn't tell anyone. It was hard to keep that bottled up. Right before she left, Lilian called me to tell me that she was leaving and that she wanted to be the one to tell me I was the new *RAW* announcer, which I thought was very cool of her. I thanked her for the news and wished her luck on her new journey.

On September 24, 2009, I flew from Oklahoma to Madrid, Spain, with the *SmackDown* crew for what would be my final *SmackDown* tour. The locker room had changed so much from years previous. All the bullies had disappeared or changed their ways, and great guys like Tommy Dreamer made the environment so much better. There was a friendly atmosphere and a feeling of it being okay to belong. I actually think Tommy Dreamer was single-handedly the guy who changed the entire locker room on those tours. For that, and for many other things he said and did, I will always be grateful. Tommy is the funniest person I have ever met in my life. If it weren't for Tommy's influence on the locker room, I don't think we ever would have had the majority of the shenanigans that took place, like Tommy Ball, Mr. Fuji…and the Kane Ram. The 4'4" Hornswoggle asked Kane if he thought it would hurt to get rammed by a ram, so Kane put two paper horns on his head in a locker room in South America, got down on all fours, and rammed Swoggle. He got his answer. So, from my first *SmackDown* tour to my last, things were completely different.

That last tour was great. I enjoyed Madrid, Nice, and Paris. We had two nights of shows in Paris, and I had to leave before the final one. The office wanted to make sure that I was in Albany, New York, on September 28 for my first episode of *RAW* as the new announcer. We even had a special guest host, Reverend Al Sharpton. I left the crew after the Paris show to a Gatorade-like goodbye, but I was sprayed with the ice and waters instead by my *SmackDown* friends. It was hard to leave that group, but I knew *RAW* had a great crew as well, and I'd see most of the *SmackDown* roster at the combined pay-per-views.

The transition to *RAW* went well. I knew that as the new announcer, I was under the microscope a bit, so that made me a little nervous. I was no longer filling in temporarily; I had taken an open spot. I mentioned that I couldn't say the phrase "...and his opponent..." at my tryout. That was because Vince would make crazy little rules from week to week, and one week he decided he didn't like the word "opponent," so the announcers were not allowed to say that. If I ever pitched an announcement referring to "the fans," I was quickly reminded that he did not want the fans referred to as "the fans," but rather "fans" or "our fans." Vince is the same guy who decided Ryback couldn't be billed from Sin City (which sounded cool) and decided he was from Las Vegas instead. No state like most wrestlers get, just a city introduction. When Vince made a rule, that was it until he changed the rule shortly after. Or forgot the next week and yelled when he heard me saying something odd that he had actually come up with in the past. There was a time when the Canadian talent lost their Canadian hometowns and had to be announced from the States. We would be told something by Vince, or someone who Vince gave an order, or a memo, and that was the rule for the moment.

No one gave me direction or told me what to do (or what not to do), so I started making my own style. I wanted to say "opponent" since it made sense to say the word (after all, that's what that person was). No one told me to stop. I also heard "the following contest is scheduled for one fall" year after year and started saying little things like "this contest is set for one fall;" "this bout is set for one fall." Just my own little changes. If Chuck Palumbo rode a motorcycle to the ring, I said, "Riding to the ring from San Diego, California..." I was making my own rules, and it wasn't anything bad, just small details that I thought should be said a little differently. I was the "head ring announcer" on the flagship show, so why not? I respected but didn't want to be Howard or any other established announcer. I wanted to create my own style. I recall Howard calling me shortly after I got into my groove and letting me know that when he introduced a team of wrestlers, he would start with the name of the person whose music was playing. I respected his style, but I felt if you had two different talents that each have their own music, when they're getting just one song played at the end of their match, the last name I announced should go along with the music that was playing. Every word, every tone, every pronunciation of my announcements were different and had meaning. If Vince or Kevin didn't like something that I tried, I would definitely hear about it as they listened to every word of my announcements. Yeaton would always relay, "Vince wants to know why you said..." or "Kevin asked why you said ..." A lot of times they questioned why I said words that I had gotten from the script, and my response was, "It's in the script!" Then they would tell me not to listen to the script, but other times insist on going by the script. I learned that the best way to handle those situations was to apologize and take the heat, pretending I was dumb. I got really good at that. Not only was I playing with the words of my standard introductions, I began having fun with the announcements. Maybe I would announce Minneapolis, Minnesota, with a Minnesotan accent. If Tyson Kidd was from Calgary, Alberta, maybe I would add the dramatic pause as a tribute to the talented Lance Storm, who he paused during his promos. I was doing a lot of little things that didn't hurt anyone's credibility but added some fun so my announcements wouldn't get boring. There would be many "little things" a few fans would catch if they listened closely. The main thing, though, was that I wanted to introduce the bad guys and make them sound like bad guys. I wanted the good guys to sound like good guys. My tone was leading the crowd toward a certain direction. They were going to go there with or without me, but I wanted to lead them there. I wanted my tone to build up that huge reaction with the announcement and build toward the booing that was about to happen. I wanted special moments to feel special.

The night after my *RAW* debut, I also announced *SmackDown* for Tony. I would always watch every show back and pick out what I liked or didn't like about all my introductions. I loved the difference on announcing *RAW* versus *SmackDown* in the audio. *RAW* was live, and the sound you heard in the arena was what you heard on TV. The sound on *SmackDown* was usually altered for crowd noise and whatever else they did. It was weird sounding and just unnatural. The following week, I covered the pay-per-view. I was set in my new position. *RAW* was a lot of fun, and at this point in the show, we had different celebrity guest hosts each week. We had guests like Snoop Dogg, the late Florence Henderson, David Hasselhoff, Buzz Aldrin, Rob Zombie, Mike Tyson, Snooki, Bradley Cooper, Dennis Miller, Don Johnson, Napoleon Dynamite, Jewel, and one of my favorites, Pee-Wee Herman. When I was a child, I watched *Pee-Wee's Playhouse* every week and *Pee-Wee's Big Adventure* over and over. When he was there, I showed him the Polaroid of me as a 10-year-old kid wearing Pee-Wee pajamas. He got a kick out of that.

Jerry Springer was one of our guest hosts. I said hi when I passed by him in the hall. JJ, the WWE rep working with him, told me to "tell him." I said, "No, it's okay," and Jerry asked, "Tell me what?" She pushed again, and I admitted to Jerry that I was on his show back in the day. He laughed as I took out my cell phone and showed him the video. We had a laugh together, which was pretty cool a decade later.

Growing up, Mike Tyson was the guy we loved to watch in boxing. He was unpredictable and unstoppable. The Tyson I got to work with was like a kid in the candy store. In the middle of a rehearsal, he ran out of the ring to approach Ricky "the Dragon" Steamboat. He, too, loved wrestling, and it was awesome to see this badass boxing face destroyer so excited to meet his heroes.

Similar to Mike, I like to do things now, as an adult, that were just not possible as a kid. Whether it's meeting television personalities I always liked and grew up watching or even talking to that girl who I never asked out when I was in junior high, there was just something so fun and fulfilling from being able to finally do it! I used to watch the *Golden Girls* on Saturday nights while I helped my sister on her babysitting gigs. Even back then, I appreciated the stories and characters on the show. My grandma loved it as well, so it was nice to have that in common. I was also very vocal about being a *Golden Girls* fan throughout my years in school, and I never really cared if I was teased. I found out that Bea Arthur was doing a live piano show in Chicago when I was home from college for winter break.

At this point in life, I was an independent wrestling ring announcer. I didn't even have WWE on my résumé yet. But I used that angle to talk to her manager while she was in the building performing. I told him that I would love to meet her and left a photo I had made, which I used to sell at wrestling shows, to autograph for her. The merch tables are key at indie shows. It was a collage of me standing with various wrestling stars that I had met and a couple that I had actually worked with, which gave a little credibility at the shows and now to Bea Arthur's "people." I thanked him and stood outside the trailer as she came in following her show. A minute later, the door opened, and he waved me in. I could not believe that I was walking into Bea Arthur's trailer! She immediately said, "Well, hi there. Why do you want to meet me? I'm not a wrestler." I told her how much I loved her and the show. We spoke for a few minutes, and she was everything I could hope for and just as funny and warm as she was on television.

I had hoped to meet all four *Golden Girls*; unfortunately, while Estelle Getty and Rue McClanahan passed away, I was determined to meet Betty White. The first time I worked a WWE show at the Staples Center in LA, I tracked down her management company and wrote a note, inviting her to the show. Unsurprisingly, I never heard back. Fast forward to February 2014: Betty White was booked to appear on *RAW*! A friend tipped me off about her appearance, and I flipped out. I was determined to meet her, and not just because she was a Golden Girl. I always loved Betty White. Obviously, I'm not the only one. Everyone at the arena, including everyone backstage, wanted to meet her. I knew that I would have to put in some serious work to make sure I did not miss out on this opportunity.

I planted seeds all over the place. I sent a text to my friend Melody from the gym in Arizona. Her mom was the set designer for Betty's show, *Hot in Cleveland*. She mentioned that if I were ever in LA on a Friday when Betty was there, she would try to arrange something. But whenever I was in LA, it was usually for less than a day, and Betty was not around. I let her know that Betty was doing our show that next week, and she told me that she would talk to her mom. I followed up with her throughout the week and again on that very day; I didn't want to drop the ball. She told me that they had a meeting before she came to WWE and that her mom had mentioned me to Betty. This was great! I also asked Ryan at ProWrestlingTees. com if he could make a Betty White-inspired *RAW* T-shirt. They had developed an incredible business. They printed and sold wrestling-related merchandise that gave fans an opportunity to purchase more than just what WWE offered. They started printing merchandise for former WWE wrestlers as well as independent wrestlers. On top of it, they would take great care of the talent, doing all the work, yet giving the talent a cut from all the merchandise they sold. It was great for the company, the talent, and the fans. Ryan designed a Betty White wrestling-inspired shirt for me, and it was awesome. I wore one with my suit and brought an extra as a gift for her.

I saw some people roaming around the building I did not recognize, so I assumed they were her people. Turns out, they were. I introduced myself and told them how much I love Betty. They complimented the shirt, which I couldn't have made any more obvious as I made sure to keep my jacket wide open during our conversation. I gave them one and asked if they could please give it to her. They asked if I would prefer to do so myself if I was able to meet her later on, but I knew that if I did get to meet her, a) there's a good chance I wouldn't have time to grab it from my dressing room, and b) if I left the shirt with them, that might help my chances of getting to meet her if she liked it. I played it cool throughout the day and kept in touch with her people. Time was passing quickly, and it was getting way too close to show time. I knew that if I didn't meet her before the show, she would be long gone by the time I got to the back once TV ended. Fifteen minutes before I walked out into the arena to start the show, I stopped by her dressing room area. Her people told me that she was reading her lines and could not be disturbed at the moment. I thanked them anyway, but couldn't just give up. Without saying it, they made it clear that it wasn't going to happen, and they said that they even had to turn down Stephanie McMahon. I thanked her manager and mentioned that my friend's mom had talked to Betty about me earlier in the day, plus I added that I hoped she liked the T-shirt. I guess one of those was a trigger word. She told me to hold on and walked into the room. She came out shortly after and said, "We can't let anyone in because we have said no to everyone, but we are going to let you in as long as you don't tell anyone until later in the night. Come on."

I walked into Betty's dressing room, and she stood up from the couch. She was just as sweet as she was on TV. I had wondered if she would be the Hollywood type and would leave me disappointed, but she was awesome. She was so thankful for the shirt, and we had a very natural conversation. I gave her a hug, we took a picture, and I was on top of the world. I ran out to the arena and started the show by introducing her. That was a hell of a day. I just couldn't tell anyone how incredible it was until later in the night, as I had promised her people. Once later came, the world knew, and anyone who knew me was definitely happy for me! Follow your dreams...

Back on the road away from all the stars in LA, I had just fallen asleep in my hotel room in Elizabeth, New Jersey, ready for some new dreams. We were doing an east coast house show loop, and I woke up in the middle of the night, literally unable to breathe. I finally started breathing again shortly after, but wondered why that happened. I was traveling with my one of my good friends at the time, Dr. Chris Amann, a WWE physician, but did not want to call his room and wake him. The next morning, I told him what happened. My throat simply closed while I was sleeping, and I couldn't breathe. He suggested I see my ENT doctor when I got home, so I did. The doctor diagnosed me with a "laryngospasm," which meant the vocal cords close and block the air from flowing into your lungs. It can last as long as two minutes, and my doctor told me that mine was caused by pertussis, or whooping cough, and would most likely be around for about two months. This meant that at any point in the next two months, my throat could just close up unexpectedly. If I couldn't start breathing soon enough, I would simply pass out, and then I would be okay once I came to. That wasn't very comforting, nor were the next two months of working a full schedule while having that weighing on my mind. A lot of the times it would hit me right before a show. I would cough or sneeze or anything at all, and my throat would just close up, and I couldn't talk or breathe. It would slowly come back while I made my way to the ring, and I could get a few words out and then breathe, then breathe again, and then speak a little more, always hoping the crowd would cheer to buy me a couple of extra seconds. Luckily, it never caused any major problems in the ring, and nobody really noticed. But every time it happened, it scared the hell out of me.

I was at the gym on one of my off days at home when I got a call from Kevin's right-hand man, his friend John "Big" Gaburick. He said they wanted to offer me a new deal, and it would basically be the same deal as before. I explained that I went from announcing ECW to *SmackDown* and now *RAW* all on that same contract. The deal offered nothing new really, which made me feel pretty bad. I didn't take time off. I worked my tail off, announcing my shows as well as covering other shows while other announcers went on vacations. (I did not get paid extra anytime I covered additional shows.) I announced the ECW TV show, which was typically three matches and then the two-hour *SmackDown* show and now the live two-hour *RAW* show. In addition, I was doing all the little things at shows to help with everything possible. I rang the bell at live events so they didn't have to pay someone else to do it. I took ring gear to the back at house shows when the guys disrobed before a fight, whereas they used to pay someone local to do it. I knew I was an invaluable guy to have at the shows on top of busting my ass to do my actual job. I was still getting the same salary. I was very insulted that they wanted to offer me the same deal that I had been working on for the past two years. Immediately after I signed the last deal, they promoted me to *SmackDown*. That deal I had just accepted as was without asking for any changes.

I asked Big to put the offer in writing and send it over to read through. For the first time, I would use an entertainment lawyer to look over the contract and help me out as an agent, despite the company's dislike for dealing with agents.

Big sent over the contract, and I sent it to my lawyer. I discussed a very slight pay increase that I felt I deserved for doing my job, for doing it well, and most important for being on the road five days a week, every week of the year and for generally giving the company my entire life. I know the presumption is WWE folks get paid top dollar because they're on TV, but that is not the case at all. Since they are the biggest, most well-known wrestling organization, and they know it, they don't have to pay you a certain actor's union (SAG/Aftra) rate; they pay what they choose to pay, and most people still choose to take it because it brings stature and prestige.

On January 31, 2010, I got to the Royal Rumble in Atlanta and was notified that Kevin wanted to see me in the truck. I met him, and he told me to take a walk with him. We went into one of the crew buses, and he told me that he was not happy with me. "You told Big you had a deal. And when he sent the contract, you went to a lawyer and asked for more." I tried to explain that was not the case, but he did not want to hear it.

I asked for two weeks off. I explained that I never had any time off and that I worked every week on every show. Once in a while I just needed to hop off the WWE rollercoaster for a few days. Delayed flights, connections, cancellations, all of the fun that comes with just the travel alone can get to you. This wasn't a job that I could work 9 to 5 and get errands done at night or during lunch. When I was on the road, I was away from the world. On top of that, what most people have no idea about is what I actually did on television nights. My job came off as the easiest in the company by far. While it's not as hard as the wrestlers busting their asses every night, ring announcing on live television for WWE carried its own stress. I would sit in the corner with Mark Yeaton and a floor producer, both of whom are on headsets and hear conversations between Vince, Kevin, and the match producers. When the script changes as we go, I was usually not notified. Many times, Vince would tear up the script right before we went live, and they would rewrite the show as it went along. There was a time that the script said the upcoming match was a six-man tag-team match, but the match sheet said it was a tag-team match accompanied by their managers. I asked the guys on headset what was going on, and they didn't know. As I stood in the ring to get the cue to announce what the match was (and I had no idea what it was), I asked the ref. He didn't know. It got to the point that the ref asked one of the wrestlers as he got in the ring what type of match it was. If I even got a script before we went on the air (as I mentioned earlier, there have been many times when I start the show without one, or even receive one covering just the first hour and await the rest), I know that it's just a rough idea of what might happen. I use it loosely. Most of the changes happened on the fly, and sometimes they were mentioned on headsets. Other times, not so much. Even if the changes were mentioned on the headsets, it was still about 50/50 whether someone with a headset would tell me.

Most of what I did was guessing what my bosses would want. I read the script to get an idea of what might be happening on any given night and then tried to read my bosses' minds to do what I thought was right. They were typically so busy with important issues that they didn't want to be bothered with my questions. If I messed up, it would have been seen as a big deal, but until then, ring announcements were not a priority or even a concern. If I guessed incorrectly, I'd hear about it. If they were okay with an announcement, I wouldn't hear anything.

I was not usually told "good job" or "thank you" or anything like that. I just continued to get a decent paycheck that paid the bills. It wasn't enough to set up a retirement, but it was good. I feel like the last time I got a thank-you was when I was covering *RAW*, *SmackDown*, and ECW all in the same time period. I was also "thanked" when *WrestleMania* was in Phoenix. My family had never been to a *WrestleMania* before to see me, and when the office asked all the talent about family tickets for the skybox and for the after party, I let them know that I needed three for my mom, my sister, and my brother-in-law. I didn't think anything of it. I was the announcer for the show and while I was told early on how good Mania paychecks were, I did not get paid $1 extra to work the biggest event of the year. Plus, my family and I lived in the city it was being held in. Days later I heard back from Sue, who told me that Kevin responded to my request by saying, "You should know better than that." He denied me tickets for my family. Every other talent and even production person had their families, friends, buddies, and whoever they wanted there, but I couldn't have my three family members. Luckily, we pulled some strings and made it happen. (Even better, while Triple H was never high on me, his parents and sister were among the nicest people I have ever met. They allowed my family to join them at ringside.) I shouldn't have been shocked at that point, but the truth is, I still couldn't believe I was treated that way.

I had all this in mind while discussing my new deal. The bottom line was two weeks off in a year is needed. Kevin noted that it was frowned upon, but agreed to it. "Yes. Of course. Everyone needs at least two weeks. We'll give you that, including time off of TV," he said.

"You also say here that you want benefits." We were all independent contractors— the wrestlers, the refs, and I. We were treated as employees, 100% in every way, but considered contractors. I got the same paycheck every two weeks, I was on every show, I was told what to do and when to do it. We had employee rules to follow, mandatory meetings, dress codes. There was nothing remotely contractor-ish about what we did. So, I asked to become an employee with benefits so my insurance and savings would be taken care of.

"Justin, I just can't make you an employee now. In three years when this deal is up, I promise I will make you an employee." That's all I needed to hear. We shook hands, and they made the couple of minor changes to the contract. Kevin told me that any diva could do my job. They might not be as good as me, but they could get the job done. I didn't agree with him, but I understood his subtle threat. I thanked him and signed the new deal. He was right, any diva could. Anybody could. Not everyone would put their heart into it and think about each announcement, but anyone could say names. As I walked out of the truck, I tried to lighten the mood by asking if I could announce that night's Royal Rumble match rules and end with (as I projected my Howard Finkel signature impression), "And now, let us all find out who drew number one!" Kevin laughed, and I walked away feeling good about our conversation and my job.

CHAPTER 15
NOW YOUS CAN'T LEAVE

Throughout the year, we would do various international tours. We would fly to South Africa, China, Japan, Australia, and Portugal. It might be for two shows or four shows, or it might be one of our major European tours each year, both of which are about 11 shows each. We could work live events domestically and then do TV and then head overseas and work the shows. We might possibly work a TV while away and then finish the international shows and go right back to the US for a domestic TV before we came home.

On April 5, 2010, we worked a *Monday Night RAW* TV and then embarked on a journey to Vienna, Austria. Each day, we had a new show. Vienna on the 7th, Newcastle, England, on the 8th, Glasgow, Scotland, next, then Dublin, Ireland, then on to Liverpool and London, then on to Sheffield and Strasbourg, France. Sounds crazy so far, right? It gets better. Not only did *RAW* take place in London, England, on April 12, 2010, but I also became the Divas Champion.

Wait. What?

Before they reverted to a Woman's Championship, Eve Torres won the Divas title that night, and we had been playing a series of Gin card games on the tour bus. We decided that we needed to put something on the line to make this game different and more meaningful than all the rest. I asked her to put her newly won title on the line. I don't remember what I wagered, but it didn't matter because she lost the game, and I was the new Divas Champion! Our ongoing joke was pulling aside the future ladies that won the title and letting them know that it's cool for them to wear the belt, but it was actually mine since I won and never defended it.

The day after the Strasbourg show, our buses took us to the airport to fly to Liévin, France, for that night's show. We sat and waited. And waited. And played more gin with Eve, where I refused to defend my title. We finally got word that the airport was giving our charter's crew a hard time about a part that supposedly wasn't needed but that the airport wanted. It did not seem like the issue was going to get resolved. At the same time, we got word that a volcano had erupted in Iceland. Our producer on this tour was Mike Rotunda (who was my dad's favorite wrestler when I first got into wrestling, as Irwin R. Schyster, or IRS). He broke the news that we might not be able to fly later that night from Liévin, France, to Belfast, Northern Ireland. I'm not sure what he said, but in my head it felt like we would take a bus somewhere to a ferry to another bus, to a skateboard, to a ferry, to a bicycle to roller skates to the arena in Belfast. Great.

Our buses that had dropped us at the airport from the hotel earlier that day came back to get us. We stopped at a McDonald's and got a boatload of food for the two tour buses. We were on our way to Liévin, and it was a good four to five hours for the buses to get us there, so this was going to be close.

With a decent amount of drive time still remaining, the two buses pulled over. Rotunda, William Regal, MVP, Chavo Guerrero, Evan Bourne, and I were led into a minivan so we could speed ahead of the crew. On top of that, a motorcycle cop met us down the way and gave us a police escort to get us to the building even faster.

The show was to start at 8:00 sharp. Our minivan pulled up to a sold-out arena with a hot crowd. We quickly jumped out and got ready. It was about 8:30 when the show actually started. This crowd was excited to see WWE live, and they had no idea that when we began the only people in the backstage area were the first two matches! The four guys put some extra time in and delivered a great opening to the show. To be fair, those guys always delivered. We got word that the buses had arrived, and once the third match was ready, the second match went to their finish. The rest of the show was great, and no one ever had any idea what was actually going on behind the scenes. It was a long, challenging day, but we did it! We got through it. Little did we know that the adventure had not even started yet.

We were drained from that day and walked onto our buses to find the schedule for the next day, which was very typical. This itinerary, however, was not.

We were to leave Liévin on buses at about 10 pm and drive one and a half hours to a ferry departing from Calais, France, to Dover, England. Then we would drive another seven hours to Holyhead, Wales. Then we drove to a hotel in Chester, England, for breakfast. Then we left Holyhead on a 12 pm ferry and arrived at 2 pm in Dublin, Ireland. The we drove three hours to Belfast which got us in at 5 pm, just in time to eat some catering, shower, and work the next show.

The following night we were still in Belfast for show two. This would be the final night of the tour, so we didn't have to worry about flying or traveling to the next stop. We did, however, have to worry about getting back for *RAW* on Monday. There were talks about us traveling to Iceland where the volcano had erupted and attempting to fly out of there. Luckily that wasn't the case.

We kept hearing about plans that the company was looking into to "rescue" us, but once they realized that there was no way to get us back for TV, we stopped hearing about any sort of plan. They used *SmackDown* talent and whoever else was available to cover the show.

We were on standby for a few days and just hung out at the Belfast hotel. Eventually we got the memo we had been waiting for and had another crazy travel day of buses and ferries to meet our charter plane. I guess the plane couldn't fly to us, so we traveled to it. The good news was that we were flying to Newark and would be able to land and catch direct flights home, for the most part, since it was a major airport. That was, until we landed and found out the company had changed the plan to cater to the top guys. They flew us to Hartford where the company jet was waiting to fly Cena, Batista, and a few of the Tampa guys home to Florida. The rest of us would stay overnight in Hartford and take one, two, or maybe even three flights home the next day—just in time to fly out for that week's pay-per-view. We were held up for a bunch of days at the end of an already long tour, but WWE did take care of us. The same way airlines give out drink coupons for an inconvenience, WWE was nice enough to pick up a bar tab one night for some of the guys who were out at the bar as a thank-you for the extra travel and extra days on the road.

Over the years, Lilian, Howard, and even Tony had all been involved in various storylines. From matches to love affairs, they had gotten caught up in various situations. I always enjoyed being the ring announcer—no allies, no enemies, no history with anyone. I was just there to do my job. People around me got beat up, and I just announced it! That could only last so long as I was about to add an element to my history, which would disappear until right around *WrestleMania* 30. On June 7, 2010, I showed up for *RAW* in Miami, Florida. I had no idea that this would turn out to be a night that made history. Throughout the day, I walked around the building and, as usual, had no idea what was happening on the show. I had been told nothing out of the ordinary. Within a half hour of when the doors were about to open, a giant black curtain was hung around the ring that blocked everyone from seeing it. This was only done when top-secret events were going to happen on a show, and they didn't want any word leaking out. Arn Anderson was grabbing talent, mostly the newer guys from the NXT show who were still training in FCW (WWE's newest developmental territory) and bringing them behind the curtain. As I was about to leave, he looked at me and said, "You, too."

Okay? Maybe I needed to see how an ending was going down so that I could make a complicated announcement. I usually didn't like to see how things were going to end because I liked being genuinely surprised so that my reaction would make for a natural, genuine announcement. The NXT guys worked with the producers and referees, and no one was talking to me, so I wasn't sure what was going on or why I was there. I finally overheard Arn say, "You'll get the ring, Cena, and everyone else, and the very last thing you'll get is him." He pointed to me. "He has never been touched, but tonight, even he is not safe. Rip his suit off and take him down. He will be the final victim before we go off the air."

That was it. I didn't ask for any specifics, and I didn't know any specifics. I had an idea that after watching everyone around me at ringside get beat up after all these years I was, as Arn said, no longer safe. Tonight, I wouldn't and couldn't run! I was very happy to participate and do whatever I needed to help. During the main event, while John Cena wrestled against CM Punk, all of a sudden, the NXT guys came down the aisle of the arena looking like a vicious gang. Wade Barrett, Daniel Bryan, Michael Tarver, Darren Young, Heath Slater, Justin Gabriel, and Skip "Ryback" Sheffield approached the ringside barrier.

It was a very intense moment. I knew something big was about to happen to spice up the show, but I didn't know what. The gang immediately jumped in the ring and beat down Cena. Punk left, and they destroyed the ring. I mean, they tore the entire ring apart. The ringside area looked like a war zone. Then they knocked out Mark Yeaton, as well as all of the commentators. I stood there and watched until they grabbed me. They held me as Justin Gabriel knocked me down with a punch. Then they ripped my suit jacket off. Then my shirt. I wore a pink tie that night that knotted up when they pulled on it. As I laid on the ground with my suit pants and just a pink tie, Daniel Bryan did what he thought he was supposed to do: make an impact. He saw an opportunity to get one last shot in on "the last victim." He sat behind me, pulled on my tie, and strangled me. To this day, I still get messages about that night. I've seen pictures, cartoons, and memes that made fun of the "tie violence." I have even seen a double action figure set of Daniel and me made by a fan that looked so real I almost convinced myself that I had an action figure.

The choking was real. For anyone who commented about the face I made or the noise I made or anything else that people claimed to know, that tie was tight around my neck and that was 100% legit. These guys, later known as the Nexus, made their mark and left. The show went off the air with the war zone and its destruction of materials and people strewn about. I was walked to the back by referees, and when I came through the curtain, I started dancing around like *Jackass'* Party Boy with my tie/no shirt combo. Vince immediately reached over to shake my hand, which was really cool but rare. Of course, when you work there, you always want his approval, and it doesn't happen often.

Everybody from Vince down was happy with what took place, and I went to the locker room to get dressed. The Nexus came to the door and shook my hand and apologized as we all exchanged thank-yous, instead. I told them that was great, and I thought it went well, and the bosses seemed to be happy. It made for awesome TV, and everybody was fine, so it was perfect.

Well that didn't last very long. As the week went on, our portion was removed from the highlight package. That Thursday night I was out in Scottsdale, and I got a message that Daniel Bryan was fired. Wow, I thought to myself. I wonder where they're going with this storyline. The next day, word was going around that this wasn't a storyline. I immediately got Bryan's number and gave him a call. I asked him what was going on, and he explained that Vince had called to tell him that he had to let him go. Something about choking not being allowed, and it was out of his hands. This was a typical example of a rule being broken without anybody knowing that it even existed. It wasn't like guys haven't choked each other before, but for some reason this choking incident got Bryan terminated. Bryan was a very talented guy, and I knew he would be okay. Time just needed to pass, and this incident would be forgotten.

The next morning, I began receiving all sorts of hate messages. I heard from fans that I had "told on Bryan" for choking me; that I had gotten him fired because he choked me; and all sorts of crazy assumptions spun by people and their imaginations. The Internet really is a giant forum where people make things up daily and spin these stories that just become the truth because the real truth is kept quiet by the company guys. Anytime I was in the ring to announce, the fans would direct Daniel Bryan chants at me. Fans went from liking me, or at least being indifferent, to instantly hating me. They blamed me for him getting fired! Fans would constantly ask me about the incident and couldn't understand why I would do such a thing. I got choked in a storyline. I didn't fight back. I just laid there and took a beating. Why was I getting blamed?! The Internet can be rough. One person makes up and reports a story, and the world runs with it as fact. It wasn't a fun period because I genuinely felt bad for Bryan, but there was nothing I could say to convince the masses.

Daniel was allowed to work independent shows, and he loved doing so. After TV time on NXT, plus the controversial firing, he was an even bigger name. He came straight off TV and made a ton of money on merchandise. I even heard that he sold neckties at shows. He spent his summer working every week all over the world and making a killing. At the end of the summer, he was brought back to WWE, given a new deal, and returned directly to the main event of *SummerSlam*. From there, he went on to greatness in his WWE career, which, as the talent he is, he deserved. It's safe to say that the firing worked out for him in the long run.

I had done an interview with the local newspaper back in Chicago after all that had passed. I loved being able to tell my story in hopes of inspiring others to follow their dreams. Anyone who knew that I was a fan and had gone on to chase my dream and become the announcer thought that was an amazing story to share, and I was proud of it.

I pitched the story to *WWE* magazine about being a fan that chased his dream to get there. I explained that other media outlets loved the inspirational story and how wrestling fans would probably like to hear that story more than any other demographic out there. I explained everything to the editor of the magazine, but he hesitated. "I think you have something. I just can't put my finger on it." I explained that they have to come up with stories every month, and this is a great story about a kid who loved *WWE* and chased his dream to get here. "Yeah. There's definitely something to this. Maybe a 'how-to' piece," he said.

"What?"

"You know, like how to make something or like when we do weight-training tips, maybe you can do something like that." I told him we are not on the same page. I thanked him anyway. So that never happened.

What did happen was a call from another writer at *WWE* magazine. She explained that they were going to be doing a story on the people who work behind the scenes at the company. Jen from catering, Tom from props, Mark Yeaton in the production office. I just looked at the ceiling. "So let me get this straight, you want to do a story on people who work behind the scenes, and you want to do a story on me as a behind-the-scenes guy? I show up, drink coffee, talk to everyone at the arena, throw on a suit behind the scenes, and then go and do my job right in the center of thousands of people?" "Yes." And they did. My one mention in *WWE* magazine was for the work that I didn't do behind the scenes because I guess that the company viewed me as a behind-the-scenes guy rather than an on-air talent.

In the fall of 2010, Vince's wife, Linda McMahon, ran for senate. Her opponent and the media were starting to attack WWE. They weren't really making up allegations; they were just bringing up facts about WWE and past actions. They held a meeting for the talent and told us about a campaign called "Stand Up for WWE" in which employees (the people at the office who didn't endure the brutal travel but did, however, receive benefits), the talent (brutal travel, no benefits, no insurance, no 401k), and fans could stand up for this wonderful organization. Many of us felt the company wasn't one that took good care of us, but we were happy to have a job. Many employees were let go once they were there too long, but for the folks who were still employed, they were able to speak up for the company. The talent were told they could go into the pre-tapes room where the camera was set up and speak freely, if they would like.

We endured some pretty brutal loops on the weekends. Traveling to a smaller city on the first day meant sometimes leaving the night before and taking two to three flights plus a drive. We had many nights where we had a long drive with an early show the next day or travel that would keep us from getting sleep before having to work again. It wasn't rare on TV days for the higher-ups to fly in on the jet and talk down to the crew that had been touring all week. On top of all that, and despite almost feeling like a ghost at WWE, I knew what the company meant to me as a fan and how the superstars helped my dad when he was sick. I lived for WWE, and despite some of the mental abuse I was taking, I was the first to go in the room and talk on camera. I told my story and told them what WWE meant to me and my family. There were times that I wrote letters to Oprah and Howard Stern and even a blog, defending wrestling, because I really do hope others can understand what it's like versus seeing it as "that fake stuff on TV". Oddly enough, I was one of the only people who took advantage of the pre-tape time. In our next meeting, we were all now required to go in and speak. I guess not enough talent felt like standing up for the company the first time around. I went again, and this time, of course, it was more of a structured interview where we didn't tell our stories; instead we were asked questions. My interview, which was one of the few to come from the heart, by someone who spoke up by choice, was never aired when they played a series of the interviews as part of their campaign.

CHAPTER 16
I'M RIGHT ON TOP OF THAT, ROSE

During a November 2010 tour of Europe, I could no longer deal with a nagging shoulder injury that I had been working through for quite a while. Training in the gym hurt, sleeping hurt, and throwing my suitcase in cars and planes hurt. Every time I raised my arm, the bone would rub against another bone, and it hurt. Even sleeping hurt, and nothing I did in the gym helped. While in Cardiff, Wales, I scheduled an appointment to have shoulder surgery when I knew I had an extra day at home.

I asked the company for permission and assured them I would not take any time off. I flew into Arizona from *RAW* on a Tuesday and went straight to the hospital. They put me under and made an incision to shave down the bone and then scoped the shoulder in a different spot. They numbed it up from the nerve at the very top of my shoulder so I couldn't feel anything from my shoulder to my fingertips. What a weird feeling it was to wear a sling containing an arm that doesn't feel like your own, as I had no feeling in the limb whatsoever. I laid in bed poking at my arm, just waiting for the feeling to come back. I stared at the bottle of pain pills but chose to wait it out instead. By that Saturday, I was still in pain but had to fly to Las Vegas for a live event. I had chosen that week because it was the one week where we did not have a Friday show, which gave me three rather than two days to recover.

I wore the sling during the show that night as well as the next night in Ontario, California. When I got to TV the following day in Louisville, Kentucky, I was still wearing the sling, which the doctor instructed me to do for two weeks. I walked into the building and immediately went to find Kevin Dunn. I waited outside the production meeting as Kevin and Vince both walked out together. "What happened to you?" Vince asked. I told him that I had surgery on Tuesday and would be working with no problem. I just wanted to know if they preferred I wear the sling or not. As I expected, Kevin did not want me to wear the sling, and I did the show, letting my arm hang to the side despite never being on camera that night.

A friend had mentioned that after the conversation I had with Vince and Kevin, the two talked among themselves with Vince saying that he liked how proactive I was. The next thing I knew, Kevin told me that he wanted to talk to me. He didn't tell me if it was good or bad, just that he wanted to talk. The following week I went to meet him in the production truck. He told me that we would talk when he wasn't busy. Week after week I would try to talk to him, and finally I approached him after the *Tribute to the Troops* show in Fort Hood, Texas. The holidays were coming up, and I was paranoid. I wanted to get the conversation out of the way. Kevin barely talked to me outside of discussing the show questions, so I had no idea what to expect. I asked him if I was in trouble or what, and he laughed and told me that it was a good talk and not to worry. I was relieved, but was still anxious to find out what this was all about.

Finally, on January 3, 2011, when we were in Phoenix for *RAW*, I caught Kevin outside the truck. I asked if he was able to talk, and we went for a walk. He told me that he and Vince were very happy with my work. He mentioned that I was proactive and that they liked that. He asked if I wanted to just be a ring announcer for the rest of my life, or if I wanted to grow in the company and start making some real money. He told me that the company needs people like me and asked what else I wanted to do. Talent relations? The creative team? He warned me that creative is rough, but gave me any option that I would want. I thanked him and asked if I could take a couple of days and get back to him.

I was honored that he talked to me and said the things he said. I had never really received much praise, but this job offer was the highest compliment that I could ask for. I thought about it for a long time. I started thinking about the aspects of the company that I really liked and how I could help out in addition to ring announcing. At any company that I worked for, I loved doing anything I could to help them grow and be the very best possible. I wanted to earn my stay there and help in any way I could. If you ever wondered why so much of my social media was pushing WWE, it was because I was trying to help promote everything we did.

I submitted an idea to Kevin: I wanted to be the live event liaison. That position didn't exist, but I thought that it should. Every week there were two live tours. The referees changed; the producers changed; and the wrestlers changed. The only consistent element was that I was the only person at every *RAW* live event (Chimel handled all of the *SmackDown* house shows). I watched each show, each night, each week from start to finish right there with the fans while everyone else caught parts of the show from behind the curtains. I cared about those shows and wanted to fix what was broken. I wanted to make a lot of the little things that I do official. I called Kevin with the idea but could never get him on the phone. I put my idea in writing. I didn't want to choose one department to work in. I wanted to stay where I was and contribute to numerous other departments—marketing, security, fan services, talent relations, creative. I wrote him a thorough email explaining everything. I told him about various things I was doing at the shows and how I would love to make that an official part of my job. Helping with sick and disabled kids that I spotted in the crowd to make their night extra special, promoting merchandise effectively, making the marketing announcements work at live events because the way they were written at the offices didn't translate well. I wanted to make sure that live shows were consistent from week to week. They're written one way, but executed differently each time as different producers came through, and I knew what worked and didn't work. We would start the live events, and the crowd would be fired up, waiting for the opportunity to cheer. But the shows didn't give them that opportunity. We start the show dark and immediately give a quick opening announcement before going right into something that kept them down, cutting their chance to cheer. By the time the first good guy came through the curtain, the crowd wasn't at that same level. It was so minor to most, but I wanted to help get the crowd an opening that flowed.

Reports were turned in by the producers, which would discuss feedback from the shows. The next weekend, the plans were usually copy and pasted exactly same, not taking the feedback into account, which would have made the shows better. There were so many elements that I wanted to fix, and I couldn't wait for this to come into fruition. Sure, I could do and did many of those already, but some higher-ups would question why "the ring announcer" was doing it. If it was part of a job description, I might not have to defend myself or worry about getting heat.

Well, time went by, and I never heard back. I asked him about it when I caught him in the hallway at TV a couple of weeks later in Little Rock, Arkansas, and he told me it can't happen overnight, but that he would eventually get back to me. I never heard about it again or anything else about moving up and doing something to contribute in addition to my current role.

WrestleMania 27 was in Atlanta in April 2011. I was scheduled to announce the entire show myself, which meant that I had all the matches as well as any and every extra ring announcement. In this case, the attendance announcement was of particular concern. I was told that Vince would be getting my verbiage regarding attendance to me at some point during the day, but right before the show started, I had not received anything. I was never even told when to head to the ring, but knew that it would be at any moment. I was informed that Vince wanted to see me. Now I had the common panic of if Vince wanted to talk to me, but Kevin wanted me at the ring, they would not know because of that lack of communication. I was told that Vince was disappointed that I had not brought my own announcement to him for him to approve or modify. I had never been expected to write my own announcements; I was given a script and went off of that. I would pitch changes but was never told to come up with my own announcements, especially when I was told that Vince would be getting me what he wanted me to say.

I understood where he was coming from as far as pitching an announcement outline myself. A lot of times, I wished that I could write my own announcements as I never knew if what was written by the writers could be modified—if they came from a writer who didn't think it through or from Vince himself, meaning it had to be read verbatim, or if I was allowed to alter it. I always wished they would just give me bullet points to hit and let me make the announcements. So many times what I was given was confusing to me and to the audience. In this case, I was told that Vince would be sending me the exact wording for the attendance announcement, so why would I suggest my own? I didn't even have the number or any details. It's not like it was an easy thing to submit my own announcements to him in general. Sometimes he was cool and willing to help. Other times, it was like I was wasting his time, and he didn't care one way or another about what I said. Then other times he would nitpick the exact weight of a wrestler I announced. I couldn't win by asking or not asking. Sometimes he gave me a script that was worded in such a way that only college professors could understand, and I would ask to make it a bit easier for the rest of the world to comprehend.

On the topic of announcements, as I mentioned, a lot of times the marketing department created them for me to read during the live events. There was a huge disconnect between the marketing department (and the "office" overall) and the actual product. Aside from the live event reps who were on the road, I don't think a lot of the people in the office knew our audience or really knew the product. So I took it upon myself to rewrite the announcements to make them more digestible for (and less insulting to) our fans. I enjoyed doing that. I felt like I was looking out for the office and the fans.

In this specific case, at *WrestleMania 27*, I was very anxious to speak with Vince as I had no idea what he wanted out of me, and he was not in a very good mood when we met. He began dictating the announcement to me quickly, much faster than I could write. Midway through it, while I was writing, he asked me to read it back to him. It seemed to me that Vince respected those who were not intimidated by him but at the same time enjoyed making people uncomfortable in his presence. I tried to read my chicken scratch as best as I could, and then he continued. When he was done, he told me to read it back to him. We had always been serious in our conversations; I had never once made a joke to Vince. But this was *WrestleMania*, and I was announcing the whole show. As the day went on, and as we worked on this announcement, I kept hearing in the back of my head Howard Finkel's voice doing his signature *WrestleMania* attendance announcement. I read the lines back to Vince. When I got to the attendance number, I decided to do it in Howard's dramatic voice (how I always heard the attendance announcements in the past). It worked once to make Kevin laugh. He gave me a disgusted look, which, at that point, was something I had gotten used to. "What was that?" he asked. I apologized and told him that was my inner Howard Finkel coming out. He was not amused. That was uncomfortable at the time, but looking back, an amazing moment. He approved the announcement as the disclaimer was playing in the arena, which meant that I should have snuck out to the ring by then. When I said there was a lack of communication, I wasn't kidding. Most pay-per-view events gave no direction as far as what I would be saying when cued to talk during the welcoming announcements. Sometimes I would be in the ring waiting and just never given a cue to talk. That actually happened a lot during the matches, too, when Kevin wouldn't call for the bell, and I would just be standing in the ring with a look of fear on my face thinking, "Do I get out now before the guy gets to the ring, or do I wait because he's eventually getting in an introduction?" Feel free to look back at *Survivor Series* with Miz and Truth versus Rock and Cena. I never got a bell to give me "permission" to announce the match, so it was never announced! That happened a lot on *RAW*. I would look over at Yeaton, and he knew the look and would try to ask Kevin on the headset if he should ring the bell. Kevin would sometimes respond with a "yes" or just ignore him.

On this night, I asked the floor producer what I was supposed to say when I welcomed the crowd and asked if I should mention the pre-show match or if that would be a separate announcement minutes later if Kevin was going to be playing a video to the arena. I was told it would be a welcome announcement and go straight into the first match, which was Sheamus and Daniel Bryan in a lumberjack match for the US championship. I welcomed the huge crowd of over 70,000 people and went straight into the US title match announcement. At the end of the announcement, nothing happened. I stood in the ring, confused and alone. No music, no wrestlers coming to the ring, and no idea what to say when the bell rang right after. The bell rang, which meant that was the cue to make a match announcement. The only problem was, I already had, and there were cameras there to catch it as well as over 70,000 people. So, not being able to ask Kevin or anyone else about what to do, I went with the flow and made the same announcement again. I can't stress enough how uncomfortable I was at every event because of the lack of communication. Part of that was due to all the plans being so disorganized. The other part, it seemed, was Vince and Kevin enjoying giving a lack of direction and watching their own reality show of who would sink or swim. Rather than type all of that out in the script the week leading up to the event, everything would just come together as the event started. WWE always ripped on how disorganized WCW was toward the end, but I don't think they realized that it wasn't much different there.

The show went well, and I was having fun. You could hear the enthusiasm in my voice. I took that ball, and I was running with it. They started to shoot me on camera a lot less and chose to shoot the crowd for long periods of time during long announcements which meant I would still be heard but unseen for the most part. I mentioned being somewhat of a ghost at WWE, and this was part of that.

I was at all the events, and you heard me but wouldn't see me or know who was making the announcements.

For the most part, I would try to avoid running into Vince unless we had to talk, like before *WrestleMania 27*. In general, I tried to keep a safe distance from him. If you have a discussion with him that goes back and forth more than twice, there's a good chance he will get frustrated, impatient, and angry. I'd make a point, see how he took it, and then back off. It's amazing that with everything on his plate he still listened to every word, every hometown, and every weight in my ring announcements. Sometimes he would ask Mark Yeaton to ask me to repeat a weight for him, and then he would question why I used a certain weight, even if it was something that I had been doing weekly for a number of years.

I always loved listening to him as a commentator. When I first began in WWE, my announcing was inspired by Vince. The growl, the over-the-top announcements, the "welcome everyone to (insert city), welcome everyone to (arena), welcome everyone to (insert show name)!"

I loved when he called a match that featured an enhancement talent taking on an established or about to be established superstar. Vince made that enhancement talent sound like a million bucks, so when the opponent defeated him, it made the win much more meaningful, which helped to make the winner an even bigger star. Every announcement he made was over the top, and I always felt like his announcing really helped the superstar seem larger than life.

I subconsciously took note of that and applied it to my announcing. On some of the shows he did commentary for, he went over the top for every performer. When I started announcing ECW, I assumed that they wanted the WWE version of ECW to be similar to the real ECW. I mean, they did bring in all the former ECW talent at the beginning. I watched ECW, so I knew how those performers were introduced, and I tried to up my style. I went from being the *SmackDown* back-up guy to being what Kevin Dunn called the "face of ECW." I gave everyone big introductions. Even that early on, I was eventually told to tone it down by Vince. It was "too over the top" he told me. I refrained from asking him how Vince the announcer would have introduced them. Anyway, I toned it down. He said it was still too much, so then I really toned it down. As I wrote earlier, this would become an on-going challenge.

During my ECW years, I would go to town on the "extreme rules" and Sabu announcements. In the *SmackDown* years, I would accentuate the introduction of the widely popular Jeff Hardy, Batista, and Undertaker—later on at *RAW* it would be John Cena and Brock Lesnar—until I was told to bring those down as well. They actually removed me from the ring to do introductions from the outside for Brock and Triple H at *SummerSlam* after Vince said my announcement was too big in rehearsal.

WWE was known at one time for the gimmicky characters and one of the biggest ever (both in front of and behind the camera) was Vince McMahon. This man was a very interesting character. The guy who created *WrestleMania* and turned his family business into a global empire does not believe in sneezing. Sneezing, according to Vince, is a sign of weakness. Early on in my WWE run, when I had bronchitis and my voice kept cracking at a *SmackDown* TV taping in Columbus, Ohio, Vince told me to just let them know if I'm sick. I assumed he was sincere about that. I once had a high fever at a *SmackDown* taping in Canada and told him before the show started. His response was: "There's no such thing as being sick." Vince tore his quadriceps muscles on both legs by walking to the ring on a live pay-per-view, didn't sell it, and walked to the back afterward. Since he did not believe in showing weakness, the soldiers working for him couldn't either. If he could get through an entire live PPV segment with both legs torn to shreds, then there was no way a puny little ring announcer could "call in" sick. Prior to Canada, I had a Sunday pay-per-view in Chicago to announce. I had a high fever and could barely board my flight to Chicago. Fortunately, I only had a match or two to announce and then I was able to check into a hotel and sleep until Tuesday when I had to be at TV again before then leaving the next day for a two-week European tour. While at the hotel that night, I received word from the office that Lilian's band would be performing in Grand Rapids, Michigan, the next day, and they wanted me to introduce her. I explained how sick I was, but Kevin insisted that I should be in Grand Rapids. So, the next morning, I got in the car and drove an hour. I pulled over to sleep on the side of the road, drove a little more, slept a little more, and eventually made it there. Kevin thanked me, and we practiced my introducing her band from the stage. No problem. But because Lilian would be performing as a singer on this night, she did not want to have to be a ring announcer. So, I had to announce the show and then announce her on my one day to rest before my TV show and then two-week tour. I got the cue to announce her, and I just froze. I couldn't think straight and had no idea what the lines were. I made it up, and no one noticed. John Laurinaitis called me into the office because he knew how sick I was. He saved me. He called Howard to work the tour and sent me home to actually get some rest while they went overseas. I feel like I have talked a lot about being sick in this book. The problem is, we were on the road every week and did not have time to be sick; we did not have time to let our bodies break down from the constant travel and shows. There's no such thing as being sick, though…

There was a night in New Orleans when I thought I was getting fired. We were doing the *Hell in a Cell* pay-per-view. The script did not come out until I was heading to the ring to start the show. I looked through, and there was one part that wasn't clear. Since most of the material I was given wasn't specific and was completely and likely subject to change, I often didn't know what I was supposed to do, even as the show started. In this case, I wasn't sure if there was an introduction for Alberto Del Rio's personal ring announcer or how that was going to play out. A writer came down to ringside early in the night, and I asked him to please find out for me whether I was to announce him.

During the battle of the two Sin Cara's in the ring, Yeaton handed me his headset. Vince was in a mood. He berated me over headset (which means that everyone on production headsets could listen in), and he asked if I knew how to do my job. When I started to respond, he angrily asked if I knew what I was doing. I obviously knew how to do my job, but I didn't know what was going on for that Del Rio introduction, so I said "no," simply because I did not know how to do my job…for that match. That got an "oh, wow!" reaction from everyone listening in on the conversation. "Well if you don't know how to do your job, then maybe we better find someone who does." I put down the headset and went back to my seat. I still had no idea how that segment was going to play out, and now I wasn't sure if I still had a job!

I saw Kevin Dunn after the show, and he asked me what the hell happened. I explained and asked if I should talk to Vince. He said that he would and that it would be fine. My guess is that he never said anything, and it just blew over.

It never ended, but I still had a job. I was working the *Payback* pay-per-view event in June of 2013 when I was given a long, long announcement with the rules for an ambulance match between John Cena and Ryback. When I received the sheets at ringside (just as the show is going live), it was hard to ask questions for direction. I had a way to simplify the announcement and shorten the announcement (which the bosses usually prefer), so I called and texted the producer of the match, John Laurinaitis. I got a text back from him saying the wording came straight from Vince and to announce it as written. So I memorized the whole announcement, which was about a minute long. Mark Yeaton read along on that piece of paper as I made the announcement in the ring. I got back to my seat, and he told me that it was perfect, word for word. Then I got the dreaded uh-oh sign: Mark holding his headphones to hear what someone important was saying to him. It was either Vince or Kevin, and whoever it was, was angry and questioned why I mentioned something about ladders being set up at ringside. I pointed to the piece of paper from Vince and said, "Because it says that right here!"

Every night I would go out and do the best possible job with little, or, more likely, no direction. I had to read my bosses' minds since I usually didn't communicate with them. For the most part, I usually guessed correctly. There were many times when everything would be fine, but policies, names, rules, or minor details would magically change overnight. I was never told about the changes until I violated some new rule I didn't know existed.

In this instance, regarding the ambulance match, I decided to cover myself for once rather than play dumb. I wasn't dumb, so why continue appearing that way… oh yeah, because that's what they wanted, and it would have prevented this…

I took a picture of the script from Vince to explain why I said what I said. I emailed the picture to Vince and Kevin. Before this, the only time I ever emailed Vince was a couple of times on his birthday. The next day at *RAW* I was called into the production truck. Kevin told me not to ever email Vince again. "He is the chairman of a publicly traded company. You are a ring announcer."

Shortly after, *RAW* was about to go live, and I got the script. It was very unclear, and there was an unusually high number of variables left up in the air. The specific announcement I'm referring to was about a Battle Royal for the US championship. The script didn't include anything about the guys who were already in the ring or who were going to be coming to the ring shortly. I asked one of the PAs on headset to ask Kevin if I should announce any of them, and he relayed from Kevin to do what was on the sheet. So I did. On live TV. Then Mark and the same guy were yelling for me to introduce the guys in the ring, so I did, even though that wasn't on the sheet. When I got back to my seat I asked what happened. They told me Kevin wanted to see me in the truck the next day (I wasn't there on Tuesdays). When I asked what the issue was, they told me that Kevin had told me to do what was on the sheet, and that's what I did. Winning was never an option; failing was typically preferred.

The bottom line was that the bosses were always right. That was frustrating when you do everything in your power to do the best job possible, and you would still get in trouble for doing what you're told to do because someone suddenly changes his mind. Everything had to be memorized (even though they weren't showing me on TV at this point, so notes wouldn't have been a big deal, really).

Please, enter the mind of a ring announcer: You have to look left at the timekeeper in case he's trying to tell you something, but also straight toward the cameras in case they decide to shoot you, but not into the cameras, because Vince didn't like that (we weren't supposed to know the cameras were there). You also have to look to the right at the entranceway to see if anyone is coming out because that can be a cue in itself, but also back left at the timekeeper in case he's trying to cue you to say something about that person coming out or anything else. In addition to all that, you have to memorize what could, at times, be very lengthy announcements with long explanations, rules, and introductions. Sound stressful? It was.

The job would have been so much easier with an IFB. An IFB is a small intercom that fits in the ear. It allows producers to give cues through an earpiece. That way your boss could give you messages directly instead of relaying things from sound guys or timekeepers or camera people or whoever else. Kevin once demanded that I use the IFB (I was given one for the non-televised shows) after the floor director kept feeding me wrong messages at ringside during commercial breaks. I was relieved and knew most of the stress would be taken out of my job since I wouldn't have to read Kevin's mind; he could now tell me exactly what he wanted and when he wanted it! I was finally looking forward to working TV and being comfortable out there!

Well, it was a rib…just a big joke on me. For about three months I wore it, and for about three months, I never once heard Kevin speak into it. I would test it out with the audio guys to make sure it was working before I went to the ring, but Kevin still chose to tell the timekeeper and floor producer to cue me. *RAW* used to be a half hour of tapings for other shows followed by two hours of TV. But when *RAW* increased to three hours and you factor in all the other shows they were taping for the *WWE Network*, it just got to be too much for them. It was too much of a demand to organize everything. If we were lucky, we would get a script before we went live. It was usually incomplete. As the show went on, we would get more and more scripts, revised even as the show was happening. That was usually due to Vince changing his mind late in the day and completely rewriting the shows. All of these different factors made my job challenging. I didn't get beat up in the ring like the wrestlers did, but after all the travel and chaotic shows I went through, by the time it was TV day, I felt like I had been.

PART IV

26/09 WWE Backlash Live on Pay-Per-View – Providence, RI   4/24/09 WWE SmackDown/ECW
mackDown/ECW Live – Birmingham, England   4/21/09 WWE SmackDown and ECW TV – Lor
ve – Vienna, Austria   4/18/09 WWE SmackDown/ECW Live – Salzburg, Austria   4/17/09 WWE
14/09 WWE SmackDown TV Taping – Knoxville, TN   4/13/09 WWE Monday Night RAW – Atl
r-View – Houston, TX   4/4/09 WWE Hall of Fame Ceremony – Houston, TX   4/2/09 WWE Fan
lls, TX   3/28/09 WWE SmackDown Live – Amarillo, TX   3/22/09 WWE SmackDown Live –
nackDown TV Taping – Corpus Christi, TX   3/15/09 WWE SmackDown Live – Waco, TX   3
8/09 WWE SmackDown Live – Columbia, SC   3/7/09 WWE SmackDown Live – Augusta, GA
27/09 WWE SmackDown Live – Cornwall, Ontario   2/23/09 WWE Monday Night RAW – Nash
Seattle, WA   2/10/09 WWE SmackDown TV Taping – Fresno, CA   2/8/09 WWE SmackDown
ennewick, WA   2/2/09 WWE SmackDown Live – Tupelo, MS   2/1/09 WWE SmackDown Live
ndianapolis, IN   1/25/09 WWE Royal Rumble Pay-Per-View – Detroit, MI   1/19/09 WWE Sma
ve – Charleston, WV   1/13/09 WWE SmackDown TV Taping – Omaha, NE   1/12/09 WWE
nackDown Live – Poplar Bluff, MO   1/9/09 WWE SmackDown Live – Hot Springs, AR   1/5/0
WE SmackDown Live – Tyler, TX   12/30/08 WWE SmackDown TV Taping – East Rutherford,
/27/08 WWE SmackDown Live – Greensboro, NC   12/26/08 WWE SmackDown Live – Charle
WE SmackDown TV Taping – Baltimore, MD   12/14/08 WWE Armageddon Pay-Per-View – Bu
V Taping – Bridgeport, CT   12/7/08 WWE SmackDown/ECW Live – North Charleston, SC   12
C   11/30/08 WWE SmackDown/ECW Live – Johnstown, PA   11/29/08 WWE SmackDown/ECW
ries Pay-Per-View – Boston, MA   11/16//08 WWE SmackDown Live – Dortmund, Germany
urembourg, Germany   11/13/08 WWE SmackDown/ECW Live – Zurich, Switzerland   11/12/08 W
ngland   11/10/08 WWE SmackDown/ECW Live – London, England   11/9/08 WWE SmackDo
nackDown/ECW Live – Brussels, Belgium   11/6/08 WWE SmackDown/ECW Live – Nice, Franc
ping – San Diego, CA   10/26/08 WWE Cyber Sunday Pay-Per-View – Phoenix, AZ   10/25/08 T
X   10/20/08 WWE SmackDown/ECW Live – Hidalgo, TX   10/19/08 WWE SmackDown/ECV
nackDown/ECW Live – Aguascalientes, MX   10/16/08 WWE SmackDown/ECW Live – Monter
Spokane, WA   10/5/08 WWE No Mercy Live Pay-Per-View Portland, OR   9/30/08 WWE Smac
WE SmackDown/ECW Live – Munich, Germany   9/26/08 WWE SmackDown/ECW Live – Bowling G
              Portugal   9/22/08 WWE SmackDown/ECW

OK, YOU CAN WAKE ME UP NOW...

eneva, Switzerland   4/23/09 WWE SmackDown/ECW Live – Glasgow, Scotland   4/22/09 WW
nd   4/20/09 WWE SmackDown/ECW Live – Cardiff, Wales   4/19/09 WWE SmackDown/ECW
wn/ECW Live – Strasbourg, France   4/16/09 WWE SmackDown/ECW Live – Cologne, German
4/7/09 WWE SmackDown TV Taping – Austin, TX   4/5/09 WWE WrestleMania 25 Live on Pay
ouston, TX   3/30/09 WWE Supershow – Dallas, TX   3/29/09 WWE SmackDown Live – Wichita
ns, MO   3/21/09 Little Rock, AR – WWE SmackDown Live – Little Rock, AR   3/17/09 WWE
VE SmackDown Live – Beaumont, TX   3/13/09 WWE SmackDown Live – College Station, TX
WE SmackDown TV Taping – Uncasville, CT   3/1/09 WWE SmackDown Live – Glen Falls, NY
2/17/09 WWE SmackDown TV Taping – Portland, OR   2/15/09 WWE No Way Out Pay-Per-View
ersfield, CA   2/7/09 WWE SmackDown Live – Yakima, WA   2/6/09 WWE SmackDown TV Taping
le, AL   1/31/09 WWE SmackDown Live – Dothan, AL   1/27/09 WWE SmackDown TV Taping
ve – Muncie, IN   1/18/09 WWE SmackDown Live – Lexington KY   1/17/09 WWE SmackDown
vn Live – St Joseph, MO   1/11/09 WWE SmackDown Live – Springfield, MO   1/10/09 WWE
mackDown Live – Alexandria, LA   1/4/09 WWE SmackDown Live – Bossier City, LA   1/3/09
/08 WWE SmackDown Live – Richmond, VA   12/28/08 WWE SmackDown Live – Raleigh, NC
2/22/08 WWE Monday Night RAW Live and SmackDown Taping – Toronto, Ontario   12/16/08
12/13/08 WWE RAW SmackDown/ECW Live – Hamilton, Ontario   12/9/08 WWE SmackDown
E SmackDown/ECW Live – Florence, SC   12/5/08 WWE SmackDown/ECW Live – Greenville
te College, PA   11/25/08 WWE SmackDown TV Taping – Albany, NY   11/23/08 WWE Survivor
WWE SmackDown/ECW Live – Berlin, Germany   11/14/08 WWE SmackDown/ECW Live –
kDown/ECW Live – Nottingham, England   11/11/08 WWE SmackDown TV Taping – Manchester
Live – Cardiff, Wales   11/8/08 WWE SmackDown/ECW Live – Luxembourg   11/7/08 WWE
ECW Live and WWE SmackDown TV Taping – Orlando, FL   10/28/08 WWE SmackDown TV
down charity wrestling event – Chandler, AZ   10/21/08 WWE SmackDown TV Taping – Laredo
exico City, MX   10/18/08 WWE SmackDown/ECW Live – Mexico City, MX   10/17/08 WWE
0/14/08 WWE SmackDown TV Taping – Las Vegas, NV   10/7/08 WWE SmackDown TV Taping
Taping – Green Bay, WI   9/29/08 WWE SmackDown/ECW Live – Stevens Point, WI   9/27/08
stria   9/25/08 WWE SmackDown/ECW Live – Barcelona, Spain   9/24/08 WWE SmackDown
/08 WWE SmackDown TV Taping – Columbus, OH   9/16/08 WWE SmackDown TV Taping –
gomery, AL   9/14/08 WWE SmackDown/ECW Live – Jackson, MS   9/13/08 WWE SmackDown
9/9/08 WWE SmackDown TV Taping – Milwaukee, WI   9/7/08 WWE Unforgiven Live Pay-
Cleveland, OH   8/31/08 WWE SmackDown TV Taping – St. Louis, MO
kDown/ECW Live – Jonesboro

CHAPTER 17
THE BEST THERE IS, THE BEST THERE WAS

The *WWE Network*, had been talked about for a good while. The talent would constantly be asked to sit down and do interviews for network content. We were never asked or told about pay while we did these. After their own network became official and available, talent would no longer be making their bonuses off pay-per-view buys. During one talent meeting, Triple H told the talent (when asked) that buy rates would be averaged from over the years, and talent would be paid based off that. At the same time, the current and former talent who were all over the network, as WWE's library of past shows were available to subscribers, were never paid royalties for usage of that content. Even if the talent didn't agree with how the network was rolling out without the pay being addressed, when we were asked to do interviews. I knew that the network would be a game-changer in both scheduling as well as affect an already demanding schedule.

The idea of announcing TV once a week like Lilian had done started to sound like an appealing idea. I wouldn't have to worry about travel on Friday, Saturday, and Sunday, plus the shows on top of that. I could fly in, announce one show, and fly home. Obviously, I had some venting to do, and being on the road all those days gave me too much time to vent. With that schedule, you weren't really "on the road." The idea was really growing on me, but for some reason, I didn't think that would fly with management.

While the storylines could get stale from week to week, things really heated up at TVs in August 2011 when CM Punk's contract was about to expire. He had become a very big star in WWE and would be taking on John Cena for the WWE Championship on what could have been his last night in the company. On top of that, the match would take place in his hometown of Chicago. The atmosphere in that building is indescribable, but when you factor in the storyline and CM Punk's entrance, it was brought to even a whole new level. The morning of the show, I headed to the gym in the neighborhood where I grew up. On my way out of the hotel, I opened Twitter and noticed a tweet in which Smashing Pumpkins singer Billy Corgan had made a comment about how he was looking forward to the match later that night. Corgan was from Chicago and a friend of Punk's, but most important, he was a big wrestling fan. His tweet also mentioned that he had hoped a match of that caliber would have been announced by Howard Finkel. Now, I get where he was coming from. He's an old-school wrestling fan, as am I. We grew up on Howard, and that's what we were programmed to hear. I never let it bother me when people told me they preferred Howard over me. Everyone has their own preferences, and some people liked my style, some disliked it, and many were indifferent. I'm glad that people have their favorites. I have not and will never claim to be the best ring announcer; I am just happy to be one of the options to choose from in the history of WWE. In this case, Billy was going to have me as the announcer that night, but that did not mean he wouldn't hear Howard announce the match.

Right before the show started, I walked into catering and noticed Corgan sitting down at a table. I walked up behind him and covered his eyes. I don't think that happens very often at WWE catering, especially to a rock star. Without any hesitation, I did my Finkel impression (based on his announcing and slightly exaggerated as most impressions are) and announced the entire John Cena/CM Punk/WWE Championship ring introductions just as I would be doing later that night in my own voice. You can't make every single fan happy, but I definitely tried. I don't think Corgan was impressed or amused, but I felt I had delivered. I left catering and headed out to the ring. Standing in the center of the Rosemont Horizon, I mean, Allstate Arena for the main event was incredible, even more so than I had expected. The crowd was so loud for Punk's entrance. I loved being in there for moments like that.

The same went for standing in the ring in January 2010 when Bret "Hitman" Hart returned to *RAW*. The crowd was hot, and again I was able to introduce the Hitman's return. I almost felt what those in the popular Attitude Era felt. Part of the appeal with the still popular Attitude Era was that stars were built up and the audience was allowed to care about the characters. The company got behind the guys who were getting reaction, and they let them run with it. Nowadays, those reactions were rare, as most characters getting a reaction were told to stop doing whatever got them those reactions or just pulled from television completely. I couldn't understand why the company was trying to take the thunder out of guys who were finding ways to get over.

The return of Bret Hart to WWE was rare in itself. He had left WWF for WCW in a controversial manner years prior. Vince McMahon walked to the ring and had the referee call for the bell while Bret was in a submission move but before he actually tapped out to give up. Shortly after, his brother Owen tragically died in the ring during a WWF pay-per-view when a stunt where he was to propel from the ceiling went wrong, and he fell instead. There had been a lot of animosity, but he had accepted a WWE Hall of Fame induction and now had returned to *RAW*. I didn't know Bret at all, and this would be his first night back, but I had to invite my friend Craig from the cruise, who swam in his Bret Hart T-shirt and idolized him. People can claim to be the number one fan of whoever all they want, but Craig was truly the Hitman's number one fan.

When Bret's return was made public for Dayton, Ohio, I immediately called Craig and invited him out. I owed him from the first time we met as kids, waiting for Bret in the cruise ship theater, and I knew that. This time, Bret really would be there. Craig and his brother drove from Chicago to see Bret's incredible return, and when the show ended, I introduced myself to Bret and asked if he wouldn't mind meeting Craig. Bret was very cool and had no problem with it. The two met, and Craig was on top of the world.

Bret had never seen Craig's Bret Hart hat, and he liked it. Craig immediately gave it to him. The moment was so surreal for Craig—to actually meet his idol. His hero was everything he hoped for and more. I think I redeemed my dad and me from our original meeting. In an ironic turn of events, Bret had been coming to shows once in a while, and he happened to be at a show right before I would be going with my family on a cruise around Hawaii. He told me that he was heading to Hawaii that week, and I mentioned I was doing the same. He told me that if I would be in Kona to call him and gave me his number. Sure enough, one of the stops was Kona, and I gave him a call. I left the ship and headed over to the restaurant where he was at to watch a hockey game with him and his lovely wife, Stephanie.

As we sat on the patio of this restaurant, I just kept looking at the cruise ship in the distance. It was unreal, thinking about the cruise story with Craig and Bret supposedly getting on the ship. He wasn't my cousin nor did I even know him in high school, but now Bret was two miles from my cruise ship, and we were sitting at a restaurant together, catching up. I had to tell him the story about Craig and the irony behind everything. "Hey, remember that kid I introduced you to in Dayton…" As soon as I got back on the ship, I immediately called Craig to tell him. Craig appreciated the story but had something to tell me. He had been diagnosed with testicular cancer. I knew how down he was and called in a favor from Bret. Bret took Craig's number and gave him a call to check in and wish him well. I'm happy to say that Craig is doing well and idolizes his hero even more these days—and rightfully so.

CHAPTER 18
ARE YOU EXPERIENCED?

Having the ability to use the influence of my job to help people was amazing. I just needed a silver lining in my actual job to make things better at work. In October 2011, I thought my opportunity had arrived. A job listing was posted online. The title was Live Event Producer. This was amazing. This had a lot of similarities to the position I had pitched to Kevin. It was a show producer for the overall show, not like the current producer position held by former wrestlers that put together matches and finishes with the wrestlers based on what Vince and creative wanted. This person oversaw the entire production. These shows take you through an emotional up-and-down rollercoaster. They run on psychology. It's not something that can be taught; it's something you learn to feel over many, many years. I had been at every live show every weekend for all of these years, and I knew I was perfect for the job. I had been pitching ideas every week at all the live events when the office would send out a script with lots of holes. I'd discuss the idea with the production manager and producer or agent in the meeting, and 8 out of 10 times they would agree, and we would make the small but significant changes. When John Laurinaitis was booking the live events, he would ask me for feedback since he wasn't there to see the execution, and I would always give him my opinions. It was cool that he cared and just as cool that he considered my input. Now I wouldn't be "just a ring announcer" making suggestions each show, I could be the Live Event Producer and make all the wrongs right in order for every single WWE live event be the consistently amazing and the best experience a fan will ever have. I was a fan and saw the show as a fan. I knew when the crowd was getting a quality show versus a poorly thought-out show production wise. My job was simply to show up and announce. That's what I was there to do, but I couldn't just do that. I had way too much passion and couldn't let mistakes written by guys who weren't there to see it hurt the show. I wanted to help with production so the fans got the very best show possible. I wanted to announce, but I wanted to love the product I was announcing so the fans would as well.

I walked into Kevin's truck at TV and handed him the job printout. I confidently told him that the company did not have to look any further. The guy for the job was right there. He read the description and told me he would get that to HR and make sure that I got a shot.

Shortly after, HR gave me a call. They asked me to tell them about myself. After two minutes into the call, I had to ask if she knew that I already worked for the company. Surprisingly, she claimed that she knew. She told me about the schedule and asked if I would be okay with that. She told me the proposed salary and that my expenses would be covered on top of that. I explained that the company already covered my expenses, so they would be saving a great deal of money. On top of it, I told her that I only wanted one-third of the salary. Just add one-third to what I was currently making as a ring announcer. Man, this was perfect. She continued to tell me I would work Friday through Sunday, and they would fly me home on Monday. I explained that I would just drive to TV from the Sunday show and fly home after that. I really don't think she understood that I worked there or what I did, despite explaining it at least twice. She ended the call by telling me that I would be speaking with a gentleman by the name of Duncan Leslie.

While I knew most people that worked at TV, I had never talked business with Duncan before. He was just someone I said hello to when I saw him in passing. As you know, I don't sit back and wait for anyone, so I hung up with her and immediately went to find Duncan. We talked for a while, and I explained why I was perfect for the job. I started explaining all the elements of live events and what I wanted to help with. The problem was, this was all foreign to Duncan. Duncan is a technical guy. He knows things like the staging sizes and the equipment needed at live events. He doesn't attend the live events, nor does he understand the psychology of taking the fans on a nearly three-hour journey that's based on our TV shows. He also doesn't understand that unlike the continuing television variety show we did week to week, a live show has a very distinct beginning, middle, and end. He asked me to write him an essay on why I would be good for the job, detailing what I've done, what I'm doing now, and what I would do if offered the position.

I went on an overseas tour right after that conversation and used my downtime to sit and write a four-page essay explaining my background. I listed everything I had done up to that point, my experience, what I wanted to do with their new concept of bringing in video screens as part of the live events, and anything else pertinent I could think to write. I was very happy with what I submitted. I was confident. If there's one thing I knew better than anything else, it's the wrestling business. I lived it every day as a fan and still continued to do so as well as someone in the business who was at wrestling shows 52 weeks a year. As I've stated, I was the only person from the show that sat and watched the entire production from start to finish from ringside, seeing everything that the fans saw.

I heard that Stephanie McMahon had some involvement with the position, so when we were in New York City at Madison Square Garden, I asked if she had a minute. I explained that I loved my job and treated her company as my own. When my father passed away, I had the opportunity to continue the family business but chose to move on to my dream career at WWE, her family business. She asked about my experience, and I explained how I had been announcing since age 16. I had been at ringside for WWE live events every weekend for years, and for a position running WWE live events, I thought that was the best experience to have. She asked what outside experience I had, and I told her that I had been to sporting events and seen numerous concert and productions and had a great understanding of what a live event experience should be, especially a WWE live event experience. I also explained that I ran an independent organization prior to working at WWE full time. She told me that this position did not fall under her but that she would talk to Duncan.

On November 28, 2011, we did a *RAW* TV in Columbia, South Carolina. I flew early that morning from Phoenix to Charlotte and then drove from Charlotte to Columbia. After the show, we had a charter flight take us to New York City. Once there, we had a couple of hours in a hotel before we headed back to the airport for a 14-hour flight from JFK to Narita, Japan. After landing in Narita, we took a three-hour bus ride to the arena in Yokohama. After a couple hours of sitting around, we worked a show and then took a bus an hour and a half to a hotel in Tokyo. That was kind of a long day.

The next day we took a bus back to Yokohama (maybe they don't have hotels any closer?), worked another show, drove an hour and a half back to Tokyo, spent the night there, and then took a two-hour drive back to the Narita airport to catch a flight back to Los Angeles to catch a flight to Miami for a show the next night in Fort Lauderdale. If you lost track, and I don't blame you if you did, that was all from Monday to Friday, and I went from the west coast to the east coast, west to Japan, east to the west coast, and then back to the east coast, nonstop travel and shows. Insane travel was actually very common for us. The folks booking these tours did not have to live them out, so they could not possibly understand how grueling it was. The only reason I gave the specifics here is so you could try to imagine how tired and mentally exhausted I was by that Friday night after finally landing in Miami. A group of us had planned to take advantage of being in Miami on a Friday night and make the most of it before Saturday's show. I was looking forward to this and wasn't going to even think about the past few days of what I'd done or where I'd been.

I got to my hotel room in Miami, and around 8:00 pm, I was getting ready to go out. My phone rang. It was "Big," who had been handling the commentators and ring announcers. He called to tell me that Lilian had been rehired, and she would be coming back to ring announce. He told me that she would be announcing *SmackDown*, and I would be staying on *RAW*. I didn't know if that was temporary or if it was the long-term plan. I had always known that the company didn't place much stake in a ring announcer. As much as I overanalyzed every little thing I said and did, I felt the company just wanted someone who would get the job done, preferably an attractive female. Lilian had previously left to pursue her music career, and when that did not take off like she wanted it to, she returned to get a spot in the WWE. I just hoped as the guy who never left and worked every TV, non-televised event, and overseas tour, that my passion would shine through and keep me on *RAW*.

Over the years, Lilian was always the one that you saw on TV and a part of storylines, so fans knew her as the ring announcer. When it came to all the other shows, non-televised events, and most of overseas tours, she was not there. That's because that is not what she wanted to do full time. That isn't a shot at her; it's just the truth. I'm sure she had no problem admitting that, either. Her passion was her singing career; mine was wrestling. At *WrestleMania* that year, she was happy when she approached me to tell me that she would be singing "America, the Beautiful" and that I would be ring announcing. "It's perfect," she beamed. "I get to sing, which is what I love to do, and you get to ring announce, which is what you love to do." It was definitely the truth.

After Big told me she was coming back, I sent her a "welcome back" text, and her response was, "what are you talking about?" I wrote, "WWE." She responded with, "huh?" I texted back, "Never mind."

That Monday, Lilian came to *RAW* in Tampa to do an interview about her return to *SmackDown* the next day. When she approached me for a hug, I just looked at her. She apologized for the texts and told me that "they" didn't want anyone to know. Minutes later, I heard from Duncan that he wanted to talk to me in the truck. We went in and had a meeting about the live event producer job. He explained that they were going to move forward with two outside prospects. He told me that the company would like me to work with these guys and teach them everything I knew. Their experience was outside wrestling. One came from the NBA, and the other had worked music concerts. Each weekend tour, we would have one of these guys. Duncan said that I should pay it forward, and then a few months in, I would be added as a third live event producer. He wasn't sure how I would be able to produce and ring announce, but I explained the majority of producing the show is handled before the event. If needed, I could always give cues from the ring. When the production managers were running the events, if they didn't know how to feel out the crowd for when to draw out pauses and when to hit music, I would cue them by switching my mic from one hand to the other when it felt right. I knew that it was possible to do both. I just needed a shot to show them.

Duncan was sincere in his delivery, and I took him at his word. I was happy to help these new guys enter my wrestling world and teach them everything I could. The NBA guy, Jonny, was very open to taking my suggestions into the mix, whereas the other guy didn't want to hear my input. He was the boss and was doing things his way. Rather than apply psychology to the show, he threw elements in just to throw them in. There was no reasoning or logic behind where videos were played or anything else. At one show, he even told me that he didn't care what I did, he just wanted to "get this stupid show over with." That was a pretty hard pill to swallow when you were as passionate about the shows as I was, and the guys calling the shots weren't "wrestling people" and didn't really care about the quality of the show. One was just wanting to get the job done, but at least the other was trying to learn the business as he went along.

I give Jonny credit. He always wanted to try new things and pushed me personally to become better on every show. No one before had ever pushed me to become better. No one could ever give me real feedback because no one had ever done my job. A "good job" here and there from the producers won't make you any better. Jonny and I would still butt heads when it came to certain show elements, however. He would argue that sporting events do things a certain way, and I would try to explain that wrestling wasn't a sporting event. It's a show; it's theater; it's a psychological roller coaster that takes fans on a journey as the night progresses.

A few months came and went, and I never heard anything about the position again. Kevin once assured me that I was going to produce a live event that we had in Lakeland, Florida. My flight wasn't going to make it on time, so I called the office, switched flights, and ran from one end to the other to get to Orlando to drive to Lakeland so I could make it to the show. When I got there, I had taken the script that was emailed and made a bunch of changes so I could show them my ideas, but I was stopped in my tracks as they had one of their new producers there. And he was running the show. Duncan said I could give him my ideas, which I started to, but he wasn't interested.

They ended up making a couple of guys from the studio the back-ups, and I could tell they weren't going forward with me. I even asked Triple H, who at that point was running numerous departments in the company, about the job, and he told me that I didn't have enough experience. That was the norm, though. As he was taking over, experienced guys were getting let go, and people who had no idea about the business were being brought into positions of power. The person brought in to hire talent had no experience in the wrestling business. How do you scout new talent when you don't understand the type of talent the wrestling business needs? Discussing the actions of the company were always the topic of conversation backstage between talent and even employees. The decisions the company continued to make were laughable, and we could never understand how business continued to strive. The live events still sold tickets, but most nights, I would walk away feeling like the fans were robbed of a show that made sense. I assumed that Hunter wasn't interested in having someone like me who would question direction; he just wanted puppets who would do what they were told to do.

Unless you're at these live events, you don't understand the science behind them. Some aspects of the shows fall under the category of "wrestling psychology," and other things are as simple as not playing a *WWE Network* commercial in Canada when the *WWE Network* wasn't yet available in Canada. Even a lot of the guys who work the live events are backstage or at the sound table, and they don't get to see the full show from center of the arena.

Live events just have so many details that can either make or break the show. Lighting cues are crucial. Music is a huge part of the show, as is turning it on and off at just the right times. When a guy is getting beat down and certain music hits, the audience is immediately caught up in that moment, and they know someone is coming to save the day. There should be a solid flow that takes you on the ride. When a superstar enters the ring, the music should play just enough—not too long, but also not too short. There are times when the first guy comes out, and he sets the tone so when his opponent's music hits, the crowd erupts. There are certain guys whose music makes the crowd want to chant. You have to know how to read the audience, and you have to feel this to give the audience what they want and what they deserve.

At TV, it was a totally different ball game. The shows were written for the television audience, and there wasn't much thought put in to what the live audience had to endure. If you've been to a television taping, you know that it's filled with music videos and commercials in the arena. Rather than keeping the crowd happy, the show was focused on what the TV audience saw, and lately that has continued to be insulting to fans as well.

Now when you take a TV writer and let him book live (non-TV) events, and he has only been to a handful of them and doesn't really understand the psychology of the shows he is in charge of putting together, the product suffers. There is no question, and there is no way around it. The product suffers hands down 100% of the time. So the local producer running the event, the show runner, if it's Jonny, and the ring announcer would take what they wanted and make it work. I'm not pointing fingers, but there's a long-haired gentleman I just described as said TV writer. He got bullied by the powers that be all the time, so he liked to talk down to everyone below him and bully everyone who would take it. He was a free bird, so to speak, and he joined us on a tour of Australia. I was looking forward to it because the show runner on that tour wasn't the one who cared about running a quality show; he's the guy that just wanted to get it over with. I thought for sure the free bird would finally pick up on what I had noticed on these events and finally fix the problem going forward. It wasn't that I wanted to take his position; I just wanted him to work with us for the benefit of the show. He could be the boss, but I wanted him to hear me out if something was off. I was trying to help him for the sake of the company, wrestlers, and fans to do his job, a job that I knew and he did not.

Often the problem in WWE was that were a lot of people who really cared and really did know how to make things better, but usually they just didn't speak up. If they did, these people knew that the company would go the direction they wanted to go anyway. Unfortunately, no matter how talented and intelligent guys are in the wrestling business, it's the "Yes Men" that are kept around. The company throws out a horrible idea, and the Yes Men just go along with the plan so they can keep their jobs. They nod their heads mindlessly so they can keep cashing their paychecks each week, and I get that. It's just sad. Fans generally blame "creative" when they're unhappy with a wrestling show. The writers use logic and pitch well-formed storylines to appease their bosses. The end result is creative versus what Triple H and Vince want to take place.

Well, on this night in Australia, the main event was CM Punk versus Daniel Bryan. Bryan came to the ring, and the crowd erupted with enthusiastic "YES!" chants. With something as white-hot as his entrance and the rabid chants that accompanied it, he should have been able to lead the crowd in some fun, especially since there were no television time cues. What was the rush? That's what the people bought their tickets for! But, as soon as he got to the ring, the guy producing the show immediately crashed Bryan's music with Punk's, rather than let him get in the ring and keep the chants going. I thought to myself, what did he just do? I looked back by their table where I fully expected to see commotion, the free bird scolding him for killing off Bryan's entrance, but instead, free bird was rocking out to Punk's music and playing the air drums. No wonder things never changed for the better!

Whenever I would ask him questions that were in the best interest of the show, he would usually start with, "What do you want now?" in a irritated but joking way followed by, "That's actually a good question. I'll get back to you."

When he continued to let the same flaws slide week after week, you couldn't go over his head, either, as Triple H was now in charge of live events (as well as seemingly every other department). When John Laurinaitis ran live events, he worked with the producers and used their feedback to make everything better. Triple H was busy with everything else he was in charge of, so busy, in fact, that overseeing live events was not something he invested much time into, or if he did, he wasn't doing a very swell job.

Triple H did, however, make sure that the opening video at international live events was him as the COO of WWE welcoming the crowd. This sounds cool at first: the COO of WWE, who for many years was (and still is) a main character on the show, welcoming you on a giant video screen. The problem, however, was that he was pretty much the top "bad guy" on the show at the time. So when he comes on the screen, the audience is conditioned to boo him mercilessly. When he welcomes them as a good guy, but they know him as the guy they hate from TV, then he tries to get them amped up like a good guy...the whole thing is very confusing. For some reason, that's how most overseas events started just so he could be a part of those shows and make sure his face was the first thing the foreign fans saw, even if he wasn't there. He didn't get to witness, nor would he notice, the video of his "bad guy" self, saying "welcome, are you ready" into a new voiceover they had made that also says "welcome, are you ready," then into the ring announcer coming out to actually welcome the live crowd. Mind boggling. There were so many elements that I picked up because I was fascinated with the psychology of these shows. Those elements were quickly dissipating.

As I mentioned, many years earlier, Paul Heyman got on me for playing on my phone at a house show instead of talking to everyone, picking brains, and trying to learn everything possible about the professional wrestling business. I thought back to that day and realized that no longer would Paul's advice hold true. I felt like I really did have a grasp on the business and that I knew live events from every direction and angle possible, but now my knowledge was pointless because the show was being run by guys who didn't have any of those experiences (and one guy who openly just didn't care). I listened to the guys cutting their promos in the ring, and I could feel what they were trying to say. So many times after shows and even during promos, I offered them my feedback or even a line or two to use. Thankfully, most of the times the guys knew I was trying to help them and were receptive to my suggestions, as they knew that I was a fan and knew the business. The problem was, maybe I now knew too much, and there was nothing I could do with that information because the people who should have embraced the input could care less and booked shows based on ego. I wish I could have just shown up, announced, and kept my mouth shut. Unfortunately, I cared way too much about the product.

Live events were fun when John Laurinaitis was booking the show with an agent or two and a production manager running the event. No detailed script from people who weren't at live events, overbooking, and booking segments over and over that confused the crowds. Guys were given the basics of what was needed of them, and they more than delivered. That's where guys had the chance to try new moves, new catchphrases, and develop as performers. It was a lot more fun. But it was also great to have guys who just wanted to have fun in the ring and do what they loved. By doing so, the fans would have fun. Dolph Ziggler, who was beyond talented and should have been a star years ago, was fun. The incredibly talented and entertaining Chris Jericho made it fun. Even I got to have fun. Sometimes I would make subtle changes to basic introductions—whether it was changing a weight or a hometown to make one of the guys laugh. The crowd never caught it. If one of my friends was in a rest hold right in front of me as I sat by the bell, I would use the Blurt app on my phone to perhaps type a message that would light up and scroll across my phone to amuse them. Guys all throughout the years liked to have fun. Tomko, a vicious-looking wrestler, used to walk into the ring every night and walk straight across the ring right in front of me to pose as he would stand on the ropes. Every night, he would do the Napoleon Dynamite weak kick that Dynamite did in the movie after a bully pushed him against a locker, and I laughed every time. Christian would take off his entrance gear and hand it to me the way Razor Ramon used to hand ring attendants his gear back in the day and tell me, "Hey, Chico. Something happen to this? Something. Gonna happen. To you." And then he would flick an imaginary toothpick at me (which I would "sell" as if he really did it). A guy like CM Punk wanted to have fun. He would go out and have a match and incorporate the late Earthquake's finishing move. He would do the late Yokozuna's bonsai splash finisher on his opponent. (Yokozuna was over 500 pounds and would place his opponent under the turnbuckles, climb to the second rope, and then land on their chest with all his weight.) Punk was 200ish pounds, and it was fun. It was entertaining. He would do these tributes and more mid-match to the legends that paved the way before him, and he would have fun, and the crowd would have fun.

Punk was one of the few guys who also did a Greg Valentine for me. I always remembered Greg Valentine getting eliminated from the 1992 Royal Rumble and slapping the ring in anger from the outside. He truly looked upset that he wasn't going to win the match, and it always stood out in my mind. Whenever we had a battle royal or even the Royal Rumble event, I would ask one of my friends to Valentine for me. I recently watched the 2010 Rumble where Punk was on the verge of getting a huge push and was dominating the match. Of course, Triple H came out and let everyone know that Punk was no match for him and threw Punk over the top rope. He was gone, out of sight, and suddenly came back in the frame to Valentine for me. I immediately sent him a text confirming what I had just seen to be what I thought it was. There were numerous Battle Royal's where a friend would Valentine for me; Punk's just happened to be caught live on pay-per-view.

On the subject of Punk...We were in Istanbul, Turkey, one night, and for whatever reason, he forgot to put his actual gear on. He had speedo-style underwear that would be on under his shorts. He forgot the shorts and came to the ring in the speedo in his match with John Cena. It was funny among those of us who knew it, but I guess it wasn't funny to the office. A ref came out and said something about him needing his shorts, and I ran to the back and grabbed his shorts from the locker room. I tried to be discreet and hid them in my suit jacket. I walked to the ring and threw them under the ring. At one point, Punk got out of the ring and went under there and threw his shorts on. That was a first and one of the memories I'll always have of Punk and his sense of humor.

It's funny when people ask me about Punk and refer to him as Phil. Or Undertaker and they refer to him as Mark. "What do you call each other backstage" is a very popular and also, an excellent question. I would say with me, and for the most part-you call each other what you know each other as. For instance, I met Cena as "Prototype" so he has always been Proto to me. John Morrison who had a few different names, is Nitro to me-since I first worked with him as Johnny Nitro. Miz is Mizard due to his Mizard of Oz move from the indies, Batista was always Tista to me, Ricky Steamboat-Dragon, and Hulk was Hulkster. When guys like Ted Dibiase and IRS were my bosses, I actually called them Million Dollar Man and

IRS whenever I spoke with them as that's who they were to me. However I knew the guys, was what I called them-but it was more often a ring name, than birth name-because that's what you knew them as.

CHAPTER 19
DID I DO THAT?

WrestleMania 28 was in Miami, Florida, and I was able to announce the John Cena versus Rock match. It's amazing to announce two of the biggest names in wrestling that bring on the loudest audience reactions. Right after, I traveled home to Phoenix and was running around like crazy trying to get everything situated before I left again for the upcoming European tour just a week away. I rarely kept food in my house aside from a pantry full of every sugary cereal you could imagine because I was never home to eat it, and it would just spoil. Count Chocula was always number one with everything else as a close second. I planned to have dinner with my family, and I hadn't eaten all day, so I picked up a frozen pizza from the grocery store. I bolted home and threw it in the oven while I got ready. As soon as I got out of the shower, I ran in the kitchen to turn off the oven and take it out. I'm not used to cooking and even though it's common sense, I took the pizza out. It smelled really good, and I was really hungry and not thinking straight, so…I cut into it and threw a small bit into my mouth. As expected, it was hot. Wildly, dangerously hot! I was so hungry that I chewed and quickly swallowed the little piece of pizza as fast as I could. I waited for the rest to cool down and ate it. I went for dinner that night and was fine.

By the next day, I was feeling like my mouth had been numb, and it was starting to hurt from a burn. You know that feeling when you burn the roof of your mouth? This felt like a variation of that, only much, much worse. I flew out to DC for TV, but the roof of my mouth was completely burned and blistered. Mark Yeaton had a runner in the production office go out and get some medicinal liquid so I could try and numb it. I went for dinner that night with Miz and Doc, but I couldn't eat; my mouth hurt too much. The next day, after not eating, I was eager to get some food at the airport before the journey to Europe. Punk and I grabbed some Chili's at the airport, but I could only think about how good it would taste because I couldn't chew to eat.

Then we flew out to Moscow, Russia, followed by Gdansk in Poland, then Berlin, Nottingham and London, Rome, Milan, Toulouse, Paris, and Merksem and Belgium. During the tour the entire roof of mouth was seriously burned. I took pictures and sent them to two of my dentist friends back home. Neither had seen anything like it. Doc was with us on the tour but couldn't do much until we got to the UK where the medications could translate better. When we got to London, he planned to find a pharmacy where he could make some sort of medicinal concoction to treat me.

I could not eat any solid foods, and talking at a normal volume hurt. Announcing hurt even more because my tongue pressed against the burned palate when I annunciated certain words. I had family from Poland, so to be there was such a great experience. The fans there were also very, very kind to me. During the main event championship match introductions, they started chanting my name. That was a first. As usual, I instantly got shy and red in the face because I didn't want to upset anyone on the show (it wasn't about me, after all). I moved on and tried to ignore them, but that was actually pretty cool. I was in Poland, it was an awesome show, I was thrilled to be there, the crowd was phenomenal, but my mouth was killing me!

I was in a lot of pain but got through the shows and got through the tour. I remember Mike Rotunda noticing the garbage bin in our locker room in Nottingham, England, and seeing the all the blood that had come from my mouth. "Is that all from you?" he asked. It was. The mouth tissue wouldn't heal, and it got worse after each show. I lived off protein shakes and Vickie Guerrero's protein pudding that she brought for herself on the tour. Sometimes good food from arena, hotel, or bus food catering was hard to come by on these lengthy tours. Vickie was kind enough to donate her entire stash to me so I could switch off between the shakes and the pudding. She was so easy to hate on TV, but so fun and truly easy to love behind the scenes. Dr. Amann got some meds to help a bit, and my dentist friend called in a prescription for me for when I got back to the States after the two-week tour. That medicine started to help immediately. Unfortunately, the new tissue must be very thin or sensitive, because every time I eat something even remotely hot now, the wounds still open up for a couple of days.

I mentioned that we were in Moscow on that tour. You would think that flying in and going straight to the arena and straight back to the airport would mean that Moscow was no different from any experience we might have in the US. Despite the circumstances, I was able to see Red Square from the bus, and on top of that, I was able to witness a moment with the fans in Moscow that no one had expected, or especially understood.

You see, it was Kane's birthday that day. Kane's character is that of a monster. Monsters don't typically celebrate birthdays, nor does Kane, especially in the ring. The previous night, there was a sign in the audience wishing Kane a happy birthday by using his real name. I quickly ran backstage to have Grant, our hardworking tour coordinator, look up Kane's birthday on his passport. We learned that his actual birthday would be that next night in Moscow. At the time, Kane was teaming with Daniel Bryan. Their team, "Team Hell No," was the epitome of throwing an idea against the wall and watching in amazement as it stuck. Their chemistry was incredible, and they created amazingly entertaining moments every night.

Bryan decided he would be in charge of Kane's surprise celebration and handed me a bag before the show to leave under the ring. I did not open the bag but assumed that whatever he had planned was going to be good as Daniel had a great sense of humor. There was a six-man tag-team match that night with Ryback, Dolph Ziggler, and Big E taking on Kane, Daniel Bryan, and John Cena. After the match, the bad guys went to the back, and the shenanigans started. Bryan included Cena in his nightly routine where Kane and Bryan would argue about who was the tag-team champions (they were champions together), and it was so much fun to watch night after night as it never got old. At the appropriate time, I handed Daniel his bag. Inside was a Russian hat. Cena had given the birthday monster a Russian hat, and now Bryan had done the same. Bryan had Kane close his eyes and hold out his hand as he wore his Russian hats. I couldn't wait to see where this was going. I wondered what the payoff could be. Bryan gave Kane a banana.

The big red monster Kane, wearing two Russian hats, held the banana, and Cena and Bryan left the ring.

That was it.

That was the whole plan that Bryan had come up with. They left Kane in the middle of the ring with his eyes closed, holding a banana. I have to tell you, when you tour, the oddness in that is entertaining. To the rest of the world, that is not normal. Or entertaining. Cena convinced Bryan to come back to the ring, and they shared a group hug with Kane and walked back with him. No aspect of that celebration made any sense, but Kane standing in the middle of the ring in Moscow with his hats and a banana won't ever be forgotten, but now you might understand what happened—despite still not really understanding. The crowd sang "Happy Birthday," and we bolted out of the arena to catch our plane to the next stop before our flying curfew.

Some tours allowed shenanigans. Some more, some less. It usually depended on who the agent or producer were. Some of the producers were Dean Malenko, Mike Rotunda, Ricky Steamboat, John Laurinaitis, Tony Garea, Sgt. Slaughter, Arn Anderson, and Fit Finlay, who I mentioned from the first international tours. David "Fit" Finlay was an unbelievably gifted wrestler from Belfast. William Regal always spoke very highly of him, even when I interviewed him with my video camera in high school, and I finally got to see him in the ring when I was a fan watching WCW. His sense of humor was always on. Always. He liked to make everything funny and just plain fun. Even long waits at airports were fun when Fit was around. He once saw a lady who fell asleep in a massage chair. He was kind enough to stick a dollar bill in the chair as hers must have expired, and she woke up to a surprising extra round as the group tried to keep from laughing. As one of the WWE producers, he was my boss for numerous non-televised shows. Vince doesn't attend the non-televised shows, so his producers run the shows. While Fit was wrestling and producing, it was common for him to wrestle against new talent that was just getting brought up on the road to their first WWE matches to make sure they were ready for television. Wrestling in general isn't an easy job, and leading a newcomer in a match definitely isn't an easy job. Being the producer, running the show, wrestling, and leading a new talent is a wildly challenging combination. Unless you're Fit, then there's still room for more.

During Fit's matches, I participated in something I'll call the Fit Challenge. While producing and leading the new talent through a good match, Fit would call for a various sport, whether it be baseball, basketball, football, and so on. He and I would have an imaginary game of whatever sport we decided to play that night. He would be climb to the top rope and get thrown off by his opponent. Everyone in the arena saw it. But no one noticed him pretending to dribble a basketball in the meantime and get the imaginary shot off just before he was thrown off the top rope. While his opponent had him in a chin lock, Fit was taking swings at the imaginary ball I was tossing to him. Sometimes Hornswoggle would be at ringside and join in on the fun as well. To be able to do that among everything else he was juggling in the process says something about Fit's genius as well as his sense of humor. When I mentioned I was being harassed by the old *SmackDown* crew, Fit told me not to give up. It wasn't a deep conversation or even a conversation at all. He made it a point to put that out there, and I appreciated him doing so. I was heartbroken when the company once fired him for having a heel's entrance music interrupt the National Anthem. Whether it was right or wrong, it was classic pro-wrestling and how shows would be booked to get the crowd to hate the heel for years. Eventually the "babyface" would prevail and then could lead the anthem in its entirety. This was an example of someone breaking a rule that wasn't actually a rule but taking the heat for the company when their National Guard sponsor was upset—very similar to the Daniel Bryan situation. Luckily, later down the road, Fit and his brilliant wrestling mind and sense of humor was brought back to contribute behind the scenes.

Fit had a rare sense of humor, and I loved and appreciated it. My sense of humor is also very odd. I try to find entertainment in everything. I love the Andy Kaufman/ Sasha Baron Cohen idea of just getting a reaction. I loved picking Jerry "the King" Lawler's brain about Kaufman, as he was so unique. Lawler would tell me story after story that gave me a genuine perspective on him, not just what was told on TV or in books. This was direct from his friend and very cool to add to the legend. Lawler was a legend himself and was always good to me. The scariest night of my career was when Lawler collapsed at ringside in Montreal during a live *Monday Night RAW*. We were sitting at ringside, and I noticed Cole waving to me. He signaled for me to get the doctor's attention. As I nudged the doctor, I noticed Lawler had passed out on the table a few feet away from me. Doc immediately ran over to him. We at ringside wanted to help, but didn't know what we could do. I felt helpless as I moved the rolling chairs out of the way so paramedics could come through. There wasn't enough room for a stretcher to come to Jerry, so a crew of guys lifted Jerry to bring him to the stretcher. He was up and out of there within a minute and getting the medical attention he needed instantly.

The rest of the show was hard to get through as I kept staring at his chair when I was in the ring and wondering how he was doing. Yeaton would get updates over the headset, and it turned out that he had a heart attack but would be okay thanks to the immediate and good treatment from Doc and the paramedics. Long live the King.

CHAPTER 20
I'M NOT A DOCTOR, BUT...

In May 2011, my good friend Mike and I came up with the idea of HandsToGo, which is a portable massage device similar to a TENS unit. This contracts and releases your muscles to help blood flow to areas that may be experiencing knots, cramps, aches, or spasms. I had that shoulder issue that made working out impossible, and eventually even sleeping became painful. My mom saw a portable massager and thought that might help, so she picked it up for me. I had never seen anything like it before, but Dr. Amann, "Doc," was familiar with it, so he set it up for me. When I put it on my arm, I was blown away. This little battery-operated unit completely took control over my body. I felt relief in my shoulder, and the next day I contacted the company that sold the massager. I told the guy that I worked with athletes, and they would probably love his product, and we made a deal for him to send out a case. I planned to let some of my coworkers (not just wrestlers) take them and try them out. Once I got my credit card bill, I noticed that he charged me a lot more than the price we agreed on. I loved this device and the concept, but knew I couldn't do business with this guy, so I called Mike.

Mike is a very intelligent, business-savvy friend of mine from college who has contributed in the launch of numerous successful companies. I always wanted to collaborate on a business with him but never had an idea of what. When I explained the concept of the personal massager, he was very interested. We began talking to his contacts in China, and we had a similar product made. The initial prototype didn't blow me away, so we went back to the drawing board. They sent out a revised model. This was it. We called it HandsToGo since it feels like hands that are massaging you, and you can take it with you wherever you go. We were on our way to helping the world feel better, one massage at a time. There were similar products that sold for around $150. Or, people in need could pay to go to physical therapy and have a doctor use a similar medical device on them, which was also expensive. We decided to charge $89. Mike and I weren't out to get rich; we were just trying to help people feel better. The technology had been around for a long time, but we wanted to have the very best and most helpful unit.

It wasn't just the wrestlers who used HandsToGo. Seamstresses, bus drivers, referees, and people all throughout the company enjoyed the product. Outside of WWE, HandsToGo became popular with professional athletes, recreational athletes, and everyday people's common health ailments and even helped with speeding up recovery times from injuries. We offered the product primarily on Amazon at first, and it did really well. I contacted the manager of my local Bed, Bath & Beyond, a friendly guy named Greg. He had a HandsToGo unit and loved it.

Greg and I discussed the possibility of Bed, Bath & Beyond carrying the product, and after lots and lots of calls to the buyer I was told to contact, they were interested in giving it a shot. I sent out a unit, and after they tried it, and after me staying on top of them, I got a meeting for Mike and me in New Jersey at the Bed, Bath & Beyond headquarters. They agreed to give us a test run in a number of stores, and we were ecstatic.

The reps from Bed, Bath & Beyond asked us to make some design changes to the product, and we did. Then they wanted more changes, and we appeased them again. Over the next 14 months, we made every little change they requested, and we jumped through every corporate and design hoop they placed in front of us. We were very good about keeping in touch with them, and we were very timely and efficient with revisions no matter how tedious it became.

Finally, after lots of money had been spent on making every change to appease them, the HandsToGo unit was approved by Bed, Bath & Beyond, and we were ready to launch the product in stores when...they just stopped responding to us. None of the reps, none of our contacts (or anyone in the company for that matter) responded to any of my follow-up calls or emails. Eventually, I went over the buyer's head to the corporate office, and I was informed that the deal was off. That was frustrating (and costly). I questioned the move and mentioned that, at one point, the buyer had emailed me to say that her husband had injured himself playing football, and HandsToGo was put to the test and passed as it helped him recover. I asked that if they knew this was a good product that might help people feel better, why wouldn't they at least give us the chance to test it out in the 30 stores to help their own customers? We were given the runaround as the units were selling on their website, but eventually realized that though we fought hard in that battle, they weren't going to put us in their stores.

CHAPTER 21
TURN THE PAGE

HandsToGo was useful on the long drives we would have from city to city or the plane rides from state to state and country to country. The car rides were sometimes the most entertaining part of the job. You traveled for long periods of time with guys that you talked to and saw more than your family and friends from home. I've driven with a lot of guys over the years, whether it was a short one-time drive or hundreds of miles. I drove with everyone from Edge, Christian, Matt Striker, Viscera, Mark Henry, Todd Harris, Jimmy Tillis, to Hornswoggle, Tommy Dreamer, Ezekiel Jackson, Eugene, Matt Bloom, Curtis Axel, John Cena, Randy Orton, Arn Anderson, Dean Malenko, Christian, Chavo Guerrero, Mike Chioda, Tony Chimel...and the list goes on and on.

In my later years, I was riding with a combination of our doctor—Chris Amann—Zack Ryder, Miz, and Dolph Ziggler, depending who was on the tour each weekend. It would get tricky because some guys would start Friday and some on Saturday and some would finish Monday, while everybody else would work through Tuesday. When the company combined the *RAW* and *SmackDown* rosters, it meant that guys might have to work Friday through Monday on the *RAW* loop, go to *SmackDown* Tuesday for TV, and many times go from there to Florida to work NXT and then head back out Friday to start *RAW* again.

I'm not sure how the wrestlers in the industry ever had time to rest or recover from injuries. There really wasn't much time to heal, and the only break most guys would get would be when an injury got bad enough for surgery. Then they were forced to take time off. They're on TV every week, but there's no SAG union for wrestlers, so they don't get that guaranteed good pay or even benefits. In fact, since wrestlers are classified as "independent contractors," the talent that keeps the company in business does not get any health benefits whatsoever. On top of having to pay for their own cars, hotels, gas, and tolls, now they were required to have health insurance (which they must pay for on their own). The icing on the cake was that because WWE runs a virtual monopoly, they could do whatever they wanted, and if you didn't like it, you didn't have anywhere comparable to go. You could probably make the best money there, but it was not the amount you thought you deserved from what you put in and what you helped draw In fact, most of the wrestlers would tell you that they don't know their pay scale. They know their minimum guarantee and some numbers agreed to in their terms, but with pay-per-view buys being a thing of the past, since those are now included in the WWE network, the guys don't know what their bonuses will be from each event or even how royalties are decided. It's not an easy lifestyle, by any means, to put your body through the training, let alone full matches on top of the travel, gym training, and appearances. I have the utmost respect for everyone who does it.

I was usually the one who planned the hotels for my car on our tours. For each loop, I mapped out the towns and figured out the best cities and best hotels to stay in. The formula included how long the travel day was that first day, how far the second town was, if that third town would allow two nights in the same town, and of course, the gym and restaurants we liked going to and what time the shows were (sometimes they would be 7:30 or 5 or 3 or 1 pm). Availability was never really an issue, as I had mastered the routine of finding the hotels I wanted to stay at, plus being able to negotiate a good rate. WWE paid for my hotel, but I still liked to get the best possible rates as the other guys had to pay for theirs. I would use every discount code that I knew to find a low rate, and when those weren't applicable I'd speak with a supervisor and try to work my magic. Almost 95% of the time, it worked. I explained that I was the announcer from WWE and we were headed to their town for a show and would like to stay at their hotel. Once they told me that the offered rate is the very best they have, I'd either ask for the discount code or even the rate I received the last time I stayed there. Once those rates presented themselves as better than the initial "best rate," I would have them just where I wanted them. "But I thought you said that was the best possible rate?" I would innocently ask. From there, we would make sure that the very best possible rate was negotiated. We had fun riding together, but I'm sure they also appreciated the fact that they saved a lot of money by not having to rent cars or pay for all the gas, tolls, or parking by riding with me. Those Madison Square Garden loops could be costly for the guys. Expensive hotels, expensive tolls, and they even had to pay to park in the public parking garage across the street to come to work. The one-way rentals between Canada and the US were also expensive due to drop fees, but the talent had no choice but to pay them. If a charter got in late and only one rental car place would be open when they landed, the talent was stuck with those high fees.

I was leaving Boston with Chris Jericho who was trying to find a hotel room in Lafayette, Louisiana. He called up a Hilton property and attempted to book a room for two nights. They only had a room available for one night. He told them that he had a Diamond membership status. He thanked them and hung up. No room. I asked him if I could call back on his behalf. He had been around for a long time, and he knew the drill. He just gave me a look which said, "Sure, go ahead," as I sensed his doubt. I told him that I enjoyed this type of challenge. I called right back and was very polite. I asked for a room for two nights, and the woman on the phone informed me that they only had one night available. I laid it on real thick and told her how much I enjoyed staying at that hotel, which she could probably see from my Diamond status. I asked her if she could work any magic. I was polite, I was cheesy, and I was making conversation in a fun way. After a short while and a few keyboard clicks, I, Justin Roberts posing as Chris Jericho, had just gotten myself a room for two nights.

Chris was impressed. But I wasn't done. I thanked her for getting "me" the room, and then I asked what the rate was. It was pretty high, but I knew Chris was just happy to have it, and he was, of course, paying out of his pocket despite this being a company expense. I asked her what the best rate she had was. She dug around and gave me her best available rate. Chris was pleased. I asked her about a company rate code. She plugged that in, and it went down even more. Chris mouthed, "Are you kidding me?" I thanked her, and the room was booked. Chris told me that he hadn't seen anything like that since Bubba Ray Dudley back in the day, and I should work as a line producer. I loved those kinds of challenges. They were fun for me and rewarding for all of us who could benefit.

You see, I learned that airlines, rental car companies, and hotels can always make things happen by pressing a button. Sometimes they'll tell you they have to charge you. Sometimes they tell you that there's nothing they can do. The truth is, all they have to do is press a button. If you're friendly, polite, and you push just a little bit but not too much, they can press that button for you.

Rental car places are a good example. When you reserve a certain car and then are given a completely different car that won't work for you, "That's all we have" is the common line. I promise, if you dig around a little bit and politely work them (even while they work you), there's a very good chance they're going to find at least one other choice despite that vehicle being "all they have." When airlines want to make you pay this fee and that fee and then pay to have a seat despite already having a ticket, all it takes is a polite conversation with someone who could easily "press that button" for you. Chris and I discussed this after the conversation, and I told him that people are typically lazy when we call for reservations. It's a bold statement, but it's true. Not many people that we encountered want to do their job. It's easier to just say no. It's easier to just say, "This is the best rate," without even looking for others. It just is. So, in order to make things happen, you just have to push a little.

Pushing was most common when jumping on all of those planes every week. You get tired of being told stories by ticket and gate agents when you fly enough to know what's really going on. It's kind of similar to the way parents will lie to young children—it just gets the passengers off their backs. I had to work overtime on international flights. The company would book us in coach and in "group space." The WWE travel department would tell us that we couldn't call ahead to change our seats or else it would affect the whole group. That claim was denied by any airline employee I ever spoke with, by the way. So we were basically told that we would have an aisle or window on these long flights in coach, and if we didn't like what we got, we could change our seat at check in. By the time we checked in, the flights were usually too full, and there were no seats left. Every tour, I would politely ask various folks at the in-house WWE travel department for a window seat. Just about every time I got to the airport, I had an aisle seat. I just wanted to sleep as much as possible to make the flights go by quickly. If you sit in an aisle seat, there's a good chance that you will have to keep getting up to let people out for the bathroom, and that the cart is going to come by and bump into you. I just wanted to sit at the window and not bother anyone. On a 16-hour flight, if I had a window seat, I could sleep and not even have to get up to go to the bathroom once. When Seth Rollins discovered that, I became his favorite person to sit next to on overseas flights. With that in mind, you might be able to imagine the frustration of the company getting me an aisle seat every time. So that just meant extra work at the check-in counter and at the gate. It meant that I had to work my magic to persuade them to give me a window seat. And they did, every time. It just would have been easier if the company had simply placed me in a window seat when I had asked, months before.

We were flying into Los Angeles from an international tour and had less than a couple of days before we would have to fly out for the next tour. That time off went by real fast once you landed in the US, and it was important to get a flight home as soon as possible. I had a four-hour layover and then would finally fly home to Phoenix after being gone for quite a while. As soon as I cleared customs, I called Delta as I walked through all of the terminals to get there. I asked about jumping on an earlier flight, and if I walked fast enough, I would make it just in time. They put me on standby, and I got to the counter with just enough time, maybe less. I pleaded with the ticket agent, and she approved me. As I was about to walk away, Daniel Bryan walked into the terminal. There was a long line, and I knew he was going to Phoenix as well and had less than one day at home. I called him up to the counter and asked the same agent to please put him on my flight as well. She told me that there wasn't enough time and refused to switch him. I explained that it was a minute after she approved me, and it wouldn't make a difference to do the same for him. Bryan was getting nervous about making waves and told me to go ahead, that he would be okay. I knew that it was possible and even an easy switch, but the woman did not want to help. I cleared security and approached the supervisor by the gate. I explained the situation and how my friend would barely have any time at home if he had to wait for the later flight, and she agreed to switch him and even upgrade him to first class. It all worked out, just took a little time and persistence.

I never sit back and wait on anyone. I stay on top of everything, step by step. It might be an annoying personality quirk, but when you're persistent, you get things done. People have other things to do, other customers or patients to take care of; the point is, it's very easy to get distracted. I feel that if you stay on top of whatever it is you need, step by step through the process, you stand a better chance of preventing that customer service rep or nurse or whoever from forgetting about you, and you'll get what you need much sooner. My motto has always been to not wait on anybody, to go after what I need, and to be polite. I'm never forceful or threatening, but I'm stern and make it known that I'm going to stay on top of things. I also like to surprise my friends and make life fun...

Dolph and I had been invited to a party at the Playboy Mansion in Beverly Hills, and since we had a show in Ontario, California, that night, the stars aligned. I thought it would be cool to invite Amann since he had never been there before and Adam, who as a kid took me to my first wrestling show. I told Adam that we were going to do our show in Ontario and head to Beverly Hills as soon as it ended to pick him up and head to the mansion. Chris, however, we wanted to surprise. My friend Nick was working with the Harlem Globetrotters and casually mentioned a big party where someone was paying to have them perform. That inspired me to tell Chris that we would be going to a big party after the show, a bar mitzvah party of some kid who hired the Globetrotters to perform, and Nick was inviting us to join as the adult's party was going to be just as big. I kept reminding him to bring a black suit, and throughout the day we would tell him all of the rumors we were hearing about this bar mitzvah and who was going to be there. We grabbed food before the show, put our black suits on when the show ended, ate as we drove, and hauled out to Beverly Hills. We picked up Adam, pulled up to the house where security greeted us with their list, and informed Chris that he was actually at the Playboy Mansion for their party. He silently looked down at his phone, googled the address, and looked up with a big smile on his face. "We're at the Playboy Mansion," he confirmed. Needless to say, we had a fun night and a rough wake-up for an early flight to Oregon. Luckily, we had a bit of a drive to the town, so we could sleep and Miz could drive. This was the first time he got the keys, and it was also the last. I've never been so nauseated in my life, and it was 100% due to his jerky driving. He probably did that on purpose. After that, he was banned from driving.

Miz rode with me enough to know about my drive to get things taken care of and to look out for fellow consumers. He also knew that I would shoot to accomplish anything I put my mind to. He once bought a new dishwasher that broke shortly after he installed it. The company tried to take advantage of him by charging him to come out again and fix what should have been under warranty. He naturally felt frustrated and helpless. Some companies will just take advantage of customers.

I went to battle for him and got his dishwasher fixed for free. In doing so, I also became his go-to guy when he had any type of trouble like that.

Satisfied with my service, he reached out again shortly after. He bought his wife, Maryse, an expensive piece of luggage. Of course when the zipper broke along with some other minor damage, the manufacturer made excuses as to why his damages were not included in the warranty. I like when companies are fair, and I hate when anyone tries to take advantage of their customers.

He had tried to get things done over the phone and lost the battle; they weren't going to budge. The loop we were on was over, and I went home while he went to the *SmackDown* taping. I landed, went to the gym, and then to the pool. When I got to the pool, I sent him a text asking if he wanted to dial up the luggage company using a three-way call. He immediately called me. Keep in mind since it was a Tuesday, I probably had not slept the night before after *RAW*, flew once or twice with short naps, landed, and went straight to the gym. So I was a bit delirious and in a fun mood. I also like to make myself laugh, as well as my friends. This was going to be a fun phone call.

I told Miz to mute his phone. If they asked anything that I wouldn't know the answer to, he could unmute it and just start talking. I would be calling as Miz, but periodically throughout the call his voice chimed in to answer certain questions. Keep in mind that we sound nothing alike, not even on the phone. I told him that we wouldn't acknowledge that there were two of us. I loved the idea of the person on the other line being confused by this. We called and spoke with a customer service representative. As is usually the case when I'm on a mission, I requested to speak with the supervisor. (How else am I supposed to get some rule-bending done?)

The supervisor came on and asked how she could help. I kindly explained the situation of how "my" bag had been damaged, that it was sold to me with a lifetime warranty, and now that I needed to use it there was supposedly fine print that prohibited me from taking full advantage of it. The woman was very stern and explained to me that the bag had been inspected, and they were sticking to their argument. That zipper, among other damages, were from wear and tear and getting thrown around by airport baggage handlers. I kindly responded by telling her that a piece of luggage is constructed with the understanding that it should hold up during travel. This includes the hands of airport baggage handlers picking it up, putting it down, opening it, closing it, and the chance that it may shift around during flights and in baggage claim. I said, "Ma'am, with all due respect, this bag was sold to me with a lifetime warranty. I've had the bag for a year, and it's damaged." She told me that she would give me a credit toward the purchase of a new bag, or I could pay to have it fixed.

I asked if she had Twitter. She was thrown off. I asked again. I explained that I (or rather, Miz) had a lot of Twitter followers. At the time, it was around 1 million. I mentioned that I would love to send out a kind tweet letting the world know how much I appreciated her company as well as the good customer service. I told her that if just one of the million-plus followers is inspired to buy a bag, her company would make a lot more money than she would make from the credit she offered me, because I would definitely not be buying another bag, and I would rather say something positive.

She put me on hold and came back about five minutes later. "Sir, I am going to..." I knew exactly where this was going. I even said it along with her in my head. "...make a one-time exception." That was it. I got it. She informed me that rather than repairing the damages, she was going to just send me a brand-new bag. We spent the next five minutes exchanging information and making dumb comments to her that I knew was making Miz laugh on the other end. None of our jokes made any sense to her, but she played along. I apologized for the handling of the bags and told her that I should look into hiring an assistant who would watch after my bags and personally place them on my flights to prevent this from ever happening again. When Miz chimed in to answer questions that I didn't know, she thought she heard a different voice talking to her, but we never acknowledged it. Afterward, Miz told me that he had previously tried everything with that woman, but nothing worked for him. He was blown away.

Miz and all his hometown friends that I met were always really good, quality people. Any friend of his could be a friend of mine, so I once traveled on a tour with Miz's wife Maryse. We flew in from a Mexico tour to work a show in Hidalgo, Texas. We arrived early in the morning and had the entire day until our live *SmackDown*/ECW event that night. The next night was TV in Laredo, Texas.

Maryse just needed a ride to Hidalgo and then to Laredo where she would meet up with the other girls. At the time, I was driving alone, and she knew that she could trust me, so she asked if she could hop in. I didn't mind at all. Maryse had a great sense of humor and was fun to hang out with. I just didn't know what to do to kill six hours with her before the show. Usually I would go with the guys to the gym, but I didn't think that's what she would want to do, so I asked about going to a mall. That idea appealed to her, so that's what we did.

As soon as Maryse and I entered the mall, I approached the cellphone case kiosk. I assumed the folks in Laredo, Texas, had not seen in the *Borat* movie outtakes. I decided to make this long day at the mall as entertaining as possible for both of us. The sign clearly read, "Cell phone cases: $12.99, 2 for $20."

A foreign accent slipped out of my mouth as I asked the gentleman how much the case was as I pointed. "$12.99," he said. "And this one?" I asked as I pointed to another. "$12.99. They are all $12.99 or 2 for $20." I nodded as if I clearly understood and then pointed to another case. "And this?" "$12.99," the frustrated salesman said. I spent the next couple of minutes testing his patience, but Maryse couldn't hold in her laughter anymore, so I thanked him and left.

I told her she wasn't being a good sidekick. I was used to Tommy Dreamer always telling me that I was a horrible cohort. He was hysterical and could keep a straight face while he messed with people. I would laugh before he said anything, because I already knew that whatever he was about to say or do was going to be funny. While in a random part of Texas, I knew that now it was my job to keep the straight face and mess with people and hoped they could laugh at me.

Next, we walked into an extravagant dress shop. Maryse was the epitome of a diva, both WWE and otherwise: tall, long blonde hair, drop-dead gorgeous. As we entered the store, I could tell the sales associate was scanning her mind and deciding which dress to sell her on. I began speaking with a slightly effeminate voice and explained that we have a party to attend and need something flashy, but not too flashy. Something that gets attention, but not too much attention. Something wow, but not too wow. She began to point out various gowns to Maryse. I had to let her know that the dress wasn't for her, it was for me. She was thrown off by this and, I should add, extremely uncomfortable. Maryse loved it. I was ready to let the poor woman off the hook, so I threw a little tantrum and said, "You know, I'm never going to find anything. I'm just not going to go to this party. Let's go. Thank you." And we left.

We spent the next couple hours wandering the mall, and for every store we went in, I had a different accent and a different routine. She went from being my daughter to being my girlfriend to being my wife to being a complete stranger. It wasn't about making fun of other people; it was about making myself look ridiculous for their entertainment and for Maryse's entertainment. The company liked to rib us, so the joke was on us, but we liked to rib ourselves and put the joke on us. Everyone was confused, amused, entertained, and time flew by. This was the first time we had ever hung out, and I figured that she would either think I was nuts and would never talk to me again, or I'd find out that she had a great, odd sense of humor and would appreciate and enjoy the day. Go figure, she had an odd sense of humor! A few years later, I was honored to "announce" them at their wedding.

CHAPTER 22
SHARP DRESSED MAN

You'll notice that most of what's written is about work, and I haven't talked much about my personal life outside of work. That's because I didn't have one. It was like Groundhog Day, every single day. I was a zombie just going through the motions. Earlier I mentioned that Chimel and Chioda were in a WWE bubble and oblivious to everything outside. Well, the same thing happened to me. I didn't have time to watch TV. I'd fall asleep if I went to a movie. I was living in a bubble. Gym, laundry, haircut, errands, and then back on a plane again. I got used to flying very early on and was programmed to get on a plane, head to a window seat, and pass out. As I mentioned, I never bothered anyone to get up so I could use the bathroom or walk around. I just wanted to use that time to rest and to make the trips seem faster so I could keep a shred of my sanity. Because I flew out of Arizona each week, the flights were usually pretty long.

As odd as it will probably sound, I consider myself an introvert. While I am okay with addressing huge crowds of people, in my downtime, I usually prefer to lie low. I feel out of place at big dinners or parties and have always been the type to hang out with a buddy, maybe two. I don't like to do what's trendy or popular or what everybody else likes to do. If it's not something I'm into, I just don't leave myself open to it.

I've often been asked about my love life. As a 37-year-old man (wow, where did the time go?), I can safely say that I have always been single. I am straight (and support whatever anyone else out there might be), although I'm sure my family wonders about that after never really bringing a girl for them to meet after all these years. Until I do, I'll stick with being single. I have met many women over the years, but they were never really "the one," so I didn't want to settle. I've seen too many people settle, and I refuse to do that. You only live once, and you have to be happy. I don't think I should settle down with a girl just to settle down and get married. I'll make a move when I know it's right and when the right girl comes along. I look for way too many qualities in someone, and it may or may not happen, but I will be happy being single or with someone and knowing that I never settled.

When I was on the road, I never went for any of the divas. Part of me thought dating a diva could be good because they understood the life and the issues that popped up in travel that other girls might not fully understand. They knew the politics as well and everything else associated with the job. The problem was, if something happened, and we broke up, it could get weird and interfere with the job. I had to put the job first and not take that risk. Before the couples in the company were glorified on a reality show, they would usually split couples up and put one person on one run of shows and their significant other on the opposite tour. If you dated within the company, at least you could see your significant other on the road, and it makes it easier only having a day or two at home, since you have more time with them on the road. It also seemed like management didn't take too kindly to certain guys dating their divas, and it could harm that guy's career. I avoided dating the divas and tried to avoid any politics that came along with that.

When it comes to women, I am very picky, and I can read people really well. I know within the first 30 minutes of a face-to-face conversation if there's anything to it. If there is, I'll continue and feel it out. Eventually I know if it's a temporary thing or if there is hope for a legitimate future. If a girl catches my attention physically, I'll make a move and try to get to know her. If she has a great personality, she will keep my attention longer. Being on the road all the time, it was somewhat easy to meet women. At the same time, it was very difficult for anything to come of it. At any point, I could leave in a matter of hours and not be back in town for months. There wasn't an off-season in which we could spend time together, either.

My life was a complete rush. I rushed through the tours, and I rushed through my days at home. Now that I'm in one place for a normal period of time, maybe it will be easier to attempt a relationship when the right woman comes along.

I didn't have an office or a workplace in Arizona, so the only places I consistently went were gyms and restaurants. I don't talk to girls at the gym, because it bothers me when I see a guy approach a girl mid-workout and flirt with her. I also don't approach anyone at a restaurant or a bar. It just seems like women are bothered enough by that as well. That kind of put me in a hard spot to meet anyone at home.

Looking back, I think the majority of girls I have talked to over the years were servers. The conversations were natural. They started out about business, and then they would turn into normal, casual conversation. Once in a while they carried on after that. A lot of times when I was home and could go out, I would meet a server that was cute and then use my time on the road to talk to a mutual friend who worked with her. She would feel it out for me, and if there was mutual interest, she'd connect us. I could use the time on the road to get to know her and maybe meet up when I was back, if it went well. Just like anything else in my life, if I were interested in someone, I would go all out to try. The dating scene, as anyone knows, is hard, and it's that much harder if you're always away. Girls are chased by guys all the time, and they all come off the same: uninterested unless you have a friend introduce you first. I also used social media while I was away to see who was out in my area. If I was talking to someone, I would try to have "dates" over phone to see if I was interested in using my limited free time at home to further a relationship.

Sometimes I would talk to a girl knowing full well that it wouldn't turn out to be anything long-term, but I would give it a shot and hope that I was wrong. Even if we enjoyed the conversations and if it was a long-distance thing (which it always was), it was just impossible to make it anything more than merely a flirting or a sexual thing. I think with my schedule and the crazy experiences I had just traveling the world, it made it hard to connect with anyone. I couldn't relate to everyday things they spoke of, and they couldn't relate to what I was talking about either or why it was hard for me to talk every day.

One of the things that got past me with the lack of time on my hands was watching television. I used to live for TV, and now I wasn't watching any! I found that crazy as TV influenced my life for so long. I could be missing out on the next *Saturday Night Live*, a show that I loved growing up. If there were one show that could match my love for wrestling, it was *SNL*. From the moment I first saw the show as a child (it was a sketch with Kevin Nealon, Dana Carvey, Dennis Miller, and Jon Lovitz), I was hooked. I had the show opening memorized. I imitated Dana Carvey's "Church Lady" character on a daily basis. As soon as I saw who the guest host and musical act was, I knew every sketch that was on that episode. I loved every season, but my favorite was the Phil Hartman, Dana Carvey, Dennis Miller, Jon Lovitz, Kevin Nealon crew mixed together with the newer Chris Rock, Adam Sandler, Chris Farley, David Spade crew. To me, this cast was the All-Star Team. I have seen Kevin Nealon do his stand-up show in Arizona. I met Adam Sandler, one of my all-time favorites, on a beach in Malibu, Janeane Garofolo at a comedy club in Los Angeles, Victoria Jackson at a stand-up show in Tucson, Rob Schneider at *RAW*, Norm MacDonald at a bar in Scottsdale, Tracy Morgan on the set of "The Tracy Morgan Show", Dennis Miller at a different *RAW*, and Chris Farley in a shopping area in Los Angeles. Each one of those encounters was incredible for me.

It went a step further when Jon Lovitz was the guest host on *RAW*. He was great, and we had a brief conversation. He talked a little more with Dolph, and they exchanged numbers. Dolph had moved nearby a while back, and we became good friends after both traveling with Dreamer. We shared a lot of the same interests and always had fun when we went out. While feeling insecure is common, Dolph was very rare in that regard. He wasn't not the type of friend that constantly took jabs at you or made fun of you, even though we all did that. He was the type of guy that was secure enough to just be positive and supportive. We liked talking wrestling and possible ways storylines could go that would make for great WWE TV. We also loved making *SNL* references and talking about our favorite characters and sketches from over the years. Lovitz had arranged tickets for us when he was in Arizona doing stand-up. He put us right in the front row, which is never good at comedy shows, and immediately called Dolph out when he got on stage. As the show ended, the audience applauded, and he came over to grab us. We walked with him to his dressing room and sat and talked from that point until the knock at his door about 90 minutes later when it was time to do his next show. He asked us about wrestling, and we asked him about *SNL*. It was a lot of fun and mind-blowing sitting there with a *SNL* cast member we grew up watching every week as kids. We had gotten used to that with wrestlers we idolized, but an *SNL* legend? That was awesome. Then the next time he was in town, we checked out the show, and he jumped in my car to grab dinner with us. Another unreal moment for the kid in me and probably for Dolph as well.

That night motivated me to see Dana Carvey live. He was the guy. He was responsible for me doing voices, which led to the announcer voice, which led to my career. He was the master impressionist. I had messaged him when he joined Twitter and Facebook, and he wrote back! He told me in the message that I might notice I have a new follower. I looked and saw he was following me, which was really cool! Within the next day, he was following everyone on Twitter, but regardless, it was cool.

I was determined to see a show, and I'd do so even if it meant having to travel. I only had a couple of days at home each week (if I was lucky), so I didn't usually take any trips whatsoever unless they were business related or if I had to. I saw that Dana was coming to Las Vegas, which is a quick flight or a pretty easy four-hour drive for me. I had asked my friend Mike if he would want to do a Vegas trip to see some shows. This was the perfect excuse to go and do that. He agreed, and he said that it's better to do it than to regret it. I knew if I didn't go, I'd definitely regret it.

We went down and saw my friend, the hilarious George Wallace. We were talking in his dressing room when I heard the opening video that he played to the crowd. My introduction when he did a WWE show was part of his legendary reel!

The next night I purchased tickets to see Dana Carvey. This was a big deal for me since I idolized him growing up. I was really good at talking my way into most things, including meeting someone when I wanted to meet them, but this was a challenge because I wanted it more than any other time. A lot of the concerts where I landed backstage, it was simply about trying just for the challenge. This was a challenge I didn't want. I would rather have someone tell me that Dana was a friend and set it up. That wasn't the case. When I know that a friend is a huge fan of someone, and I know that I can do something to connect them, I love to help. I don't usually have people who offer that to me, but I go out and find a way.

When I arrived at the venue to pick up the tickets, I asked to speak with Dana's "people." The gentleman outside of the Orleans Theater brought out a woman from the venue, a very nice lady named Stacey. She asked how she could help, and I told her that I was hoping to speak with someone from Dana's crew. She said that Dana was his crew, but she was the showroom manager and asked what I needed. I explained that I was the ring announcer from WWE, and I spend my weeks introducing people to their favorite wrestlers, and I had taken the weekend off of work and traveled to Las Vegas to see and hopefully meet my *SNL* idol. I wrote him a note just saying hello and thank you for the entertainment throughout the years, and I wanted to give it to him along with a HandsToGo gift for his travels (I always thought any performer who travels could benefit from traveling with one) in the event that meeting him wasn't a possibility. Stacey was extremely personable and knew that I was sincere in everything that I had said. There was no "working" here; it was just being friendly, polite, and honest. She asked where I was sitting and took my tickets to the box office when I handed them to her. When she came back, she told Mike and me to follow her into the theater. Our original seats were in the back. She pointed them out and walked us down to the last two seats in the second row. "Here," she said as she pointed these seats out, "These are your new seats. Dana doesn't usually meet anyone; he does his show and heads out. I have some guests coming tonight that he has already agreed to meet. After the show, I'm going to grab them and you two, and we will meet up with Dana." I couldn't believe that. I doubted my ability to make this happen, but Mike assured me that I would. And I did.

His show was awesome. He took all his old material and made it relevant to 2013. I loved every minute of it. When the show ended, Stacey grabbed us, and we walked backstage. She brought her friends in to meet him first, as she knew I would want to have some time to talk with him. As they walked out, Stacey called us in. There was my *SNL* idol standing right in front of me. Of course, I wanted to tell him how my third grade teachers Mrs. Malis and Mrs. Wituckee knew me as the Church Lady. I wanted to tell him how much I liked everything he did on *SNL*, Wayne's World, etc. But I had to play it cool. I told him that I was a big fan of his work, and I thanked him for getting me hooked on *SNL*. He was very laid back, and the three of us had a normal conversation for a few minutes. I told him that I always record a video for Twitter before we begin *RAW* and asked if he would have any interest in being part of it. He probably didn't, but he was cool and played along anyway. I quickly produced a 15-second video that would a) give me an excuse to record a video with Dana Carvey, b) have him do his Church Lady and George Bush characters, and, most important, c) allow me to be in the video with him. I pitched him the idea, he was on board with it, and we did it. I watch the video every once in a while and think to myself how amazing that was!

Adventures like that were fun, and so were a lot of the car rides with our crew. We were four friends laughing nonstop at times or bored out of our minds at the end of a grueling tour. Now, I didn't take bumps, I didn't get beat up, and I didn't have to beat anybody up. To the casual fan, I had the easiest job in WWE. As far as they knew, I made a few announcements and that was about all I really had to do. Along with an easy job, I was able to travel the world alongside the WWE superstars, and I got paid millions of dollars to sit there and watch wrestling shows. (People assume you make millions of dollars if you're on TV, but that isn't the case.) I absolutely admit that my role was much easier than that of a wrestler. But the travel itself was a whole different monster. You might be in a city each day or even four cities in a day. The travel days can last longer than 24 hours (it really is possible), and it never stops. After three or four flights in a day, with the hours of flying and delays and cancellations factored in, the travel really takes a mental and physical toll on you. You can't forget about the airports either, dealing with security and lines and anything and everything that can—and will—go wrong before you even get to your gate. I always liked walking behind the 7'2" Great Khali in security lines though. TSA would be so enthralled by him that they would just stare and not nitpick anything about my bags.

2013 was my worst year of travel as it seemed almost every week, no matter how short or easy flights were supposed to be, I was getting delayed or encountering cancelled flights or connections. I was flying to a Friday night show in Syracuse, New York. Daniel Bryan and Brie Bella were also on this 5 am flight to Charlotte to connect to Syracuse. It was to be a long, but easy, day. The guys in my car had planned to do the show and then drive afterward to Rochester. We sat in Phoenix for a while and took off late. By the time we landed in Charlotte, we had missed our connection to Syracuse. Daniel was rebooked on the next flight which would get him to the city in time for the show. Brie and I, however, were booked on a flight to Philly, to connect to Ithaca, to drive to Syracuse. When the Friday shows were booked in large markets, the talent had an easier time starting the tour, because it was easy to get to those major cities. When they started booking more sporadically, many Fridays were challenging travel days. Brie and I ended up going from Phoenix to Charlotte, to Philadelphia, to Ithaca, then finally to

Syracuse, where we did the show and then had to immediately drive to Rochester for the next day's event. That's one hell of a day. Oh, and our bags didn't make it. Of course. Days like that were common, and those of us who cared about making the show did whatever it took to get to the venue. It was not uncommon to fly to the closest city 200 miles away and jump in a rental car to get there if the original plan fell through.

After a long travel day, even after landing, it wasn't uncommon to run into more problems. There were long lines at the rental car counter, no car when you got to your rental car spot, or you could check into a hotel at 3 am after a full day and find that no one is at the counter, or they're doing their daily audit so they can't check you in yet, or they gave away your room, or you have to wait for the computer to finish before they can check you in, or the "Do Not Disturb" sign doesn't work (meaning, housekeeping still barges in to clean while you're trying to get just the tiniest bit of sleep), or the alarm is going off in the room next to you two hours after you fell asleep, or you got in at 3 in the morning but you have to be at the airport by 7 for your next flight...the list can go on forever! I'm proud to say, though, in all the years flying numerous times a week, I never slept in or missed a flight due to my own actions.

Travel wasn't all misery. Like I said, it could also be the most fun part of the job at times. There were ways in which we made things fun. I'll let you in on a few...

"The Pineapple Story" was one of our main recurring games we played to help with boredom on the road. Doc and I had been riding together for a while, which means we shared every meal and car ride together. Eventually you just run out of things to talk about. But we always had The Pineapple Story to break up the monotony.

Here is how it went down. We would be at a restaurant. I would order my food, and then Doc would order his. He would end his order by asking the server a simple question: "That doesn't come with pineapple, right?"

Most of the time his orders weren't even in the same ballpark as pineapple, so the confused server would always answer no.

He would then say, "Oh, good."

Then came my part. Each time, I asked him to explain why he asked about pineapple. And each time, he would decline to tell us the story. And each time, I would push him. He would say no again. I would push him again, back and forth, until finally, he would say, "Okay. I'll tell you the Pineapple Story."

Each server would just stare while he or I regaled her with a wild, unbelievable story. He or I would begin:

"Picture this. It's straight out of a movie. I'm on the beach with my girlfriend of two years. We're having the perfect vacation, the sun is setting, and the time was right. I got down on my knees and asked her to marry me. She was holding one of those foofy drinks with a piece of pineapple on the glass. She just looked at me, handed me the glass, and ran away crying. I sat there looking at this pineapple wedge just staring me in the face. It was a horrible experience, and I haven't been able to look at pineapple ever since."

Nobody ever knew how to take that. There were so many different variations, and we would trade back and forth between who would do the Pineapple Story. I even did that once when a server brought an unsolicited giant cotton candy over to the table. This variation came to be known as the Cotton Candy Story.

The idea was not to upset or offend anyone, just to get a reaction. If I could get someone to go home at the end of the day and scratch their head and ask themselves, "what was wrong with that guy?", then I did my job. The joke was always on my friends and me, not on the servers.

A common, unspoken rule was to stay awake while riding in the passenger seat of a car. It was out of respect for the driver. If one of us had to stay awake driving, then the passenger should, too. Anything goes in the backseat, but a comfortably sleeping and snoring passenger can make it hard to fight those heavy eyelids.

Sometimes it was too hard not to sleep in the passenger seat. It was especially hard on those 19-hour days. We could travel all day and night, work a show, and then keep on driving to the next town. When you're the one driving and you look over and see that other guy in the passenger seat so comfortable and just snoring away, it really does make you want to rest your eyes, too, but you know you can't.

So we came up with a fun little game to play if we were bored and someone had fallen asleep in the car. As long as the road was clear and it was safe to do so, we might just quietly count down from five and on zero slam on the breaks and scream at the same time. Oh, and we would also capture the sleeping beauty's reaction with a camera. Ryder was the victim of this more than anyone, but at least sleeping kept him from being awake and eating pistachio nuts. The cars around us could probably hear the sounds of him sucking the salt off the shells, cracking them open and chewing.

I wish the big bosses were as fun as my riding partners, or even fun like most other people in the company, but that wasn't the case. In 2013, the Royal Rumble (my favorite event since I was a kid) was in Phoenix. That year, the headline match was CM Punk going up against the Rock. I was excited for a lot of reasons, but especially since my old friend Punk had climbed to this incredible position in the company. Not just anyone got to wrestle against the Rock, and I was happy for him.

Rain is pretty rare in Arizona, especially rain that lasts all day. It might rain for a bit, just enough to mess up your car, but it's usually quick to clear up. The day before the Rumble there was a WWE fan festival right outside the venue, the US Airways Center where I shared camera time with Syxx/Xpac when it was the America West Arena years prior. The marketing director for the event asked me if I would host the event. I was really excited about that. I loved hosting these types of events. It was always a pleasure to be able to say words other than "the following contest is scheduled for one fall." Plus, this was my hometown now! I was thrilled! That is, until I saw the weather forecast for nonstop rain. The event was advertised as rain or shine, and there didn't seem to be any chance of the sun coming out. I am a proactive person and a meticulous planner, so I planned to work this outdoor event completely in the rain, meaning that instead of a suit, I wore a WWE rain jacket with a nice WWE shirt, jeans, and boots. I thought I was doing the right thing...until I arrived at the arena and found out they just decided at the very last minute to move everything inside without informing any of us. Rather than the hosting work that was described, I was scheduled to announce a continual slough of NXT matches throughout the day.

I loved announcing, but announcing NXT matches presented a slight problem. I had all the WWE superstars' weights and hometowns in my head, but I had never before worked a NXT show. This was an entirely new roster of talent that I wasn't at all familiar with at the time. It was a challenge enough to stay on top of the full WWE roster, let alone an entire roster of the developmental wrestlers. On top of that, I still didn't have a suit, and the rain jacket and boots weren't going to fly inside. We were an hour away from starting when I found Triple H, who was the man in charge of the fan fest. As I attempted to explain my suit situation, he cut me off, ignored me, and decided to stay true to his usual behavior by making jokes, mocking me, and making me look like an idiot. "Your suit's your gear, and you didn't bring your suit," as he rolled his eyes. I assumed he would do that, and I also assumed that I should just drive home and get my suit.

I sped home and grabbed a suit. That took me about a half hour. Driving back to another 30 minutes. As soon as I got to the building, it was time to start. I worked completely on the fly and hosted the entire event without a hitch. When I was asked to host the fest, I really didn't expect that I would be ring announcing NXT matches; I thought I was hosting an event. But, after the suit debacle, it went smoothly. They had a lot of great talent, and it was good to watch them work. Once the matches ended that day and I had a chance to collect my thoughts, I think I realized for the first time that Triple H really didn't like me. It wasn't just a joking thing, he really seemed to dislike me. He liked to pick on guys, but we never really took it personally. This had never been a major concern in the past, but at this point, he was the one who was starting to make a lot of the decisions, and Vince had given him a lot of power. Vince's "soldiers" were starting to lose their power and Hunter began bringing in his friends and lining up his own "soldiers" into place.

The following night at the actual Royal Rumble event, I welcomed the crowd and then introduced the commentators and Lilian. I was to walk to the ring in darkness, but Lilian was given a big entrance with a music video and announcement. I didn't mind that or even the other major differences between two people in the same role. If Lilian were to do something wrong, Michael Cole might make a joke on commentary and Kevin might joke on headset, but she never got reprimanded or questioned. I would try my hardest every week to not make any mistakes and to read Vince and Kevin's mind when I wasn't given direction and when Kevin

SHARP DRESSED MAN

wouldn't respond to my texts asking what to do. They would still find reasons to reprimand me on nonexistent mistakes, for instance "why did you say....?" And it would be something that they had told me to say the last time the topic was discussed. Or the announcers would get an email from the studio or Kevin's team (and he was on the email) that read "going forward, announcers should refer to __ as ___." So when it came time to refer to the situation as instructed, I would be asked why I said it.

So on this night, after I welcomed the crowd and handed Lilian the mic, a National Guard video played to the arena. They were a sponsor at the time and after the video, we would acknowledge the men and women in uniform and thank them for everything they do for our country, which was very cool. After the video played, Lilian had welcomed the crowd, which I had done not long before that, rather than making the National Guard announcement. It happens. There's miscommunication. The floor producer was trying to get her attention, but she didn't catch on. I don't recall her being reprimanded for that. After all, it was an honest and trivial mistake. However, I can only imagine how much grief I would have gotten if I had done the same thing, especially considering the grief that I got for making mistakes that weren't even mistakes but things I was told to do. It's funny sometimes how there are politics everywhere, even in something as innocuous as ring announcements.

Politics aside, I was really looking forward to the main event. Rock is the man. He was a standup guy when I first met him, and now that he had moved beyond wrestling and was a huge Hollywood megastar, he was still the same standup guy, maybe even nicer if that's possible. If you've ever wondered what he's like in person, I can assure you that he is more friendly, positive, and approachable than he seems. He shows that side in his Instagram posts, and you can assume and now know for sure that the kind of guy he portrays is exactly the kind of guy he is. Plus, he's good to his family. As I mentioned, his opponent at the Rumble was CM Punk, the kid from Chicago who had worked his way up from the very bottom of the business all the way to the very top. My introductions for that match were exactly how I thought they should have been: two huge announcements for two huge superstars. Because of how short it is, Punk's name is hard to verbally blow-up. In other words, it's a challenge to make it larger than life. Because of that, I would regularly hold the "C" and the "M" and stretch out the "Punk" as much as possible, but not a lot. Rock, however, has an even shorter name, but I knew I could take the "R" and really growl it out. So I did. As the match began, I sat down ringside. Yeaton wiped the perspiration off his earphones and handed them to me. Uh oh. I was in trouble.

I never knew what the issue was when I was handed the headphones, nor did I ever know who was going to chew me out. Would it be Kevin to impress Vince? Or would it be Vince himself? Or would it be both? In this case, it was Vince. "Damnit! What the hell was that? We've talked about this before, and now you went back to going over the top. You're just trying to get yourself over!" Well, you can't argue with Vince. No matter how wrong he was, because as anyone who has worked with Vince knows, he was never wrong, and the same goes for Kevin. They can tell you to jump. You can jump. They will ask you why you jumped, and the correct answer is not "because you told me to jump." The answer is, I'm not quite sure why I jumped. It will never happen again. It was mentally taxing, constantly getting reamed out for trying to do a great job. I tried to stay on top of everything (every little detail, no matter how minuscule) and did my absolute best to make the ring announcements as perfect and as meaningful as possible night after night after night. But I still seemed to get chewed out each night. The other announcers weren't getting the same treatment for actual mistakes. They were usually joked about over headset, but not talked to. The bosses knew how much I cared and had to keep me in check. I apologized and let him know that it wouldn't happen again. It was time, once again, to bring all the introductions "down."

I hated going out there and being told not to give 150%. I wasn't even allowed to give 100%. This sounds preposterous, but in order to make my boss happy, I had to go out there and give 60%. I would do a decent job versus a great job and ask Vince if that was better, and it was. I began to receive backlash from fans on social media. They demanded to know why I wasn't giving the big, fun, action-packed introductions anymore. People seemed to enjoy the "Johhhhhhhnn Ceeeeeena" introduction that Mick Foley even mentioned on the back of my trading card. It didn't matter, though. I knew I was just following orders, but personally, it just wasn't good enough for me. No matter what my opinion on the matter was, when it came down to it, I had no choice. I was basically told to give unenthusiastic match introductions by Vince, the most enthusiastic, over-the-top commentator I had enjoyed listening to as a kid. He ordered me to go out there and do a mediocre job. I hated it. My passion and love for the company and for the art of ring announcing were slowly being sucked out of me. I was a guest on Colt Cabana's podcast at one point, and my stomach dropped when he asked if I was going to be a lifer. Of course I would be, right? A lifelong fan in a great position—I cringed and went along with it, but knew in my gut that wouldn't and couldn't be the case.

I was always amused by a fan named Rick, who became known as "Sign Guy." He always came to lots of shows. He would take hours and hours to create a huge portfolio of poster board signs to hold up for the wrestlers. He might attend four shows in a row on a loop, and he would have fresh signs each night. He had been going for years and was a huge fan. One night, we were in Tyler, Texas. I loved that town. The large barn-looking building was called the Oil Palace, and we would change in the trailer out back. In September 2004, Travis "Tyson" Tomko came into the trailer and told us that Sign Guy, who was at our show the night before in Waco, would be in Tyler. Some of the guys knew how big of a fan he was and now the others were learning. Tomko made a sign that said "Sign Guy Sucks," and we all signed it for him. During the show, Tomko pulled it out from under the ring and handed it to him. It was really cool, and he was blown away by that. In recent years, the powers that be decided that they didn't like having him on camera. I don't know who specifically, but Steve, who coordinated audience seating, was in charge of moving people when Kevin didn't like how they look on camera. That seemed to happen a lot with audience members who dressed up in costumes or even wore shirts or held signs that the company didn't want in the shot. The floor producer and timekeeper would hear Kevin mention these people, and someone would move them, bring them a shirt to put on, or take their sign away. So now, this meant that Sign Guy would spend his money on awesome, on-camera, and often front row seats and would be relocated somewhere else in an off-camera section where he wasn't allowed to hold up his signs as they might block the camera shot. He really spent lots of time and even money on signs and props to hold up to have fun and be playful with the talent. The fans, and even the wrestlers, took a liking to him as he was respectful and "sold" for the heels he was insulting after they gave him a threatening look. As the passion for WWE started to dwindle on my end, I wondered how this man, who didn't even work here, could still spend his hard-earned money and travel all over the country on a company that treated him so disrespectfully. Each time I saw him being forced

243

to another seat off camera just because they had the power to do it, the more that passion continued to be sucked out of me. I feel when people have enough money, sometimes that's not what drives them any longer. The power can drive the higher-ups to use the talent and even fans as their own personal entertainment since they are able to pull the strings.

Sign Guy's treatment was just one of many examples of backward thinking I saw in the company I once loved. When Vickie Guerrero was on the roster, crowds in every city around the world booed her to the point where you couldn't hear anything else in the entire arena. Great reaction for a heel (bad guy) character, right? Wrong. Even as her reaction—her "heat"—was white hot, Vickie's role in the company was quickly diminished until she was moved off TV entirely. Santino Marella and Vladimir Koslov were an extremely entertaining in-ring duo. They were very popular with the fans and were only becoming more and more so. I guess they were too popular as they were taken off TV as well. After Ryback's debut, he was obviously growing to be a humongous star. His merchandise started to sell really well, too. Apparently, he was too popular or sold too many T-shirts, because he was "taken care of" as well. No more "feed me more chants" at the time. Anything where the fans got to chant along with the wrestlers wasn't acceptable like it was in the Attitude Era when catchphrases were encouraged. Now if something caught on, something would be done creatively to prevent that from happening, unless they were the rare handful of guys "chosen" by the company that they wanted to get over. Whatever happened to managers like Jimmy Hart and Bobby Heenan? Armando Alejandro Estrada was a manager who caught on with the crowd, but he caught on with the crowd and lost his catchphrase and not long after, his job.

I started to wonder if the company really wanted to make money or if they were just writing TV to favor their own personal preferences, whether it was good for the fans or for business. Instead of the crowd getting what they really wanted, it got what the company decided they wanted. The Monday night shows felt flat to me as a fan. There were so many talented guys and girls backstage, but the focus only reached a handful. The company had all the potential in the world to put on the absolute best show, so why did it seem from week to week that the decision-makers didn't care. Talent and writers would all pitch logical ideas, but Vince ran the show he wanted to run with the talent he wanted to run with. The inconsistency from week to week and the same storylines over and over didn't seem to matter, it was the show they wanted to produce.

My love for the company continued to diminish. I pondered possible ways I could get out of my contract. I really, really wanted to get fired, but without doing anything bad. I considered calling in "sick" for work. Maybe if I did that a couple of times, it would work. Or maybe I would just say no when they asked me to do something, because as a perennial team player, I had never really done that before. When I requested not going back on *SmackDown* international tours while I was getting bullied, the office told me I still had to go. Maybe a solid no from me would earn the termination that I wanted. There was a part of me that didn't want to quit, as I really had nothing else to fall back on at the time, but I had become pretty miserable.

CHAPTER 23
STANDING TALL, ON THE WINGS OF MY DREAMS

I always found it amusing that I was never acknowledged, but when we had a guest "celebrity" that needed a spot on the show, there was always a "guest ring announcer." Well, if they were a guest, who was the actual announcer? Why didn't I have a name? When Lilian left WWE, she got a nice send-off and was acknowledged as leaving. When I took over, it was never announced anywhere on the website and definitely not during the show. The transition just sort of happened without any mention whatsoever. In some ways, the company treated that position as a nothing position. There were even times when I saw the script specify the type of shot to take with a note instructing production to not shoot the ring announcer. I was told toward the end of my run that a writer wanted to have one of the wrestlers mention in a Malaysia promo that being a ring announcer was the "very bottom position in the company." There's my answer.

The claim that ring announcer is the bottom rung in WWE, however, kind of makes sense if you look back at past ring announcers. I was the only mainstay ring announcer to come in as a ring announcer and be a ring announcer. Howard Finkel was an usher. Tony Chimel was ring crew. Lilian was a singer. All these people were just put in that role from a different position or vocation. I, on the other hand, had a very real passion for it. Lilian once told me at ringside that I really analyzed every announcement. I overanalyzed every announcement. Every little word I spoke meant something. Everything I did had a reason. It was ring psychology at its finest, and I was always touched when fans picked out subtleties in my work and mentioned them on social media. I would keep track of the entire roster's weights and hometowns for all the ring announcers and commentators. If everyone were 215 pounds and from the same cities, it would sound a bit mundane. I would try to keep every announcement different—214 pounds, 213 pounds, and so on. I was a part of the show every week

STANDING TALL, ON THE WINGS OF MY DREAMS

for over a decade and was passionate about the product and the position. Some announcers might only want to work one show, a single TV taping each week. I wanted to be a part of that world full time—every show, every taping, every event.

I've said that I never considered myself to be the best—that is entirely a matter of opinion. I always thought it was pretty amazing that I got to work with so many other ring announcers from different worlds. Looking back, I have worked with Michael Buffer, Bruce Buffer, Howard Finkel, Gary Michael Cappetta, and Mike McGuirk She was the female announcer who I watched on Saturday and Sunday mornings as a kid. We used to do a deal where Diva Maria Kanelis would throw out T-shirts during intermission, and the last person to catch a shirt could come in the ring and be a guest ring announcer. When I saw Mike in the crowd in Tulsa, Oklahoma, I asked Maria to throw her the shirt so she would be able to ring announce. She walked in the ring, and I handed her the mic, stood behind her, and fed her exactly what to say so she would nail it. I can't even explain how cool it was to hear her announce again and doing so literally right in front of me. I've also worked with David Penzer, Lilian Garcia, and Tony Chimel. In addition, there were announcers I really looked up to and got to work with, like Sean (Edmund) Mooney and "Mean" Gene Okerlund.

By the time Lilian left the company to pursue what she was truly interested in, music, I had trained about five women in the craft of ring announcing. They didn't have any knowledge of the business—most didn't have even a slight interest in the business, actually—and not one of them had any idea how to ring announce. There was a lot to teach them, and I definitely tried, but it seemed that no one truly wanted to learn. We started with learning the talents' names. Yep, I sat in the arena with a program and asked them to please learn the names of the superstars in WWE. I would also walk around the arena and point to the men and women and ask them to tell me their names. There were many times when you entered the ring for a match, and the match would change, so you had to be familiar with matching names to faces. From there I would teach the cues and then what phrases to announce. Winner by "pinfall, submission" and those terms. It usually went in one ear and out the other because going for hair and makeup was a higher priority than learning the job. In a lot of the higher-ups' opinion, anyone could be a ring announcer. After two years of seeing all these women come and go, I wondered if my bosses realized that simply wasn't the case. There are no notecards, no ear pieces, and no real direction. You're on your own in that ring. You have to make a lot of judgment calls on what to say and do. Plus, something you did every match for years could all of a sudden be the absolute wrong thing to do, and no one would every bother to let you know until it's already too late.

I never went down to WWE's developmental territory when it was NXT. I went when it was called FCW (Florida Championship Wrestling) to help the company choose a ring announcer and to also train them and work on their TV pilot. Ty Bailey was in charge of recruiting new talent at the time. The company was high on finding a female ring announcer. They had three for me to choose from. All of the women were attractive; they each had a great personality, and I know that they would be excellent in other roles, but ring announcing just wasn't for any of them. You need a certain presence, a certain voice, and even a certain kind of attitude. I worked with them during the day, and at the end of the session Bailey asked me to pick one. I asked if I had to. He told me that, yes, I did. So I picked the one I thought would be best for that spot at that time. I worked the pilot and never again went back to developmental.

Later, I was casually asked about going to NXT to work with the announcers, but I explained that there was not anyone in NXT striving to be a ring announcer. There were women who wanted to be divas who were made into ring announcers. I'd love to sit down with anyone who wanted to learn and share what I had learned, but no one down there at the time wanted to be "stuck" in that position. A total of zero of the five girls I had worked with over that two-year span had wanted to be a ring announcer. Rather, they put up with it to get their foot in the door.

While trying to do my job correctly, the same job I was trying to teach others to do as they came in to the company, I would continue to get berated by Vince and Kevin for my announcements. "Too over the top. Too melodramatic." After the Royal Rumble scolding, I just had to bring all levels down once again, but we were approaching *WrestleMania*.

On March 5, 2013, I was at the airport in Buffalo, New York, having breakfast when the Undertaker walked by. He sat down with me. I was a 33-year-old professional who had worked with him for many years; it wasn't that big a deal for him to sit down with me. He was my coworker; we texted here and there, no big deal. Admittedly, however, there was still the little kid in me smiling that Undertaker just sat down. I let him know that Vince had just talked to me about toning it down. Undertaker's match at *WrestleMania* was always a main event on its own merit regardless of where it's at on the card. Even though Vince asked me to tone down my intros, I asked Vince, that since it was Mania…and that's where he cut me off. He said, "Don't do anything at *WrestleMania* that you wouldn't do at *RAW*."

I never discussed intros with any of the guys. No one ever said, "hey, I like how you," or "hey, can you change my intro to…" They just trusted me to give them a good introduction. A lot of the guys are in a zone when they come out to the ring, and they don't even hear their own introduction. I told Undertaker that his intro was my favorite. It really was. I watched him as a young fan. The entrance was eerie and memorable back then. Now, as an adult, I got to stand in the ring and watch his entrance live, with the scary music, the lighting, the fire, the smoke, and my voice saying his name. His name also has four syllables, which helps a lot. Because the crowd exploded when they heard his name, I always went over the top and growled the first "r" sound. "The Un-derrrrr....Takerrrrrr!" I loved hearing from others that I gave them chills, and I'll admit, I gave myself chills announcing his *WrestleMania* matches.

So while we talked, I really wanted to know, was I allowed to still give him, the freaking Undertaker, that big introduction? The one that he deserved? He didn't know what to tell me. He alluded to Vince changing his mind quite a bit on a daily basis. He told me to do whatever I thought was right. So I did. I went overboard. Just not as bad I normally would have. (By the way, the Rock and John Cena were the main event that year, and as per Vince's strict orders, I gave them both mediocre ring introductions.)

It was a very memorable breakfast. We discussed a lot of those inner fan questions I always had, such as why he wore his grey gloves at *WrestleMania 13* in Chicago where he won the title from Sid. "Nostalgia" was the answer he gave me. Awesome. He ended the meal with a couple of Percy "Paul Bearer" stories. Percy was his manager for a long time, and they traveled together quite a bit. I had once met Percy at a show in Chicago, and we took a picture together. The poor guy was also a victim of my unsolicited wrestler-hotel-room-phone-call habit. If

I suspected a wrestler was staying at a certain hotel, I would ring up and ask for him using his real name. Here is how the Percy call played out:

Paul Bearer: (sleepy) Hello?

Teenage me: Hello. Is this William Moody?

Paul Bearer: (sleepy and also angry) Yes. Who is this?

Teenage me: My name is Justin, and I wondered if I could interview you?

Paul Bearer: What the hell you doing calling my room at 1 in the morning?

Teenage me: I'm sorry.

Paul Bearer: (slangry and now hang-up-y) Goodnight!

I kept that story to myself my entire career and always felt bad when I saw him over the years. Finally, Percy and I were at a TV in Calgary together. We were hanging out, talking in a hallway together. He called me his little buddy as he loved the photo of us from my childhood and said he was so proud of me. When I first I showed him that photo, he posted it on his Twitter and Facebook accounts. I felt comfortable enough with him at this point, so I told him the phone call story. He laughed hard! He didn't remember the call, but he got a kick out of the story and as if it was planned, Undertaker walked by right after that. Percy stopped him and made me tell him the story, too. Undertaker laughed and said that's why he'd always use a different check-in name.

Unfortunately, the night of my "Underbreakfast," Percy passed away. I was at home and about to sleep when my phone lit up with the notifications. I was devastated, as was the entire wrestling world. Everybody began to share their thoughts and their stories about Percy's life. I messaged his son Daniel to send my condolences. He asked if we could talk, and we had a brief phone conversation. I felt terrible for him and his brother, who unfortunately also passed away shortly after. They were really good, respectful guys. We talked for a bit, and then I just stayed up to read what people were sharing about him. We had done a live event building up to *WrestleMania* not long before this in Biloxi in mid-August. I was able to introduce Paul Bearer as a surprise guest. He got in the ring for an interview about Undertaker's upcoming *WrestleMania* match and began by telling everyone in the crowd about the history between him and me. He told them that I was a little wrestling fan and had followed my dream and made it to the WWE. The crowd applauded. I always shied away when attention was brought to me, whether it was a mention, a sign, or a crowd chant, but, coming from him and that he took time out of his promo to tell the arena our story was amazing. It was a huge honor and a moment I will never forget, nor will I ever forget him and how wonderful of a person he was.

CHAPTER 24
WHAT A MANEUVER

While Percy was great with me in my fan years, I did not have that fan picture with the Ultimate Warrior—or an autograph or even the memory of him being cordial. Despite this, I still dressed as him for Halloween and still proudly wore his jacket throughout my childhood. I'd be lying if I said I wasn't thrilled when I heard that he had signed a deal to be in the new WWE video game. Warrior had been at war with the company for a long time, so I knew that this was a big step. There were many rumors going around that this step was also indicative of him being inducted into that year's Hall of Fame class. The fan in me was excited for what this could mean for the company. The fan in me was also excited for an inevitable third meeting between the two of us—one in which Warrior would not blow me off. Maybe I'd tell him what he did back then and how it's bothered me for years. I was angry, excited, and curious. But more than anything, I was determined to re-meet Warrior.

I picked my spot. We were at the Staples Center in LA for *SummerSlam*. Warrior had a WWE2K video game appearance nearby. I had a friend at the event who gave me the heads up on when Warrior's appearance was. No one knew that he would be there. Unlike the first time I met him, nobody else would be around; it would be just him and me. I anxiously waited for him to pull up, and when he did I was standing by the door. He walked in and was greeted. Then he was introduced to me as, "Justin, the WWE Ring Announcer." I had so many things I wanted to get off my chest. I couldn't wait to lay into him.

I opened my mouth and really gave it to him. It went something like this: "Hello, it's very good to meet you. Would you mind if we took a picture?" He said, "Sure, and then make sure it's okay; if not we'll take another." We took the picture, and

I thanked him. Okay. The grudge had finally been dropped. The fan in me was the only one left!

I loved doing my job, and I can't say that enough. The actual job and the interaction with the fans was the best. I used to give 150% and was told to bring it down. Then even at 100% I was told I need to tone it down, because apparently doing a good job is considered "trying to get myself over." That was never the case. My job was always to give the best introduction possible using the most appropriate and fitting deliveries. Each week I went to the shows and tried to do what was best for the fans because I, myself, was a fan, and that's how I saw the shows. It was never about me; I knew my role was to make stars sound as big as possible before their matches. Some announcers might do it for the attention, the fans, the TV time, and the exposure and make it about themselves, but I was truly there to willingly and happily contribute to the show in a supporting role.

Later on, I often had to "politic" (i.e., creatively tiptoe and work with and around) with guys who weren't from the business to do what was right for the show. Unfortunately, I got shot down a lot in those situations. Sometimes it felt like I didn't exist. I referred to myself as the Ghost of WWE, and by now I really truly felt that way. I would show up to TV and receive zero direction throughout day or during the show. I would have to guess what was going on, and I would only hear from the bosses if I had guessed wrong. I enjoyed talking with the talent, the lighting and sound people, and the production crew—everyone but my bosses. To them, I just didn't exist. They treated me as if I was just a meaningless, replaceable ring announcer. I was never comfortable at my job. Ever. Every week from the beginning felt like it could have been the last.

Despite the politics and the treatment, I did enjoy being able to live out my dream. Toward the end, I had become worn out from traveling every week, year after year. The schedule, which was already pretty insane, had somehow gotten unbelievably worse. Distance between towns had grown, which meant more hectic flights and airport days versus simply driving from show to show. I still felt like a zombie. I went through the motions on my few days off in order to get all my errands finished before I headed right back to work. We were no longer being flown in business class. I don't mean that in a snobby way. We took many international flights in which everybody, even the countless giant superstar wrestlers, were all smooshed together in coach. The guys could barely fit in the seats, and the rest of us were smashed between them and the other passengers. We were told not to call ahead to move seats either, so many times that resulted in our group sitting together. Imagine that group of huge wrestlers sitting in the same row together for 14 hours.

Executives boasted about how many millions of dollars each tour made as we sat uncomfortably in coach for one, two, and sometimes even three flights in one day. We would show up to an overseas show, work the show, and then all these men and women who had busted their bodies in the ring would hop right back in tiny seats on the cheapest flights possible, with guys like me packed right in between them. It wasn't fun. The food situation overseas wasn't fun either. For the most part, I was with a large group of health-conscious athletes. Most of our meals were given at catering, except for lunch when everyone was on their own. We could be in countries known for their food, but we would have to eat dry chicken or fish with other disgusting catering choices at arenas and hotels. If we were doing a show and then taking a bus to the next town, it would be fast-food options…But at least there was lots of candy on the bus. Good thing they made protein powder.

We would build storylines and angles the whole year up to *WrestleMania*, which is the "Super Bowl" of the industry. The company books hundreds of appearances and signings for the talent that weekend, and by the time the show starts, the guys are already worn out. Even so, they give it their all. Then the show ends, that's it. *WrestleMania* is over, and there's no off season. There's no month sabbatical. There's no week off. There isn't even a single day off, because the next night is *RAW*, and the "next season" begins. By the way, that *RAW* after *Mania*? It was brutal. Everyone was so beat, and adrenaline was so high from the night before. That Monday was probably the hardest *RAW* to get through, until the post-*WrestleMania 29* New Jersey *RAW* with the audience that had travelled from all over the world, bringing the *WrestleMania* feel to *RAW*. That crowd completely transformed the "downer" of a *RAW* to its own spectacle. Even so, after building to that huge show and then going right into the "next season" that next night, the guys and girls never get a real break. I was glad that there was drug testing to look out for the talent, but not giving them time off unless they're already injured wasn't very healthy. There was no reason, with all the talent under contract, that they couldn't cycle talent off every once in a while to rest and recover.

In December 2013, it was time to discuss a new contract. I hadn't heard anything from the office, and I knew that I was up soon. I was burned out with everything that happened with trying to move up in the company and having been given the runaround. I was almost hoping they would just forget, and my contract would expire so I could be done with them. I flew out to work Tribute to the Troops and a *RAW* TV. When I landed, Sue called me and asked if I could fly to Connecticut to meet with Big about my contract. I was already out on this trip and had family commitments. I did not have an extra day to go to New York, drive to Connecticut, and have a conversation that I could just as easily have on the phone. I declined. It was the first time I ever felt that if they wanted to let me go after this contract, then that was fine. I was over it, and my contract was almost up. Up to the last minute, Big and I went back and forth over email, and right before my contract ended, we met at the arena in Tampa.

I wanted to explain how I helped with live event execution. I tweeted out everything that was going on to help spread awareness that live events existed because at that time most of our audience thought we only ran shows on Mondays and Tuesdays for TV. Before they hired social media people, I was doing this on behalf of WWE during all the shows. Even after they were hired, I would still post photos and updates from the ring or even backstage on Facebook, Instagram, and Twitter. I even gave the fans a peek into the world of travel by tweeting pictures of buses and flights. I was doing all these cool things in order to bring the fans along on the adventure and to also promote whatever it was we were doing.

If you lived in that town, you could find out about the show and come out by following my posts on social media. If not, you were aware that this event was happening, and while you couldn't watch on TV, you could see what was going on through following me online—which the WWE account would typically repost for their fans to see.

I let Big know that over the past few years, five different women were trained as ring announcers, and all five had come and gone. No one had the passion, no one cared about the business, and surely no one could handle the position the way I could. I wanted to let Big know that not just "any diva" could do what I did, as the bosses had put it. I had been on every single pay-per-view since 2007. I never missed one. Whether I was sick, healthy, drained, or whatever, I was there and gave it my best. My work ethic was always good. I announced the highest grossing show of the year, *WrestleMania*, along with every other TV and pay-per-view, yet I did not make $1 extra from doing so. Those events were all included in my salary. Between the shows, the talking megaphone, trading cards, DVD programs, and video games I was on, I literally had not made $1 in royalties during my entire WWE career. I explained that nobody puts into this role what I do. I travelled to make sure I got to the towns no matter what. (I did miss a non-televised show in Sacramento after a blizzard drove the company to get a last-minute flight from Reno, and they forgot to put me and Big Todd on the flight. We drove 132 miles over 8 hours to get there, but it was too late.)

I was eager to let Big know how I felt and very curious to see what he had to offer. My contract was set to expire in just a few weeks. We sat down in the empty arena. *RAW* was a three-hour live TV show that came together on the fly, and I did a hell of a job rolling with the punches and knocking all of my stuff out of the park. I felt somewhat good about what Big was about to say.

I was wrong.

I had sent Kevin a text on January 31, 2012, that mentioned I get a vibe from Vince that he hates me. I asked what I could do to fix that. Kevin's response was basically that Vince didn't hate me, and that I was the best ring announcer in the history of the business and to enjoy the run. His words, not mine.

Less than a year later, I was working even harder and doing an even better job, but rather than mention Kevin's thoughts from that text, this discussion had taken a whole new turn, and the new tone was coming from Big, who spoke regularly with his friend Kevin:

"Kevin says you have become complacent. You are not as hungry as you were three years ago. He wants you to focus more on your ring announcing at TV."

I wasn't expecting that. Yes, I understand that they try to make you feel as worthless as possible when signing a deal, but still! I told Big that I had changed my style monthly, weekly, yearly, and I always try to find new ways to announce and continue to do so until Vince or Kevin go out of their way to tell me that they

Standing in the exact spot where I used to meet my heroes, my number one hero, my dad, got to meet his.

At Chili's with E! talk show host Michael Essany, sidekick Mike Randazzo, and Colt Cabana.

Backstage in San Diego, CA, with one of the greatest minds, best talker, and biggest character in pro wrestling, Paul Heyman.

On the bus in Tokyo, Japan, with the most special character in wrestling history, the Undertaker.

Our group entering one of the ferries after an exhausting day and night of travel, trying to make it to Belfast while grounded by the erupted volcano in Iceland.

Back on the road a few days after shoulder surgery in Las Vegas with Florida promoter Bill Brown and the legendary Nick Bockwinkel.

Curtis Axel, Zack Ryder, Miz, and I, proudly wearing our Members Only jackets of pro wrestling from Ribera, thanks to Chris Jericho.

The winner of the Divas Championship (in a card game).

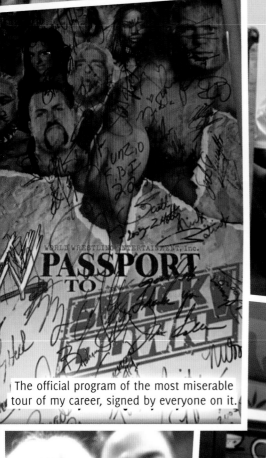

WORLD WRESTLING ENTERTAINMENT, INC.

PASSPORT TO

The official program of the most miserable tour of my career, signed by everyone on it.

The "Million Dollar Man" Ted DiBiase (right) was always one of my favorites, and IRS (left) was my dad's favorite. The fan in me loved it when they were my bosses at various points in WWE.

Pulled over on the road to Liévin, France, so a group of us could jump out of our buses and into that minivan. We would then speed over to start the sold-out show until the buses caught up.

Saturday morning wrestling ring announcer Mike McGuirk came to watch a show in Tulsa, but had no idea she would be getting back in the ring that night

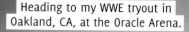

Heading to my WWE tryout in Oakland, CA, at the Oracle Arena.

Our car. The group I shared and enjoyed the road with on most weekends: Dolph Ziggler, the Miz, Chris Amann, and Zack Ryder

HandsToGo: A miracle worker or speeding up muscle-related injury recoveries-plus an intense way to battle aches, pains, knots, cramps, and spasms.

Announcing the Undertaker in my first WrestleMania main event in Orlando, FL, just one year after announcing my first WrestleMania match.

It is normal for Tommy Dreamer to place a lettuce wrap on his head mid-meal. Anything to "pop" his friends and make them laugh.

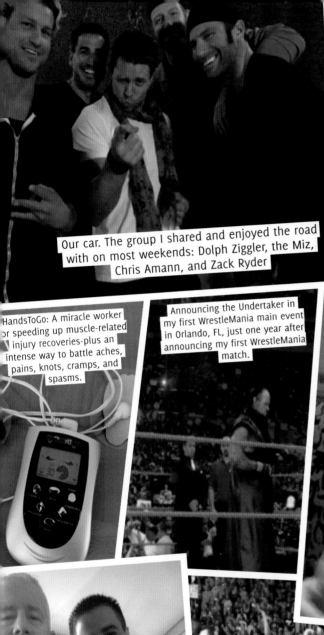

A tough man, gifted wrestler, and creative producer, the hilarious David

I watched the very first episode of RAW as a kid and was at ringside, announcing for the 1000th episode of RAW with announcers Howard Finkel

Daniel Bryan and John Cena celebrating Kane's birthday in Moscow, Russia.

While my boss did not grant tickets for my fami to come to WrestleMania my friends still made it happen, and the surprise upgrade couldn't have gotten them any closer.

It wasn't comfortable on many international trips for someone that's just average height, so I always felt bad looking around at my co-workers and seeing them trying to squeeze into their seats for the long flights.

Backstage at RAW with friend an mentor William Regal.

I used to sit in the crowd and watch them, but at my final WrestleMania 30, I was able to perform in front of legends Harley Race, Bruno Sammartino, Dusty Rhodes, Bret Hart, and Bob Backlund.

For the 1000th episode of RAW, I was able to work with the announcers I grew up watching: "Mean" Gene Okerlund, Sean Mooney, and Howard Finkel.

Meeting and holding my niece for the first time, 10 days after she was born.

I treated the company as if it were my own family's business and always wanted to help. I sent the office this photo from the highway in Florida after noticing the WrestleMania billboard gave no indication of where the event would be. It just had the date and John Cena and the Rock, but did not mention Miami, FL, or the stadium.

When Rick the "Sign Guy" got moved, it was usually to these seats off camera. At least they were near the ring.

It's amazing the people I have been fortunate enough to meet and get to know. One of the best examples is Mr. Las Vegas, legendary comedian and friend, George Wallace.

Pre-WrestleMania 24 with security and friend, Big Todd.

My tag-team partner, timekeeper Mark Yeaton holding the WWE Championship, and I couldn't think of a more deserving champion.

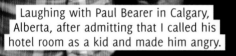

Laughing with Paul Bearer in Calgary, Alberta, after admitting that I called his hotel room as a kid and made him angry.

Watching the Ultimate Warrior's WWE Hall of Fame induction speech.

The first wrestler that I met, but this time it was t ultimate experience with the Ultimate Warrior.

The chairman of World Wrestling Entertainment and my favorite host of Prime Time Wrestling, the commentator who made everyone and everything mean something, Vince McMahon.

GI Joe and wrestling legend Sgt. Slaughte who was a big help over the years.

At the Royal Rumble, Connor and Steve Michalek were surprised to meet various superstars including company executives Stephanie McMahon and Triple H.

Backstage in Washington, DC, after Connor "the Crusher" Michalek's very special day.

With Daniel Bryan's music blaring from the speakers and his own name in lights, Connor and Daniel make their big entrance toward the ring.

Sitting on his dad's shoulders, Connor is on top of the world while ringside at WrestleMania 30.

Steve Michalek and his father Steve Michaelek, Sr. were always by Connor's side. They did everything they could for him. Two terrific fathers that I am honored to have as friends.

Walking out of the WWE arena for the very last time with WWE security guard, Scott. (Photo Credit: Matt Cardona) didn't like something. Every time I got momentum, Vince told me that I was too over the top and to tone it down. I told him that I was always trying.

His response was, "It's not that. You should write a manual on how to ring announce, like Michael Cole wrote a manual on how to do commentary. You should hold seminars. You need to teach other people how to do your job so the future can provide new ring announcers." At this point, I was looking for the hidden cameras and waiting for Ashton Kutcher to pop out and tell me I was being punk'd. When that didn't happen, I said, "But if I'm not doing a good job ring announcing and have not been as good as I was three years ago, I don't feel right trying to teach others how to do the job that I'm not doing a good job at myself."

"It's not that. You do a great job. Kevin says you are a great ring announcer. [I start looking around for those cameras again.] He wants you to focus on TV, any diva can announce live events." He offered me a three-year deal with a 3% raise. I looked at Big. "So you only want to offer me 3% more a year, and you want me to focus just on announcing at TV because any diva can do live events. And live events are a grueling schedule. We jump all over the place and have numerous long days. If you want me to focus more on ring announcing and my ring announcing at TVs, pay me less than what you offered and have a diva host all the live events, and I'll just work TVs."

As I write this, I cannot stress enough that these are real, actual quotes. This is not exaggerated or taken out of context. This is a real conversation that took place between a WWE executive and me. I needed to make that clear because it's hard for me to even believe it, and I was there. I thought I came up with a hell of a solution. Big's response?

"We don't have anyone to do that." He just told me that any diva could do it. We have lots of divas on the roster and lots of divas in developmental, and he said that any of them could do it. But he doesn't have anyone to do that.

I asked Big if he had any idea about all of the other roles I play unofficially. I told him, and he didn't care. He was eager to tell me his big contribution to live events. He told me a story of how he pitched an idea to Vince about getting rid of intermission at live events. "We don't take intermission at TV. Why do we need intermission at live events? It's a waste of time."

There you have it. The guy that I'm pouring my heart out to about my passion and everything I did just made the most mindless comment I had ever heard. He was so far removed from what we did at live events and oblivious to the live event world that I now knew he couldn't relate to any of what I was saying. Intermission gave fans a little break from that psychological roller coaster that we take them on at the shows. If we did a show without an intermission, you could feel it in the air. People got antsy. They needed a drink, a snack—some sort of a small break, even a bathroom break. Otherwise, by the time the main event comes on, they are tired and zoned out. On top of that, intermission is when the company sells the most merchandise. Get rid of intermission, Big? What an awesome idea from a guy who didn't come to live events regularly and was now one of the top officials at another wrestling organization.

I mentioned to Big what Kevin had told me three years prior in the bus at the Royal Rumble in Atlanta about becoming an employee and getting benefits. He told me I would have to discuss that with Kevin. I also told him that I would like a little more time off to be with my family. My mom had been diagnosed with Parkinson's Disease, and I just wanted a weekend here and there to spend more time with my family. You miss so much when you're on the road, and you only really have a brief window of time to see loved ones or have time to yourself. There's no reason to be imprisoned when under contract, but unfortunately, that's what you are. They rule your life and book you whenever and wherever they want and don't take "breaks" into consideration.

I emailed Kevin and told him about this new contract not containing the benefits. Shortly after, I received a call from Big. I asked if he made any changes. He did not. "Kevin did not remember telling you that he would make you an employee."

"How about the days off?" I asked.

"Sure. Every once in a while, when you need days off, just let us know, and we will work with you." I had asked for a weekend a month, and he told me, "That's too much. Nobody gets time like that."

I wanted to be home for an extra day or two here and there. They told me I could ask every six to eight weeks. "Well, you want me to focus on Mondays and said any diva can do live events, how about having me do just TV on Mondays?"

His response? "I don't think that's an option. We like having you there because you're a presence from TV, and we like having you at live events so it feels like TV."

I said, "So it's basically take it or leave it?"

"Yes."

I was standing outside Bed Bath & Beyond with my phone planted firmly on the side of my face. I did not say anything. He was waiting. I waited. I wanted to tell him how I felt and end it right there. I really did. In that minute, I was ready to be done with the job I had dreamed of. I was underappreciated. I gave them all my time and energy. They did not want to play fair. That brief 15 seconds of silence felt like 10 long minutes of awkward silence.

I just said thank you and hung up.

I signed an extension that bought me an extra month. Two days later, I was on the road. I had two flights, a live event, and then a long drive to the next town. Around midnight on February 9, 2013, we stopped to get some dinner.

My phone lit up with an email from Big. He asked where we stood on the issue and had expected a response that day and needed an answer by Saturday.

Well. It was late Friday night, and I was on the road. I needed to give them a yes or no by the next day. I was in a bad spot. It wasn't like I had anything else to jump into. HandsToGo was doing just okay. I felt like I should just stay and take their abuse until I had a reason to really leave because there was probably no going back. They took Lilian back, but I knew they wouldn't take me. I thanked him the next day and accepted the new deal that locked me in for three years but gave me zero benefits.

In what would be my last year with the company, I wasn't getting excited to get in the ring anymore. I was so worried about my bosses picking on my announcements for being too energetic, too melodramatic, or too whatever that I was scared to announce. I hated getting picked on by the higher-ups. I hated trying to help make sense of a show by asking the smaller but meaningful questions (so things in the show would make sense once in a while), only to be mocked by my superiors. Usually after they made fun of me, they would take my input into account and make a change. But they had to get their bullying in first.

When we had rehearsals, a lot of the time I wasn't told what I was going to be rehearsing. I would be told to get in the ring and go. I'd look at the writer and ask, "what am I saying?" I was never called, told, or texted to come for many of the rehearsals, but when needed, I better be there! Entrances, promos, and blocking would take place, but many times, we wouldn't have scripts just yet or have any idea what was going on in the segments that were being rehearsed. One day, we were in Philadelphia, and I was sitting in the locker room watching the monitor. Talents were casually going over their matches with the producers just like every TV day. All of a sudden, Kevin started paging me over the arena. Not, "Hey Justin, you're needed at ringside." No call, text, or anything. Instead: "That's okay. We will all just wait until Justin's ready to start." He continued doing this in front of everyone. As I ran into the arena, he had the camera guys shooting me for the jumbotron to see my reaction to his rib. I was ready again to quit, right there, right to his camera. Kevin Dunn, the man who sits on the board of directors for this publicly traded company, and the man who at one point gave me my first shot.

CHAPTER 25
FAVORITE EVENT BECOMES LIFE-CHANGING EVENT

Toward the end, I was so disillusioned with the job that my focus shifted. Instead of advancing my own career, I decided to use the position I was in to help other people. At the Royal Rumble in Pittsburgh in 2014, Frank Bullock, the audio engineer, came to visit all his friends. Frank worked in the TV corner with Mark and me on shows. He would keep an eye on all the audio equipment and make TV nights fun. Unfortunately, he had been sick, and there was a part of me that knew it would be the last time I would see him. It was a very depressing day, and we all hated to see a friend who was loved by everyone at the company in this type of situation. I got through the show, but I couldn't stop thinking about Frank.

As I thanked the crowd for coming, I took some pictures with fans at ringside. I walked down the aisle toward the back as the crowd was filing out. I noticed a little boy with a bald head, and it looked like maybe he, too, had gone through some depressing days. He had a very cute personality when he spoke. His father was trying to tell me something, but another kid kept yelling out. This little boy explained that I was talking to his dad, and he would have to wait his turn. His father whispered to me that he didn't have long to live. He then handed me a note for Daniel Bryan:

"Daniel, Connor is nearing the end, baring a miracle. If u could facetime it would cheer him up greatly. UR info would be secure with my life."

The little boy's name was Connor, and he was a very big fan of Daniel's. He mentioned a YouTube video, and then I realized right away that I had seen that video and immediately sent Daniel the link, just like I'm sure many others had. It was a video where he hoped it would spread and allow him to meet Bryan. His father, Steve, told me that they were able to meet Daniel through a local radio station a while back because of that video, which was very cool. I asked Connor if Daniel was the only superstar that he liked. He immediately said, "No, I like everybody!" And I knew how genuine his voice was. He sounded like me as a kid—just a big wrestling fan.

One of the greatest parts of my job was to be in a position where I see a kid in the crowd that could use something to make their night just a little extra special. I gave the guys and girls a heads-up so that maybe they would hand out their arm band, elbow pad, or even just to give a special little kid a high five. I loved seeing faces light up, and I knew how easy it was for the talent to do that to people.

Once in Fargo, North Dakota, there was an entire section of wheelchairs seated behind me at ringside. The arena was cool enough to give them a great section for the wheelchairs and their able-bodied friends. I immediately went back to find our marketing guy and asked about setting up an impromptu meet-and-greet. The way I looked at that was just knowing that the ailments these fans had obviously impacted their lives, and while they could do everything they were physically able to do, they still had challenges that other people didn't have. I just wanted to do something to make this day extra special for them. He said that he would try to find a room. He also asked if that would be okay with the guys and girls on the show. Every single wrestler that I asked said yes. No talent that I had ever worked with ever hesitated in helping. I had tears in my eyes watching the long line of wheelchairs head back to a room where a parade of WWE superstars and divas took pictures and signed autographs for all of them. It was so easy to help someone, and in this case, a whole group, have a good night.

I never forgot when Mr. Garibaldi gave us basketball tickets, and I tried to do random acts of kindness whenever possible, whether it was help someone out with tickets to a show or help people I met outside of shows when they already had tickets. I remember one time in particular when a family was with a little boy wearing a John Cena T-shirt. I asked him if he liked John Cena and told him I was the guy who introduced him to the ring on TV. They already had tickets and were so excited to take the boy to the show that they had their seat info memorized. I made a note of where seated and made sure they had a nice package of gifts at their seats. They were not into wrestling, but the whole family was so excited to take the boy to the show. I just knew how much wrestling meant to him, and I wanted to make his first show amazing.

I always tried to do something special without bringing people backstage, except for a handful of times. On this night in Pittsburgh, however, without any hesitation or permission (I was trusted after being there for so long, and the company knew I used good judgement), I took Connor and his father, Steve, backstage. Connor had used his Make-A-Wish gift to go to Disney, but this wasn't a wish: This was just the right thing to do, and the stars had aligned for him. A lot of the talent had already left. The show was over, it was late, and we had a long drive to Cleveland ahead of us. I approached Sheamus, Randy Orton, and Batista, who were the last few still in the building. They were all more than happy to say hello to Connor and give them their T-shirt, towel, or whatever they had right off their backs. Most important, they hung out and chatted with him for a bit. There was something special about this little 8-year-old. He was battling brain cancer, and doctors didn't have a positive outlook on him beating the brutal disease. Batista was in the middle of being interviewed for his upcoming DVD when I approached him, and without any hesitation, he walked away from shooting to meet Connor.

While Connor and the guys were talking, Triple H's bus driver, Terry, told me that he and Stephanie would be coming through momentarily. I asked if that meant I should move out of the way, and he said no, they'd probably like to meet him. Sure enough, Stephanie came through and immediately got down to the floor and began conversing with this little man. I can't say it enough, how special this little guy seemed to me. To everyone, really. I never wanted to bother Stephanie because everybody else did, and our conversations over the years were brief. But seeing how great she was with Connor really made me have a whole new respect for her. She was the head of numerous departments, and as if her life weren't busy enough at work, she was a wonderful mother to three little girls.

Triple H joined us, and Steve asked about taking a picture of Connor with Triple H and Stephanie. Steve didn't know if his camera would work in the dark area, so I immediately volunteered my phone. Of course, this gave Hunter a chance to make a wisecrack because I liked taking pictures at ringside (to promote the company's shows). I took the picture, and Sean Cleary from HR who was standing there observing quickly gave Steve his business card to arrange for getting the picture by emailing him. I immediately asked Steve for his email address, which was on his note to Daniel, and said that I would send him the picture so he wouldn't have to wait or go through any extra channels.

After Connor had met everyone and gotten his two commemorative folding chairs signed, I walked them back into the arena where they could exit out to their car. In any other situation, I would have hoped they had a special night and said my goodbyes. Something about this night was different, however. I had tears in my eye from seeing his face light up. I walked back to the dressing room, and CM Punk and I were the last two guys there. I sat down and immediately sent Steve the pictures from my phone. The vibe in the room was off. On top of that, I had Frank on my mind, and now I was happy that the little boy had a good night, but I also felt horrible for him. The next day on my way to the arena in Cleveland, I received a very touching email back from Steve, thanking me for Connor's special experience at the Royal Rumble. As soon as I got to the arena, I handed Daniel Bryan the note from Steve.

I saw Punk in the hallway and put my hand out to shake his. He ignored me. I didn't know if that was due to his feelings toward the company or if it was personal. At one point when he was using HandsToGo and having the trainer use it on him for an injury, I asked if he wouldn't mind tweeting something about it, just like any of us would tweet about someone else's product that helped us or that we generally liked. He told me to text him something to say in the tweet, so I did, assuming that would make it easier on him to post. Well, he took a screen shot of that text and posted that instead, which really bothered me, but I never said anything. I also remember doing an interview with a newspaper reporter from back home in which I was adamant about repeating facts so the story would be correct versus an interview that is more about creative writing. Well, they took the creative writing route and slightly changed the story I told about being in the ring with Punk at *WrestleMania* to make it more entertaining, I guess. He once got in the ring during *RAW* and made a sarcastic comment about a "quote" they used, so I assumed that it bothered him. Whatever silly beef there may have been over nothing, I had a feeling that would be the last time I would probably see him for a while. I knew he needed a break and hoped he would get it, and he did. He left the building and WWE that day.

I went home the next day and told my friend Mike about Connor. He was so outgoing and witty, almost like an adult in the body of a child. I told him that I passed along Connor's note to Daniel, and nothing against Daniel, but I had a feeling that he wouldn't reach out. I'm sure the superstars get bombarded with requests, and some people choose to reach out and others may not. I didn't know what Daniel would do, but I felt that I needed to do something for the boy just in case. I took a picture of the note that Steve wrote—it wasn't folded but was written on piece of packaging. I kept looking at the note and knew I had a rough decision to make. There was a chance that if I stayed in touch with Connor and his father, there could be a sad ending in the future. I also knew it would be selfish to not try and help because of what I might be feeling if or when that happened. I decided at lunch that I wanted to make his possibly short but hopefully long time here on earth as happy as possible. I decided to stay in touch with Steve and Connor.

At the time, I did not know exactly what was wrong with Connor. I knew he was sick, and I knew he liked wrestling. When we first talked, I didn't ask him about anything negative or anything about the hospitals; we only talked about wrestling and fun topics. It was all positive. Stephanie would ask me questions, and I just didn't have the answers, and honestly I didn't want to talk about that just yet. I talked to Steve and Connor almost daily. I used FaceTime to chat with Connor throughout the week. I especially liked doing that on Mondays (his chemo days) because I was with the majority of the roster at TV, and I could have the guys pop in on FaceTime and say hi to him. I usually sat in the stands or on an equipment case in the back, and as anyone walked by I grabbed them and introduced them to Connor. They all took the time to have a conversation with this excited little boy—a little boy who may have possibly forgotten about his battle with a deadly disease for that brief moment while he talked to his favorite wrestlers about their in-ring battles. His father later told me how awful Monday's were, but to make them better, they would discuss the possibility of a FaceTime call later that day from *RAW*.

Stephanie asked me to keep her updated on Connor as well. We were in Green Bay, Wisconsin, when I told her about my plan. I was going to use the power of WWE to help him and do what medicine could not do for him. I said that I wasn't aware if she really knew how this company affected people because she was brought up on the inside. I explained how when my dad was sick, wrestling on

TV cheered him up and hearing from the wrestlers lifted his spirits like nothing else. I could see her just staring and processing everything I was explaining. I knew her wheels were spinning. I was happy to keep her posted as Steve gave me the scoop each week, and I started to learn more about Connor's battle. I sent him photos from ringside at the live shows and even FaceTimed him during *RAW* to show him what was going on during a commercial break. I did whatever I could do, just to keep in touch and keep him positive. I knew that Connor was living for WWE, in a sense, and I wanted to use that to give him motivational fuel and, therefore, do what medicine could not do for him, help make him happy. Talking to the little man made me forget about being unappreciated and pretty much nonexistent at work. At that point in my career, they pretty much stopped showing me on camera during *RAW*. I wasn't mentioned by name or included in anything. I was part of the background ambience, and there was a very clear choice made to not utilize me for anything beyond that. Working with Connor, however, gave me some motivation, something to work for, and that other stuff didn't matter anymore. I knew what I was doing meant nothing to the company, but what I was doing for Connor meant the world to him. I did anything I could to help.

Steve mentioned that *RAW* would be back in Pittsburgh in June, but according to Connor's recent medical scans, they weren't sure he could wait until June. So on March 31, I invited Connor, Steve, and Steve's father to *RAW* in Washington, DC. Steve didn't know if it would be too far to drive, so I got them a hotel right outside of DC and made sure they could have flexibility if Connor needed a nap.

I was at the gym one day and had an idea that I wanted to pitch to Stephanie. I reached out to Steve and ran it by him, and he was okay with it. Then I approached the wrestler Big E and did the same. I wanted to ask Stephanie about possibly announcing Connor to the ring early in the day. I wanted him to be able to walk down the ramp, across the aisle, and into the ring, just like the superstars he lived for. Rob Van Dam was at the arena one day when he wasn't with the company, and I knew he was one of Connor's favorites. He let me record a video message for Connor in which he said the Intercontinental Championship would be renamed the "Inter-Connor-nental Championship" once he won it.

I approached Stephanie when we were in Chicago prior to the DC show, and she asked if there was anything special she might be able to get him. I asked her about an intercontinental championship replica and then asked if I could run an idea by her. Now, this wasn't a storyline pitch; I had an idea of something fun we could do just for Connor earlier in the day. I wanted to know if, before doors were open, Connor could walk down the entrance ramp and into the ring. I would announce him like a wrestler, and he could experience what that felt like. On top of that, if it would be okay, Connor would be in the ring, and Big E, the intercontinental champion, would join him. Big E would offer to defend the title against Connor. Connor would push him, he would fall over, and I would get to announce him as the new intercontinental champion! But then the Authority's music would hit. The name given to Triple H and Stephanie, the bad guys from TV, but the people who were so nice to him, would come out and declare that title was now the Inter-Connor-nental Championship and present him with the belt. I ran the idea by Big E, and he was cool with it. As far as Stephanie, I knew it was a bit much, but even if she said no to the in-ring stuff, the entrance would seem easy enough to get approved. I knew in my mind that he would love it! Stephanie, however, was worried about legalities so I had to run it by Triple H's assistant at the time, Jane. I immediately approached Jane about the idea and then emailed her to follow up. She said that some forms needed to be signed. I asked Steve about my plan and if he would be okay with signing the forms, and he said yes. I followed up a couple of times about my plan, but she stopped responding, so I dropped it as I didn't want to push anything with the office. Just in case my plan would eventually come to fruition, I had T-shirts made for him, again by Ryan at Prowrestlingtees. com, who donated them as well as the drawing of Connor and his concrete letters inspired by his dad's concrete business as well as Daniel Bryan and his Yes! Arms. I sent the graphic Ryan used on the shirts to our stage designer. That way they could use it on the video wall for his big entrance if he ever got the chance to come down to the ring.

Less than two weeks after our conversation in Green Bay, Stephanie approached me as I was about to go through the curtain to announce a house show at Madison Square Garden. "Justin! Um…Uh…What's our little friend's name?"

"Connor," I replied.

"Yes! I want to invite him and his father to *WrestleMania*! I will pay out of my own pocket for them to fly out and come to the show. I want to give him something to look forward to!" I was blown away. I was using DC to do the same thing, and now Stephanie was covering an event after DC! She asked me to invite him, and I asked if she would rather give him the news, but she declined. I couldn't wait to have that conversation. I called him on FaceTime and asked him if he would like to come to *WrestleMania*. For some reason, he wasn't as excited as I thought he would be. I was perplexed. He asked if he could call me back. I was then in the car with a couple of the other guys, driving to the arena and looked at them like, hmm that was strange. He called back immediately and gave me the Daniel Bryan YES! chant and put his hands in the air like Daniel. He also ran around the house, on top of the world! It turns out that he was a bit hesitant when I first extended Stephanie's offer because he first wanted to check with his dad to make sure it was okay. Once he cleared that with his dad, he was ready, but his next adventure would be DC.

Connor, Steve, and his grandfather, Steve Sr., got to the arena early that the day. My friends in marketing pulled some strings and arranged for them to sit front row center at *RAW*. I met them with their tickets and passes and brought them everywhere. I had never brought anyone everywhere. Not even my family. They met everyone. The first person we saw was John Cena who immediately went into the merchandise cabinet on his own merit and grabbed some apparel which he signed and gave to Connor. It was such an incredible afternoon. Connor took pictures with everybody he saw, and he got their autographs and even gifts from his wrestling heroes. It was the first time I ever introduced anyone to Hulk Hogan, Brock Lesnar, and even the Undertaker. Nothing and nobody was off limits for Connor. He was familiar with all the talent, and most of them were familiar with him, too, from the FaceTime calls. I texted Stephanie to let her know he was there, and she couldn't wait to be on the receiving end of one of his giant hugs.

We all walked toward the Gorilla Position, where he met our friendly giant, the Big Show who was so good with the little guy. Stephanie then gave him a tour which led out to the stage. He ran into the New Age Outlaws, who requested to see his big "New Age Outlaws" ring intro in person. They had seen it on FaceTime, but the real thing was even better. This was incredible: The kid was a superstar to his own superheroes!

Triple H approached us and said hello to Connor's family, but as the ghost, he never looked at me or acknowledged that I was even standing there. He asked Connor about coming to the ring and what entrance music he likes. If you knew anything about Connor, you knew the answer was Daniel Bryan's music. As Connor told him that, Triple H began talking in his headset and walked away. I called out his name, and he looked back. I mentioned that I had emailed the stage designers an image, and they might have that to use if he were getting an entrance. He didn't say anything. He just walked away, talking into his headset.

A few seconds later, the graphic popped up on the jumbotron. I stood there as the plan unfolded. I was standing on the entrance way with my camera to record it, but I was no longer a part of it. I was just glad that it was happening for Connor. Daniel gave Connor the sweatshirt off his back to wear. Bryan's music hit, and the Connor graphic filled the back video wall. Daniel and Connor walked to the ring together. The entire roster surrounded the ring. They cheered for Connor and chanted his name. I had never seen anything like it. Ever. There was no doubt that this was a surreal moment for Connor straight out of his dreams.

Rather than the IC Champ, Triple H got in the ring and had Connor punch him and pin him. The ref ran over and counted to three. Connor had pinned Triple H. I didn't get to announce him to the ring or as the winner the way I thought it up, but regardless, it was an amazing day for a huge wrestling fan who had shown incredible bravery in the face of a life-threatening illness. It was very special and without a doubt the most rewarding day of my career.

While all this good stuff was going on for Connor, I was pulled into the bathroom of the talent relations room, for extra privacy, I guess. I asked Connor and his family to wait in the hall. Michael Cole and Mark Carrano of talent relations wanted to speak with me.

A little background: Previously, I reported to Kevin Dunn to discuss contracts, but other than that, I worked with his assistant for the majority of my time there. After that, the ring announcers (me included, obviously) were handed off to Big who then took over our contract negotiations. Then we got handed over to a guy named Will (who didn't do anything with us), and then at some point later we reported to Hunter who took over many other departments including talent relations. But Hunter didn't deal with ring announcers directly, so then Michael Cole took over, but he didn't want to deal with the announcers either, so he had Tony Chimel handle scheduling and would only get involved to approve certain things. Confused yet? Me, too.

Anyway, Cole and Carrano, acting on behalf of talent relations, but as they told me, were talking to me as a "friend," pulled me into a bathroom to tell me that my HandsToGo unit was no longer allowed to be brought into the locker rooms or even talked about. I told them that I wasn't trying to sneak around anyone. I had previously given Cole a unit for his wife's back, which he told me helped her. I had also given one to Carrano. They told me that this came from "high up," and I could get fired if I didn't stop bringing the units around. I told them I would stop, and I did.

I had given a lot of these devices to the guys for free. I just wanted to help. They told me that was part of the problem. A trainer told them I had given one to a guy who was recently injured at a show, and apparently that didn't fly with him. I was just trying to help. This trainer had even used it on talent in the past! There were numerous men and women on the roster with bumps, bruises, and injuries, and often being on these long tours prevented them from really getting the care they needed. If HandsToGo helped them feel better in safe and legal way, what was I in trouble for? I can't even count how many times guys were injured, and despite the company knowing, they still had to go out and work. I wanted to help them as much as possible before they had to work again the next day. The list of what you couldn't use to help with pain or recovery was growing, so I thought this device was great because it helped injuries and recovery time and did nothing bad.

I wasn't doing anything illegal. They claimed it helped them when they were injured and if they were, I was giving it to them, not selling it to them at this point. A referee and two wrestlers were hurt before a European tour, and I got all three of them HandsToGo units to get through the tour. What was the problem? On top of it, I had given one to Hunter, to Kevin, to Vince, and again, even the trainer who at one point asked to borrow one while he worked on the guys. Hunter's assistant asked for one, NXT head trainer Bill Demott used one for an injury, and so on. Numerous people were using HandsToGo and claimed that they helped them feel better. This only benefitted the company. I didn't understand why they wouldn't allow something that was legal and helped talent to feel better, but that's what they wanted, so I obliged.

Talent will very regularly be injured, and the company usually doesn't give them time off. They are expected to work through the injuries. So why not let them use something that could help the healing process and give them some relief? The HandsToGo incident is just one of countless examples of someone trying to help, trying to be proactive, trying to help the company, and then needlessly being punished for it. Another example that comes shooting into my mind is Zack Ryder.

At one point the company held a meeting to tell talent to reach for the "brass ring." Zack reached higher than anyone. He wasn't being used and feared he was going to be fired. He worked his tail off on a YouTube show to entertain fans and save his character and job. It worked. The show blew up, and he was a star. But WWE didn't want guys to become stars if it wasn't "their guy." Zack definitely wasn't a chosen guy. So despite being way over with the crowd (at a time when the company desperately needed popular stars), the company buried him in awful storylines. It was so bad. At one point, when Triple H was a "good guy" and the roster "walked out" on him, Zack came to the ring, stood by the boss, and said he was still there for him. Hunter hit his finishing move (The Pedigree) on him and laid him out. It was utter nonsense. The company also made him move his insanely popular show to WWE's YouTube channel as part of a deal they made with YouTube (which weighed heavily on the popularity of Zack's show). Despite the time and the money, it cost him to produce the show each week. When he asked for pay or even small reimbursement for the props he purchased, the company denied him. Keep in mind that this company was making millions of dollars off this deal. To all of you hungry men and women out there, let Zack's story be a warning. Only go for the brass ring if they want you to get over. Just like me, Zack was just trying to do what was right and got punished for it.

It was mind boggling to people within the company that they had such an incredible roster of talent, but they would constantly cut their wings off. When a move got over and the people were starting to get behind that talent, they would be told not to do that move anymore. It happened at first with the Cesaro Swing, In fact, Cesaro was SO good (If I ran a company, he would be my first champion–

he is incredible), they made him yodel to the ring on top of controlling what he could and could not do. When fans caught on to a catchphrase, so many times the talent would be told to stop. Feed me more? There was a roster full of hungry talent, and every time they built up momentum, if they were able to do so under the radar, they would be put back in their place unless they were the chosen ones. They would continually endorse NXT as the future of the business and promote how wonderful they were but ignore the present stars. They would make *RAW* a boring three-hour show with the same talents doing the same things and cutting the same promos, but they would let the NXT shows be what a good show should be. Damien Sandow had been given some horrible gimmicks that guaranteed him failure. He was so talented that he made them work, and not just work, but thrive. Fast forward to his pre-*WrestleMania 30* battle royal when the entire stadium was chanting for him in the perfect situation to have him turn on the Miz and become a "babyface"…and then win! Instead, he was eliminated and given a new gimmick to sink with and then was released shortly after.

I felt bad for the guys killing themselves in the ring on the main roster night after night only to be told indirectly on Steve Austin's podcast by Vince himself that they weren't hungry and they weren't having fun. They got in trouble for having fun. They were putting on incredible matches at live events when they were allowed but were not allowed to do so on television. Triple H, who was the VP of talent, cut a promo on the Undertaker basically saying he looked at the locker room (of the talent he is in charge of developing), and there was no competition for him, which is why he was challenging Undertaker. How does that do anything for the roster? Then he lost the match, and Undertaker disappeared for the year. The show goes on with that talent that Triple H buried. He did the same thing when the roster walked out on the company in a storyline. But the way it was spun, the talent walked out on the company which would get the crowd to boo everyone except for the handful of guys that stayed around. Hunter looked like the sympathetic character and said, "I'll wrestle a broomstick for two hours. Hell, I've wrestled a lot of the guys in that parking lot; the broomstick will give me a better match than most of them." That's the head of talent development, burying the talent rather than building them up and making a case about how he and the fans should hope that the talent returns. You can call that the character of Triple H, but many of the fans, many of the talent, and I would take that as Triple H burying the talent. Over the years, he gained a reputation of constantly turning the crowds against everyone and making him look like the hero, even as a "bad guy." These can be considered storylines and not personal, but regardless, what it does to the talent is nothing but detrimental. Many of us within the company thought that creative decisions were made to appease the egos of the powers that be rather than entertain the fans and give the fans what they wanted to see. They already won the battle. They became the only game in town, and the competition took away their drive. Now it was to do what made them happy. It was amazing to see how Triple H had become this hero by holding down the current talent and allowing "his talent" to prosper. He would even blame Vince for what happened on the main roster, like that wasn't not his fault, but hey, wasn't his NXT great? From the outside, you would think he really was trying to help the business, but those that were there knew better since most of them had probably felt his wrath. He always looked to be in top shape when standing with the talents he was working with, and it makes you wonder, if the full-time talent had to be natural, then did the "part-time" talent (that was there full time) have to be natural?

I found it funny that Hunter joined Twitter even though he would constantly mock it, including on Jimmy Fallon's show. Then he got an account and tweeted that he also got his wife to join the "nerdfest." While he also used to make fun of indie guys, he was now signing established indie guys off the indies to give NXT credit and use guys that actually knew the business rather than stick with their model of taking everyday people and turning them into wrestling robots. Now you can see him constantly taking selfies with these "indie" guys and posting them to the "nerdfest." I have nothing against the NXT guys at all, and I hope they do well. The treatment, however, that they get from him is totally different than what the main roster gets because those are his "students" and his projects. The locker room mentality had changed significantly from the old-school mentality to even the fun times when Dreamer was there to much less camaraderie. I was trained to shake everyone's hand and just say hello and be polite; that's the way it was. Now, it wasn't like that anymore. The new talent came in as if they belonged there and didn't have to show respect to anyone else, to any of the established guys. It wasn't everyone, but it was a lot of people. We had heard that it was encouraged in Florida, and the talents didn't know any better nor know that it was frowned upon by the current roster. I liked the NXT talents, and there were a lot of talented people coming out of there. I just wish they all had come in the way everyone else had over the years: respectfully.

The Washington, DC, *RAW* was special because Connor sat front row center, and the Bella Twins and other talent went out of their way to acknowledge him. The twins always went the extra mile with everything they did. There was a long period when the company didn't know how to use them, and each week they would show up to live events and get thrown into a random spot. Whether it was hosting, announcing, managing, or sometimes wrestling, they always knocked everything out of the park and ran with every opportunity that came their way. They already had my respect, but their treatment toward Connor cemented it. He wasn't feeling well early into the show, and they ended up leaving so he could rest after a long but incredible day. I sent a cryptic tweet that night, thanking my coworkers for everything they did, as I truly appreciated it.

CHAPTER 26
THE WORLD DON'T MOVE TO THE BEAT OF JUST ONE DRUM

On the few days off after DC, an extremely unique opportunity arose. Adam Jones, the incredibly talented guitarist from the legendary, Grammy-award winning band Tool, was a wrestling fan and had been coming to shows over the years. He even played an amazing rendition of the National Anthem at *SummerSlam* 2011. I had heard of Tool, but I didn't know their music or even how big they were. You wouldn't be able to tell from talking to Adam. He was so down to earth and was nice as anyone could be. He was always friendly, and I enjoyed talking to him and his wife when they came by. When we were talking at *SummerSlam* in LA that year, he had asked about announcing them when they went on their next tour. I told him I would love to do it if they were in Arizona when I was there, or if not, I would fly out on one of my off days to wherever that show was. As it turned out, they were in Arizona on one of my days off between *RAW* in DC and *WrestleMania 30*.

To get an idea of what I was getting into, I started listening to their music. It turns out, I owned a couple of their songs, and a friend had added his collection to mine since their songs aren't easy to find. I loved this music and was immediately impressed and hooked. It was very unique to the point that it was even mathematically different. You couldn't nod your head to it, as the counts aren't standard. The music, lyrics, and live visuals at a show really take your mind on a mesmerizing adventure. I was immediately a fan and listened over and over, not just to get psyched for the concert-but because I really got into it!

I met up with Adam the night before and then again on that afternoon before the concert. I had been attempting to get him to try Portillo's since we first met, and they actually opened in Arizona. So I picked it up for us and brought it to the arena. He invited me to his VIP session where I learned his story and a lot of background on his music, which was very interesting. When he wrapped up, I headed to his dressing room to get our food ready. I made a video call to Connor and Steve while I waited for Adam to come back. Any other eight-year-old who didn't know of the music group I was working with probably would have just blown off the fact that I was there. Connor, despite not being familiar with Tool, thought it was cool that I was introducing them. We talked a little wrestling, and, as usual, he was the one making me laugh and lifting my spirits while I was attempting to do the same for him.

Adam came back, and we spent the rest of the day hanging out, drinking our chocolate cake shakes, and then meeting the other three band members. I brought them HandsToGo sets for their tour because I knew it would help, and it wasn't WWE, so that was allowed. Someone asked if I was nervous, and I explained that I did this pretty often, so I was okay. Adam quickly commented that this would be different than announcing at WWE. Right away I looked at him with an expression that suggested this was a challenge. Then I started to wonder, could this be different?

My friends came to watch me and, of course, see the show. I explained what Adam had said and filled them in that this was going to be a good test for me. As the show was about to start, I actually became nervous. Tool doesn't need an introduction, and that crowd was ready. I took a quick picture with the group to tweet out and ran up the steps onto the stage (I didn't realize at the time that this isn't something Tool usually does as they are somewhat mysterious and do not produce many photos). The crowd was up, not because they knew who I was, but because a guy was on stage, and the show was surely to begin soon. I brought them to complete silence. Then I brought them up. Then down. Then up, then up more, then down, then UP!

Well, I still had it. I was able to control that sold-out US Airways Center like a puppeteer. The power of that microphone and truly knowing how to use it was such a thrill. I introduced them and watched the show with my eyes glued to the stage. What an incredible opportunity and honor. Not only was the music mind blowing, but the visual effects were amazing as well. They are very unique, and I highly recommend going to a show when they're out your way.

The next week was *WrestleMania 30* in New Orleans. I arrived at the company hotel where talent would typically check-in and receive standard packages from WWE. Usually we got a T-shirt and hat and maybe a sweatshirt if we were lucky. We worked hard all year, and this was the one big show where the company made lots of its money. The talent would make lots and lots of (unpaid) appearances that the company booked, making the *WrestleMania* weekend days very long and very busy. It was nice of them to throw us some WWE merchandise as a reward.

When I asked for mine, I was told that I wasn't talent. Now, I had heard this for years—that ring announcers weren't included in the corporate umbrella of "WWE Talent," but I kind of assumed that since I was officially labeled as working under talent relations (under Triple H and Michael Cole), that I was now officially considered "talent." I mean, let's think about this: I was part of the show (every show, in fact). I talked on the microphone and was physically present in the ring. If I wasn't talent, what was I? They didn't have an answer for me or a gift bag. Not receiving a gift bag wasn't the problem, despite always getting one in the past. I could care less about a T-shirt or a hat. The problem was that, once again, I was made to be invisible by the people I worked for.

I discovered that I was also left off the list for transportation to Axxess (the *WrestleMania* fan fest) where I was booked to announce alongside the NXT ring announcer. What's odd is that even with both of us there, they had me announce the entire NXT show and did not have anything for her to do. This was quite strange since she was the NXT announcer and the one familiar with the NXT stats. I was also left off the list as there was no ticket for me at the Hall of Fame ceremony. Typically, someone from talent relations would get ahold us before Mania and ask how many people were coming with us to the Hall of Fame ceremony, and we would all be placed in assigned seating. Unfortunately, despite that, no one had my ticket. Apparently, no department wanted to claim ring announcers anymore in Triple H's talent relations. Sue used to always take care of us when we were under Kevin. Luckily, Fandango was booked at Axxess during the ceremony, so I just sat in his seat.

It was still unreal to see the Ultimate Warrior standing in front of me as he was inducted into their Hall of Fame. I watched him live as he made his speech. We all wondered how that would go. Years before, WWE released a DVD that ripped him apart. It was basically a story about how horrible a wrestler he was. He was truly bothered by that and mentioned that in his speech, which was understandable. He also mentioned that he had moved past it, which was very admirable. He loved his family; he had his daughters up there on stage with him. I got to know wrestlers primarily as how they behave at work, and it's always really interesting when you see them in different roles. Most of them were very passionate about their families and loved ones. I found out that night that Warrior was no different.

The next night was the big event. Now, I was a huge wrestling fan. That night I got to announce *WrestleMania 30* in front of over 70,000 people with the majority of my childhood idols in the arena. But I was under Vince's, Hunter's, and Kevin's microscopes, and pretty much all the passion had been sucked out of me at that point. It wasn't fun anymore. I didn't get those butterflies or any of the excitement I used to feel.

The show was cool, but for me, it was more about Connor getting to be there. Prior to Mania, Stephanie had also begun contacting him as well. Right before we went live, Stephanie walked past her family and Connor, who were all seated ringside. She walked over to me and grabbed my hand in the dark, as if to say, "we did it." Connor was on top of the world. He got to see all his new WWE friends wrestle live on "the biggest stage of them all" and sit in the front row to watch his number one guy win the WWE World Heavyweight Championship. While Steve had written Daniel a couple more letters, pleading for a call at some point, Daniel's call came from after he won the match by going over to Connor to give him a hug, which meant the world to him.

I announced the main event, and I was able to introduce some of the guys that I had grown up watching, like Bret Hart, Hulk Hogan, and "the American Dream" Dusty Rhodes. I even got to announce the winner of the Undertaker versus Brock Lesnar match. Undertaker had never before been defeated at *WrestleMania*. He was 21-0, but, on this night, Lesnar ended that streak. Did I know that was going to happen? Not at all. When the bell rang, I thought there was a mistake, and my stomach dropped. I just looked at Mark Yeaton. The cue from him to announce the winner was about a full minute after the bell, which was not normal. The most impressive streak and one of the highlight matches of Mania each year was "the streak match," and it was just...over. The crowd was shocked. I was shocked. Everybody was shocked. My announcement that Brock Lesnar had won was one of the strangest things I had ever said into a microphone before. I could typically anticipate the reaction that would join in midway through an announcement, but not this one. It was one of my biggest announcements ever, and it wasn't greeted by a stadium full of cheers or boos. It was greeted with more of a "Huh? No. This can't be right." That's the only time I could ever classify a reaction in that fashion. If I'm not making it clear here and we ever meet in person, ask me to describe it for you with sounds. It's a lot easier that way, or maybe listen to the audio version of this book.

The show felt big because it was Mania, and there was a huge crowd. Basically, every top star was there, but my overall feeling was that it was just another opportunity to be told that I did something wrong, or something I did or said was too much or not enough. The one and only thing that kept me going was watching Connor at ringside the whole show. He was so excited, and unlike at *RAW* the week before, he never showed fatigue. He had all the energy in the world. When Bryan hugged him, it was the perfect way for that night to end.

The following night was *Monday Night RAW* in New Orleans. I read through the show, and it read "Ultimate Warrior Entrance." I was jumping up and down. Literally, I jumped up and down. I was losing my mind. I was just happy that he was going to be on *RAW* after all of these years. But, now, on top of that, what if I got to announce him? I announced Hulk Hogan at *WrestleMania* the night before, and now Warrior on *RAW*? What a fulfilling 48 hours that would be. The only problem was, the way this was written out, it seemed like it might just be music, meaning no verbal ring introduction. In my head, I imagined that sweet guitar riff and Warrior speeding to the ring. That would be enough. No need for an announcement. I was just excited as the fan in me and the other fans just like me; however, it worked out didn't really matter.

I had only seen him from a distance at *WrestleMania* and the same that afternoon for *RAW*. When the show was live and his music hit, that probably made the moment that much more special for me. He wasn't bolting to the ring like he used to. He took his time and walked down the ramp. That didn't take away from the palpable excitement, but the crowd coming down from the initial pop did allow an opening for me to make an announcement. I didn't have one prepared, but I was immediately cued to announce him.

"Ladies and gentlemen, please welcome WWE Hall of Famer, the Ultimate Warrior!"

Wow. I could've thrown the towel in right there. I just announced *WrestleMania* 30, and now I have announced just about every superstar there was to announce. (If I couldn't do it live, like in this case with Warrior, there were always the video game voiceovers.)

The weekend was surreal for Connor and for me as well. I constantly tried to look past the issues with the company and focus on the good points. I was ready to get back to Arizona that Tuesday morning and soak it all in. I hadn't slept much, but at this point no matter how much or little sleep I got, I was always tired. Energy drinks, coffee, sleep—nothing worked. I just always felt average. I never tried using sleep-aid drugs, but I doubt even that would work on me. My body clock was completely out of whack, and I was happy to have a few days off before the next tour. I went out for sushi that Tuesday with a couple of my friends who were in town working on "Total Divas." As we sat down and started talking, my phone started lighting up. I picked up my phone to see if it was anything important. The Ultimate Warrior had just died from a heart attack. This was awful news. He was young, and in addition to all of his fans, he had a very loving family.

The company sent company representatives to be there immediately for Warrior's wife. Maybe it was to look out for her or maybe it was to make sure that the company looked okay to the media. If they were kind to her in her time of need, it also made it easier for WWE to produce anything Warrior-affiliated, knowing that his wife would be appreciative and happy to go along with their requests. Either way, I am very glad that over that past weekend, Warrior had gotten closure with the company and with the fans. I am glad we had that brief but defining moment on *RAW* and that I was able to introduce him during his last appearance. What an honor. Rest in peace, Warrior.

I was hoping for positive health news when checking in with Steve that week. It seemed to me like the dose of WWE medicine that Connor had that Sunday really helped him from the previous week in DC. Connor loved the beach, and after *WrestleMania*, he and Steve flew directly to Florida where they had plans to spend some time on the sand. We continued to FaceTime, and Steve sent me updates and pictures. Connor had been doing okay; however, toward the end of their trip, Connor started to grow weak. I was in Birmingham, Alabama, right before *RAW* started when his aunt messaged me about trying to fly him home from Florida. She didn't think the airline would let him fly. I ran out to start *RAW* and tried to stay strong as they showed Connor from the *WrestleMania* video package for the live audience and I thought about our conversation.

Luckily, he had pulled through and made it home, but shortly after, Connor was given hours to days to live. Steve messaged me and told me that he was holding his hand, waiting for him to give up and let the pain stop. I had tears in my eyes as I typed a message, thanking Connor for his friendship. He really showed me how incredibly brave he was. Later that Thursday night, Steve texted me that Connor had passed away. That hit me hard. I had lost family. I had lost friends. I had lost acquaintances. I had never lost anybody like Connor. He was only eight years old and so special, so mature, and so unbelievably brave. I slept a few hours and woke up to fly out to a show in Toronto. I emailed Stephanie to let her know the news. I sat on both flights and looked up articles, news stories, and videos about Connor on the Internet. I learned some things that I never knew and watched all the good that his family, friends, and community had done for him. I knew how blown away the wrestlers and I had been, and now I saw that all of these people were touched by Connor as well.

When I got to the arena in Toronto, I only told a couple of my close friends. I didn't want to tell all the wrestlers. When I decided on that day to keep in touch with Connor, it was my decision, and I felt that it wasn't fair to tell the others and make them feel bad. One of the wrestlers who frequently met Make-A-Wish kids told me what makes it easier on him was not knowing what was wrong with them and not asking what happened after they met so that it was meeting fans who liked him, and he liked them. I always kept that in the back of my mind and chose to keep it from most of the guys.

Connor fought really hard and never once complained. He was always so positive and loved that he became friends with his superheroes. He felt like he was on top of the world—and he was. It was painful to lose him at such a young age. He was so special that I selfishly wanted to see him grow up so I would know what he chose to do for his career. It made me feel a bit better knowing that the last few months of his life were extremely special and better than any wrestling fan could have ever dreamed of. While he went through the treatments and horrible things that came along with his condition, his dad would tell me how he looked forward to our phone conversations.

WWE put together a video of Connor's DC experience. The week before he passed away, they decided to do an "in-house" video, which was explained to me to mean it would to show the employees of WWE what goes on behind the scenes and what WWE means to its fans. I knew what was going on and the real reason that video was being produced. It was to show the world what WWE did for people, and I was okay with that and knew that Steve would be as well. WWE wanted to tell Connor's story. WWE did give Connor his strength and motivation, and a sick child who becomes friends with his heroes is a special story. They sent a producer and camera crew to talk with Steve and Connor, but Connor was too sick. The producer called me and said I was on the top of the list of people to interview. I watched the full story unfold, everything that happened with Connor, from the Royal Rumble until that point. I knew which superstars and divas he had conversations with on FaceTime and every detail I thought that he should know. I explained all the details over the phone, and then the producer was going to come to TV the next week and conduct interviews in person. I was happy to share my story and hoped that everyone who had contact with Connor over the past few months would do the same.

I had so many memorable interactions with Connor. I loved telling him that Stephanie invited him to *WrestleMania*. One of the last times we talked, he was eating an Easter basket full of candy and got a good amount of chocolate on his face, which was adorable. I have an office wall full of signed photos of wrestlers I have worked with over the years. Lots of them. The first time we talked in there, Connor instantly noticed that I did not have a photo of Daniel Bryan. I was sitting with Connor, Steve, and Steve Sr. in catering when they came to visit in DC. Ryback joined us. He was unknowingly one of Connor's favorites even though he was a bad guy. (Connor asked me why WWE had bad guys. I told him that it's part of the company deal: they're allowed to have a company with good guys as long as they have bad guys under contract as well.)

Ryback looked at the box of Connor "the Crusher" T-shirts that I had brought with me to DC. I gave Connor the box and told him to give them out to anyone he wanted. Ryback, in a playful way, was trying to convince Connor not to give them away. He told Connor that he's a cute little kid, and everyone would give him money for them, and he needed to charge everybody for the shirts. Connor would not have that! He stuck to his guns. He was giving those T-shirts to his friends, no matter what. Then Miz walked in. Despite being a good guy at the time, Miz is...Miz. Every time he tried to talk to Connor, Connor stopped him with Miz's own "Really? Really?" catchphrase. Take that, Miz! It was a really cool moment watching Connor team up with Ryback to block Miz's teasing and fire back.

Kane was enemies with Daniel Bryan, so Connor regularly threatened to break Kane's finger if he hurt Daniel. When they finally saw each other in person in DC, Kane saw Connor and said, "I have a bone to pick with you!" Connor didn't even flinch. The two kind of became friends despite Kane also being a bad guy.

Vickie Guerrero had said hello to Connor on FaceTime. He told her right away that he hates when she says, "excuse me," and if she did that on the phone, he would be forced to hang up on her. So she got bunches of "excuse me" in there in a totally playful and fun way. I introduced Connor to Road Dogg Jesse James, and he told Road Dogg that he could do the New Age Outlaws promo. Dogg was blown away, and we got his tag-team partner Billy Gunn so he could watch. Connor was announcing the New Age Outlaws for the New Age Outlaws. It was awesome. As I mentioned earlier, Connor didn't shy away from performing this intro in person as well!

We once FaceTimed in Brooklyn. The arena was really loud during the day, and the WiFi connection was very weak. Mick Foley walked by, and I asked if he wouldn't mind talking to my friend. Mick is one of the nicest guys in the world, and I already knew the answer before I asked. Unfortunately, like many people, Mick accidentally called me Josh a few times. (Since I wasn't typically shown on television, people assumed I was interviewer Josh Mathews who was on camera.) Connor couldn't get over this mistake to even let Mick say what it was that he wanted to say to him. Between the music and the bad connection, all Connor wanted to do was correct Mick and tell him that my name was Justin. Unfortunately, Mick didn't understand what Connor was telling him, and he just kept trying to have a friendly conversation. My second to last *RAW* was in Brooklyn. When I walked past that area of the building, I immediately thought of Connor, and I shared that story with Stephanie.

Connor's father told me that he was buried in the "Connor the Crusher" T-shirt that I had made. It was signed by everybody imaginable in WWE. He was proud to wear that T-shirt, and I was so happy to see what that shirt became. WWE offered anything he wanted to Connor, and his father asked for a *RAW* microphone so that I would always be close to him. It was hard to tell people that when I found out. It's still hard to even write it. Knowing that Connor is gone always makes me sad, but I'm very glad that he came into my life. He gave me a stone with his picture on it to hold on to whenever I want to think of him. And I do, and it helps.

At *RAW* in St. Louis, Daniel Bryan and Stephanie were interviewed for the in-house video. I received an email that the plan had changed, and they would be the only two people interviewed for this piece. I thought that was odd, but knew the video would be done very well as the WWE production team was the best, and their work was exceptional.

I assumed the staff would receive the video, and shortly after it would "leak" online. The staff did receive the video, and later that day it was sent to me. The producer who put together that video sent it in an email letting me know that while it wasn't mentioned in the piece, Steve was very grateful for everything I did for Connor. I knew at that moment that something was off.

I watched the video and noticed that I had been completely removed from the story. Wow. I was sad watching this video about my buddy, and I was hurt that my own company omitted me from the story—probably because I wasn't a superstar. It also seemed that apparently they didn't want to acknowledge that I existed at all. The video told the story about my friend and how the WWE stars helped to give him happy times at the end of his life and left it at that. I had found out that Stephanie and Steve both talked about my involvement and how integral my relationship with Connor and his family was, but I guess that wasn't the story

WWE wanted to tell. I spoke with Connor sometimes on a daily basis, but Daniel, who had only seen him a handful of times at the arenas, was a more meaningful and marketable name to showcase for the company. I was happy to help Connor and Steve in any way I could, and Connor's enjoyment of everything that he experienced made it all worth it. Being omitted entirely from this video package was definitely a slap in the face, but it didn't mean that the work to make Connor happy didn't happen.

At TV in Albany, Triple H called for a talent meeting at ringside during the day. As the talent came around, he looked at Daniel and casually said, "It's the Connor thing." Though I was sitting right over Daniel's shoulder, once again, Triple H wouldn't even look at me. He told the talent that he wanted them to see the power of WWE and pointed to the large video screen in the arena where the video began to play. I really wanted to get up and walk away so I wouldn't break down, but it happened too quickly. It was already playing. I couldn't even look. I listened to the video as I held back the tears and faced forward. Everybody else—all the talent and crew—faced my direction and watched the Connor video play. When the video ended, I went outside to get some fresh air. Triple H never had the decency to say anything to me about the situation.

Stephanie decided to start a fund in Connor's name at the children's hospital in Pittsburgh. That was a very thoughtful gesture, and hopefully that fund will raise money to help find a cure so no one else has to go through what Steve Michalek has gone through. This is the point when things got even harder for me. They had been playing that video every night at the live events and even at TVs. I'm glad that they were raising money for Connor's fund. I truly am. Each night, however, I had to watch that video. And each night, it made me sad because Connor was gone. It was also a nightly reminder of what that and also of what WWE had done to the story: completely eliminating me and twisting around the facts. It's not that I ever wanted or needed credit, but the idea of how the story was spun really bothered me. It gave the illusion that this was a Make-A-Wish story as that's their partner. I love and respect that organization, but when Steve reached out, they couldn't help. That's not a knock on them; they just couldn't help. Interviews with people who never took the time to talk to Connor outside of when he was in front of them really bothered me because they didn't know him. At the same time, I know they're just going along with what the company asked of them. The video was placed in the middle of the show, so when you're at a WWE event, a place I used to think was for fans to go escape their problems in the real world and enter a world of imagination, now you are watching a video that's unbelievably sad. Internally, many talents asked me about why the video was shown here or there as it was hard to get the crowd to rebound after they watched.

The concerns were supposedly brought up to management, but the video was still being shown at the events. They liked to instill emotion in their fans. In my opinion, rather than just doing a good deed, the company wanted to shove how great they were down people's throats. It's my opinion that if fans are at the show, they probably think that the company is great to begin with. They might not treat the people very well who work for them, but they support breast cancer awareness and raise money for that and now this. At the same time, I always felt horrible when I saw a sick child at ringside, and they, along with their family watched the video, which ended acknowledging that Connor had passed away.

Throwing to, or, in layman's terms, directing the crowd's attention to, that video never got easier as time went on. I watched it every night, and every night I had to fight the tears back to make the post-video announcement letting fans know how they could donate. On the surface, the point was to show the video and then go to the screen where it gave information on how to send a text message that would make a small but meaningful donation. In my head, I assumed there was a way to mention the foundation and show that screen without showing the video, and it may have been just as effective. Looking around the ring, I never noticed people on their phones donating. They were wiping away the tears. I would get choked up on most nights, so I just kept it brief and usually got through it. At TV, however, I was given an announcement to read.

Kevin Dunn even got on me a couple of times about making the post-video announcement faster. I guess he didn't care how hard it was for me to do that, but I never said anything, and I sped it up for him. He even started timing me. I watched Yeaton countdown while we were in commercial and ended the announcement with two seconds to go. He told me I still took too long, and if I didn't make the announcement, which was extremely long, in less than 30 seconds, he would cut my mic. So, as I was reading, I had to skip most of what was written in order to not have my microphone cut. From talent to crew, Kevin Dunn verbally abused lots of people from his seat in the production truck. The powers that be ran the company with a complete bully mentality, so I guess it made sense for them to start an anti-bullying campaign. They could run it and promote it; they just didn't have to follow it.

Kevin would order the timekeeper to cue me to talk, which meant that I had to keep my eyes on the timekeeper in case it was a hand cue. However, when I was looking the opposite direction at the entrance ramp, I was in trouble. (Bell ringing meant to announce the first person; the next announcement was to start when I saw the next participant on the ramp, so I would look there for that cue.) So, I apparently had to look in two completely opposite directions at the same time in order to make him happy. When I looked straight at the ramp, I wouldn't see the cue from the timekeeper and, thus, wouldn't know when to speak. "Get me a small caliber gun. Find out what's going on. Smack him. Put him on headset when he gets back." What a boss. If I asked him a question on the headset about something important in the show, he would make a big deal out of it and knock me for it. He would make everyone be a part of the embarrassment. He got on me about the Connor announcement just because he could; he had all the power and let it be known.

I told Stephanie that I had recorded Connor's name in my 2K video game voiceover session. You can design your own character, and I let Connor know when he was fighting for his life that he had something to look forward to because I planned on recording his name in the new WWE video game. I told Stephanie about that and asked her about either having his likeness in the game so people can build Connor and take his journey to the championship. I even suggested having him as a downloadable character so that the money could be used to go to his fund. She told me that she passed that on to Vince's office, but I never heard anything about that again. I realized that no matter what I offered, they did not want to hear it. Almost like the old "suggestion box" in Gorilla that was actually a paper shredder, the company only wanted to run with their ideas. If it didn't come from them, they didn't want it.

On September 6, 2014, I was at the gym in Dayton, Ohio, when I realized that I would be in State College the next day for a show. I had been talking to Steve on a pretty regular basis. Steve was an unbelievable father to Connor. He was always by his side and did everything he could for him. He would even send Connor gifts and letters and sign them from Daniel, which meant the world to Connor. It was buying the expensive seats that he couldn't afford at the Rumble that put Connor in my line of sight and made everything possible. I lost my buddy of a few months, but he lost his son. Steve was such a caring person, and I enjoyed talking to him and helping him stay positive. I assumed he wasn't too far from State College since he lives in the Pittsburgh area, and I asked if he would want to come to the show the next day. Luckily, he had Connor's brother Jackson with him that evening. So that night, Steve, his father, and his son Jackson came to the show. It was my first time seeing them since Connor had passed away, and it was my first time meeting Jackson in person. He knew me through Connor, and we had also FaceTimed a couple of times. Jackson's favorite wrestler was Kane, and Kane was always willing to take the time and talk to Jackson, which was awesome. Kane was a bad guy, and Jackson idolized him. Steve and I always got a kick out of the irony: Connor liked all the good guys; Jackson liked all the bad guys. We were at the Philadelphia airport on Jackson's birthday for an international flight, and Kane had asked to talk to him. On FaceTime at the crowded airport, the "monster" Kane sang Happy Birthday to Jackson. It was amazing.

At the show, Steve and the gang came in the back, and Jackson got to meet a bunch of the roster before they sat in their ringside seats. I knew we would be showing the Connor video that night, just like we did every night, but I didn't know how I would feel, or, more importantly, how they would feel. I discussed this with the bosses the night before. Since they couldn't seem to make a decision one way or another, I emailed Stephanie. Unfortunately, when Stephanie responded, she didn't acknowledge that question in my email, so we were back to square one. The efficiencies of working in a corporately structured hierarchy.

I took it upon myself to ask Steve about the video and said they would be okay with showing it. I then asked if we should acknowledge them in the crowd. He said they would be okay with that, too. They were enjoying the show, and I even handed Jackson a Wyatt sheep mask to wear during it, which he loved because they were bad guys. He was having a blast. Then it was time to show Connor's video to the arena. I was emotional each time I saw it without them there, so I didn't know how I would feel with his family sitting ringside. I got in the ring and glanced over. Emotions ran wild, and I knew that I just couldn't do it. I never backed down from announcing anything, but I couldn't make the announcement about them being there, and I also knew I wouldn't be able to make the post-video announcement that I normally made. Our security guard was by the ring. I asked her to relay to the show runner to go straight from the video package to the donation screen and then to the next commercial video without coming back to me.

The fund was such a great thing for such a great kid and, beyond that, such a great cause. But the video package and announcement forced me to relive the sadness of losing Connor over and over each night. I missed my conversations with Connor, and I missed seeing the joy on his face as he interacted with his larger-than-life friends.

Steve was very thankful for how great WWE treated him and his family. Everyone who took part in helping Connor was amazing. It was just a slap in the face, really, that the company continued to eliminate my name from the real story. Steve had done an interview for the *Consul Energy Center* (the arena in Pittsburgh) magazine. He told me that he had talked it over with his family and the magazine and that he wanted to get my name in there. Well, WWE edited the interview before it was printed, and apparently the only change they made was removing my name. Instead of reading, "Justin Roberts brought Connor backstage that night," it now read, "WWE invited Connor backstage, and he was introduced to all of the superstars who were on hand." Even in a magazine for an arena in Pittsburgh, WWE's reach extended and altered my existence. They didn't even want me to exist outside WWE events. I'm just glad that his last few months here on earth were as good as possible with everything he was fighting through.

The constant slaps to the face from the company, the frustrations with the live events that were written without being thought out, and the chaos at TVs didn't add up to a whole lot of fun. When you factor in domestic travel being worse than I had remembered in the past with shows all over the map plus a bunch of constant international tours mixed in, things weren't dreamy at my dream job. I had a long call with Sue, who I practically begged to work there just a decade earlier. Over time, I smiled and nodded and went along with things that were said and done to be a company guy. On this call, I poured my heart out to her and committed what could have been career suicide if she relayed this to Kevin or anyone else by telling her how much I hated working there now and how horrible the few people in upper management were and how terribly the talent was being treated. While I trusted her, part of me hoped she would tell them.

I looked around on a plane from San Francisco to Washington, DC, to see everybody from this tour next to me in front of me and behind me in coach. There were some huge guys who destroyed their bodies for this company. The company makes all its money off guys busting their butts, and they fly around the world in coach. When I first started, everyone was flown in business class. Again, I don't say this in a snobby way, by any means. On long flights when you are going overseas for work, sitting in cramped coach seats, six to a row is rough for anyone. When the guys are huge and their bodies are sore from nightly matches, it's simply cruel to do that to them. The international flights were rarely direct as well, even if we were flying from a hub, as it was cheaper to connect. On that particular tour, we had an hour ride to the airport, a two-hour wait once we got there, a ten-hour flight from Osaka, Japan, two-hour layover in San Francisco, a five-hour flight to DC, and a two-hour drive to Richmond, Virginia, for the next day's TV.

Before we headed out on that Tokyo tour, the forecast showed a major typhoon heading toward Japan. The company didn't seem to be alarmed. They usually weren't in those situations. I remember being in San Juan, Puerto Rico, years ago. Shelton Benjamin and I had gone out there a couple of days early instead of going home for a day between tours. We sat in a restaurant and watched the news as the radar showed a huge hurricane heading right for us on the island. We thought for sure the shows were going to get cancelled, but instead the company flew everyone out early to make sure they got there rather than fly the few of us that were already there safely home.

While in Tokyo, we were relieved to hear that the typhoon was not going to hit. We had spent two nights there, and on the third, I went to bed pretty late. Two hours later, I was woken up by a Japanese voice coming through my iPhone. Then the emergency alert went off. I knew something bad was going to happen or was happening, but both warnings were in Japanese. I put my phone down and went back to sleep; 10 seconds later, the huge hotel we were staying in began to sway like a boat! I assumed it was an earthquake, but I had only been in one earthquake and that was 11 years earlier at the same hotel. We moved a bit, and I just thought that I was dizzy. This time, we were swaying for a few minutes. You could hear the creaking of the building, and it was definitely an experience that I don't ever want to go through again. I turned on the television to see what was happening, and, again, everything was in Japanese. What I could tell was that something bad was happening, and the map showed the coast flashing, which made me wonder if there was a tsunami heading in. I was hesitant to go near the window, but eventually we stopped moving, and I looked out to see a rainbow. We were fine, but being in a situation like that in a foreign country is pretty rough, especially when you're thinking about a tsunami or even a nuclear power plant getting hit!

There is a famous steakhouse in the Tokyo area called Ribera. For years, wrestlers touring in Japan have stopped to dine at this incredible restaurant. Legendary wrestling photos covering the walls prove this. When I used to stand outside the arena waiting for wrestlers to pull up, so many of them wore the classic satin Ribera jackets. I never knew what Ribera was as a kid. I just knew that while I had an Ultimate Warrior jacket, the wrestlers all wore Ribera jackets, and I would have loved one of those. Seeing as my earlier trips to Japan weren't very fun, I had never even considered going with the guys to Ribera until this trip. I went with Chris Jericho, Miz, Zack Ryder, and Curtis Axel.

Side note: Axel was the son of Mr. Perfect, and I instantly liked him when he first came around to induct his dad into the WWE Hall of Fame. He's a talented guy who the company never truly got behind, and it's a shame. I found myself working with a lot of the kids of guys I grew up watching—Ted Dibiase Jr, Nattie Neidhart (who used to enter the ring, and we would both grab our nonexistent goatees like her father, the Anvil), Bray Wyatt and Bo Dallas (sons of IRS), Harry Smith (son of "The British Bulldog" Davey Boy Smith) and Dustin and Cody Rhodes (sons of Dusty).

Traditionally, the guys who stopped in and ate at Ribera were given the satin jackets, and I couldn't wait to have my own. We arrived, looked around at all the photos, and were treated to an excellent steak dinner. Chris, who had been working in Japan for a long time, was generous enough to ask about the jackets. When they brought them to the table, it wasn't the usual satin jackets that I had seen on all of the wrestlers over the years. It was a maroon jacket that had the Ribera logo on the right side and a gym logo on the left, possibly from the 70s. I thanked them and went back to eating when Jericho called me out on being disappointed. I was, because that wasn't the jacket, but I was still appreciative of the gift. Jericho actually said something to the gentleman, and he returned with the official Ribera jackets! After all of those years of seeing the wrestlers wearing them and after being in Japan for numerous tours, I was proud to eat at Ribera and wear their satin jacket, thanks to Chris Jericho.

We headed into a hurricane once in Monroe, Louisiana. Everyone was home because that was the first show on the tour, and despite the reports showing a hurricane heading right through there, the company decided to proceed with the show because they had sold a lot of tickets. That was the rockiest landing I had ever experienced in the US. You would board the plane knowing that the conditions were bad elsewhere, and it was scary. I would ask myself, do I get off the plane and play it safe or do I go and keep my job? Is this worth losing my life? I asked that over and over throughout the years, but I always did what the company asked.

In 2010, huge snow storm hit the east coast on Christmas night. Rather than cancel the show the night after Christmas, they had us scratch and claw to get to Madison Square Garden for the show. It didn't matter if we ran the risk of an accident while driving from whatever city we flew into, the company wanted the show to go on so they could make their money. I understand that business is business, but when the risk of danger is high for the talent, it made for some scary situations. There's nothing like sitting safely at home watching the news and seeing how dangerous the weather is elsewhere and knowing that you have to head right into that because of a company's greed. I understand that they would claim that the show should go on for the fans, but the safety of the performers never seemed to matter to them. When Owen Hart died in the middle of the ring during a show, the show continued, and if that didn't stop it, I don't think anything could.

One time I actually brought up a tour being dangerous. That didn't go over very well at all. I mentioned my concern for an upcoming tour to Vince's assistant simply to protect the talent and protect the company. We had a Friday show in Lakeland, Florida. There isn't a direct flight to Lakeland, so right away day one is a long day. Then after that, we had an early morning flight to San Juan. We would do the show that night and then leave early in the morning to fly to Charlotte where we would get in, go to the arena, do the show, and then drive to Atlanta to do a TV. It may not sound awful and if it doesn't, trust me, it was. There was nowhere in the schedule for sleep, just long days. We weren't driven around in the US. We had to stay awake behind the wheel of our rental cars. Years ago, legendary wrestler/broadcaster/promoter and all-around good guy, Gorilla Monsoon's son, referee, Joey Marella was killed in a car accident, driving to the next town. We weren't invisible. I wanted to prevent that rather than have them fix the scheduling after it was too late.

On this tour, they were all long days on no sleep and ended with a long drive from Charlotte to Atlanta. I was called into John Laurinaitis' office. He mentioned he heard that I said the upcoming tour was dangerous. He explained, in a non-threatening way, that if I didn't feel safe, there was someone else who could take my spot. I stood up for us as a group, which was frowned upon. That was how it was dealt with, so I told him I understood and worked the tour. David Taylor once spoke up in a meeting about the travel, and he disappeared or was released from the company shortly after. That's how it was. It was their way, and if you tried to stand up for yourself or for your peers, you would suffer the consequences. Now we were all given coach tickets, and we were lucky if we didn't get middle seats. Many guys did get stuck with middle seats, and the office would tell us that meant someone called in and changed their seat which affected the group. The tours were brutal, and there just wasn't a break in the schedule to regroup.

I was at a gym in DC when my email alert went off along with the schedule for October. I had really been burned out on the road and needed a break. The way October was looking, it wasn't just a full schedule ahead, it was all over the place. Arizona to Toronto, Ontario for a show, then to Boston for a Providence, Rhode Island show, to a Bridgeport, Connecticut show, to TV in Brooklyn, NY on Monday night followed by a drive to Philly for a flight out on Wednesday to head to Malaysia for two shows, and then back in time for another TV in Atlanta.

My head was ready to explode. I needed a break, and missing the two Malaysia shows would keep me from just two shows but equal to a few days off, which would be perfect. My sister had another baby, and I wanted to be around a little bit more for my family. I was on autopilot so many times when I had a day or two home. Months before, I had received a text from my friend Reid. He was crazy in a fun way—always having a great time and making the most out of life, traveling around the world every chance he got, and talking to everybody along his journey. I knew him from college. He was my sister's age, but always really cool to me at school and then afterward as well. He always texted me about joining him and his friends at this place or that event. I always had to decline because I was always working.

Reid messaged me when I was in Moline, Illinois, working a house show. He was clearly drinking and texted me to come hang out in LA. I got frustrated. I didn't get to sit around with my friends on a Sunday afternoon; my schedule was too packed. I didn't have the laidback lifestyle that he had. I explained that I couldn't go to LA, I was at work. I was always at work. His response was that my friends wanted to see me. I just stopped responding because I was working and didn't want to have that conversation. Work dominated my life, and I sacrificed having freedom to work the job I had dreamed of.

The next day I received a text right before *RAW* started that Reid had passed away the previous night. He was gone. That really hit me hard. He was such a great guy and just wanted to see his friends. He was a flight attendant and had offered in the past to fly with me to Dublin where I was headed for the day to work just so he could get me upgraded. He was always up for an adventure, but friendship was the foundation of that.

He messaged a few of us the night he died, almost as if he knew. That really made me think about my life and my job. I was living to work and was missing out on my friendships and my family because every week revolved around only being at this job and living just for work. Work with even a little bit of life would have even been okay!

I immediately emailed Michael Cole when I saw that upcoming tour in Malaysia. As much as I would love to go to Malaysia for the first time, I really needed a break. I had asked to take off a Saudi Arabia tour earlier in the year, which was the first time in a decade that I ever asked for an international tour off because I had recently become the go-to guy for every international tour. I asked in advance and was assured by multiple people in the office that I could have the tour off. I swapped tours with Tony, and I worked his domestic shows, and he had the week off since the tour got postponed. When it came around again, I confirmed that he was doing it, and Cole and the office told me he was. At TV in Memphis, Mark Carrano asked me to sign a document for the Saudi Arabia work visa. I told him that Chimel was doing the tour, and he asked me to sign it just in case as a back-up. I told him that if Chimel was doing the tour, I wasn't going to sign the paperwork. I knew that signing could result in me working the tour. He then told me that I had heat (meaning, they were upset with me) with the legal department because I was giving them a hard time. I use this term a lot, but what I haven't really mentioned is that, overall, heat was used as a threat. Heat was usually not real, but you had to pretend it was and then pretend to do penance to pretend to be absolved of your pretend heat. Keep in mind this is the first time I ever questioned anything, and up until this point I signed every document they ever sent me. I called Sue to double check with her and to relay what Carrano said. I also went to Cole and Chimel who all said Chimel was working the tour. Two weeks before the tour, I got an email from Carrano that said they still didn't have visa clearance for Chimel, and due to the conflicting lists and visa issues, I would be attending the tour.

I then contacted one of the heads in legal who happened to reach out earlier that day, and I told him the situation. He told me he would take care of it and to not worry—no heat, no problem.

He did take care of it, and Tony worked the tour, despite supposed "visa issues." Tony also made a joke to me about how he almost got out of it. Talent relations told me one story, but at the last minute, they were going to pull strings anyway and make me go.

Back to Malaysia. Cole checked with Tony Chimel and Eden (who was back on the road to learn the ropes and to fill in when needed). The email exchange went as follows:

Chimel said he would be in Hawaii from October 2 to 13 for his 25th wedding anniversary. Cole asked, or rather assumed, it was covered in advance and added that if all his dates are covered by Eden, then I'm going to Malaysia unless I had another idea. Chimel added that it was June, and he was going to put in for it in August.

I suggested alternatives but was shot down, and I got it. I knew the dates had no merit since Chimel hadn't asked. I just thanked him and asked for the next weekend off after Malaysia, which was a regular domestic tour. I was granted that weekend and booked a trip to Hawaii.

I understood that it was Tony's anniversary and that my request was simply so I could have a break, so I was okay with that. The way it was handled showed me that Cole as my new boss and alliance with his friend Tony probably wasn't going to be good for my future. Sue was always very fair when coordinating our dates and travel; unfortunately, this was no longer Sue's department.

I was in the production office later on that day in the Verizon Center. JBL, who was back in the company, had walked in the far side of the room and didn't see me sitting there. Chimel spent a lot of time in the production office, and even though they were all friends, they all made fun of each other. JBL started telling the story about how "stupid" Chimel is. He then proceeded to tell the story of how we had all emailed earlier, and I asked for the time off before Chimel did, but Cole tried to cover for him and give him the "ol' wink-wink", but Chimel was so stupid that he responded saying he just hadn't asked yet.

I'm not good at keeping my mouth shut. I had to let him know that I heard the story, so I just added a "yep" out of nowhere. JBL's smile got real big when he realized I had heard. I then went to change for the show, and Cole was in the locker room. He thanked me for being a team player and proceeded to tell me that he thought he remembered Chimel asking him a long time ago for that week off but had just forgotten about it.

I just smiled and nodded.

Scott Fishman had written a story in the Miami Herald about HandsToGo. He had asked me about doing an interview. I cleared it through WWE talent relations and PR. PR had actually cleared it the day that Carrano had talked to me about not promoting my product at work anymore. We decided not to do an actual interview, and he wrote a story about it instead based on his wife and him using and liking it. The story was worded as "WWE Announcer Justin Roberts: HandsToGo." I received a phone call from Carrano in which he told me that I was in trouble and would be talked to at the next pay-per-view. The threat of heat would now consume me until then.

I immediately contacted Scott and asked him to pull the story from their website, and he did. I was never sure about where I was and wasn't allowed to promote my product. I was an independent contractor and knew lots of guys had side projects. I thought that I could use my own social media accounts to promote it, but Carrano had told me to pull everything, including my own social media, so I did. The whole independent contractor thing always confused me. Dress codes, arrival times, a full schedule, a biweekly paycheck, can't do this and that...I guess I should have just assumed that I was an employee (except without the benefits, of course). I stressed over that pay-per-view for days, as Carrano loved instilling fear like that, but this time I thought I really was in trouble. However, no one ever talked to me. Sometimes letting us know we had "heat" was a better way of handling an issue for management versus tactually discussing the issue. Discussing and solving issues and misunderstandings would make too much sense; the bullying management system preferred to stir the pot and think what they wanted and handle it how they wanted instead. The talent typically got punished publicly if they had heat, whether it was getting squashed in their match, an embarrassing stipulation, or anything else that would humiliate them.

After this situation weighed on my mind a bit, I really wanted some clarity on what I could and couldn't do with HandsToGo. On September 22, 2014, I asked Hunter if he could help clear it up for me. I asked about what I was and wasn't allowed to do as far as having HandsToGo. He said he would have to talk to legal as he walked away from me. So, that didn't clear anything up.

I had gone with Dolph to a Diamondbacks game, and we ended the night having dinner with our buddy Zach who worked with the team. He posted a photo on Instagram and Twitter and tagged Dolph and me. Unfortunately, my two handles were different, so he had to repost it using separate names. I told him that I wished I had the "JustinRoberts" Instagram name like I had on Twitter.

So the next day I set out on a new mission. I checked with Nicky, my favorite WWE social media guy. He asked if I owned my name, and I told him I had the rights to it but never trademarked it.

He told me if I trademarked my name sometimes they could easily acquire the social media rights to it, but in this case, I should just try talking to the owner. So I did. I sent @JustinRoberts a direct message on Instagram, and he responded. I told him the situation and that I would love to have his user name. We went back and forth a bit, and he didn't seem to be married to the name. I asked what he would want, and we started trying to figure out what he was into and what I had connections to. It came down to two tickets to two Diamondback games and mentioning my old user name, which would be his new user name in hopes that he would get some new followers. We had a deal, and we both got our new Instagram names.

The process made me realize that after all of these years of using my name publicly, I needed to trademark it. If WWE let me go, despite having the rights, they could see the name wasn't trademarked and trademark the name themselves, which meant I would have to use a different name for whatever I did next. I just wanted to play it safe and legally own the name. I didn't want to be Enzo Reed again! I called my lawyer, and a few weeks later the name was trademarked.

Using social media the way I did as I worked with WWE was amazing. It allowed me to be myself and share my thoughts and photos. I was able to take everyone on my adventures and also fill everyone in on photos from the past as well as random thoughts that others may appreciate and be able to relate to. The audience was able to see a different side of me. I wasn't just a guy who stood with a serious face and said, "The following contest is scheduled for one fall." Twitter also gave me the opportunity to talk to my childhood crush, *Charles in Charge* star, Nicole Eggert. Did I tweet with *Coyote Ugly* star, Piper Perabo? Yep. Anyone I have ever wanted to talk to and possibly wrote a love note by using the fan address in the back of *Teen Beat* magazine I tried to contact on Twitter. Stephanie Tanner's bad influence friend on *Full House,* Gia? Yep, we tweeted. Topanga from *Boy Meets World*? Check. Mick Foley even tied us in together on the back of one of my trading cards. Twitter has been awesome for corresponding not only with my celebrity crushes, but also for talking to other performers who I'm a fan of and, most important, communicating with fans!

CHAPTER 27
NOBODY LEAVES THIS PLACE WITHOUT SINGING THE BLUES

As we approached the end of September 2014, it was nearing the 10-year anniversary of my dad's passing. Of all the cities we ran all over the world, TV happened to be in Chicago, where my dad was buried. I knew it would be an emotional day to get through. Being there on that day would be hard, but in a way, I figured it might be therapeutic. Chimel and our backup ring announcer-in-training, Eden, were working the live events that weekend. Eden, or Brandi, was the stunning wife of Cody Rhodes, who I had trained a few years previously.

It was nice having her around. She understood the job, pulled it off well, and was a pleasure to work with. Having her join the team finally gave Chimel and me a break now and then so that he and I could have a day (or maybe two) off. She had left in the past because she didn't want to get stuck just being a ring announcer. She had trained to wrestle and wanted to do more, and was capable of doing more, but now she was back as a ring announcer. She filled in on live events for Chimel and then became the announcer at the Tuesday TV tapings for *Main Event* which aired on the *WWE Network*. Lilian was also there on Tuesdays to announce *SmackDown*.

All of us had one common friend and lifeline at work, my tag-team partner at ringside, timekeeper Mark Yeaton. Mark was an extremely hard worker who was there early in the morning, taking care of everything and everyone in the production office. People were constantly coming to him, needing this shipped and needing this and that, and he accommodated them all and handled the logistics. Then he sat ringside and handled the bell for each match, as well as cues for the ring announcers and communication on headsets with the bosses and also on a walkie-talkie to communicate with any other departments that could be needed during a live show. In general, Mark helped the show run as smoothly as possible. A lot of times, commands would come in from the bosses, but they were so stressed from the live TV that Mark would take what they said and translate to what he assumed they wanted me to say and do. After being there for so long, he knew what they meant despite what they might say. He was a great right-hand man and a good all-around person. He was loved and respected by everyone.

In the summer of 2014, on the eve of what would have been his 30th anniversary with the company, Mark was fired. And not even by his boss. His boss didn't show up but had someone else do it and cite "budget cuts" as the reason. I was sitting on the floor in an Australian airport when he messaged me. I broke the news to some of our friends that had been at the company a long time, and it made a giant dent in our morale. After 30 years of nothing but pure dedication to WWE as their most loyal employee ever, he was fired. I talked to a few of the guys about putting some money together for him, but I was talked to and told that wouldn't be a good idea since the decision came from high up. Morale hadn't been great to begin with, but losing Mark was a huge blow to all of us. It was funny that the company would do things in the media's eyes (anti-bullying campaign, Connor's Cure, Susan G Komen) that made them appear to be such a quality, caring company, but in many cases, they were bullies and treated their own "family" so heartlessly. The people who give their lives to this job were treated like chewing gum that lost its flavor and was spat out. Vince even used that analogy in a promo once, but that seemed to be more real than a wrestling promo. He said, "When you chew gum, you chew it all up, and then, when you're done with it, you spit it out. Why? Why do you spit it out? Because it lost its flavor! Just as simple as that. Bret Hart lost his flavor. I spit him out." Over the years, it seems that's what the company did. Use guys for whatever they could get out of them and then kick them to the curb. WWE did start a program for former talent that needed to go to rehab, and they would cover the costs. Perhaps if the talent were better taken care of during their tenure, those problems and rehab could have been avoided.

When Mark was let go, he was replaced by a young man who had been working the bell in NXT. Working the bell wasn't as easy as ringing a bell. It involved taking direction and passing it on to others. You had to give cues, stay alert, think on your feet, and work with the team that was at ringside, including the referees. The new timekeeper was yet another member of the team that had wrestling in his blood, which I thought was great. His father was a wrestler who worked as Tugboat/Typhoon Shockmaster, a super nice man. This also meant that the new timekeeper was the cousin of Cody Rhodes.

I hoped he would be good in this spot because this was a tough position that required someone special. Because he was a fan of the business and it was in his blood, I knew there was definitely hope. We explained as he was coming up that this was different than his position at NXT. There was a lot more pressure, and the bosses on headsets were Vince and Kevin. When I was new and for about 10 years after, I would always grab waters and bring them to the guys in our corner.

When he came in, I was hoping that out of respect, since he was the new guy, maybe he would do little things like that. At first I hinted at it. Then I even flat out mentioned it. He wasn't interested. Instead of humbly coming in, he took over that position like he deserved to be there. He talked down to the fans and even to his coworkers as if he had a right to do so. That really rubbed me the wrong way. I even spoke to him about it. I told him that when fans at ringside ask him questions, it was probably best to not to be a jerk to them. He came and talked to me, and we discussed why I said that. I never noticed that happening again, which was a good sign.

As far as being comfortable right away and not working with the team at ringside, that's another story. I got very frustrated working with him because I had no communication with Kevin unless I sent him a text during the show. Usually he would ignore those, but sometimes he would respond to the timekeeper to relay to me. I would look through the show at the upcoming segment, but the ring announcer's notes were never usually written out. So if I couldn't assume how something was supposed to play out, I would have to ask. Rather than ask Kevin on headset for me, this new guy would tell me what he thought was the right answer. This became a problem; I couldn't go off his assumptions. I needed to know the actual direction the bosses wanted. That way I wouldn't get in trouble, and I could do what was best for the show.

The final week of September 2014, I invited my family to come with me to Chicago so we could all be together for that tough weekend—the anniversary of my dad's passing. We could see as many of our close friends and family as possible, and we could do it all together, something we had not done in Chicago for a long time.

We caught up with everyone—friends, neighbors, and family. We visited our old stomping grounds, our favorite restaurants and had so much fun together. With my schedule, we mostly saw each other on Tuesday nights (unless I was on an international tour). That was about all the family time we had before I ran around getting ready for the next week's tour.

My mom came to the show and hung out backstage for a little while before going out to her seat. I introduced her to Stephanie McMahon, who had walked by. We talked about the trip, and Stephanie commented on how important family time is. I agreed, but I also knew how I never got enough of that due to my work schedule. Stephanie also mentioned to my mom that I was a great guy, and I had done so much to help so many kids over the years. Maybe she was actually aware of the little things that I had done for others just as I had with Connor.

The Chicago show was fun mostly because we were at the Allstate Arena. It truly is one of the greatest arenas in the world. I say that partially because that's where I grew up attending shows and also because of the smaller, more intimate size and also because the Chicago fans are always amazing. At one point, I noticed Reverend Jesse Jackson walk in. I grew up seeing him on TV and thought that was pretty neat. I said hello and even took a photo with him. I always tried to accommodate fans waiting around in the parking lots of the arenas for autographs because I used to be one of them, especially in Chicago as that was the actual area where I used to wait and remembered how cool it was to meet everybody. The past couple of shows at that arena, I even recorded voicemail greetings for fans that requested it. I never even liked recording my own, but I was happy to do it for them.

The show was going flawlessly until the timekeeper and floor manager told me to go into the ring during a commercial break. I had asked the floor manager throughout the show how the next segment was going to pan out. When they told me to go in, I did so, and stood there with the referee. We watched as the timekeeper pointed to me, which was always my cue to talk. Usually before I got that cue, I was also given a topic. I had three announcements in my pocket that I was given before the show that could be called for at any point. There was the "Thank You" announcement, the "Sign of the Night," "Goodnight," "Welcome," and "Cut-in" announcements. All those standard ones on top of the three special ones I had in my pocket. There were all those announcements to cue me on, and all he did was point. Then he pointed again. I calmly looked at him and said I knew I was supposed to say something, but what was I supposed to say? He pointed again, and frustration overwhelmed me as the floor manager finally shouted, "Sign of the night!" Then I calmly made the "Sign of the Night" announcement and watched as the fans held their signs up for the cameras to show them off on the giant screen.

After that segment, we came back from break and went into a match. I returned to my seat and was fuming inside. I calmly asked the timekeeper what happened. He told me that he cued me. I told him that yes, he did indeed cue me, but he never told me what to say. He then told me that he told me what to say and then pointed. I explained that the referee and I both watched as he pointed over and over again and never once told me what I was supposed to say. Then he said that since the floor manager was right by me, he assumed that the floor manager told me what to say, so he just pointed. Now I explained that he had just given me two different stories and to pick one.

I asked him if he "buried" me to Kevin. I knew that Kevin's reaction to him cueing me and me not talking would make Kevin scream and swear about me using derogatory names and threats. This was usually followed by him telling someone to hit or shoot me. Just another day at the office. This new timekeeper told me that he did not put any blame on me or bury me to Kevin. At that point, our new audio guy Tim, who had taken over for Frank, spoke up. He said that the timekeeper told Kevin that he cued me four times. That would also be referred to in the wrestling world as a burial. That meant he did his job, and it was my fault for not saying anything. That placed all the blame on me. According to what I was told by others, this apparently wasn't the first time that he threw someone under the bus and had acted dishonestly. Other guys on the crew had heard him bury them as well to save himself. I was extremely upset. I tried talking to him, but he just wouldn't admit any wrongdoing. I was beyond frustrated with him. He was young, he was new, and I was frustrated by everything at this point. It just wasn't a good combination.

I'm sure he was an ok guy. That was just a rough position to be in, and he did what many there do, he protected his spot rather than accept responsibility. I don't blame him, as those were the types of people who kept their job longest.

Since that break didn't come for the Malaysia tour, the next week I was off to Malaysia, starting with the Toronto show. I flew to Chicago for a connection, which ended up being cancelled. In these situations, I always tried to be proactive and would call the office right away before everyone else got off the plane and took those spots on other airlines. I immediately called travel to try and find a new flight to get me to Toronto in time for the show. The new flight they found left late, and I got to the building exactly two minutes before the show started. I kept the producer, Finlay, posted, and he gave me an extra five minutes to get there. I ran into the building, threw on my suit, and within three minutes was standing in the ring, welcoming the crowd. It had been a mentally grueling day and only day 1 of this very ambitious tour. A few hours later, I was up for an early morning flight to Boston to drive to that night's show in Providence.

From there, we ran Bridgeport, Connecticut, and then TV Monday in Brooklyn. I saw the timekeeper early in the day, and he told me that Kevin had called him into the truck the week before to find out what happened with the cueing incident. He told me that he took the blame. His cousin, Cody Rhodes, sat down at the table with us in catering while was going on, and I explained to Cody what happened and questioned the story about the truck. I knew how dishonest the timekeeper had been with me the week before, and I was skeptical about his story on this day. I didn't want him make up a story and tell Cody, who was a friend of mine. I figured if we discussed this in front of him, he would hear the full story and understand everything.

After we hashed things out, I left catering and ran into someone from production. This person told me that the timekeeper went into the production truck last week and threw me and the floor manager under the bus. He blamed us for everything. Despite what the timekeeper told me in catering, I now heard this completely different story. I assumed I knew which to believe. I was very upset. But no matter how upset I was, guys like this were the future of the business. This type of behavior was now becoming the norm, and as much as I understood yet disagreed with it, there was nothing that I could do.

A couple of hours later I was approached by Zack Ryder who told me that he was in a weird position. Cody sent him to tell me not to talk to him for the rest of the day. I worked with Cody on his first night at WWE, and through all these years we were always buddies. I was even invited to his wedding. He was very angry, probably because I called out his cousin in front of him and apparently alluded to Zack that he almost hit me. I immediately sent Cody a text to apologize. I explained it probably did put him in a weird spot, and I did not mean to do that. I did not say anything to him the rest of the day. When I saw his wife, I apologized to her as well and tried to explain that I just wanted Cody to know what was going on.

Monday night after *RAW* I drove to Philly so I could catch the flights on Wednesday morning to Malaysia. We flew to Doha, Qatar, to connect to Kuala Lumpur, Malaysia. The total travel time was about 22 hours. We got in at night and had the next two nights for our shows and even a little site-seeing. I never really saw anything other than gyms, hotels, airports, and arenas when overseas. There just wasn't time usually. But with two nights in the same hotel, for once it worked out. Miz, Derek from merch, Sami Zayn, Paige, Sin Cara, Neville, Big E, Larry the trainer, Rich the photographer, and I went to a cave that was filled with crazy monkeys, which was awesome. Miz and I got down to pose for a picture with a monkey while another one came from behind and attempted to take my bag off my back. They would prey on unsuspecting tourists. As soon as someone walked by with food or even a bag, the monkeys would run out and grab the treasure and run. Then they would look back at the victims like "what are you gonna do about it" as they rummaged through their belongings. It was fascinating to watch.

The fans in Singapore were awesome and totally into the shows. After the second show, a group of talent began their journey to Germany to connect to Atlanta, which wasn't so bad. Our group had a flight back to Doha at 3:30 in the morning after the show and then one from Doha to Chicago, then a final leg from Chicago to Atlanta. That took about 32 hours. Again, I had pleaded with travel for a window seat so I could try to sleep through most of it, but again I was booked in an aisle seat and had to do some sweet-talking at the airport. By the time we got to Atlanta, we were fried. It was time to sleep because the next day was TV. They would teach us to act like superstars, and that perception is reality, but then they would have us travel like cattle. It really was brutal.

I woke up that Monday not only feeling stiff and jet-lagged (which I normally pretended that didn't exist), but I also had a really bad feeling in my stomach. The last few times that happened over the years, something bad happened. This, in a weird way, was a gift. But what was not part of the gift was knowing what that bad thing will be.

Doc and I went to the gym. Everything seemed to be fine, but I still had that feeling. We arrived at the arena in Atlanta where I at one point became the full-time *SmackDown* announcer back about seven years prior. I walked into talent relations to turn in my passport. The company handles talent passports in order to obtain the correct visas and permits for each tour—and possibly to keep us from leaving the country. I'm kidding. Maybe. Mark Carrano told me that I could keep it since they had my second passport. Immediately a red flag popped up. They liked to keep both passports at all times and were very adamant about holding on to both.

I went to catering and noticed Sean Cleary walk in from HR. He was looking around catering. I watched to catch his eye. He saw me looking and nodded hello, and I noticed he was no longer looking around catering. I took that as a red flag as well, but maybe I was just reading into everything.

I was quite beat from the Malaysia travel, but by this point in my career, I was tired all the time. My body got used to jet lag and that just became the norm. I grabbed a coffee and headed out of catering. I was approached by a couple of guys in suits from the *WWE Network*.

The shorter gentleman mentioned that he produces one of the series on the network and had enjoyed my interviews from the past and had used quite a few of them on the shows. Once in a while, network representatives would come to the arena on TV days and grab us to do various interviews for network shows or DVDs. They requested me quite a bit because I was a longtime fan and knew about most of the material they were covering. He mentioned the topics that he would be asking about, and as usual, it was everything I loved digging up in my memory to discuss—various old-school wrestling characters and topics. He was used to guys making him wait to do interviews and was shocked when I asked if he wanted to do it right then. He quickly took me up on the offer, and we went to the room that they had setup.

The lack of sleep had really kicked in, and I was delirious but having fun discussing childhood wrestling memories. It was a great combination, and the adrenaline was waking me up. I was giving the greatest interview I had ever given. I was singing, yelling, and making surprisingly funny jokes. They didn't have to choose which topics to ask me; I was hitting every one of them.

We had a lot of fun in there, and they had gotten a lot more footage from me than they could have ever expected. The passion I had as a fan came back when I talked about all of those old memories. It's funny that the company put so much emphasis on the "Attitude Era" when guys were allowed to have fun and not get reprimanded for doing things that the crowd went crazy for. They always built network shows about that era and brought in guys from that era rather than let the current product become just as entertaining. It was fun to talk about the past, but then I had to get back to the present. When the interview ended, it was time to return to 2014 and start the night's live *RAW*.

Right before we began, I got the sheets and looked through to see if there were any long announcements I needed to memorize. There were a couple of parts that were written with holes, meaning that, as usual, I wasn't sure what I was supposed to say during those segments. And just like usual, I found the producer of the segment in question, who referred me to the writer, who referred me to Vince, who was in a meeting. I was then told that someone would get back to me. As usual. I saw William Regal, who was mostly working in Florida at this point, and we had a rare moment to say hello and talk. He was so good to me while I was trying to get to WWE, and this opportunity would prove to be a special treat.

I walked out into the arena as the lights went out so the disclaimer could play. The disclaimer let fans know the rules and legalities about cameras and filming. I made my way down the aisle in the dark. The next thing the fans in the building experienced was usually a highlight video of the previous *WrestleMania*.

When I got to ringside, I noticed Evander Holyfield sitting in the front row. Years back, he had made an appearance on *SmackDown*, and we took a picture together at Madison Square Garden. My phone reset, and I had lost it. There he was, and I had another chance to grab a new picture with him, so I did! Some people would frown upon that, but I am a fan, and I don't hide it. With that out of the way, it was time to start the show, so I got into the ring.

I was no longer allowed to welcome the fans by using their city name because that would generate a "pop," or loud cheering reaction from the crowd. Vince and Kevin were adamant that the fans only had so many pops in them. As a ring announcer, I was not to steal the pops from the matches and wrestlers by wasting them on my announcements. I understood. I greeted the fans each show with a simple, "Good evening ladies and gentlemen," keeping my excitement down to a minimum so they wouldn't cheer as loud—and so I wouldn't get chewed out. In any other live event setting, I would want to get the best reaction possible, but at work, I was hoping they wouldn't cheer too much because I did not want to be accused of stealing pops. Sometimes they would even chant my name at shows, but I would give a subtle wave and quickly start announcing so I could not be mistaken for trying to get myself over during a show. Your job is to hype up the crowd, but it isn't your job to hype up the crowd, and you aren't allowed to because they only have so much hype. That's like asking fans not to cheer for the first three quarters of a close basketball game because they might not have any cheers in them for the fourth quarter. Vince supposedly likes "real men" that will stand up to him. And I wanted to stand up to him and tell him that his opinion on this was ridiculous, but there's a fine line. If I did that, he could have easily canned me right there.

During *RAW*, a writer came to ringside and gave me the wording I would need for an upcoming part of the show. In the main event, or very last match, I announced Dean Ambrose versus John Cena in a "Contract on a Pole" match. My very first WWE match was the pre-show, "dark" or non-televised between John Cena and Shelton Benjamin, and it's amazing how everything comes full circle. I remember standing in the ring for what seemed like an eternity before the main event. The crowd of thousands of people were out there in what seemed like silence. I had this lonely feeling in the ring, just standing there and taking it all in. I never knew when it would all end, but I knew eventually it would, so I always took it in. Stephanie and Triple H were sitting at ringside, and I just looked down at them while giving the look of disgust that I usually gave to the "heels" of the show. Inside, I felt the same way about

Hunter as he had been such a heel to me and others over the years. I continued to take it all in, and while it wasn't rare to have a long break, this one just never seemed to end.

Finally, we were back from commercial, and I made my announcement, introducing Ambrose and Cena before I sat back in my seat. Halfway through the match, a referee approached the corner where I was sitting and told me that I was to go to talent relations after the show. I knew right then exactly what my bad feeling was as it immediately came back and felt even worse. This was the moment I always feared and also expected every week since I began with the company, but in the past couple of years, I had really needed. I asked a couple friends nearby if I was getting fired, and no one seemed to know or at least admit it. I sent a couple of texts, but again, no one knew.

I was 99.9% certain that I was going to be let go after the match, yet I had a live microphone on me during that whole main event. I could have easily let out some of the frustration that I had by talking into the mic and simply quitting before they let me go. I pondered the idea of walking into the ring and telling the world how the company treated their talent, but that's not how I wanted to go out, so I refrained. I made the final announcement when the match ended, and we went off the air. I took out my phone for whatever reason and just made a video saying that if this was my last night, it has been fun. Overall, in the long run, it truly had been fun. I looked around the arena and took it all in once again, perhaps for the very last time. I made my standard goodnight announcement and, as I always did, alluded to coming back in the near future. I almost wanted to make a comment about that, but again, I refrained. I told them to please drive safely, and that was it. I had a friend come that night, but I apologized for not being able to talk because I had to go in the back to most likely get fired.

Normally I would stick around ringside and meet fans after the show ended, but I knew that I had to walk that plank. I typically did not walk back through gorilla position because I tried to avoid seeing Vince. On this night, I walked back there. He was gone. I walked through and to the back where I saw Vince along with Jim, the head of security. I asked him if I was getting fired; Jim acted surprised and said he had no idea. I saw Stephanie and just shook her hand, saying hello and waiting for her to give me a sign or say goodbye. She just looked me in the eye with a smile and said hello. I approached Vince, shook his hand, and simply said, "Thank you."

"You should tell them to travel safely. Not everyone drives," he said. I thanked him.

I walked into the talent relations office. I saw Michael Cole standing with Sean Cleary and Mark Carrano. This was it.

Right off the bat, a nervous Cole told me that they were going a new direction, and that I wasn't part of that direction. It wasn't anything I did; they just were not renewing my contract. The WWE contracts are designed to protect the company, not the talent. Whether it's a 1-year or a 10-year deal, they have the right to terminate you at any point with with some amount of notice. Cole offered to have the company make me a reel (a highlight package of my on-camera work) if I was interested. They told me that the door was always open, but I should probably refrain from doing any sort of "shoot interviews" that a lot of talents do (once they have the freedom to talk about their experiences and treatment). I told them that I thought I was getting fired and had recorded a video at ringside. Cole quickly corrected me that I wasn't "fired," my contract just wasn't being renewed. Sure, I showed up to work, did my job, and didn't give them a reason to "fire" me, but since things don't work like a normal company, they do things to make a statement. They made their statement, and my time was up. I simply thanked them, shook their hands, and walked out.

There were still a few guys left in the building, and I was glad to be able to shake their hands and give them a hug goodbye. I wasn't angry. I wasn't sad. I just felt very neutral and okay with everything. It felt like a huge burden was lifted off my shoulders. The upcoming schedule was brutal, and the nonstop shows, week after week and year after year, had been too much. I came in at 22; I was now 35. I felt 50. Where did that time go?

A couple of guys teared up, which brought a tear to my eye, but I did not want anyone to be sad. I was ready to be done for a couple of years now. I just couldn't seem to jump out of the roller coaster on my own. I needed a nudge. I got my nudge. I do wish the scene was just a tad different. If it was truly wrestling, one of my favorite bad guys like Bad News Barrett would have been the one to deliver the news. But even wrestling isn't wrestling sometimes.

I went to change, and then I sent a quick text to Kevin Dunn and thanked him for the opportunity. He didn't reply. I sent Vince an email thanking him for the opportunity. He didn't reply. I had temporarily forgotten in the moment what Kevin told me, that Vince was the chairman of a publicly traded company, and I was just a (former) ring announcer. After 12 years of doing everything they had asked, pulling off the show that they were producing as they went along with no direction whatsoever, I didn't need a thank-you from them. I would have been happy with any reply.

I sent John Cena a text. He and I had been in WWE for about the same amount of time. He was my first and last match to announce in the company, from an opening dark match to the main event. We always had a good relationship. He loved his job, and at one time I had loved mine. Regardless, he knew that I always put my heart into my work and knew that I cared. There weren't a lot of people who would give John a suggestion, but he knew I was out there for all his matches, and if something ever stood out, I would let him know. He knew he could ignore my input or consider it. He knew I wasn't being a jerk, and he was always cool about it because I was trying to help a friend. He also would sit down before the shows and autograph a bunch of photos that they would sell at the merchandise stands. I would make the announcement about them and do it in a way that would drive people to run to the stand and buy them until none remained. I know he liked when I made that announcement, and I enjoyed assisting him. It was obviously John's autograph that sold the photos, but if nobody knew they were there, they couldn't sell at all. The merchandise guys showed me the numbers for their sales when I was announcing the merchandise versus when I wasn't. They were significantly different, and I was proud of that. He had just heard and said this one was beyond his comprehension. He complimented my work and told me not to lose my passion. Unfortunately, it was too late.

On this night, I also sent Stephanie a text. I had tried to say goodbye to her when I got the news, but she was talking to our friend Chili from the music group TLC, and I did not want to interrupt. Hunter was nervously texting away on his phone, and the more he texted, the more the security guard who was waiting with me tried to suggest that we head out of there. He was in a bad spot because he was my friend for all these years, and now he was standing by my side to make sure that I didn't cause any problems. I simply wanted to thank for her help with Connor and to say goodbye, but Hunter was presumably texting with someone who was in the security guy's ear. We walked back to the dressing room, and from there I sent her a text thanking her for everything she did with Connor. His father told me that she had called him the next day to let him know I had been let go. He told me she said it was just business and that they offered me a different job working within the company. This was news to me as nothing of that sort was ever offered.

Dolph, Miz, Zack, and Doc came into the dressing room where Mark Henry and I were talking. I was glad to have my good friends there at that moment. We talked for a bit, and while they were concerned, I assured them that I was truly okay with this and that I had a great run. I did everything I had wanted to do and much, much more. Scotty, the WWE security guard, had been at my side from the time I walked out of talent relations until I left the building. It was weird, but I know that's how it goes. He didn't rush me, and he let me say goodbye to a couple of production friends who were tearing down the arena.

We walked out of the building, and while I'd normally sign autographs for the fans out there, this time I didn't. I couldn't. The reason for that was, well, I no longer felt the autograph would mean anything anymore. I was no longer a WWE announcer.

My phone blew up on the drive to the hotel. I was alerted that Jim Ross mentioned me in a tweet. He responded to the news of my departure with very kind words. A few of his tweets that popped up were: "WTH? A classy kid. Damn shame. Great kid. Shocked & sad. @JustinRoberts loved his job." Very kind words from the very talented, well-respected legend.

I guess word had gotten out. WWE issued the classic "best of luck in your future endeavors" statement, and the world of wrestling was starting to find out and to comment publicly. I thanked some people, and some others thanked me. I stayed up all night and through the morning just reading what people were saying. I was responding to friends until my flight at 7:30 the next morning. When I landed, I couldn't keep up with the messages. I never realized how many people cared.

PART V

ANYTHING AND EVERYTHING IS POSSIBLE

Innsbruck, Austria   9/25/08 WWE SmackDown/ECW Live – Barcelona, Spain   9/24/08 WW
9/21/08 WWE SmackDown TV Taping – Columbus, OH   9/16/08 WWE SmackDown TV Tapin
/ECW Live – Jackson, MS   9/13/08 WWE SmackDown/ECW Live – Monroe, LA   9/9/08 WW
8/31/08 WWE SmackDown TV Taping – St. Louis, MO   8/30/08 WWE SmackDown/ECW Liv
n/ECW Live – Canton, OH   8/23/08 WWE SmackDown/ECW Live – Erie, PA   8/19/08 WW
N   8/12/08 WWE SmackDown TV Taping – Norfolk, VA   8/10/08 WWE SmackDown/ECW Liv
TV Taping – Atlanta, GA   8/4/08 WWE SmackDown/ECW Live – Macon, GA   8/3/08 WW
7/29/08 WWE SmackDown TV Taping – Hershey, PA   7/28/08 WWE Saturday Night's Main Eve
own/ECW Live – Poughkeepsie, NY   7/22/08 WWE SmackDown TV Taping – Philadelphia, P.
p Wrestling TV Taping – Tampa, FL   7/15/08 WWE SmackDown and ECW TV Taping – Charlott
ugusta, GA   7/12/08 WWE SmackDown/ECW Live – Savannah, GA   7/8/08 WWE SmackDow
ackDown/ECW Live – Albany, GA   7/1/08 WWE SmackDown TV Taping – Tulsa, OK   6/29/0
, TX   6/17/08 WWE SmackDown/ECW Live – Brisbane, Australia   6/16/08 WWE SmackDow
WWE SmackDown/ECW Live – Adelaide, Australia   6/13/08 WWE SmackDown/ECW Live
E SmackDown/ECW Live – Auckland, New Zealand   6/8/08 WWE SmackDown TV Taping – Sa
Los Angeles, CA   6/1/08 WWE One Night Stand Pay-Per-View – San Diego, CA   5/27/08 WW
5/24/08 WWE SmackDown/ECW Live – Cheyenne, WY   5/20/08 WWE SmackDown TV Tapin
/ Taping – London, Ontario   5/4/08 WWE SmackDown/ECW Live – Saint John, NB   5/4/08 WW
8 WWE SmackDown TV Taping – Atlantic City, NJ   4/27/08 WWE Backlash Live on Pay-Per-Vie
vn/ECW Live – Glasgow, Scotland   4/18/08 WWE SmackDown/ECW Live – Newcastle, Englan
ningham, England   4/15/08 WWE SmackDown and ECW TV Taping – London, England   4/14/0
2/08 WWE SmackDown Live – Geneva, Switzerland   4/11/08 WWE SmackDown Live – Torrevieja
- Boston, MA   4/1/08 WWE SmackDown TV Taping – Miami, FL   3/30/08 WWE WrestleMani
WWE SmackDown TV Taping – Fayetteville, NC   3/18/08 WWE SmackDown TV Taping – Bilox
lexandria, LA   3/11/08 WWE SmackDown TV Taping – Chicago, IL   3/9/08 WWE SmackDow
vn TV Taping – Cleveland, OH   3/2/08 WWE SmackDown/ECW Live – Muncie, IN   3/1/08 WW
WWE SmackDown TV Taping – San Diego, CA   2/17/08 WWE No Way Out – Las Vegas, NV Pay
Live – Santiago, Chile   2/12/08 – WWE SmackDown/ECW Live – Quito, Ecuador   2/10/08 – WW
emala   2/6/08 – WWE SmackDown/ECW TV Taping – Houston, TX   2/5/08 – WWE SmackDown
SmackDown TV Taping – Reading, PA   1/27/08 WWE Royal Rumble Live on Pay-Per-View – Nev
WE SmackDown TV Taping – Charlottesville, VA   1/21/08 WWE SmackDown/ECW – Uppe
WWE SmackDown TV Taping – Charlottesville, VA   WWE SmackDown/ECW – Salisbury, MD   1/19/08 WW
WWE SmackDown/ECW – State College, PA   1/15/0

CHAPTER 28
YOU TAKE THE GOOD, YOU TAKE THE BAD

The Internet has a way of letting one person make a statement, and before long that statement spreads like wildfire and becomes the truth. In this case, the Internet stories varied, but the one I saw most was that I had flipped off Michael Cole during the show and yelled at him, resulting in my getting fired. While the irony is that Cole delivered the news, he and I never even talked or looked in the same direction during that show. He was focused on commentary and that aspect of the show, as usual. He and I never had any issue whatsoever, and I always respected his work. He did so much background work and put so much thought into everything he did. I think he's one of the best to be in that challenging—and I mean challenging—position. I would never flip him off, especially not during the show. I would also never yell at him. I would give him information as I got it during the show and let him know what certain announcements would be if he needed to touch on it during the matches. Since he was in constant communication with Kevin on headset, sometimes I would ask him to clarify something coming up, but for a guy in the know, he never seemed to be able to tell me. Still, though, even with the scheduling, I had no issues at all with Cole.

I also read a story that said I wanted too much money for my new deal and that there were complications with that. That story is especially funny because I never had any say; there was no negotiating with WWE in this situation. Plus, my contract was not up yet, -as some speculated that it was. I still had some time to go, and it was their choice to end the deal early.

Now that this is all cleared up, I should also clear up another Internet rumor from the past. Lilian and I supposedly had a heated shouting match during a pay-per-view. People love to create dramatic news stories, and this one made both of us laugh when it showed up on the Internet. One of us was in the ring, but we didn't know if it was my match or her match. We were both completely confused and panicking since it was live television and trying to ask each other from the ring. Our confusion together over the disorganization of the product, not against each other, created that story. Unfortunately, way too many "news" sites simply make up stories based on hot topics, and believe it or not, this is a daily occurrence.

So what was it? Was it really that they were going a new direction, and that's why they suddenly decided to not renew my contract over a year before it was up? Did they want all female announcers? Was it Triple H's general dislike for me? Did Cody, whose dad worked for WWE as one of the executives in Florida, use his pull while he was upset to help out his cousin? That would be interesting because without me around, a new full-time announcing spot opened up which could help his wife. I don't think that's it at all. Did the company dislike that I had a good social media following and was beginning to show my personality on there, even though they never acknowledged that I existed? The wildly popular musical act One Direction requested me to introduce them for a show. WWE shot it down. Connor's father was interviewed about the story, which WWE had to approve, and their only changes were taking my name out.

Was there something personal? When I explained to people in the company about the special kids that I would help out in the crowd and volunteered to do more, they kept telling me that they would get me in touch with the right people to do those things officially, but nothing ever happened. I had been working with Stephanie's assistants, and they knew what I had been doing and told me that they had talked to someone in the appropriate department, and she would be contacting me, which never happened. I was actually told that by helping kids out at the events could conflict with Make-A-Wish because they had a business deal with them, and if I was just helping people as I saw them, that could be a problem. I told them not everyone knows how to go through the proper channels, and not everyone has enough time left, so if I see someone right then and there, it's so easy to help. I thought with my heart, not with a business mind.

Was it because I entertained my fans with my ongoing Instagram podcast show? Was it because I helped my coworkers with HandsToGo? Was it because I trademarked my name? Was it because I wrote a blog on why I loved professional wrestling and not on why I loved WWE and Sports Entertainment? Maybe they heard that I wanted to write a very honest book about my experiences working there. I even heard that I had a bad attitude—that I got really good at my job but thought that I was really good and the best at my job, and it was an ego thing. I knew how to do my job, and it was frustrating when others didn't know how to do theirs or just mail it in, but I wouldn't say I was the best. As I mentioned, some people liked me, some didn't, and others never noticed. I just took pride in my job and always tried to get it done right. Could it have been standing up to them when they told me I was off the international tour and then forcing me to go two weeks before? Anything is possible.

I was not one of their chosen guys. Unlike many others, I didn't view WWE as a stepping stone; this was the only place I ever wanted to be. Despite only wanting to be there and nowhere else, those in power clearly did not want me to succeed. Unfortunately for them, I did. I lived out my dream and was able to do those side jobs unofficially, but most important, I was able to do them while helping other people. No matter what the reason was, I am happy I could do it and now share my experiences for anyone else who is a big fan and wonders what it might be like. This might not be everyone's experience, but at least you got to hear one story.

The only thing I ever wanted and didn't get in my WWE run was an action figure. When kids play with their wrestling figures, they always announce the wrestlers coming to the ring. People have shown me lots of videos of that, and I used to do the same thing when I was a kid, but there was never a Hasbro ring announcer figure, so I used Gonzo from the Muppets in a tux. I hoped Mattel would make one of me, but even though they did take my face and body scan, they said guys in suits don't sell. Oh well.

I emailed Cole about that reel he offered, and he checked with Kevin. They basically said that the studio will put together clips for me, but not make me an actual reel. Apparently that was only for the "Stone Cold" types, I was told. I was not a Stone-Cold type, but they eventually sent me some clips to make my own.

The Wednesday morning after I left the company, I shared a photo of Vince and me on Instagram. When you pressed play, there was a clip of the song "Colorful" from *Rockstar*. I always envisioned associating the end of my run with that song. A summarized version of the message follows:

It might sound cliché, but I am truly overwhelmed and humbled by the messages I've received. As a kid who grew up loving and living for professional wrestling, I was able to chase, catch, and live an impossible dream. I was a part of events I couldn't fathom with the heroes I idolized from both WWF and various favorite television shows (Hello, Betty White).

For a guy who worked in a supporting ambience role—usually unnamed and unseen—I am blown away by the number of people who apparently not only noticed, but also enjoyed my work.

Announcing was my dream until I realized the absolute best part was using my position to help others. It brought me so much joy to bring a smile to a fellow fan's face.

The superstars I've announced and traveled with over the past 12 years (and have seen more than my own friends and family) are not only extremely talented and work year-round and on the fly, but they are also the most unselfish people I have ever met. I couldn't help others without their support. Not one superstar or diva ever once hesitated when I asked them to meet a fan or sign an autograph, or take a call, or do whatever was needed to put a smile on someone's face.

I always looked forward to TV days to spend time with the production crew. That crew is at the top of their game and is made up of genuine, caring, friendly, quality people. There's no talent–crew hierarchy; we were all one, and that's the way it should be.

After reading through all your messages, I just want to say this: Please do not be angry and please do not be sad. I lived my dream! I'm glad that maybe now someone else will have a chance to live theirs.

Many thanks to everyone I have worked with in WWE. Sue, the company gem and my guardian angel. The producers, who taught me so much and constantly let me pick their brains. The referees. The refs make it look easy. It is not an easy job. Security. Props. Audio. Seamstresses. Screens. Pyro. Utilities. Truck. Merch. Makeup. Photo. Medical. Lighting. PR. Cameras. Travel. Talent relations. Live events. Catering. Production. PAs. My eyes and ears at the bell—Mark Yeaton.

Everyone I have met along the way. Everyone who has come into my life because of this job and those who I have never had the opportunity to meet but who have enjoyed my work. I appreciate and am grateful for everyone's support. To Vince McMahon, Kevin Dunn, and the Authority who gave me this incredible opportunity. I've got two words for ya: Thank You.

Minutes after posting that message, I got a text from an old friend that I hadn't spoken to in a long time: CM Punk. We worked a lot of the same shows over the years. We both went from the ECW brand to *SmackDown* and then to *RAW*. I was proud of what he accomplished and was honored to be there for most of his big moments. It's funny. He started as basically, a "backyard" wrestler. He was self-trained, at first. Well, no one trained me to be a ring announcer. I was self-trained. I was a backyard announcer, I guess. As we both went on, we learned from other people; we learned from our mistakes; we learned from what worked; and we both had a ton of passion and loved what we did and wanted to be great. He was tired and done. Now I was tired and done. He had been in a similar situation and gave me some good advice and answered my question: After driving about 50,000 miles a year, flying about 200,000 miles, working about 52 weeks for over a decade all over the world, with no real breaks, would the permanent jet-leg feeling in my head ever go away? He told me, yes, and I was looking forward to that.

The messages started coming through. The feedback from my statement was overwhelming. I was proud of what I had accomplished. The chances of getting in to WWE were not good to begin with. But getting in and staying? Come on. Getting in and becoming the go-to announcer and everything else that came along with the gig...what a journey. I was a kid that lived to watch wrestling. I toyed with the idea of being in the business as an announcer, and then I actually made it happen. I got to run to the ring and slap hands like I used to pretend to do as a kid while running through my hallway. I was in the annual WWE video game. I have trading cards and a Mattel talking megaphone with my voice on it. I was in the programs. I announced every WWE TV show that has existed since 2002. From *Superstars* to *Saturday Night's Main Event* to *ECW* to *Smackdown* to *RAW* etc. I announced at every pay-per-view. I announced *WrestleMania* main events. I introduced Hulk Hogan, the Ultimate Warrior, the Rock, "Stone Cold" Steve Austin, John Cena, Goldberg, Eddie Guerrero, "Rowdy" Roddy Piper, Shawn Michaels, Bret Hart, Undertaker, Kurt Angle, Chris Jericho, Rey Mysterio, and

YOU TAKE THE GOOD, YOU TAKE THE BAD

Ric Flair. The more I type, the more absurd it becomes. I know I didn't sleep a lot over those 12 years, but as much as it seems like a dream, I'm amazed that this was real life.

They say if you can work at WWE and for Vince, you can work anywhere. I believe that. The work ethic we were expected to have and the schedule we kept can't be described as demanding. There is no word for it. If there's a flight issue, a car issue, or whatever, there's never an excuse. You find a way to get there and do your job. Those of us who have that mentality know what it's like and have driven crazy hours on top of crazy flights and sleepless nights. It's crazy, it's insane, but it's admirable. Any other company you work for will appreciate that type of work ethic. If you truly care about your job, you do what it takes to be the very best at it and deliver all the time, every time. If you don't care about your job, just stop wasting your time. Start daydreaming about what you would enjoy doing. You only live once. Go do it.

I hopped on a plane and took the vacation I had planned. It definitely did not feel like a vacation; it just felt weird. All the pressure, stress, and frustration was lifted off my shoulders. After over a decade of having to be here and there every day, I no longer had to be, well, anywhere. I had complete freedom. I knew what I had achieved, and I was proud. I had also been miserable and was ready to move on.

I watched *Rockstar*, one of my favorite movies. *Rudy* was about a kid who chased his dream and never gave up and got it. That was appropriate when I got signed. *Rockstar* was what I needed to watch now. A guy chased his dream, got it, and had enough. I ran down that aisle. I slapped hands on the way to the ring. I lived out my childhood fantasy. Everything else was a bonus.

What's it like to be released? Well, I heard from a lot of my coworkers as well as longtime friends. The feedback on social media was really positive, which doesn't happen often. When people have an opportunity to voice their opinions, it seems many people choose to be negative. I was happy and appreciative that everybody was so kind, especially Jim Ross, who was very vocal and supportive. Eric Bischoff even sent out a tweet saying, "@JustinRoberts is a class act. Needs no wishes of luck for his future. He will excel in whatever opportunity he chooses!" Tommy Dreamer had reached out with a kind tweet as well: "Not much trended on #RAW but now @JustinRoberts is. A great ring announcer A better friend A door closes a door opens. You will survive." I always waited to contact guys when they were released to give them some time to digest it on their own, but I personally was glad to hear from everyone right away. To be honest, I wasn't down. I was happy and optimistic. You're with a family of incredible people every day, every week, and then suddenly they're just taken from you as you're no longer part of the family. It's definitely a change, but that's just how it goes. There were a lot of production people that I would make my rounds to at TV each week just to say hello and chat as we got through the long days—people who I considered friends that I never heard from once I was out. So many people were constantly in fear of losing their jobs every week, so when someone was released, they wanted to avoid any "heat" from associating with them. Some of the talent, refs, producers, and office people that I would always talk to that were fired and rehired had disappeared as well, but you just have to expect that.

As I mentioned before, I go to the same woman every week for a haircut. Stacie has been very good to me over the years and very accommodating regarding my schedule. She mentioned that she was dealing with a problem over the past year, but my release from WWE helped her get over that. I wasn't sure how, so I asked her to explain. She told me that she was trying to get over a relationship, but I had just lost my job. Not any old job, but my dream job, and that was much more traumatic. Life changing. And as far as she knew, I had been nothing but happy and optimistic. She told me if I could handle that life-changing event the way I did, she could surely get over the breakup.

I'm happy that my story helped Stacie, and I hope that I can also help other people realize that, no matter what happens, the world goes on. You have to keep going; never dwell on anything. Take the experiences you learned from and made you a better person and move on. Apply those experiences to your next journey and use them to make you the absolute best person you can be on that next mission. I know that's my plan now.

Since leaving, I have had time to digest everything. I kept the truth about Connor's story inside for a long time until I watched the Hall of Fame and saw how they spliced Warrior's speech and made it about something different from what he suggested. It wasn't as much about that as it was about him wanting to acknowledge the hardworking WWE family, so to speak, but I knew how they really treated most of that family while giving the illusion that they are a caring company on the surface by touting their philanthropies. It was announced that Connor would be inducted into the WWE Hall of Fame. He would be receiving the first ever Warrior Award, which was a tribute to Ultimate Warrior who had passed away shortly before Connor. The company must have thought this would be a good way to twist and produce a heartwarming story. You see, the Warrior mentioned starting an award the previous year during his Hall of Fame induction speech. Warrior wanted to thank the superstars that you never see. He mentioned that some of them had been there for years, and they were the behind-the-scenes superstars that made *WrestleMania* happen. He mentioned the ring guys and honoring the people that make the company work and that it would be appropriate to have a category in the Hall of Fame to honor those people. He suggested calling it the Jimmy Miranda Award, after a well-known, behind-the-scenes hard worker who had passed away. Well, the company spun that into a Warrior Award named after him, and just as they have shown over the years, their lack of appreciation for hardworking employees, the award Warrior wanted for employees was not going to an employee, but rather to a courageous individual.

They played a heartwarming video where one of the first photos was John Cena and Connor in front of a Make-A-Wish banner. Was that coincidence, or were they implying that Connor was part of WWE's Make-A-Wish? I guess that's left for people to assume what they would like.

Everyone wanted to know how I felt about Connor's induction. How did I really feel? I felt like I wanted to help Connor as much as possible to make him happy. I was the middleman that gave him all-access to those heroes, and with my phone and the help of my heroic coworkers each week, that happened. We helped Connor.

The company took his initial visit with Daniel, the footage from DC, and footage from *WrestleMania* and created a story of their own, hiding a beautiful, real story in favor of their own. They rewrote history as they like to do. Watching the coverage of Connor's Hall of Fame announcement, it seemed to me that the company had now believed their own lie. People who never reached out to Connor outside of being at work were all of a sudden heroes in this story. By telling their stories, it came off to me as a publicity stunt. It was put out there to various news outlets before the big announcement. To me, they had a heartwarming story for the public to bite on, and they were going to milk it to the last drop. On the surface, they come off looking like a caring company, but the award that Warrior wanted for an employee disappeared, just as the employees who would have deserved the award seemed to disappear. Using this story to show they are a caring company did not match up with their mistreatment of talent and employees. Mark Yeaton was the model employee. Jim Ross, who I feel is the greatest overall commentator in wrestling, a hall of famer, a legend, was forced to "retire," and that's how he was thanked for his years of service. Mike, the gentleman who was hesitant to hire Nav, had been there a long time and did everything in his power to help the company with product development and licensing, and just like Dennis Sullivan, who opened so many doors for the company to expand to new international markets, Nicole Dorazio, who worked under John Laurinaitis and helped him, the company, and talent, as well as so many other good people, the company just dropped them. This is also the same company that sent us into hazardous weather conditions because our well-being didn't matter, it was just business, and this, too, was business. I felt that they were exploiting Connor for branding purposes. I wanted to let it be known how they truly treated people and covered this up with their philanthropies.

Once Stephanie had tweeted a quote from a business conference, admitting that philanthropy was the new form of marketing in 2015, and it was how companies would get ahead, I couldn't hold it in anymore. I had kept the true story inside for a long time, but that tweet made me sick, and I couldn't sleep. That to me affirmed my speculation that Connor's induction into the Hall of Fame was exploiting him, using him as marketing and shoving their story down everyone's throats. I started typing my blog. There was a 100% chance that writing a blog explaining the story would mean backlash against me. Most people would side with the company because they'd assume I'm just bitter since I'm not working there anymore. When you consider that we are talking about an eight-year-old cancer patient, it only adds to the chance of backlash. Still, I couldn't keep it in after I saw that tweet, and I wanted to tell the real story. I felt bad that Daniel Bryan was in a position to answer questions about his friendship with Connor when there wasn't a friendship outside of seeing him at the arena. There was, however, all of the magical moments he made while they were in the buildings together, and on FaceTime, Bryan was great to him. Some people thought it was about trying to get credit for what I did with Connor. They missed the point.

Daniel Bryan was so popular, and the company tried so hard many times to shut him down. It was amazing that he was so well liked and for good reason; it was a very rare time where the fans prevailed despite what the powers that be wanted. It definitely did not come easy as his road to get there was hard and well earned, but once they had to change directions and not fight the fans anymore, like trying to make him a member of the heel Wyatt family, there was an additional price to pay. He had a concussion in January 2014 and was back in action shortly after. That March, he was handcuffed by fake police and beaten down by Triple H with his hands behind his back. They made him pay for his popularity by throwing him out of the ring without having his hands available to break the fall on his recently concussed head among numerous additional shots followed by two big matches a few weeks later at *WrestleMania* in one night. That, right there, is the true "heart" of the company, in my opinion.

I released my blog, and surprisingly, it was about 80% positive and only 20% negative. I felt the 20% didn't read the full story, and they assumed I wanted credit. It wasn't about credit at all. It simply reinforced my statement that the company wasn't a caring organization, but rather they play the character of a caring organization. I felt they were true bullies who hold anti-bullying campaigns. *Washington Post* covered the blog and got a response from WWE which basically backed up what I had said. They were offended by what I wrote and then added all the charity work they are a part of.

After the blog, I did not feel better until I talked to Steve Michalek, his father, and the other relatives that I had talked with throughout everything. They were okay with it. Steve had mentioned that Stephanie was upset and asked what he thought. He did not want to take sides and told me that he just told her what I had written was true. He was a caring and loving father who did everything possible for Connor and now was doing the same for Connor's little brother Jackson. Despite what their intentions were, WWE treated their family very well. Connor. Steve. Now Jackson. Steve couldn't take sides, nor did I want him to. He told me he felt like he was in the middle of divorce. The company was great to them and continued to have them at events and, of course, be a part of Connor's Cure.

I felt even more okay with the blog when I received a text that night from Daniel Bryan. He was put in a position that wasn't what it seemed to be, which resulted in more uncomfortable situations. We discussed what happened and what I wrote, and he was okay with it. Therefore, I was, too.

Do I think Connor would have loved the award? Yes. Do I think his family appreciated it? Yes. Do I think the fans liked it? Yes. While filling all the corporate obligations, WWE presented their story of Connor. Yes, they were showing the video before they even had a foundation to send donations because they wanted to show their fans how great they were. But, by forming the foundation, whatever their purpose was, they've created a good organization to help sick kids and their families. Do I think Stephanie sees the business and branding opportunity with that? Yes, I think it's definitely a business move, but I also know she cared about Connor even if I think she was exploiting his story. It's a complicated situation that I hope I cleared up. When I see her photo on an ad for Connor's Cure, it does make me wonder, but I also know how she felt about him. Overall, I know how good she was and still is to his family.

I also think about the Warrior Award recipient that came the following year, Joan Lunden, a well-respected television personality who was battling cancer. WWE does branding before they do wrestling, which is clear from watching their programming. The wrestling aspect hasn't been wonderful, but their partnerships and standing with large companies has been. They also don't like the word "wrestling" and want to be perceived as entertainment, not wrestling, even if it's World Wrestling Entertainment. They once told us in a talent meeting that there was no reason Britney Spears or Justin Timberlake couldn't come to WWE to brand them and run their tours. They started the World Bodybuilding Federation (WBF), the XFL football league, WWF New York (a restaurant), and even their own WWE Films company, always looking to break away from "just wrestling" and build their brand.

Awarding someone like Sue Aitchison, who has been with the company for many, many years, as senior manager of community relations with the Warrior Award would be amazing. She has done so much for helping fans through Make-A-Wish as well as independently. She is an employee and helps so many people. Joan Lunden is definitely a warrior with a fighting spirit, but is there anything that ties her in to be a part of a wrestling hall of fame? Diamond Dallas Page is a wrestler who had a great career and now lives his life promoting DDP Yoga to help not only the general public, but wrestlers, too. Everyone that I know who uses DDP Yoga swears by it, and on top of that, he took guys like Jake "the Snake" Roberts and Scott Hall into his home to rehab them off drugs and alcohol and hook them onto yoga instead. He, too, seems like a great recipient for the award, but it might not get them the branding identity they want.

CHAPTER 29
THE FINAL CHAPTER

If you get the feeling that I cared too much about my job, you are probably right. When you're there, working within the WWE machine, you don't just fear screwing up, you fear losing your job every time you go to work. Those who care and love what they do and want to contribute? They get stepped on. Others who don't care, but become Yes Men? They keep their jobs. Outside guests were treated very well. The company prefers people who come in and do what they're told and don't ask questions. That is the key to keeping your job there. When you care too much, it's hard to let that happen. The bosses were friendly to celebrities, athletes, and high-profile viewers but would talk down to talent. While guest hosts would be provided a nice dressing room and food platter, the wrestlers would be forced to change in small, crowded dressing rooms. The mentality seemed to be that if you didn't like the schedule, the treatment, or the rules, go ahead and leave because there was no real competition to work for.

The sad thing is that everybody knows about the wrong that goes on there. Everyone who works there knows. But most people who leave the company don't speak openly about their experiences. Most employees can't due to their contracts. It always gave me hope when someone would leave because I knew there was a chance that they would speak up. They now had the perfect opportunity to let the world know how things really work at WWE. It felt like the rest of us were still trapped there, and they were now in a position to shed light on us, the prisoners. It just never seemed to happen, though. Most people who left expected to come back, or at least wanted to come back. They all wanted that "last run." I don't have any desire to ever work for the McMahons again. Therefore, I am happy to be honest and open when I discuss the WWE. I hope that in doing so, things will change for the guys who are still there and still suffering from that awful treatment. It easily has the potential to be a terrific company, but the decisions made by the people in power prevent that, and it hurts the talent, their families, and the fans. I started making notes on experiences that I've had just in case I ever decided to write a book and tell my story. On a flight from Phoenix to Boston for Survivor Series in November 2013, I started typing in order to keep myself from sleeping. I couldn't print what I had written because I had to keep my job, but now that I no longer have my job, I could finally make this happen without having to sugarcoat anything. I only wanted to write this if I could write the truth. I just wanted to tell the story of what it was like to be a fan and live out my dream in a fly on the wall position at the mecca of professional wrestling.

My advice based on my experience at WWE: Be friendly. Be polite. Be persistent, but not so much that you become a pest. Follow up with people. Figure out your destination and assume the route that most people take. Once you do that, figure out your own path to make and take. When you get close to reaching your goal, stay level-headed. Be flexible, but stay determined.

Once you get there, enjoy the ride. Know that it can end at any point, so make every moment count and be good to everyone. I found that using a new vantage point to help other people can be even more rewarding than getting the position in the first place. I also took a lot of chances. Sometimes they worked out; other times they didn't. The only way to get something great is to take a chance. Great things don't just happen; you have to do something outside of your comfort zone.

Most important, you should find something you love. If you're currently doing something for work that just helps you get by or that you've chosen to settle with, put some passion into that job. Take pride in what you do. After touring around the world, I saw firsthand that it's common for people to just get through the day and get through their job without caring. They just go through the motions. Food orders have been wrong, hotel clerks give you keys to an already occupied room, rental car companies give you a contract for a car that doesn't exist—these types of things happen a lot, and I am reminded of the importance of doing a job right. I advise all of you to do your job to the very best of your abilities so that you can excel in your company. From there, excelling in your company might lead you to an even greater opportunity somewhere else.

Unfortunately, now the wrestling business has changed significantly, and some of my career and life advice no longer applies to it. WWE is the main wrestling organization, and while there is potential for other companies to rise in the future, no matter what anybody tells you, WWE is completely alone at the top. Sadly, WWE uses its position of power to phase out people who have true passion for the business.

From reading social media, it seems that so many people want to work there and think that they're better than the current guys, or they're ideas would be so good and would help the company soar. It's hard without working there for them to know that the people currently in that position are actually good but just following orders. The guys who are there also have great ideas, but the company just doesn't want to run with them. Unless you worked there, you probably don't realize that the company seems to just run things their way. So if you're constantly yelling at the TV screen on Monday nights, know that if you follow your dream and get there, it's going to be an uphill battle, but I still wish you the best of luck. It's very easy for the company to put on a great show. They have so many talented people working behind the scenes, and the majority of the people are quality human beings. The people with the most power make the final decisions, and they don't necessarily get classified with the majority. We always talked about feeling like we were part of a family, and I couldn't agree more. There was a family on the road who traveled together, worked together, and looked out for each other. I never considered those decision-makers as part of the family. I didn't feel they cared, and their repeated actions over the years proved it.

While a lot of this was written when I worked there, some right after, and a bit over a year later, I have had a chance to see things as they are. I watch the shows if I'm home as I was always a wrestling fan and always will be. There is a part of me that thinks about giving the company my all and going above and beyond only to get kicked to the curb, but there's a bigger part of me that is happy to be out of that position. I watch now and see what seems like their attempt to hire all the names that are a buzz on the independent scene to prevent competition. I think back to the Attitude Era when the fans loved every segment. There was a sea of signs and excitement on every single show. Now, with an unbelievable amount of talent, with some of the greatest producers and writers behind the scenes, the best production out there, and a huge budget, they had the potential to run an incredible show every pay-per-view, every Monday for *RAW*, every Tuesday for *SmackDown*, and every house show, but instead they continued to book shows that felt flat. When there was an opening for something exciting to happen, they seemed to go the opposite direction that fans clamored for. I've always thought the problem was knowing what the fans wanted, but doing instead what they wanted and pushing who they wanted just to prove that they could. I don't think they're money driven or even ratings driven, just ego driven, and it's unfortunate. It seems that they are more into company branding and controlling how they are perceived rather than operating their wrestling company. I am disappointed as a lifelong fan that they try so hard to get away from the actual "wrestling" aspect. Unfortunately, most journalists seem to ignore all the bad and find a highlight or two to pat them on the back as to not upset the company that gives them access to their shows and wrestlers. If more people were honest, maybe the company would realize their mistakes.

They recently split the brands again and, for the first time, made TV interesting. As a fan, believe me, I am rooting for good shows. For the talent that works there, I am rooting for them to succeed. Despite not being a fan of upper management, I still want the company to do well and deliver. I'm a wrestling fan, and I want to watch good wrestling. By keeping everyone down and only letting a few guys and factions develop, it makes it easy to develop their talent in Florida and let them shine. When you mix them with everyone else who has truly been held down, those shining stars will look great, while everyone else who had been held down will eventually fade. The only hope seems to be the chosen talents who are allowed to push to the top versus the ones that organically grew in the hearts of the fans. It has almost been a bait and switch of sorts, in which the characters who drew you to the company are there to make the new NXT talent look good. It's nothing at all against that new talent. I am happy for anyone who gets a shot at the big time. Guys like Kevin Owens, Finn Balor, and AJ Styles who have worked all over the world to make it there—I hope they all succeed. Many talents grew wings and had them clipped off, while other handpicked talents were given wings and constantly pushed despite the audience rejecting them. The other talent can only get so elevated, but then they're usually put back into place by people at the top because no one can be bigger or better than them.

The storylines had been thrown together for so long that nothing made sense. As a kid, I loved seeing when seeds were planted, and it looked like a guy might be turning "bad" or "good." By throwing the shows together last minute, fans today don't get that special appeal to the product. In the past, guys would interfere with matches and differ in the ways to build up for the big pay-per-views. You would see interference, and you would see those talents involved in buildup matches. Now when say, Brock Lesnar, has a big match coming up, he doesn't come out and interfere in his opponent's matches. Paul Heyman cuts promos every week until they get to the match. The bigger stars that remain in the industry simply appear rather than blend into the show.

My hopes for the future is that they realize how special this industry is and what it means to so many fans around the world. I hope they stop with inconsistencies and make the storylines play out like they used to in the past. I hope they stop holding talent back and remove that glass ceiling. Those wrestlers are amazing. Please let them show what they can do and give us a new era of memorable moments. Just make wrestling fun again. I also hope one day that there will be a union to protect these extremely hardworking performers who make the company what it is and deserve the protection and better treatment. They shouldn't have to be "on" every week all year with no breaks and an insane travel schedule. Despite some of the situations the talent and employees are put in, the personal goal is for them to still go out and entertain. The forum is there for everyone to do what they love.

Am I happy with my run? Absolutely. Was it unfortunate that I wasn't treated well, and the more I cared, the less I was cared for? Yes, it was. Bullies are a part of life, and we must overcome them not only as kids, but as adults as well. I'm a better person and a stronger person for everything I endured there. I have so many memories that I will cherish forever. I've met so many good people as a result. I thank everyone who has been in my path, no matter what, because I have learned from them. I am ready for a new adventure where I could have fun again. Wrestling fans are one of a kind, and I'm still a fan at heart. I hope all of the fans that I have encountered over the years will stick with me wherever I end up next.

Since leaving WWE, I have toured as a host for Tool, shot some TV shows, done voiceover work, announced boxing, written this book, and most important, I have been around for friends and family. I even announced a wrestling show in Oklahoma so I could work with WCW legend, Sting, to round out my list. I have no idea what's next, but I look forward to making the best of it. It's weird to go from being so passionate and driven to reach a goal to not knowing what your next goal is and not being able to figure out what else you are passionate about. As much as I love wrestling, there are numerous promotions with incredible talent, but nowhere at the moment where I fit in. I still watch the old 1991-1995 pay-per-views that I used to rent from Blockbuster Video, and I'm still entertained the way I was as a kid. Now I get to see the shows with the eyes of someone who has experience from working there as well as working with so many of the stars who were a part of those shows, and that makes them even more special. Did this journey have ups and downs? Of course it did. Would I change anything at all? No. I truly had the best seat in the house to watch the wrestling world from all points of view and was able to do exactly what I set out to do. With the support and encouragement of my family, I was able to live out my dream I had imagined as a kid. I am proud of everything I accomplished and hope this story can prove to you that even the most far-fetched goals are attainable. No story has ups without any downs, and the bad always comes with the good. I thank you very much for reading my story and hope that you, too, will follow your dreams. Anything and everything is possible.

ACKNOWLEDGMENTS

Thank you to my parents and sister. If it weren't for your love, support, and encouragement, none of this would ever be possible. I couldn't have asked for a better family.

Thank you to all of my family who watched every magic show, school play, and wrestling show, to my incredible brother-in-law and nieces for joining the family and bringing lots of happiness. Thank you to every teacher who put up with me and every classmate who either cringed at me or joined in the fun along the way.

Thank you to every performer who captured my imagination and drove me to dream of doing the same.

Thank you to my friends, whether the friendship was brief or you are in my life for the long haul.

Thank you to all of the wrestlers, from Kerry Von Erich, the Ultimate Warrior, and the Gorgeous Ladies of Wrestling to Bobby Heenan and all of the talent from the early 90s that got me hooked on wrestling. Thank you to every wrestler, wrestling personality, and promoter who kept me hooked and who later kept the business going, giving me a chance to be a part of it all.

Thank you to Brian Schenk and Lou Tufano for putting in a good word with Sonny Rogers. Thank you, Sonny, for the first opportunity to be a ring announcer. Thank you, Dave Prazak, for working with me on that night. Thank you to Dale Gagne for giving me a huge opportunity. Thank you to Steve Islas for taking me on the road with you and getting me booked, but more importantly, teaching me along the way and then blessing me with your friendship on top of it. Thank you to Sue DeRosa, I'm sorry I drove you crazy, but I'm glad it worked out. Thank you to WWE for giving me a chance and a run; I was able to work with and learn from so many unforgettable people and characters.

Thank you to everyone who taught me and helped walk me through the book process: Michael Essany, Jimmy Van, Adam Mock, Ryan Nemeth, Amy Prenner, Andy Fraser, Seth Mates, and Allie Golden. Thank you to Manuel Morschel and Meyer & Meyer Verlag for taking a chance on a totally different project. Thank you to Liz Evans for editing this and all of your help with a first-timer.

Thank you to all of the wrestling producers, wrestlers, and wrestling personalities who let me pick their brains or even just let me learn from them. Thank you to Tommy Dreamer for writing the foreword and also sending a funny version immediately after, making it especially hard to read with the combination of cheeks hurting and phone shaking from laughing, while hard to see due to tears in my eye from the serious version. Thank you also for changing that locker room and making work a fun place to be, making it feel like a dream job. I've already thanked the wrestlers, but the ECW guys, you have no idea how much I appreciated that summer and you. Thank you to IZW talent and fans. Also, a special thank-you to the PWI guys who were always good to me when I was getting started: Ace Steel, Danny Dominion, Randy Ricci, Adrian Lynch, Eric Freedom, the Twin Turbos Steve and Larry, Jonnie Stewart, Adam Pearce, King Kong Bundy, Sgt. Slaughter, Steve Regal, CC Starr, Vickie Guerrero, Stevie Richards, Paul London, Matt Hardy, Jeff Hardy, Eddie Guerrero, Charles Robinson, Doctors Rio, Dodson, Sampson, Amann, Bret Hart, and Jim Ross. Thank you to my friends who I rode with. Thank you to everyone I named in the story as well. The problem with doing this page is knowing that I'll accidentally leave out a name or two, and I apologize if I do. If you helped me, you know you did, and you know I still thank you to this day, because that's what I do.

Thank you to Mike K, Lissa A, Ann C, Adam Jones, Ross K, Mike F, Seth G, Bill C, Mitch S, Jen S, Jaime F, Barry H, Scott H, Paul H, Ken T, Robert F, Sean S, Todd S, Dennis Haskins, Golden Grannies, Golden Girls, Terry, Chris P, Justin B, Wade K, Ryan S, Richie S, Danny B, Bob, Paul, Matt, Jay Paul, Todd H, Jimmy N, Jimmy T, Rich Koz, Jimmy B, Joe O, Craig S, Craig T, Nicky S, Corey C,

BEST SEAT IN THE HOUSE

Heather S, Myrna V, Gia, Matt Metzer, Doug C, Phil Speer, Vic T, Todd Grisham, Jonathan Coachman, Arda Ocal, Ron B, Trevor B, Russel T, Dale T, Patrick Talty, Kirby, Nicole, Jeramie McPeek, Robert Karpeles, Bryce Yang, Mike Archer, Dave Bogart, Ryan Barkan, Jason Hariton, Mark Yeaton, the Michalek family, Ed and Francine, Blackjack Brown, Marty E, Jordan B, Ticketmaster Mark, Ryan W, Al Lagattolla Sameet, Lucas S, Scott D, HS Van Ladies, HS Lunch Ladies, Greg P, Bacine, Esther, Beverley Cheryl, Matt Roberts, Dennis Sullivan, Whitney Williamson, George Wallace, Barry Bloom, Gary Cappetta, Howard Finkel, Horshu, Hollywood, Rob Conway, Dr. Tom, Ted DiBiase, IRS, MVP, Brian Gewirtz, Kevin Kelly, King Kong Bundy, George Steele, Gerry Brisco, Jack Lanza, Justin Credible, Tony DeVito, Sue Aitchenson, Undertaker, Mick Foley, Chris Jericho, John Cena, Jon Greco, Rose Ann, Brandi Runnels, Paul Ofcharsky, Art Dore, Susan Schermers, Lydia Robertson, Janet Reed, Norma Ayon, Adam Cohen, JD, Jamie, Nic, Nick, Matt C, Mike M, Chris, Tom, Mike Garrow, Sean Wheelock, Stacie, Nicky Cachezerri, Zach Hall, Claudia Breckenridge, Mr. Meister, Ms. McEachran, Mrs. Rosenbaum, Mrs. Glass, Mrs. Mitsokopoulos, Mrs. Malis, Mrs. Witucke, Chip, Eli J, Dennis M, Paul G, Barry and Susan, Michael and Sandy, Michael and Debbie, Don and Arlene, Anita and Loy, Harry and Linda, Earl and Jeanette, Danny and Janet, Duke, Betty and Don, Nola and Harvey, Cheryl and Marc, Julie and Jeff, Edie and Vince, Gina and Louie(s), Barb and Bob, Steve and Jeri, and Marsha and Al and Shari and Lori, Darrin W and Dr. Hurley.

Thank you to everyone in my path, and thank you very much to every fan that I may have ever had!